THE DOCTOR DANCED WITH US

Jeremiah Sullivan and the Hopi, 1881-1888 And other Essays

THE DOCTOR DANCED WITH US

Jeremiah Sullivan and the Hopi, 1881-1888
And other Essays

LOUIS A. HIEB

Published by Rio Grande Books
Los Ranchos, New Mexico

Rio Grande Books
Los Ranchos, New Mexico
www.RioGrandeBooks.com

Book design by Paul Rhetts

Library of Congress Cataloging-in-Publication Data

Names: Hieb, Louis A., author.
Title: The doctor danced with us : Jeremiah Sullivan and the Hopi, 1881-1888, and other essays / Louis A. Hieb. Other titles: Jeremiah Sullivan and the Hopi, 1881-1888, and other essays
Description: Los Ranchos, New Mexico : Rio Grande Books, [2018] | Includes bibliographical references and index.
Identifiers: LCCN 2017061872
| ISBN 9781943681259 (pbk. : alk. paper)
Subjects: LCSH: Sullivan, Jeremiah, 1851-1916 | Hopi Indians--History--19th century. | Indian agents--Arizona--Biography. | Physicians--Arizona--Biography. | Ethnologists--United States--Biography. | Hopi Indians--Social life and customs. | Hopi Indians--Government relations. | Hopi Indian Reservation (Ariz.)--Biography. | Hopi Indian Reservation (Ariz.)--History. | Ethnology--Southwestern States--History--19th century. | Arizona--Biography.

Classification: LCC E99.H7 H54 2018 | DDC 979.1004/97458--dc23
LC record available at https://lccn.loc.gov/2017061872

Cover: "Dr. Jeremiah Sullivan," 1884. Photograph by Frederick Dellenbaugh. Frederick Dellenbaugh Papers, Ms 407, Special Collections, The University of Arizona Library. Only known photograph of Jeremiah Sullivan.

To Jack, Maddie, and Merryn.

Contents

THE DOCTOR DANCED WITH US

Dramatis Personae

Anawita, "Head War Chief," Patki Clan, Walpi; lived in wife's house in Sichumovi.

John Gregory Bourke (1846-1896), Army officer, visited the Hopi in 1874 and 1881; author of *The Snake-Dance of the Moquis of Arizona* (1884).

Frank Hamilton Cushing (1857-1900), ethnologist at Zuni Pueblo 1879-1884; visited the Hopi in 1881 and 1882; Director, Hemenway Southwestern Archaeological Expedition, 1886-1889.

Frederick Samuel "Fred" Dellenbaugh (1853-1935), artist, visited the Hopi and Keams Canyon during the fall and winter of 1884-1885.

J. Walter Fewkes (1850-1930), zoologist, Director, Second Hemenway Southwestern Archaeological Expedition, 1889-1894, field research at Hopi, 1890-ca. 1899

Jesse H. Fleming (1848-1929), Agent, Moqui Pueblo Indian Agency, 1882-1883.

Herman ten Kate (1858-1931), Dutch ethnologist, visited the Hopi in 1883.

Thomas Varker "Tom" Keam (1842-1904), trader with the Navajo and Hopi, 1876-1902.

William H. R. "Billy" Keam (1848-1880), trader with the Hopi, 1876-1880.

Washington Matthews (1843-1905), surgeon in the U. S. Army; ethnographer and linguist among the Navajo; stationed at Fort Wingate, 1880-1884 and 1890-1894.

Cosmos "Cos" Mindeleff (1863-1938), geographer with the Bureau of [American] Ethnology, 1882-1895; surveyed Hopi architecture, 1882-1888.

Harriet Marion Warren (Fessler) Mindeleff (1861-1933), actress, joined Cosmos for the Snake Dance at Mishongnovi in 1885 and for his survey of the Verde Valley in 1891.

Victor "Vic" Mindeleff (1860-1948), architect with the Bureau of Ethnology, 1881-1890; surveyed Hopi architecture, 1881-1888.

Polacca (ca. 1850-1912), acculturated Tewa, Mormon convert, known to Cushing and others as Tom Polacca.

John Wesley Powell (1834-1902), Colorado River explorer, Director, Bureau of [American] Ethnology; visited the Hopi in 1870.

Sa'miwi'ki "Wiki" (ca. 1850-1910), Antelope priest, Snake Clan, Walpi.

Alexander Middleton "Steve" Stephen (1846-1894), ethnologist, lived at Keams Canyon, 1880-1891; First Mesa, 1892-1894.

Matilda "Tilly" Coxe Stevenson (1849-1915), unpaid assistant to her husband, James Stevenson, Bureau of Ethnology expeditions to the Southwest, 1879-1887.

James "Jim" Stevenson (1840-1888), Field Director, Bureau of Ethnology expeditions to the Hopi, 1879-1885.

Jeremiah "Jere" Sullivan (1851-1916), Agency Physician, Moqui Pueblo Indian Agency, 1881-1882; physician and ethnologist among the Hopi, 1881-1888.

John H. Sullivan (1817-1886), Agent, 1880-1881, Farmer-in-Charge, 1881-1882, Moqui Pueblo Indian Agency.

Rev. Charles Andrew Taylor (1848-1915), Presbyterian missionary to the Hopi, 1880-1882.

George Benjamin "Ben" Wittick (1845-1903), photographer, visited the Hopi, often for the Snake Dance at Walpi, beginning in 1885.

List of Illustrations

Acknowledgements

There are a number of words used to describe the kind of research presented in this book. Persistence is one. Serendipity is another. However, without the encouragement, assistance, and intellectual generosity of many others over the past thirty or so years, this book could not and would not have been written.

The initial focus of my research was Jeremiah Sullivan. Elliot G. McIntire and, especially, Stephen C. McCluskey had published articles on Sullivan and both sent me copies of materials by Sullivan they had found. Gertrude Geraets of Madison, Indiana, and Margene Tomkinson of Rockland, Idaho, searched newspaper files for information on Sullivan's life before, during, and after his years among the Hopi. For their generosity and encouragement, I am deeply grateful.

Well over three thousand books and articles have been published on the Hopi. Only a small number are helpful. Peter Whiteley's research and insightful perspectives on Hopi culture and history have informed my work for years as have the respectful and insightful publications of Emory Sekaquaptewa, Mary Black, and Maria Glowacka. Laura Graves's biography of Thomas Varker Keam and William Lawson's dissertation of the early years of the Bureau of Ethnology have guided me to archival materials I might otherwise have missed. And not to be forgotten is Elsie Clews Parsons, whose efforts to preserve and edit the manuscripts of Alexander M. Stephen have been essential to this project.

Nor would this book have been written without the resources and generous assistance of staff of many libraries: Mary Frances Morrow Ronan of the National Archives, Washington; Patti McNamee, National Archives, Seattle; Lonna B. Seibert, Susan McElrath, Gina Rappaport, Daisy Njoku, Caitlin Haynes, and Robert S. Leopold of the National Anthropological Archives; Roger Myers and Peter Steere of the

University of Arizona Library; Mary Graham, Hartman Lomawaima, and Amy Rule of the Arizona State Museum; Ellen Alers and Tracy E. Robinson of the Smithsonian Institution Archives; Robert G. Karrow, Jr. and Laura L. Carroll of the Newberry Library; Patricia Kervick and Sara Demb of the Peabody Museum Library, Harvard University; Eileen Meyer Sklar of the Presbyterian Historical Society; Jean R. Guild of the Edinburgh University Library; Betty DiRisio of the Lawrence County Library; Patricia Hewett and Tomas Jahn of the Museum of New Mexico's Fray Angelico Chavez History Library; Deborah Newman, Arizona Historical Society Library; Kim Walters, Braun Research Library, Southwest Museum; Tommie Ann Gard, USGS Denver Library; Jeff Newman of the University of Toronto Library. In addition, there are many individuals who in various ways have contributed to my research and writing: Durwood Ball of the New Mexico Historical Review and Bruce Dinges of the Journal of Arizona History; David Brugge, Erica Bsumek, Alfred Bush, Leah Dilworth, Don Fowler, Armin W. Geertz, Linda Goodman, Jesse Green, Tony and Marie Hillerman, Curtis M. Hinsley, Jr., Pieter Hovens, David T. Kirkpatrick, A. Thomas Kirsch, Bill Korstick, Barbara Kramer, W. David Laird, John Loftin, William Longacre, Ralph A. Luebben, Frances Joan Mathien, Sally J. McBeth, Darlis Miller, Earll Murman, Peter Nabokov, Stephen E. Nash, Alfonso Ortiz, Nancy Parezo, Joyce Rabb, Theresa Salazar, Uli Sanner, Ingo Schroeder, Fr. Thomas J. Steele, SJ, Robert Titterton, Russ and Gerri Todd, Judith van Gieson, John Ward, John Weeks, Robert R. White, and Sheldon P. Zitner. In addition, I would like to thank the Inter-Library Loan staffs at the University of New Mexico General Library, University of Washington Library and the Seattle Public Library for acquiring photocopies and microfilms.

There are others whose names I have lost, among them a historian who, in a casual conversation, suggested I look at Jeremiah Sullivan's home town newspapers.

As always, my wife Sharon Aller, has "been there" throughout this entire project, patiently encouraging me. Without her love and care, this book would not have been written.

Over the past decade or more, Joe McCreery has listened and offered intellectual perspectives that have enriched my research and writing beyond measure for which I am deeply grateful.

Finally, and especially, special thanks to George E. Webb, Peter Brennan, and Rena H. Murman for reading all or part of this manuscript and to Paul Rhetts for seeing it into print. Needless to say, its many shortcomings are mine and mine alone.

THE DOCTOR DANCED WITH US

1. Introduction: Some Pieces of the Puzzle

The Puzzle

The book before you—'*The Doctor Danced With Us*': *Jeremiah Sullivan and the Hopi, 1881-1888*—grew out of my interest in the field research of the many ethnologists who visited the Hopi Indians of northeastern Arizona between 1879, when the first Bureau of Ethnology exploring expedition arrived in the Southwest, and 1894, when the work of the Hemenway Southwestern Archaeological Expedition suddenly ended.

This is a biography which, of necessity, has become a series of biographies. This is also a book about the economics and politics of ethnology—past and present—and the silencing of an authorship.

I first encountered Jeremiah Sullivan's name while reading the translation of a Dutch anthropologist's account of the Snake Dance at the Hopi First Mesa village of Walpi in 1883. At Walpi, Herman ten Kate met "Oyiwisha (He Who Plants Corn), alias Jeremiah Sullivan, M.D., an adopted son of the Moquis, among whom he has spent more than two years."[1] I was puzzled, then intrigued. Who was this Jeremiah Sullivan? How long did he live among the Hopi? Did he write anything? I occasionally fantasized finding a dusty trunk filled with his notebooks and manuscripts. That would have been too easy.

As I was to learn, Jeremiah Sullivan lived in the First Mesa village of Sichumovi for seven years—nearly twice as long as his contemporary, Frank Hamilton Cushing, resided at Zuni Pueblo in western New Mexico. Sullivan practiced medicine in all of the Hopi villages, first as Agency Physician and then as a member of the Hopi community. In an effort to support his medical practice, he compiled demographic, linguistic, and ethnographic materials, submitting some to the Smithsonian Institution's newly established Bureau of Ethnology,

---

1   McIntire and Gordon 1968:27.

sending some to potential patrons, and publishing still other materials in newspapers. For several years Sullivan recorded Hopi narratives for A. M. Stephen, a clerk at the nearby trading post of Thomas Varker Keam. Some of the material Sullivan submitted to John Wesley Powell, Director of the Bureau of Ethnology, appears to be lost. Some of what Sullivan wrote remains in manuscripts scattered in libraries from New York and Pennsylvania to California. More, however, survives in notebooks of materials "collected by" Stephen and in anonymous manuscripts attributed to Stephen by editors unaware of Sullivan's residence among the Hopi. Enough remains, however, to suggest that—were it not for other circumstances—Jeremiah Sullivan would be well remembered today for his contributions to the early development of American anthropology. In 1921 a Hopi told anthropologist Elsie Clews Parsons "the Doctor danced with us." However, the profession of anthropology has no memory of this remarkable physician and ethnologist. As the reader will discover, the silences surrounding Jeremiah Sullivan tell us much about the development of American anthropology.

The Hopi Through Time

The ancient ancestors of the Hopi were hunters and gatherers who, in the first centuries A.D., came to pursue a life based on corn agriculture. A slow but clear evolution of many aspects of the culture or cultures of these ancestral Puebloan peoples over the next 1500 years is evident in archaeological remains found throughout the Colorado Plateau and beyond. At the same time, there is evidence that some of the fundamental principles of ancestral Hopi culture have persisted essentially unchanged. However, by the beginning of the 1880s, the Hopi were at the edge of the advancing, rapidly changing Euro-American culture and many objects of its material culture had already become a part of Hopi life. Nor were the Hopis isolated from other cultures in the area, especially that of the Navajo who began moving into northeastern Arizona by the end of the eighteenth century. Through trade, intermarriage, contacts with missionaries and traders, and the increasing impact of Federal Indian policies, Hopi culture was undergoing profound changes when Jeremiah Sullivan entered the world of the Hopi. Although unintended, Sullivan's presence among the Hopi provided the occasion for the most important event in Hopi history in the 19th century—the establishment of the Executive Order Moqui [Hopi] Pueblo Indian Reservation on December 12, 1882.

"The Ancient Province of Tusayan" and *Hopitutsqwa*

As part of the preparations for the 1876 Centennial Exhibition in Philadelphia, John Wesley Powell, then famous for his explorations of the Colorado River, published an account of two weeks he had spent among the Hopi in October 1870. The article in the December 1875 issue of *Scribner's Monthly* was entitled, "The Ancient Province of Tusayan." As familiar as "Tusayan" may be to readers today, Powell's use appears to be the first published in nineteenth century literature. At least no earlier use appears in the Cornell University-Library of Congress "Making of America" full-text database searching by the keyword "Tusayan," but the place-name may have been commonly understood. For example, on June 12, 1856, Major H. L. Kendrick, in command of Fort Defiance, Arizona, wrote, "While the Zunis have descended from those who once lived in the 'Seven Cities of Cibola' of Castaneda, the Seven villages of the Moqui are the identical 'Seven Cities of Tusayan.'"[2]

Walpi, 1876. Photograph by J. K. Hillers. Bibliotheque nationale de France/Societe de Geographie. Image: #Sg Wf 5(1).

---

2   Quoted in Hammond 1970:22.

The first Europeans to visit the Hopi were Don Pedro de Tovar and his party, a small detachment of the Francisco Vasquez de Coronado expedition of 1540-1542. Tovar had been sent to explore the land northwest of Zuni and to look for rich kingdoms in that direction. Pedro de Castaneda, chronicler of the Coronado expedition, wrote, "It is 20 leagues to Tusayan, going northwest. This is a province of seven villages of the same sort, dress, habits, and ceremonies as at Cibola."[3] The two provinces referred to were Zuni, Coronado's headquarters at the time, and that of Hopi. Victor Mindeleff's "A Study of Pueblo Architecture in Tusayan and Cibola" (1891) reflects this usage and it was followed by the Smithsonian ethnologists throughout the period under consideration here. We must assume that Powell, like his friend Lewis Henry Morgan,[4] and maybe Major Kendrick as well, had read a later edition of *The Relation of Francis Vasquez de Coronado* in Richard Hakluyt's *Collection of Voyages* first published in 1600. Stephen later speculated:

> The early Spanish colonists in their journeys from the Rio Grande to the region of the Hopi employed Navajo guides, whose country they had to cross before reaching the Hopi. Referring to the locality of the Hopi villages those Navajo frequently use their own term *ta-sa-un*— isolate—hence the adoption of the appropriate term by the Spaniards, *Provinca de Tusayan*—The Isolated Province. [Stephen added] This is my conjecture and [Washington] Matthews accepts it as quite adequate— no Hopi knows ought of the term.[5]

Although the Spanish failed to gain sovereignty over Hopi land and the Hopi people and failed in their efforts to convert them to Catholicism, the Spanish did take possession of Hopi land by naming it Tusayan. Powell's revival of the name Tusayan helped him to define an area soon to be central to the work of the Bureau of Ethnology.

Few asked, as the Dutch anthropologist Herman ten Kate did in 1883, "what do the Hopi call their land?" Jeremiah Sullivan replied, "The

---

3   Winship 1896:519.

4   Morgan 1880.

5   Stephen to J. W. Fewkes, December 27, 1891, MS 4408, National Anthropological Archives, Smithsonian Institution. Cited hereafter as NAA, SI. See also Haile 1917.

Moquis call their land *Mahsootchkwuh* [*Masau-tutsqua*], 'the land of *Masawe* [*Masaw*]' (the earth god)."[6] This meaning is reflected today as Hopis distinguish between *tutsqua* (land as a geopolitical construct) and *Hopitutsqwa* ("Hopi land," a religious concept).

Indeed, the concept of *Hopitutsqwa* is fundamental, then and now, to the Hopis' understanding of who they are as a people, of how they view the world around them, and of their relationship to the land they live on:

> When the Hopis emerged from the Sipapuni into this, the Fourth World, they encountered the diety *Ma'saw* in the Grand Canyon. *Ma'saw* was the guardian of the Fourth World and he urged the Hopis to adopt his way of life, giving them a digging stick and a bag of seeds so they could live as humble and hardworking farmers. A spiritual pact was made with *Ma'saw*, wherein he agreed to let the Hopis use his land if they would act as stewards of the earth. ... By fulfilling their pact, the Hopis earned the right to use *Ma'saw's* land; *Masaututsqwa* became *Hopitutsqwa*.[7]

Hopitutsqwa is a religious concept and not one that required— at least in Hopi thought—boundaries as defined by Euro-American property laws. On the basis information gathered during conversations in Hopi kivas, Stephen "surmised" the extent of what was "Masau's land originally, the land of the Hopituh." The "exact limits are unknown" but he understood:

> [Ma'sau] started from a point about where Fort Mohave now is situated, thence south as far as the Isthmus of Panama, skirted eastward along the Gulf of Mexico and northward by the line of the Rio Grande up into Colorado, thence westerly along the thirty-sixth parallel or thereabouts to the Rio Colorado, meandering along its tributaries and so on southward to his starting point at Fort Mohave.[8]

Other Hopi traditions, especially the migration narratives of various Hopi clans, mention seven places in their descriptions of

---

6   Kate 2004:256.

7   Jenkins, Fergusson, and Dongoske 1994:1-2.

8   Parsons, ed. 1929:56.

Hopitutsqwa. These include *Tokonavi* (Navajo Mountain), the Colorado River or Grand Canyon, *Tusaqtsomo* (Bill Williams Mountain), the Mogollon Rim, *Tsimontukwi* (Woodruff Butte), *Namituyqa* (Lupton), and *Kawestima* (Betatakin).[9]

More often traditions relate that Ma'sau told the Hopis, "all this land is mine, and all that lies within the limits of my footprints is yours."[10] The "footprints" were pieces of pottery, petroglyphs, archaeological sites, shrines—"mementos," Sullivan's word—that many Federal officials have wanted to use to define and circumscribe the extent of Hopi lands. However, Hopis say the shrines, sometimes mistakenly called "boundary shrines," do not define a boundary but rather are *homvi'ikya*, a term which derives from two words:

> *Hooma* is the sacred corn meal that Hopis use for prayer offerings. *Vi'ikya* is a route or place, an actual geographic designation of something. A *homvi'ikya* therefore refers to a route used in the offering of prayer meal. The shrines that are visited on the *homvi'ikya* are used to pay homage to a greater domain of stewardship and all of *Hopitutsqwa*.[11]

In a very real sense, it is not possible to draw lines on a map to define *Hopitutsqwa*—certainly not as a domain of stewardship or as something essential to the practice of religion--but in 1882 lines were drawn to define a small geopolitical territory called Executive Order Moqui [Hopi] Pueblo Indian Reservation. The circumstances that led to this event are central to the story of Jeremiah Sullivan's life among the Hopi. Suffice it to say here, on December 16, 1882, President Chester A. Arthur signed the executive order, a narrative construction of the landscape invisible to those living there:

> It is hereby ordered that a tract of country, in the Territory of Arizona, lying and being within the following described boundaries, Viz: beginning on the one hundred and tenth degree of longitude west from Greenwich, at the point 36'30" north, thence due west to the one hundred

---

9   Jenknis, Fergusson, and Dongoske, ibid, p. 7. See also Glowacka, Washburn, and Richland 2009.

10   Fewkes 1894b:118.

11   Jenkins, Fergusson, and Dongoske, ibid, p. 8.

and eleventh degree of longitude west, thence due south to a point longitude 35'30" north, thence due east to the one hundred and tenth degree of longitude west, thence due north to the place of beginning, be and the same is hereby withdrawn from settlement and sale, and set apart for the use and occupancy of the Moqui [Hopi], and such other Indians, as the Secretary of the Interior may see fit to settle thereon.

The lines so hastily drawn and drawn without any consultation with Hopi elders had immediate legal and political implications that continue into the twenty-first century.

In 1887 the Dawes Severalty Act was passed which gave the president discretionary power to survey Indian reservations and divide them in 160-acre plots for male heads of families, 80-acre plots for single males over 18 years of age, and 40-acre plots for boys. No provisions were made for females and the unborn.

In May 1891 surveying began in the Oraibi valley as a first step in the allotment of Hopi land.[12] Soon after the surveyors left, Oraibis pulled up the stakes and destroyed the survey monuments around Third Mesa. The government responded by sending troops who arrested the "Hostiles" from Oraibi opposed to the allotment as well as efforts to send their children to school. The allotment process continued in spite of resistance by the Hopis.

On December 21, 1893, A. M. Stephen wrote:

> Tom [Keam] has gotten his friend [lawyer W. Hallett] Phillips interested in the Hopi. Phillips has taken up their case [in a letter to D. M. Browning, Commission of Indian Affairs, dated November 5, 1893] on the grounds that the Hopi have a better title to their land than the United States has.

He continued:

> At Tom's instigation I have drawn up a brief memorial for the Hopi to "sign" and put in Phillip's hands. I have stated the main objections from the Hopi standpoint to land in

---

12   Whiteley 1988a:76-81 provides a succinct account of the events between 1891 and 1894. Whiteley, however, makes no mention of the critical role of W. Hallett Phillips in bringing the allotment process to an end.

severalty. Should the principal Hopi chiefs adhere to it I will send you on a copy.[13]

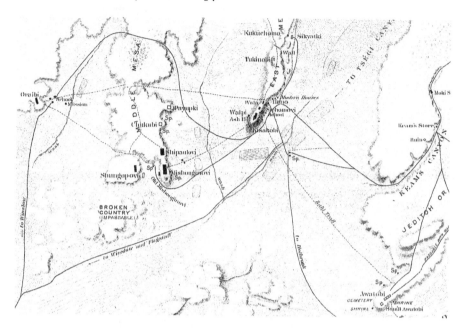

Sketch Map of the Mesa Country Occupied by the Hopi Indians, by J. W. Fewkes, ca. 1895. *Seventeenth Annual Report of the Bureau of American Ethnology*, Plate CV. Washington: Government Printing Office, 1898.

W. Hallett Phillips, a young lawyer who had argued cases before the Supreme Court, called into question the legality of the allotment of Hopi lands. In the letter of November 5, 1893, Phillips cited a decision of the United States Supreme Court in the case of United States vs. Joseph, upholding the Pueblo Indians as proprietary owners of their towns and lands and that the hold of such property in common did not affect this right. Phillips argued:

> The Pueblo Indians...hold their lands by a right superior to that of the United States. Their title dates back to grants made by the government of Spain before the Mexican Revolution. The title which was fully recognized by the Mexican Government and protected by the Treaty

---

13   Stephen to Fewkes, December 21, 1893, MS 4408, NAA, SI.

of Guadalupe Hidalgo, by which this country and the allegiance of its inhabitants were transferred to the United States.[14]

In a second letter, dated ten days later, Phillips rejected the Commissioner's contention of the relevance of the boundaries defining Hopi land in the 1882 Executive Order Moqui Pueblo Indian Reservation. Browning did not respond to Phillips' second letter. A penciled marginal notation states: "Mr. Phillips is right."[15] As this exchange was taking place, John S. Mayhugh, the allotment agent, continued the survey of lands for the First and Second Mesas, completing this work in January 1894. At the beginning of February Mayhugh received a telegram from Commissioner Browning to cease the allotment process and return to Washington. Phillips' efforts brought the allotment program for the Hopi Indians to an end.

Stephen's petition "to the Washington chiefs" used what he thought was a more politically effective logic of protest. While making no reference to the Hopi's pact with *Ma'saw* and the concept of *Hopitutsqwa*, Stephen drew on his knowledge of Hopi corn agriculture and social organization, especially its matrilineality, to provide another perspective on the meaning of "Hopi land." On behalf of the Hopi, Stephen wrote:

> During the last two years strangers have looked over our land with spy-glasses, and made marks upon it, and we know but little of what this means.
>
> As we believe that you have no wish to disturb our possessions, we want to tell you something about this Hopi land. None of us ever asked that it should be measured into separate lots and given to individuals, for this would cause confusion.
>
> The family, the dwelling-house, and the field are inseparable, because the woman is the heir of these,

---

14   W. Hallett Phillips to D. M. Browning, November 5, 1893, Letterbooks, Box 10, MSS 36087, P. Phillips Family Papers, Library of Congress. Cited hereafter as MSS 36087, LC.

15   Phillips to Browning, November 15, 1893, Letterbooks, Box 10, MSS 36087, LC. Phillips responded to Browning's letter of November 11, 1893. The pencil notation is cited in George Peter Hammond, Hopi-Navajo Relations, part II, p. 60, George Peter Hammond Collection, MSS 55 BC, Center for Southwest Research, University of New Mexico.

and they rest with her. Among us the family traces its kin from the mother, hence all its possessions are hers. The man builds the house but the woman is the owner, because she repairs and preserves it; the man cultivates the field, but he renders the harvest into the keeping of the woman, because upon her it rests to prepare the food, and the surplus of stores for barter depends upon her thrift.

A man plants the field for his wife, and the fields assigned to the children she bears, and informally he calls them his, although in fact they are not. Even of the field which he inherits from his mother, its harvests he may dispose of at will, but the field itself he may not. He may permit his son to occupy it and gather its produce, but at the father's death, the son may not own it, for then it passes to the father's sister's son, or nearest mother's kin, and thus our fields and houses always remain with our mothers.

According to the number of children a woman has, fields for them are assigned to her, form some of the lands of her family group, and her husband takes care of them. Hence our fields are numerous but small, and several belonging to the same family may be close together, or they may be miles apart, because arable localities are not continuous. There are other reasons for the irregularity in size and situation of our family lands, as interrupted sequence of inheritance caused by extinction of families, but chiefly, owing to the following condition, and to which we especially invite your attention.

In the spring and early summer there usually comes from the Southwest a succession of gales, oftentimes strong enough to blow away the sandy soil from the face of some of our fields, and to expose the underlying clay, which is hard, and sour, and barren; as the sand is the only fertile land, when it moves the planters must follow it, and other fields must be provided in place of those which have been devastated. Sometimes generations pass away and these barren spots remain, while in other instances, after a few years, the winds will again restore the desirable sand upon them.

In such event its fertility is disclosed by the nature of the grass and shrubs that grow upon it. If these are promising, a number of us unite to clear off the land and make it again fit for planting; when it may be given back to its former owner, or if a long time has elapsed to other heirs, or it may be given to some person of the same family group more in need of a planting place.

These limited changes in land holdings are explored by mutual discussion and concession among the elders, and among all the thinking men and women of the family groups interested.

In effect, the same system of holding, and the same method of planting, obtain among the Tewa, and all the Hopi villages, and under them we provide ourselves with food in abundance.

The American is our Elder brother, and in everything he can teach us, except in the method of growing corn in these waterless, sandy valleys, and in that we are sure we can teach him.

We believe that you have no desire to change our system of small holdings, nor do we think that you wish to remove any of our ancient landmarks, and it seems to us that the conditions we have mentioned afford sufficient grounds for thus requesting to be left undisturbed.

Further it has been told to us, as coming from Washington, that neither measuring nor individual papers are necessary for us to keep possession of our villages, our peach orchards, and our springs. If this be so, we should like to ask what need there is to bring confusion into our accustomed system of holding our corn fields.

We are aware that some ten years ago, a certain area around our lands was proclaimed to be for our use, but the extent of this area is unknown to us, nor has any

Agent ever been able to point it out, for its boundaries have never been measured.

We earnestly desire to have one continuous boundary ring enclosing all the Tewa and all the Hopi lands, and that it shall be large enough to afford sustenance for our increasing flocks and herds. If such a scope can be confirmed to us by a paper from your hands, securing us forever against intrusion, all our people will be satisfied.[16]

In the final two paragraphs of the petition, Stephen makes reference to the 1882 Executive Order Moqui Indian Reservation of over 2,500,000 acres and alludes—with his apparent approval but without consultation with Hopi and Tewa leaders who came to his rooms to place their "X" on the "memorial"—to a potentially disastrous proposal made by Thomas Donaldson, the "expert special agent" for the 1890 census, to redraw the lines of the reservation to form an oval of about 10,000 acres around the Hopi villages to include their agricultural land.[17]

Stephen's petition was practical and pragmatic and, ultimately, self-serving. He wanted to complete his research before more changes in Hopi culture took place. It is not clear when the petition reached the offices of the Commissioner of Indian Affairs. In his last letter to J. Walter Fewkes,[18] written just weeks before his death in April 1894, Stephen noted that Hopis continued to come to his room to sign. By then the allotting agent had been recalled to Washington. Phillips's arguments to the Commissioner of Indian Affairs had been convincing.[19] In his Annual Report for 1894, Commissioner D. M. Browning acknowledged

---

16   Stephen, December 1893, MS 4408, NAA, SI. Stephen's efforts on behalf of the Hopi began after Phillips had successfully convinced the Commissioner of Indian Affairs that the allotment program was illegal. Nonetheless, it conveys a clear sense of the potential impact of a patrilineal system forced upon a matrilineal system

17   Donaldson 1893:14. "Map showing the Moqui Indian Reservation... The oval red line suggests the reservation or grant, which should be made."

18   As detailed in Chapter 6, Fewkes was the Director of the Hemenway Southwestern Archaeological Expedition and, at the time, Stephen's employer.

19   Browning had not responded to Phillips second letter, informing him of the decision to end the allotment of Hopi lands. Consequently, Phillips continued to write to Keam, April 20, 1894 and May 26, 1894, with additional strategies to protect Hopi interests. "I stand ready to do all I can." MSS 36087, LC.

that the attempt to allot the Hopi lands had failed and he had therefore discontinued the plan, owing to the opposition of a small number of the Indians and "the formal objections to the approval of any of the allotments presented to this office by friends of the Indians."[20]

Although this battle had been won, the Hopis were to face many others in the century to follow, especially through a series of political and legal actions known as the Navajo-Hopi Land Dispute.

The Hopi Landscape as Seen by Others

In the three hundred and forty years between the Coronado expedition in 1540 and the arrival of the Sullivans in Keams Canyon in 1880, hundreds of explorers, missionaries, U. S. army soldiers, and others visited the Hopi and many wrote accounts of the people and villages of Tusayan. Still others used photographs, sketches, oil paintings and maps to describe Hopi land.

During the years Jeremiah Sullivan lived on First Mesa, a number of narratives "describing" (representing and constructing) the "landscape" near the Hopi villages were written. Each of these portraits conveys a different "seeing."

In May 1885 Herbert Welsh reached the Hopi as part of "a visit to the Navajo, Pueblo, and Hualapais Indians of New Mexico and Arizona" to secure "fresh and living facts" to inform the work of the Indian Rights Association. He wrote:

> On both days of our journey from Fort Defiance to Keam's Canyon the horizon behind us was frequently black with angry thunderclouds, so that we expected at any moment to be overtaken by drenching rain. . . .
>
> On the afternoon of Wednesday, May 21st, we reached Keam's Canyon. The storm-clouds had passed away and the evening was bright and beautiful, as our road suddenly dipped down from the dry desert tableland into a rich and narrow valley, watered by abundant springs and green with refreshing verdure. As it lay there in the afternoon sunlight, winding through the tumbled masses of white cliffs that hemmed it in,

---

20   Browning 1894:20. The "formal objections" were those of W. Hallett Phillips.

Keam's Canyon seemed to us attractive as an oasis in the desert to the eye of the wayworn traveler. ...

On the morning after our arrival, I started upon an excursion to the homes of these curious people. Dr. Jeremiah Sullivan, a very intelligent and amusing man, who for several years has lived in the Moqui village, studying the language and customs of its inhabitants, was our guide.

After emerging from the mouth of the canyon our road brought us into the open plain, which became more arid, bare, and desolate as we advanced. Lofty mountains, amethyst-colored and exquisitely delicate in outline, rose at intervals upon the horizon. A sky of purest blue hung above us and about us as everywhere fell the intense, unbroken sunlight. The heat was great, but the air so dry as not to occasion discomfort. Off to our right rose a long, rugged line of rock, like a huge antediluvian monster turned to stone. The summit of this abrupt elevation is six hundred feet above the plain. Our road turned toward it, and, as we approached, we could see high up upon the summit of the cliff the outline of the Moqui village[s], the houses (similar, in many respects, to those of the other pueblos) at first being scarcely distinguishable from the native rock on which they stood. Here and there on the roofs of the houses a dark moving object, which closer scrutiny proved to be a human being, was outlined against the sky. At the base of the cliff many of the Moqui men were working in their sandy cornfields. As we began the ascent we passed a small peach orchard. The trees, which grew out of hopeless-looking sand, were covered with pale pink blossoms that breathed upon the air a delightful fragrance. The ascent to the village, which was very precipitous, wound in and out among huge fragments of rock, and suggested the thought constantly to the mind, "What a wonderful natural stronghold, and with how little labor its approaches might be rendered absolutely secure against attack!" On reaching the top we found ourselves entering one of the three Moqui villages which crown the cliff. It is impossible to describe the strange sense of isolation and elevation which we experienced upon first coming into this curious place. I have never felt anything at all similar to it. The eye looks down, as from the masthead of a vessel, upon an illimitable sea of sand sweeping out and toward the mountainous horizon. The distance impresses the beholder with a sense of indescribable majesty and silence, while every object in the immediate foreground speaks of the peculiar customs and methods of life practiced by a people upon whom time has wrought but little change.

The summit of the cliff on which we found ourselves was quite flat, and at certain points between the villages was probably seventy-five to one hundred feet in width. Along the centre a deep furrow had been worn by the treading of centuries. The largest of the two villages which we visited was a curious collection of houses… They were piled one upon another like the cells of the honeycomb, while from doors and windows their occupants peered at us with eager curiosity. Children tumbled or wrestled with one another on the very edge of the precipice, which broke off from the sides of the village in a sheer descent of six hundred feet; others scampered over the roofs—up and down the ladders which led from house to house. I visited a number of the people in their homes. In all cases I was kindly received. We wandered at will during the afternoon through the two streets of the village and climbed from roof to roof by means of wooden ladders and flights of narrow stone steps. We were much attracted by the bright, pretty faces of the Moqui girls of twelve or fourteen years. Up to marriageable age they have a very droll fashion of dressing the hair. It is plaited in and is rolled at either side into two enormous puffs. I could not but contrast the intelligent, vivacious expression on the faces of these children with the dull, lusterless countenances of the older women. The natural fire of childhood burns to a maturity where no intelligent surroundings fan the flame and where there is no fuel of thought upon which it may be fed. Thus far our civilization seems to have offered little hope for the Moquis. Mr. Sullivan is anxious to aid them if some opportunity were to present itself. He is himself a physician and spoke to me of their need of medicines. They have at present neither agent, missionary, nor schoolmaster. The entire population on the rock numbers, he told me, three hundred. The Moquis are a mild, peaceful people, possessing sheep, goats, and some ponies. They subsist principally upon corn, which they raise in the sandy fields at the base of their cliff. About sundown we could see the men, their great, heavy hoes upon their shoulders, beginning their toilsome ascent homeward after the labors of the day were over. As night closed in upon us we retired to Mr. Sullivan's room (of which the ceiling was so low that we could not stand upright without striking our heads against it), not caring to wander after nightfall in a place where neither lamp nor candle relieved the darkness, and where one false step might plunge one down six hundred feet of precipice.[21]

Welsh's account shares an aesthetic perspective with that of several artists (e.g., Willard L. Metcalf and Frederick S. Dellenbaugh) who visited the Hopi during Sullivan's residence. There is a sense of the newness and strangeness of an encounter with the place and people living there and a "seeing" that dwells on the surfaces experienced. The land they saw was not the land Hopis saw, not *Hopitutsqwa*. For my purpose Welsh's portrait conveys an outsider's sense of the time and place in the 1880s.

The Hopi and Federal Indian Policy

There was a broad change in interest and concern for American Indians following the end of the Civil War. In 1869, early in the

---

21   Welsh 1885:34-35.

administration of President Ulysses S. Grant, a new approach to Indian affairs was developed, the "peace policy," so named because one of its central tenets was "the hitherto untried policy...of endeavoring to conquer by kindness." By an act of Congress a citizen Board of Indian Commissioners, whose members were nominated by various religious denominations, was established to oversee the work of federal Indian policy. Especially among liberals in the east, it was thought that "Christian gentlemen" could do what military generals could not—"civilize" Indian people. In 1870 Grant agreed with the proposal that Christian denominations be called upon to nominate Agency personnel. Initially, missionary societies of American Baptist, Congregational, Episcopal, Reformed, and Unitarian churches, as well as the Board of Foreign Missions of the Presbyterian Church, were included on the basis of missionary work already done among respective tribes and the church's ability to participate in the program. At the time the Roman Catholic Church had by far the largest and most successful Indian mission program. However, it was excluded, as were the Moravians and Mormons, also experienced in Indian missions. By 1872 a Catholic Bureau of Indian Missions was organized to safeguard Catholic interests and to coordinate the church's Indian mission effort. In response to complaints, the government in 1874 adopted a policy of religious exclusivity for Indian mission work, granting the sole right of evangelization to the denomination in control of the agency in question. The government's position, however, was inconsistent and uncertain, and controversy increased. The exclusivity ruling was revoked in March 1881.

In the Annual Report of the Secretary of the Interior for 1873 Secretary Columbus Delano listed the Peace Policy's five objectives, as he understood them:

> First, the Indians were to be placed on reservations as rapidly as possible. Second, those that refused to locate on reservations were to be punished for their "outrages". Third, provisions were to be made for guaranteeing that items supplied to the Indians were procured at fair and reasonable prices. Fourth, competent, upright, faithful, moral, and religious agents were to be secured through the various church organizations and otherwise. Fifth,

the goal was to establish schools, "and, through the instrumentality of the Church organizations acting in harmony with the Government, as far as possible, to build churches and organize Sabbath-schools, whereby these savages may be taught a better way of life than they have heretofore pursued, and be made to understand and appreciate the comforts and benefits of a Christian civilization, and thus be prepared ultimately to assume the duties and privileges of citizenship."[22]

In a word, the government's goal was assimilation, to "Christianize and civilize" through whatever means it took to destroy communal tribalism.

The Presbyterian Board of Foreign Missions, under the leadership of its secretary, Rev. John C. Lowrie, was given the responsibility of nominating agents and operating mission schools for nine tribal groups in the Southwest under contract with the Indian Bureau, including the Pueblo Indians of New Mexico, the Navajo and the Hopi. The Presbyterians, like the other denominations, were poorly equipped to assume the responsibility cast upon them. The Presbyterian Church created no special organization to administer its agency obligations. Supervision of agents was left to the local presbyteries. While Congressional appropriations provided the salary for agents, funding for mission schools was left to the churches. Unlike the Quakers and Episcopalians, the Presbyterians did not send inspectors into the field and this lack of supervision is reflected in a series of scandals and controversies involving the two Presbyterian appointees at the Navajo Agency, William F. M. Arny who was forced to resign in 1875 and Galen Eastman who was removed in 1882.

The perceived failures of the Board of Foreign Missions led to an internal shift of responsibility in 1880 when the Board of Home Missions took over the operation of schools at a number of Western agencies, including the Hopi. The two boards represented different constituencies and philosophies within the Presbyterian Church. The Board of Foreign Missions was responsible for spreading the gospel in foreign lands, especially China where missions had been established in

---

22   Taylor 1990:656-657. Bruce Lee Taylor's dissertation includes a clear and well-documented account of Federal Indian policy.

the 1830s, and justified its role in implementing the Peace Policy by the claim that Indians spoke languages as foreign as Chinese. The Board of Home Missions was responsible for missionary activities on the frontier, including the efforts of the missionary teachers to further the Indian Bureau's program of civilizing American Indians through education. With the division of responsibility between the two governing bodies, the Board of Foreign Missions retained the right of nominating the Indian agents and, in McCluskey's words, "a new arena of bureaucratic disputes was established."[23] In 1878 the Presbytery of Santa Fe made overtures to the General Assembly of the Presbyterian Church "asking that the Indian tribes, whose reservations are within the bounds of this Presbytery, and which are not under the care of the Board of Foreign Missions, be transferred to the care of our Home Board."[24] By 1881, through the energetic leadership provided by Rev. Sheldon Jackson and Rev. Henry Kendall, the shift of the Pueblo Indians of New Mexico, the Navajos and the Hopis to the Board of Home Missions was complete. In the meantime, as this transition was taking place in the early 1880s, the consequences of these shifts took on dramatic form in a conflict at the Hopi Agency between the nominees of the two boards, the agent, John H. Sullivan (Jeremiah Sullivan's father) and the missionary teacher, Rev. Charles A. Taylor.

One of the official rationales for the churches' nomination of agents was promotion of harmony between the agents and the missionaries serving particular tribes. However, even when both agent and missionary represented the same church animosities developed. Moreover, few of the agents under the Peace Policy escaped accusation of dishonesty or incompetence. In 1877 Commissioner of Indian Affairs Ezra D. Hayt ignored the role the Board of Indian Commissioners had played under President Grant and appointed a commission to investigate the Bureau of Indian Affairs. Hayt removed thirty-five agents. Church nomination of agents was beginning to be viewed as a farce. By the end of 1882, the controversies surrounding both the Navajo agent (Eastman) and the Hopi agents (Sullivan and Fleming) contributed to the final demise of the Peace Policy.

Church participation in agent selection came to an end. Henry M.

---

23   McCluskey 1980:366-367.
24   Quoted in Taylor 1990:714.

Teller, Secretary of the Interior, did not consult the Foreign Board prior to the appointment of Dennis M. Riordan whose term of service as Navajo agent began January 1, 1883. In the turmoil that followed the closure of the Moqui Pueblo Indian Agency in the spring of 1883, oversight of the newly established Executive Order Moqui Pueblo Indian Reservation was forgotten.

2. "The Doctor Danced With Us:" Jeremiah Sullivan and the Hopi, 1881-1888[25]

The Sullivans in Madison

Jeremiah Sullivan was born in Madison, Indiana, November 19, 1851, the son of John Henderson Sullivan (1817-1886) and Charlotte Evalyn Sullivan (1827-1907), the oldest of five children.[26] The marriage of John Henderson Sullivan and Charlotte Cutler Sullivan on June 21, 1849 was the marriage of two people with the same surnames, Sullivan. Jeremiah was the grandson on his mother's side of a prominent Indiana judge, Jeremiah C. Sullivan. Jeremiah's father, a wholesale grocer, businessman and railroad contractor, was active in politics in Madison and later in Keokuk, Iowa, where his family lived from 1855 to 1867. After two years in Louisville, Kentucky, the Sullivans returned to Madison in 1869.[27] While in Keokuk Jeremiah received his education

---

25   This chapter is a revised and expanded version of material to be published in *Zuni, Hopi, Copan: John G. Owens' Letters from the field, 1890-1893*, edited by C. M. Hinsley, L. A. Hieb and B. Fash (Cambridge: Peabody Museum Press).

26   Jeremiah Sullivan's younger siblings: John (who died before age 2), Mary Isabel (Parsons) Engler, Caroline "Carrie" Brice (Boyington) and John H. "Sully" Sullivan, Jr..

27   In 1879 John H. Sullivan and his family first lived in the Francis Costigan house (1851), 408 West Third before moving into the Federal style two-story brick house built by Jeremiah C. Sullivan (1794-1870) (Mrs. Sullivan's father) at 304 West Second Street (at the corner of Poplar Avenue, known as Poplar Lane in 1879) in 1816 or 1818. It is known today as the Judge Jeremiah Sullivan House, named for the prominent Indiana lawyer and judge (Judge of the Supreme Court of Indiana, 1836-1846) who coined the name "Indianapolis" for the new state capital. Judge Sullivan and his wife, Charlotte R. Sullivan, had twelve children, six living to maturity. One of his sons was named Jeremiah Cutler Sullivan, Jr. Because of the confusion of names it was the local practice to refer to Judge Jeremiah C. Sullivan as "Jeremiah" and Dr. Jeremiah Sullivan as "Jere." At the

under "Professor" W. W. Jamieson who conducted a Classical School at the Westminster Presbyterian Church. In 1872 Jeremiah attended the University of Louisville Medical School;[28] afterwards Madison newspapers referred to him as "Dr," and as "Jeremiah Sullivan, M.D." Twenty years later changes in the medical profession led him to return to the University of Kentucky Medical School where "Jeremiah C. Sullivan" received a degree in allopathic medicine in 1894.[29] From that year until his death in American Falls, Idaho, on April 4, 1916, Jeremiah Sullivan was a physician in southeastern Idaho.

In an autobiography[30] written in Albuquerque, New Mexico, in 1883, John H. Sullivan wrote that soon after his return to Madison in 1869 he organized the Bedford, Brownstown and Madison Railroad Company, a project that involved both private and municipal subscriptions. In 1879, well after the beginning of work, the use of municipal funds was challenged in court and denied. The company failed and Sullivan's investment was lost. As a result, "I turned my attention to the far West

---

time of his graduation from medical school in 1894 Jeremiah Sullivan adopted his grandfather and uncle's name, "Jeremiah C. Sullivan." The "C" in this case was Cutler (Judge Sullivan's wife's maiden name). Jeremiah signed his name "Jer." and "Jer:" as well as "Jeremiah Sullivan, M.D."

28 "Jere Sullivan" attended in 1872 and a "Jeremiah Sullivan" attended during 1876, suggesting he might have attended medical school twice. On June 2, 1876, the *Madison Evening Courier* reported, "The Medical Society is pressing for a law for the protection of physicians and druggists to keep the quacks out." Clearly the community recognized Jeremiah Sullivan as a doctor.

29 *Fifty-Eighth Annual Announcement of the Medical Department of the University of Louisville* (Louisville, 1894) p. 23. As noted above, the Medical Department of the University of Louisville records show a "Jere Sullivan" in 1872 and a "Jeremiah Sullivan" in 1876. He would have been able to stay with family in Louisville. By the early 1800s a number of medical societies were in charge of establishing regulations, standards of practice and certification of doctors. In 1847 the American Medical Association was established and set educational standards for M.D.s including: a liberal arts degree in the arts and sciences, a certificate of completion in an apprenticeship before entering the medical college and an M.D. degree that covered three years and included three months devoted to dissection and a minimum of six months in residency. However, the certification and registration of M.D.s was slow to be established. Arizona, for example, began developing guidelines in 1891 (see Quebbeman 1966).

30 The original manuscript is in the possession of the Keokuk Savings Bank. David Attenberg, Lee County Historical Society, Keokuk, Iowa, provided a photocopy of the original.

believing there is yet a good time coming for me in Arizona or New Mexico—where I determined to go with my family taking Mr. Greeley's advice to young men—'go west and grow up with the country.'" On January 14, 1880 the *Indianapolis Daily Sentinel* published "The Indian Question" in which he detailed a new "programme...in the treatment of Indian": "...a kind, humane policy in their treatment by the United States. ...a new policy with them by first strictly performing all promised them, by treaty or otherwise."[31]

In February 1880 John H. Sullivan wrote to the Secretary of the Interior requesting an appointment to an Indian Agency in Arizona or New Mexico and three months later he learned of his appointment as Agent at the Moquis [Hopi][32] Pueblo Indian Agency. On July 7, 1880, in recognition of the senior Sullivan's turn of fortunes, the *Madison Evening Courier* published the following humorously inaccurate announcement:

John H. Sullivan's Agency
The Indian Agency awarded by the Government to Mr. John H. Sullivan is a desirable one. He will not depart for the West until sometime in August, taking with him one clerk.—The Indians placed in his charge are the Moquois tribe. They are located in the north-eastern section of Arizona, on the southern part of the Colorado plateau. Their chief village is located at a station on the St. Louis & San Francisco railroad. They are direct lineal descendants of the Montezumas, are the largest cattle and sheep raisers in that section, have five schools and two

---

31 John H. Sullivan 1880a.
32 Most writers in the nineteenth century referred to the Hopis as the Moquis or Mokis. The source of Moqui or Moki seems to be Keresan, but what was probably *mokwi* (referring to Hopi) was transformed through Spanish pronunciation and orthographic conventions into *moki*, a spoken form offensively resembling the Hopi *mo.ki* (dies, is dead) (Schroeder and Goddard 1979). It was at A. M. Stephen's insistence that J. Walter Fewkes use "Hopi" in their publications after 1891. See Stephen to Fewkes, 21 January 1892, MS4408, National Anthropological Archives, Smithsonian Institution. Cited hereafter as MS 4408, NAA, SI. In 1923 the Moquis Pueblo Indian Agency renamed the Hopi Agency and the term Moquis was dropped from all government usage.

churches, manufacture blankets and other woolen goods, and grow extensively small fruits and cereals. They consist of five villages, with a total of nearly three thousand. They are sworn enemies of the Sioux, Arapahos, Comanches, Modocs, Utes ad Piutes.—They are very industrious and nearly all members of the Protestant Church.

From Madison, Indiana,[33] the "Moquois tribe"—the Hopi—

---

33   The City of Madison, Indiana, on the Ohio River was first settled in 1809. After the War of 1812 it quickly grew as a hub for commerce along the Ohio River and later for transportation via the Michigan Road and the Madison-Indianapolis-Lafayette Railroad. By 1830 it had an estimated population of 3,000. As a river port city Madison continued to grow during the decades of the 1830s through the 1850s. By 1830 a floating wharf joined steamboat and railroad. A permanent wharf was constructed in 1833 and by 1851 there were six along the river's edge. The city was at a peak of prosperity in 1840 with the largest population in the state and the first railroad. Pork processing became the major industry in town and by the 1850s up to nineteen processing plants circled the city. Other related industries producing lard, bristles, skins and barrels thrived. In 1850 its population of 8,000 residents was nearly equal that of New Albany and Indianapolis. Among the residents was John H. Sullivan who had a wholesale grocery business on Main Street. At that time Madison's railroad was the only one in the state and the combined river and rail transport sustained the commercial interests of the city. In the 1850s competing railroads robbed Madison of its exclusiveness. As river transport declined, land routes by-passed the city, causing a decline and recession. It may have been this awareness of the potential of the railroad that led the Sullivan's to leave Madison in 1855 and move to Keokuk, Iowa. While the decade of the 1860s, beginning with the onset of the Civil War, brought economic hardship to other parts of the nation, Madison's economy improved considerably. Shipyards and foundries prospered all along the river. In 1863 at least thirteen new commercial buildings were under construction along Main Cross (Main Street today) as well as the United States General Hospital, one of the North's largest military hospitals treating over 8,000 patients before it was closed in 1865. It was into this flurry of post-war construction that John H. Sullivan and his family returned to Madison in 1869. In that year the top ten industries (in taxable wealth) were pork and lard, flour, starch, barrels, boats, clothing, furniture, leather, woolen goods and engines. The town had five breweries, five brickyards, and five saddletree factories, plus a number of related industries. A decade later (in order of value of product and capital investment) were The R. Johnson & Son Starch Works, two hub and spoke factories, a furniture company, seven saddletree shops, ten blacksmith shops, foundries, tin and iron works, three carriage and wagon works and two cooperages. In addition there were flour and

were unimaginably "other."

Jeremiah Sullivan undoubtedly shared his father's hopes in going west. The local newspapers—*Madison Daily Chronicle* and *Madison Daily Evening Star*—both contained frequent references to the "talented" Jeremiah Sullivan. He is mentioned as singing, often as soloist, at the First Presbyterian Church, the Jewish Synagogue, and Trinity Methodist Church where he became the music director. He was President of the Choir Union. He acted in plays and performed in the musical, "The Accommodating Gentleman." He was briefly on the editorial staff of the *Star* and a volunteer member of the Washington County Fire Department. However, there were few opportunities for gainful employment. In 1877 he was laying railroad tracks and later was boss of a squad of axe men with the doomed Bedford, Brownstown and Madison Railroad Company. The City Directory for 1879 listed him as a "bookkeeper." On January 29, 1880 the *Madison Evening Courier* announced:

> Dr. Jere Sullivan received the right to put up and equip the telephone communication between Madison and Hanover and other convenient points. Shares of stock $25.

Later in 1880 at the time his father was appointed agent he was working on the locks on the Kentucky River. Only once is he mentioned as practicing medicine: on January 12, 1880 he dressed the wound of a boy shot in the hand.

---

saw mills. In the latter part of the century, the population began to decline but its unique intellectual and cultural sophistication remained. As John H. Sullivan's autobiography makes clear, the economic opportunities and successes were not the same for everyone. His efforts to reopen the Robbins furniture factory in 1876 and his investment in the Bedford, Brownstown and Madison railroad (1877-1879) both ended in failure. In the elegant Sullivan mansion, the Sullivan family hosted parties and other social events celebrated in Madison newspapers but keeping up appearances became increasingly difficult. See, for example, the *Madison Courier*'s coverage of a charity ball held at the Sullivan residence, November 22, 1877 and a reception, October 22, 1881. Like many others, John H. Sullivan decided to "go west" in an effort to find new opportunities. Much of this note is derived from National Park Service, U. S. Department of the Interior, National Park Service, "Madison Historic District" (www.nps.gov/nr/travel/madison/madison_historic_district.html) and from correspondence with Gertrude Geraets, 1997-2014

Jeremiah Sullivan was also someone who enjoyed the give and take of humorous exchanges. On November 19, 1879, on the occasion of Jeremiah Sullivan's 29th birthday, the *Madison Daily Evening Star* published the following:

> Dr. Jere Sullivan saw the sun rise on another birthday of his this morning. It is alleged by some that he is 42 years old, but Jere tells us confidentially that he was only 37 last year. He grows a year younger every twelve months though, and we hope he may live to see the century plant bloom. The boys have been shaking hands with him all day.

His letters to the editor of Madison newspapers are often humorous or edited in a humorous manner. In a letter to the *Madison Evening Courier* published on February 12, 1881, the editor writes:

> …We take the liberty to cull and condense some of our friend's observations… Jere and a lot of his assistants at the Agency made a squaw a dress, and he says, "It was cut 'by-us.' If it is not 'gored' by a buffalo we'll venture she'll die from a fit—of the dress. Jere concludes his letter with this touching remark: 'I must now patch my pantaloons.'

Since the original letters do not survive, it is not clear whether the humor is Jeremiah Sullivan's or the editor's. Sullivan refers to the *Madison Daily Evening Star* as the "Dazzling Star." The editor of the *Madison Evening Courier* "translated" Sullivan's Hopi name—Oyiwisha or "He Who Plants Corn"—into "Sprouting Corn" as in this article of May 17, 1882 under the headline "Honest Indian:"

> Chief Sprouting-corn (nee Dr. Jere Sullivan) has sent Master Fred Crozier two bows and arrows… On this connection we wish to ask Sprouting-corn one question: Would you Kickapoo Indian?

In Jeremiah Sullivan's one surviving notebook of 1882 he addresses an unknown or imaged listener with the description of the "comical doings" of a clown ("Tutcukiya") at the close of a Katsina "dance":

> …Many funny things [happen]… One instance humorous and then we will laugh together… During this scene the laughter among the women is loud and the language rather vulgar… such that it is best not to repeat it.[34]

---

34   Sullivan's full account is as follows: "There is always one of the comical [clowns]

In 1885, during a visit to the Hopi, Herbert Welsh of the Indian Rights Association found him to be "a very intelligent and amusing man."

Government Agent vs. Missionary Teacher: "An Irrepressible Conflict"

The elder Sullivan's nomination as agent by the Presbyterian Board of Foreign Missions[35] had been approved earlier in the summer of 1880 by the United States Senate and President Rutherford B. Hayes. Like other agents, John H. Sullivan reported to the Commissioner of Indian Affairs. Delays in receiving his commission (it was miss-sent to Madison, Wisconsin) and in obtaining the necessary bond detained him in Madison, Indiana, until September 22, 1880. As he traveled to the "far off West," he reported "the country is beautiful, with highly cultivated farms" and farther on "a region of fertile lands" as he neared Wichita, Kansas. From Newton, Kansas, the train "passed over a splendid looking country with many flourishing towns and settlements" all the way to Trinidad, Colorado "where our line of travel turned to the Southwest." His letter to the *Madison Evening Courier* continued:

---

or Tutcukiya who winds up the dance with queer doings. Coming in as he does to signify the end of the dance he prances around the estufa [kiva] with a [kachina] doll in one hand to which a string is fastened. The girls make a rush for him to get the doll. Finally one captures it—his motion is suddenly brought to a stop for the string of the doll is securely tied to the foreskin of the penis of the man. Then she stands for several seconds holding on to the doll while the string is not only stretched to its greatest length, but also the man who does not take hold of the string to relieve himself suffers no little pain until relieved by cutting the string." Sullivan gave a similar description of a [katsina coming] "out with nothing on but some feathers on top of his mask and one tied to the end of his penis." Frederick S. Dellenbaugh, Diary, November 7, 1884, MS 0215, Arizona Historical Society, Tucson, Arizona. Cited hereafter as MS 0215, AHS. This form of sexual humor was frowned on by early missionaries and government representatives and seems to have disappeared by the end of the nineteenth century.

35   In response to his letter to the Secretary of the Interior in February 1880, John H. Sullivan was informed nominations for agents at agencies assigned to the Presbyterian Church came through the Presbyterian Board of Foreign Missions. Secretary of the Interior to Sullivan, April 14, 1880, Letters sent by the Office of Indian Affairs, National Archives. Cited hereafter as LS-OIA, NA.

Soon after leaving Trinidad we began to ascend the mountains, and directly the peaks, perpetually covered with snow, began to appear—to me a novel and beautiful sight. ... I noticed soon after we got into New Mexico a great change in the class of people, nearly all Mexican and Indian mixture, and also a difference in their houses, here they are nearly all one-story abode with dirt floor. ... A few miles east of Santa Fe the conductor called my attention to an old ruin, an old "Peacos" [Pecos] Indian church.[36] [He was told] They were Snake Worshippers and kept a very large snake in their church, to which it is said they fed every morning a young baby! Think of it, What a tremendous and tiresome work it must have been to furnish so many babies. Queer religion, wasn't it?[37]

In Santa Fe on September 28, "one of the Fathers (an Irishman who was very polite)" gave him a tour of the "ancient city," visiting San Miguel Chapel, the "oldest house" and St. Francis Cathedral.[38] Traveling by train to Laguna, New Mexico–the extent of the Atlantic and Pacific tracks–then by wagon, he reached Fort Wingate on October 1.[39] At the fort he was welcomed by Capt. Frank Tracy Bennett, Acting U. S. Indian Agent for the Moquis Pueblos, and the two men completed paperwork to transfer responsibility for the agency to John H. Sullivan. Later that day he met Frank Hamilton Cushing who described the sixty-

---

36   Pecos Pueblo. Located about 18 miles southeast of Santa Fe, the Tiwa-speaking pueblo of Pecos had an estimated population of over 1000 when the Coronado expedition reached it in 1540 but attacks by Comanches, smallpox epidemics and other pressures led to a migration to the Tiwa village of Jemez. There were only 17 individuals left at the time of its final abandonment in 1838.

37   John H. Sullivan 1880b.

38   Santa Fe was founded in 1608 and became the capital of the province of Nuevo Mexico in 1610. San Miguel Chapel, a Spanish colonial mission church, was built between 1610 and 1626, damaged during the Pueblo Revolt of 1680, and rebuilt in 1710 following the Spanish reconquest. The so-called "oldest house," a two-storied adobe structure dates from the mid-18th century, nearly 150 years after the construction of the Palace of the Governors (1610). St. Francis Cathedral was under construction when John H. Sullivan visited; the main part was completed in 1884.

39   John H. Sullivan's account of his wagon ride is given below.

two year old Sullivan as a "pleasant elderly gentleman."[40] Resuming his travel, at Fort Defiance, Arizona, on October 6, the Navajo agent, Galen Eastman, provided a list of supplies (and supplies missing) intended for the Moquis Pueblo Indian Agency in storage at the Navajo Agency.[41] An early snow storm lasting five days delayed the new agent's departure from Fort Defiance until October 12.

From Fort Defiance to the Moquis Pueblo Indian Agency John H. Sullivan was accompanied by the agency clerk, Edward S. Merritt.[42] A few miles east of the agency, Merritt called Sullivan's attention "to a most beautiful object to the southwest; it was the snow-capped San Francisco mountain peaks...with a strongly defined outline of the buttes, hills and valleys intervening." He added, "It is a most subline light."

However, on arriving at Keams Canyon on October 14, John H. Sullivan wrote to the *Madison Evening Courier*: "This is not a

---

40   From Cushing's daily journal (Green 1990:128). John H. Sullivan was forty years older than Cushing.

41   An "Invoice of Public Property at the Moquis Pueblo Indian Agency, A. Ty. Transferred by Galen Eastman, Acting U. S. Ind. Agent to Capt. F. T. Bennett, 9th Cavalry, Acting U. S. Indian Agent" dated July 1, 1880 reveals various discrepancies, e.g., coffee 404 pounds according to Eastman, 300 according to Bennett; 2131 pounds of hay, Eastman, "none," Bennett; 3 horses, Eastman, "not worth much," Bennett; 2239 yards brown sheeting, Eastman, 1345, Bennett. Office of Indian Affairs, Moqui Agency Correspondence, MS 1144, National Archives, Laguna Naguel. Cited hereafter as MS 1144, NA-LN. Eastman submitted another, more detailed "List of Missing Moqui Property" on September 30, 1880 that included among the missing 1281 pounds of corn, 46 pounds of indigo, 3250 needles, assorted. No explanation for the losses is given. Galen Eastman to Commissioner of Indian Affairs, September 30, 1880, Letters Received by the Office of Indian Affairs, National Archives. Cited hereafter as LR-OIA, NA. See also, John H. Sullivan to CIA, October 31, 1880, LR-OIA, NA. In this, his first monthly report, he says, "Nearly all the goods intended for this people are in store at Ft. Defiance much of which has deteriorated in quality and lost in quantity having remained and been accumulating at that place for the last fifteen months."

42   Edward S. Merritt, 1834-ca. 1906, born in New York City, served as a First Lieutenant in Company E of the New Mexico Volunteers 1863-1866, became a clerk at the Moquis Pueblo Indian Agency in 1876 and served as Acting Agent in 1879. Merritt was a 'whistle blower' and outraged by those who misused government funds and property. He once said, "I have not seen an honest Ind. Agent in 20 years on the frontier." Merritt to Secretary of the Treasury, February 2, 1880, LR-OIA, NA.

very inviting place."[43] Not in the least discouraged, Agent Sullivan immediately began attending to the business of the agency. Within the first week he held a meeting with Hopi elders at the agency and shortly after toured the villages of First Mesa and the surrounding fields. The buildings of the Moquis Pueblo Indian Agency were in a dismal state: most of the supplies were in storage in the Navajo Agency at Fort Defiance, employees had not been paid, paperwork with previous agents and acting agents (Mateer, Eastman, Bennett) needed attending to, and so on. All transactions involving money required the approval of the Commissioner of Indian Affairs and involved a continual but time-consuming flow of correspondence between the agency and the Office of Indian Affairs in Washington, D.C., sent by way of Fort Defiance.

Shortly after his arrival, John H. Sullivan petitioned the Commissioner of Indian Affairs to obtain a waiver from the Indian Bureau's nepotism rules to have his son, Jeremiah Sullivan, appointed Agency Physician.[44] Expecting approval of his father's request, Jeremiah left Madison on December 9 and arrived at the Moqui Pueblo Indian Agency on December 25, Christmas day, 1880.[45] He was accompanied by James C. Davis, Jr., who John H. Sullivan intended to be the Agency clerk, and his father Jonathan C. Davis, who posted the agent's bond and came west with the expectation of being appointed Indian trader. John H. Sullivan did not know that Edward S. Merritt, clerk and sometime acting agent, was at Moquis Pueblo Indian Agency. Nor was he aware that Thomas V. Keam had a well-established trading post on property adjacent to the agency. Jonathan C. Davis soon withdrew his bond and returned to Madison as did James C. Davis, Jr. later in the spring.[46]

---

43   John H. Sullivan 1880c. In a letter of the CIA he described the condition of the agency buildings as "destitute and crippled." John H. Sullivan to CIA, October 16, 1880, LR-OIA, NA.

44   CIA to John H. Sullivan, October 21, 1880, LS-OIA, NA; John H. Sullivan to CIA, December 1, 1880, LR-OIA, NA. Commissioner of Indian Affairs is cited hereafter as CIA. Ezra A. Hayt served as CIA from September 17, 1877 to January 29, 1880; Roland F. Trowbridge from March 15, 1880 to March 19, 1881; Hiram Price from May 6, 1881 to March 21, 1885; John D. C. Atkins from March 21, 1855 to June 14, 1888.

45   A detailed account is provided in J. C. Davis, Jr. 1882.

46   *Madison Evening Courier*, February 24, 1881 and *Madison Evening Courier*, May 27, 1881. Before leaving Keams Canyon, James C. Davis, Jr., sent a brief description of the Hopi people that the editor of the *Madison Daily Evening Star*

Meanwhile, Rev. Sheldon Jackson, Superintendent of Indian Schools in the Rocky Mountain Region, had expanded the teaching mission of the Presbyterian Church to several New Mexico Pueblos in the 1870s.[47] In the early months of 1880 he recruited Rev. Charles A. Taylor, the minister of the Presbyterian church in Monument, Colorado, and a graduate of Princeton University and Princeton Theological Seminary, to be the first Presbyterian missionary teacher to the Moquis.[48] On March 3, 1880 the Office of Indian Affairs entered into a contract with the Board of Home Missions of the Presbyterian Church to establish a "boarding school" for the Moquis.

With agents nominated by the Board of Foreign Missions but reporting to the Commissioner of Indian Affairs, and missionary teachers nominated by the Board of Home Missions but responsible to the Presbyterian Church, an arena for conflict was established—as John H. Sullivan later recognized, "an irrepressible conflict … where the Church and State meet [since those representing the Church] put in an appearance claiming superiority, in as much as God is higher than the President."[49] As historian Stephen C. McCluskey saw:

> Charles Taylor clearly viewed the missionary and teacher as directly serving the primary goal of the agency—evangelism and teaching—while the agent was

---

entitled "Mr. Lo, Whose Front Name is Moquis," April 7, 1881. The phrase "Lo! The poor Indian" is from Alexander Pope's "Essay on Man" (1734). It was used derisively in the nineteenth century.

47   On Jackson's role in the development of Presbyterian missions in New Mexico and Arizona, see Bender 1996.

48   Charles Andrew Taylor was born in Ohio, June 2, 1848. He graduated from Princeton College in 1873, attended Princeton Theological Seminary for two years. He was ordained as a Presbyterian minister in 1876 and held pastorates in St. Louis and Mount Pleasant, Michigan. He had moved to St. Louis, Michigan for his health "hoping to receive benefit from the Magnetic Springs." While there he contracted typhoid fever. In 1878 he moved to Colorado for his health. In 1879 he married Elizabeth Smith Deacon in Princeton, N.J. He was the minister of a Presbyterian church in Monument, Colorado, from 1878 to 1880. From 1885 until his retirement in 1907 Taylor served as a pastor or missionary in Colorado, Illinois and Nebraska. He returned to Colorado in 1902 and died there in 1915. The Taylors had four children, two of whom died while Rev. Taylor was a missionary to the Hopi.

49   John H. Sullivan to CIA, June 8, 1882, LR-OIA, NA.

to provide support for these activities. Sullivan, however, had a quite different perception of his task. Sullivan's appointment was largely political and he clearly felt that his first responsibility was to the Indian Bureau, not to the Mission Board.[50]

John H. Sullivan reported to the Commissioner of Indian Affairs and the commissioner supervised all aspects of his work. There was, in fact, no communication between John H. Sullivan and the Presbyterian Board of Foreign Missions after his application for the position of agent. Inspectors for the Indian Service were first appointed in 1873 and reported to the Commissioner of Indian Affairs. However, the Presbyterian Church did not send inspectors into the field. In 1880 Inspectors for the Indian Service came under the supervision of the Secretary of the Interior. The first inspection of the Moqui Pueblo Indian Agency took place in early July 1882, after the replacement of Agent John H. Sullivan and the dismissal of Agency Physician Jeremiah Sullivan.

On July 15, 1880, already aware of John H. Sullivan's appointment as agent, Rev. Taylor traveled to Keam's Canyon, inspected the agency buildings, met "Mr. Keams" (William Keam)[51] and visited the First Mesa villages. While he found the "agency buildings…certainly uninviting for a family to occupy," he was "confident [John H. Sullivan] would not winter at Moqui." In this same letter he reminded Rev. Jackson, "you encouraged me to think that I could have men of my choice around me."[52] Even before Jeremiah Sullivan reached the Moquis Pueblo Indian Agency, Rev. Taylor had begun a campaign to have the Agent John H. Sullivan removed:

> …Away with such broken down, played out politicians for an Indian agent. Our church is brought into great disrepute by the signal failure she has made in nominating agents… [53]

---

50 McCluskey 1980:369.

51 William "Billy" Keam, younger brother of Thomas V. Keam, died at Fort Wingate, October 23, 1880. He was in charge of the trading post at the time of the Rev. Taylor's initial visit.

52 Rev. Charles A. Taylor to Rev. Sheldon Jackson, July 15, 1880, Correspondence, Sheldon Jackson Collection, Presbyterian Historical Society. Cited hereafter as SJC, PHS.

53 Taylor to Jackson, December 6, 1880, SJC, PHS.

On September 7, Rev. Charles A. Taylor, his wife Elizabeth ("Lizzie"), four month old daughter Hettie, and brother William left Monument, Colorado, and arrived by wagon at Keam's Canyon on October 26. Rev. Taylor expected to establish a home and school in the agency buildings only to find them occupied by the newly appointed agent, John H. Sullivan.

While Rev. Taylor wrote to Rev. Jackson on November 16 that he would not "wish a change in agent here," a month later he was contacting prospective replacements, including Jesse H. Fleming of St. Louis, Michigan.[54] In the meantime, Agent Sullivan wrote the Commissioner of Indian Affairs regarding the condition of the agency buildings and repeatedly requested authorization and funding for building materials to repair existing buildings and to construct a school.[55] But in Rev. Taylor's view, the agent was "all promise & no perform." And in a letter to Rev. Jackson on January 20, 1881, he complained at length regarding the agent, his son, Jeremiah Sullivan, who had arrived at the agency less than a month before, as well as the clerk, Edward S. Merritt. As a consequence, Rev. Jackson, "as the Agent of the Board of Home Missions of the Presbyterian Church with whom you have entered into contract to carry on a school at Moqui Agency," wrote to the Commissioner of Indian Affairs on February 10 requesting the commissioner "to take the necessary steps to secure Mr. [John H.] Sullivan's resignation or removal." Rev. Jackson then summarized the allegations made by Rev. Taylor in a letter of January 20:

> I have it from reliable authorities
>
> 1st That he [Agent John H. Sullivan] has no business qualifications... [sic!]
>
> 2nd His physical infirmities...incapacitate him from even the lighter duties of his position. [By this date, Agent Sullivan had visited the First Mesa villages and surrounding fields, distributed "dry goods, hardware, etc." at an Issue Day, developed a road from the agency to the Mormon community of Sunset, etc.]
>
> 3rd He uses intoxicating liquors... [Only one instance is documented.]

---

54   Taylor to Jackson, November 16 and December 13, 1880, SJC, PHS.
55   See, for example, John H. Sullivan to CIA, October 17, 1880, LR-OIA, NA.

4th He is under the control of bad and designing men. (a) His son [Jeremiah Sullivan] has been there since Christmas & Mr. Sullivan allows him to do the work, gives him the keys to the stores. When the father is absent the son is practically the Agent. The son is a drunkard & very profane. [Others were to note Jeremiah's use of profanity.] (b) Mr. Merritt (of ill fame, whom you know) is still there & considered as a confidential advisor of Mr. Sullivan. [Merritt, a twenty year veteran of the Indian Service, was a highly competent clerk and did much of the Agency paperwork.]

5th He is neglectful of the instructions of the Department: (a) He made no attempt to procure the five Moqui children...to be brought east; (b) He shows no disposition to erect the school building...; (c) He neglects the Agency affairs while looking around for some other business...[56]

It made little difference that most of Taylor's perceptions were false. On February 16 the Commissioner of Indian Affairs wrote to Rev. John C. Lowrie, recognizing the Board of Foreign Missions' responsibility for supervising agents, to nominate a successor to John H. Sullivan.[57]

It is significant that Rev. Jackson began the list of charges against Agent Sullivan with the statement, "I have it from *reliable authorities*." In fact, Rev. Taylor was the *sole* source of all allegations made against the agent as well as all those to be made against his son, Jeremiah Sullivan, in the year following.

Within ten days Rev. Taylor sent a list of recommendations for agent to Rev. Jackson, including Jesse H. Fleming of St. Louis, Michigan and his own brother, William E. Taylor.[58]

John H. Sullivan only learned of the charges made against him in April when Rev. Lowrie wrote to him. On April 28, in a "straight letter," Sullivan replied to Lowrie "to be heard before condemned." His response

---

56   Taylor to Jackson, January 20, 1881; Jackson to CIA, February 10, 1881, SJC, PHS..

57   CIA to Rev. John C. Lowrie, February 16, 1881, American Indian Correspondence, Presbyterian Historical Society. Cited hereafter as AIC, PHS.

58   Taylor to Jackson, February 25, 1881, SJC, PHS.

to the charge that "he uses intoxicating liquors" makes reference to a single instance:

> As to the charge of my drinking wine with officers at Ft. Wingate. In route for Moqui I did and thought no harm of it. The circumstances were truly as follows. [In Santa Fe] On the morning of the 31st of Sept. 1880, at 7 o'clock I took a seat on a buckboard for Ft. Wingate, said to be 150 miles distant. At Laguna took supper and retook my seat to travel all night with a green German for driver who had never been over the road at night and but once in day time. The night now became cloudy and quite dark. [We] had not traveled more than thirty miles when the driver took a wrong road, one that railroad hands had been using to haul R.R. ties from the forests away up in the mountains. He drove in different directions, then said he was lost. I had him stop and we spent the night in the mountains. Next morning [we] drove back to the road and made for [Fort] Wingate arriving there that day eve at 5 o'clock in a cold, drizzling rain. [I] was hungry, cold and very tired, and under this condition of things some gentlemen asked me as gentlemen to take a stimulant to warm and strengthen me. I thought it would help me and it did.

Agent Sullivan then turned to a more general accusation:

> As to the neglect of duty, that is a sheer fabrication... No one but the Messrs. Taylor in this country would make any such charge, Indians or white men... [Sullivan details the circumstances of the Taylors' arrival and his efforts to meet their needs.] This Mr. Taylor is a strange man...
>
> I will not trouble you further with my grievances at present, only to say I have been most shamefully treated in this matter.[59]

Rev. John C. Lowrie then wrote to the Rev. Sheldon Jackson to say:

> Mr. Sullivan turns the tables on the Taylors and makes a good statement of his own conduct in the matters you

---

59   John H. Sullivan to Lowrie, April 28, 1881, MS 1144, NA-LN.

impugned. Of course there are two sides to all cases.[60]

Before the year's end, John H. Sullivan was removed as agent but not as a result of Rev. Taylor's accusations.

Jeremiah Sullivan – Agency Physician

"Dr. Jeremiah Sullivan," 1884. Photograph by Frederick Dellenbaugh. Frederick Dellenbaugh Papers, Ms 407, Special Collections, The University of Arizona Library. Only known photograph of Jeremiah Sullivan.

Agent Sullivan received notification of the appointment of his son as Agency Physician at an annual salary of $720.00 through a letter sent on January 21, 1881. Letters of support of Jeremiah Sullivan's appointment as Agency Physician were not finally submitted by Senator Benjamin Harrison of Indiana until May 13.[61] Endorsements were provided by

---

60   Lowrie to Jackson, May 18, 1881, SJC, PHS.

61   Benjamin Harrison, 23rd President of the United States (1889-1893) had become the U. S. Senator for Indiana just two months earlier on March 4, 1881. He was the grandson of President William Henry Harrison and a prominent local attorney, Presbyterian church leader and politician in Indianapolis. In the 1880 Republican National Convention he was instrumental in breaking the deadlock

six Madison doctors, including L. R. Lewis, M.D., of the Office of the Board of Health. Also included was a petition written by Jeremiah Sullivan, signed by twenty-two Hopi and Tewa chiefs and headmen, and witnessed by Edward S. Merritt and Masayantua, interpreters, asking the "Great Father" to let "our White Medicine Man…stay and live with us all the time."[62]

Jeremiah Sullivan took seriously his responsibilities as Agency Physician and soon after his arrival he spent ten days in the First and Second Mesa villages compiling a census and a report on the "Social, Physical and Sanitary Conditions" of the Hopi.[63] In a letter accompanying the report, Agent Sullivan wrote:

> …He [Jeremiah Sullivan] was advised by the head men who assisted him, he had better defer for the present his visit to Oraybe, the 7th village, as its head chief is a little peculiar, and until they could talk and tell the Oraybe people of his work in their village, and that when he went to Oraybe they would go with him, and he must take his medicines with him, as he had done when coming to them, as there are sick people in Oraybe.[64]

Before long Jeremiah Sullivan was also welcome in Oraibi. While many Hopis could communicate through Spanish or Navajo, Sullivan

---

enabling James A. Garfield to become the Republican candidate and, eventually, President.

62 Benjamin Harrison to CIA, May 13, 1881 with enclosures, LR-OIA, NA. The endorsements make no reference to Jeremiah Sullivan's medical education.

63 John H. Sullivan to CIA, February 28, 1881, enclosing Jeremiah Sullivan's report of the same date, LR-OIA, NA.

64 Ibid. By the second half of the nineteenth century many seeds of change and conflict had been introduced to the people of Oraibi through Spanish explorers, Mormon missionaries, and other contacts—direct and indirect—and the village divided into two factions, the "friendlies" and the "hostiles." The Oraibis refused to accept annuity goods and rations at "issue day," to have their census taken, to send their children to school, etc. Loololma, who became the village chief in the early 1870s was a member of the hostile faction while Jeremiah Sullivan lived among the Hopi. Following a visit to Washington, D.C. in 1890 Loololma agreed to send children to a boarding school established in Keams Canyon in 1887. However, the opposition to schooling and to allotment of Hopi lands led to factional conflict and eventually to the dissolution of the village in 1906. See Whiteley 1988a and 2008.

knew only English. It is likely that the long-time clerk at the agency, Edward S. Merritt, served as translator at times during the early months of the physician's residence on First Mesa. Jeremiah Sullivan would soon acquire a working knowledge of Hopi.[65] At the beginning of March 1881, he moved into the Government House[66] adjacent to the village of Sichumovi on First Mesa.

First Efforts in Ethnography

Ethnography is a form of writing, the product of the process of participant observation or fieldwork. Jeremiah Sullivan's ethnographic writings—letters to his hometown newspapers, translations of Hopi narratives, essays and articles—changed over time and according to circumstance, some are speculative, the best give a priority to Hopi voices. Only one of his notebooks survives (No. 6, 1882-1883) suggesting there were many others now lost. In writing his longest and most important work, Sullivan drew on materials he had collected over several years. What has survived of his manuscripts indicates his interest (and that of many others) in the biennial ceremonies of the Antelope and Snake societies, commonly known as the Snake Dance. Sullivan submitted accounts of the ceremonies in 1881 and 1883 to the Bureau of Ethnology and prepared a much fuller account of the 1885 observances for a patron. However, he also wrote a lengthy account of a women's ceremony, the Mamzrau, and his final work includes a rich description of the song prayers of the *katsinas*, the so-called Kachina Dance. What is most notable about his ethnography is the number of translations of songs, prayers and narratives and of Hopi accounts of their ceremonies, most notably the Snake Dance. Notebook No. 6 contains over thirty kachina masks drawn by his Hopi and Tewa neighbors on First Mesa.

On April 7, 1881 John Wesley Powell acknowledged receipt of census schedules from "Mr. Jere Sullivan, U. S. Indian Enumerator." On

---

65   Several Hopis knew some English, most notably Tom Polacca and Layee (various spellings), a Mormon convert from Oraibi. However, Sullivan makes no mention of Polacca in his correspondence, manuscripts, publication or one surviving notebook.

66   William H. H. Metzger, farmer and interpreter accompanying Capt. A. D. Palmer, first United States Special Agent for the Moqui Indians, constructed the "Government House" during the spring and summer of 1870. It was used to store supplies and annuity goods.

May 1, Jeremiah Sullivan sent a free translation of a Hopi narrative of the destruction of the village of "See-Cat-Kee" (Sikyaki) to his hometown newspaper, the *Madison Daily Evening Star*.[67] Over the next three months, he sent accounts of Hopi ceremonies and medical practices to Dr. H. C. Yarrow, Curator of Herpetology at the National Museum, who forwarded them to John Wesley Powell, Director of the Bureau of Ethnology.[68] In August, Powell acknowledged their receipt and invited the younger Sullivan to submit materials to be published "with like material by the Bureau."[69]

The first manuscript sent to Yarrow, an account of the "Dance of Mas-saw-yah [Mas'au], or the Rising of the Bad Man" Jeremiah Sullivan had observed on May 14 in the Second Mesa village of "Shi-mop-o-vi" [Shungopavi], begins with a brief synopsis of the underlying narrative describing Mas'au followed by an account of the ceremony. Sullivan gives the opening of the narration in language characteristic of stereotypical views of the American Indian at the time:

> ...So O-maw [the "good Chief"] called Massowyah, the bad chief, to him and thus talked. You bad man, Massowyah. I do not like you, me no want you, to come to my house any more. You have thrown much rock and sand into my good springs, you make bad birds and mice to eat up all my corn, onions, peppers, beans and melons and squashes. You make my Moquis men, women and children sick, so they die.

This is the only instance of Sullivan representing Hopi narration in this way.

Cushing occasionally chose to use an anachronistic strategy to represent a different (Zuni) cultural voice as in this passage from his

---

67 Jeremiah Sullivan 1881.

68 Jeremiah Sullivan to H. C. Yarrow, 19 May 1881, ["Mas-saw-uh"] MS 1607(1); Sullivan to Yarrow, July 20, 1881, [Medicine Men] MS 1607(2); Sullivan to Yarrow, July 24, 1881, ["Ca-che-na, or Singing Men"] MS 1607(3), NAA, SI.

69 Powell to Jeremiah Sullivan, August 13, 1881, Records of the Bureau of American Ethnology, Correspondence, Letters Sent, National Anthropological Archives, Smithsonian Institution. Cited hereafter as LS-BAE, NAA, SI. Earlier Powell had acknowledged receipt of a census schedules for the First Census of the United States Indian Division submitted by Jeremiah Sullivan on March 26, 1881. See Powell to Sullivan, April 7, 1881, MS 1144, NA-LN.

Zuni Breadstuff:

> "My warrior, take with thee now provisions for thy journey... Ere thou hast reached the land of the Moquis, thy corn shall have grown milky and full of kernel as the brother and sister plants here do." ...
>
> "Father of his people, hear thou me. Thou hast given me being, even as I and thy mothers have preserved thy old and given thee new being. Precious shalt thou be..."[70]

In general, Sullivan gives "free translations" more literal than Cushing's "poetic" representations. As Sullivan's mastery of the Hopi language matured he was able, especially in his conversations with Wiki,[71] to convey both the style and content of the narratives he recorded.

While Jeremiah Sullivan was the only physician near the Hopi villages, he was soon aware he was not the only medical practitioner. As a preface to his list of "Great Medicine Chiefs," he provided Yarrow with a brief account of the fees asked, the examination of the patient, and the curing procedure. Each village had a "Medicine Chief" (Walpi, two) as well as other "Medicine Men." Yarrow is told that the "Medicine Man" chants include the words, "I will catch him," suggesting a procedure of shaman-like extraction similar to that performed by Sikya-honauwu (Yellow Bear) in his effort to cure A. M. Stephen of his fatal illness in 1894.[72] Sullivan also indicates that the names of the men are reflective of their distinct areas of medical knowledge and practice (e.g., "Salt-Water," "Mescal Cake" or "Broken Bones").

The third account sent to Yarrow, "Ca-che-na [Katsina] or Singing Men," is of the priestly prayers and offerings that precede the Niman ceremony at the end of the season of masked dances.[73] His letter to

---

70   Cushing 1920:119.
71   Wiki, chief priest of the Antelope Society. See Chapter 2. Jeremiah Sullivan, untitled manscript, MS 5.291, George Bird Grinnell Manuscript Collection, Braun Research Library, Autry Museum of the American West, Los Angeles, published as "The Hopi Indians of Arizona" with authorship attributed to Alexander M. Stephen. Cited hereafter as MS 5.291, BRL, AMAW.
72   Stephen 1894b.
73   The Hopi have a calendar of complex ritual performances that can be divided into the Katsina season—roughly from December to July (from the winter solstice to the summer solstice)—and a season of ceremonies by other religious

Yarrow opens,

> Today being the final appearance of the 'Ca-che-na' or Singing Men, for the next six months, I was on last night formally taken into their confidence and admitted to the 'Ke-bah' [Kiva] or Man's house, to witness the most sacred of their many services, that of the prayer to 'O-maw', the Chief of the Sun and rain.

Sullivan concludes his letter to Yarrow, noting that "in twenty days the wonderful Snake dance, or as it is called, 'Tschua-ti-ki-bi,' takes place."

In late June, Cushing visited the Hopi First Mesa villages on his way from Zuni to the Havasupai in Cataract Canyon on the Colorado River.[74] To Spencer F. Baird, Secretary of the Smithsonian Institution, Cushing wrote, "I am universally welcomed in Moqui." And in his daily journal he noted, "Everywhere this morning the Moquis watched me. When I awoke, they were on the roof top to talk, and admire me." Cushing visited the agency where, in his daily journal, he noted:

> Found Dr. [i.e., Agent John H.] Sullivan, who received me cordially. [They had met the previous October at Fort Wingate when John H. Sullivan was in route to Keams Canyon.] Also his son, physician of tribe. [Cushing also noted a:] "long visit with Dr. S."[75]

From their conversations it is clear Jeremiah Sullivan expected Cushing to return in time for the biennial Snake Dance at Walpi, but by August Cushing was at Fort Whipple, Arizona on a southern route back to Zuni; he would not return to the Hopi until the next fall. In the meantime, a party led by U. S. Army Captain John Gregory Bourke[76] arrived in time for the ceremony and was joined by Stephen and Keam.

---

sodalities—from August to December, including the "wonderful Snake dance." For more on the Hopi ritual calendar, see Chapter 3.

74   For a description of Cushing's expedition to the Havasupai, see Chapter 4.

75   See Green, ed. 1990:167-168. Although Cushing made brief note of his meetings with Sullivan in his daily journals, he made no mention of Sullivan in his official correspondence.

76   Bourke was aide-de-camp to Brigadier General George Crook during the early Apache campaigns. He is best known for this work on the Hopi and for his work on the Apache. See Bourke 1892.

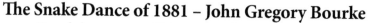

The Snake Dance of 1881 – John Gregory Bourke

Bourke's account of his visit to the Hopi in 1881 was published in the fall of 1884 as *The Snake-Dance of the Moquis of Arizona; Being a Narrative of a Journey from Santa Fe, New Mexico, to the Villages of the Moqui Indians of Arizona.*[77] Jeremiah Sullivan accompanied the party to the ruins at Awatovi[78] and shared his limited knowledge of the Hopi with Bourke. Having observed the preparations being made for the

---

77   Bourke published a preliminary account of the August 12, 1881 (1881a). For a transcription of Bourke's diary account, see Robinson 2013. Although many Anglos witnessed the Snake dance beginning with Fray Francisco Garces in 1776, Agent William B. Mateer's first-hand account (1879a) was the first to appear in print. Rev. Charles A. Taylor's description (1881b) was based on hear-say.

78   The Franciscan mission of San Bernardo de Aguatubi was established in 1629 at the Hopi village of Awat'ovi, ten miles east of First Mesa. Missions were later established at Oraibi and Shungopavi with *visitas* at Walpi and Mishongnovi. During the Pueblo Revolt of 1680 the Franciscans at Awat'ovi, Shungopavi and Oraibi were killed and the missions destroyed. In 1692, as a part of the Reconquest of New Mexico by Don Diego de Vargas, the mission at Awat'ovi was re-established. During the winter of 1700-1701, Hopis from other villages destroyed Awat'ovi, ending the Catholic presence among the Hopi. In Navajo, Awat'ovi is called Tallahogan, 'the house of singing men.' A narrative of the destruction of Awat'ovi summarized by Jeremiah Sullivan is as follows: "…just before the time of the celebration of Mu-in-wu feast [a ceremony of the women's Marau society] the priests commanded that this feast should not take place… The people were told [by the leader of the K] to prepare the Baho [prayer sticks] and feathers as before and place them in the accustomed places and if the Spaniards interfered, the people must put them to death. The Spaniards…in turn enlisted the services of some of the men of Awa-obi to aid in the demolition of the Mu-in-wu properties. The time of the feast arrived and the altar with all its features was placed in the kiba [kiva]. The songs and prayers consecrating the water and meal had been recited, leaving in the kiba only the high priestesses and two virgins. When the priests of the church made their way down into the room immediately they began the scene of destruction. The altar was pulled down, torn, broken, and thrown over the mesa side… [T]he jewels[?] were given to those Indians who assisted in the work. That night marked the commencement of the reign of terror. The priests fled for their lives and were caught and killed. The city of Awatobi (Aqua-tubi) or Tally Hogan, was destroyed and its [male] inhabitants cruelly massacred…" Jeremiah Sullivan, "The Hopitu," Hopitu Calendar, Daniel Garrison Brinton Collection, University of Pennsylvania Library. For the history and architecture of the mission, see Montgomery, Smith and Brew 1949. For a careful examination of the historical, social and religious contexts of the destruction of Awatovi, see Whiteley 2002.

Snake Dance, he told Bourke about the capture of the snakes to be used and, respectful of the secrecy surrounding the ceremony, he added: "All the snakes captured are kept concealed in one of the Estufas [kivas], no person [except those initiated into the Snake and Antelope societies] being permitted to see them or even know where they are." Bourke, "not putting much confidence in the accuracy" of Sullivan's statement,[79] entered the kiva where the snakes were kept: "Dante's Hell struck me as a weak, wishy-washy, gruelly conception alongside of this horrible, grim reality."[80] At this point Bourke's narrative shifts to the first person (Sullivan no longer accompanies him) as he "boldly descends" into other kivas where "for the sake of Science," he endures the "stench and heat which was simply overpowering" to make observations and in another kiva offers to buy sacred objects.[81] For Bourke the Snake ceremony was "horrible...loathsome...your blood chills."

Ten days later, on August 22, because of "the non-arrival of Mr. F. H. Cushing," Sullivan sent Powell a twenty page account of the Snake Dance beginning with the eight days of preparations prior to the public ceremony. With no examples to draw upon, Sullivan developed his own language of description, using "Charmers" for the priests of the Snake Society, "Singing Men" and "Chanters" for those of the Antelope Society.[82] There are minor errors of fact and meaning, most notably his reference to the Antelope priests as Ca-chi-nas;[83] however, in comparison with

---

79   In his diary Bourke (2013:299) remarked, "Dr. Sullivan is not, ordinarily, trustworthy in ethnological matters. ... This untrustworthiness is not due to Dr. Sullivan's want of capacity, but to his ignorance of Ethnology and the lack of training necessary to qualify him for the work he is really anxious to accomplish among the Moquis—a work which Mr. Cushing is doing so brilliantly and thoroughly among the Zunis." In fact, there was no academic or other formal "training" in ethnology at the time.

80   Bourke 1884:108, 128.

81   Op cit., 124-128.

82   Jeremiah Sullivan to Powell, August 22, 1881, Records of the Bureau of American Ethnology, Correspondence, Letters Received, National Anthropological Archives. Cited hereafter as LR-BAE, NAA, SI. The manuscript, "Tschua-ti-ki or the 'Snake Dance' of the Moquis," MS 837, NAA, SI, was forwarded to H. C. Yarrow without the covering letter. Because Yarrow's name appears at the top appears at the top of the manuscript, authorship has been attributed the Yarrow rather than Sullivan.

83   Katsina, kachina [*katsinum*, pl., *katsina*, sing.]; the spirit being(s) given

Bourke's book and other sensationalist accounts of the Snake Dance written at the time,[84] Sullivan's first description of the ceremony is remarkable for its empathy and objectivity. Compare Sullivan's account of the Snake kiva with Bourke's "reptile dungeon":

> At the snake house [kiva] I found eighteen men sitting or lolling around engaged in various occupations necessary for the morrow dance while in one corner one noticed the large twisted heap of snakes their little red eyes shining out like garnets, with one or two of the more restless glided from one part of the room to the other. The Charmers [sic] sat there, quiet to the extreme, not talking except when it was absolutely necessary nor allowing anything…which might possibly excite the restfulness and anger of the "Rattlers"… [Sullivan notes the presence also of Bull snakes.] As to the Racer and Garter snakes, they are seemingly but playthings in the hands of the Charmers and cause no little merriment among the Native Spectators [at the public ceremony] as they (the snakes) are as apt to go straight up ones pantaloons as to go straight when set at liberty [by the Snake priests] and knowing such is the case, I with great caution, took up my position on the housetop [to observe].

Clearly Jeremiah Sullivan was seeking to establish himself with the Bureau of Ethnology and continued to send materials, without any suggestion of payment, to Yarrow and to Powell. On September 29 Sullivan acknowledged a letter, "a flattering favor," from Powell, noting "the field [is] entirely new to me and [I have] none or very little knowledge of compiling Ethnologic Data." Given Powell's encouragement the same day he sent "a brief sketch of the Indian Syringe extensively used by the 'Medicine Men' of this section" to Yarrow.[85]

---

personification in ceremonies in the late spring and early summer prior to the Snake Dance.

84   See Dilworth 1996-21-44.

85   Jeremiah Sullivan to Powell, September 29, 1881; Sullivan to Yarrow, September 29, 1881, LR-BAE, NAA, SI. James Pilling, Powell's Chief Clerk, acknowledged Sullivan's letter and he was "sending you several volumes which I hope may assist you in your investigations." Pilling to Sullivan, October [12?], 1881, LS-

There is a lacuna—apparently more a gap than a missing piece—in the correspondence between Rev. Taylor and Rev. Jackson during the summer of 1881. The silence concerns the death of the Taylors' fourteen month old daughter, Hettie Elizabeth Taylor, on August 3 and the birth of a son, Alfred DeForest Taylor, on September 9.[86] Taylor clearly preferred to separate his personal life from his professional life as "Minister of the Gospel" but, as the next year unfolded, this wasn't always possible.

Jeremiah Sullivan was not only a physician treating sickness and injury in all of the villages on the three mesas, he participated increasingly in many aspects of Hopi social and ceremonial life. Sometime in the fall of 1881, roughly coincident with Cushing's much heralded initiation into the Order of the Bow at Zuni, Sullivan became a member of the *Kaletakwimkya*, Warriors, on First Mesa and was given the name O-yi-wi-sha (He Who Plants Corn).[87] Among narratives Sullivan recorded for Stephen is one entitled "Owaka-Ka-tci-na" that makes reference to Sullivan's initiation as a "chief," prophecy ('a thing that was promised to us') and volcanic activity (possibly eruptions ca. A.D. 1085 north of Flagstaff, Arizona, that created what is known today as Sunset Crater):

> Pau-i-ti-wa speaks. It has been many days since this dance was observed – probably 50 years ago. It has been repeated today on the occasion of a white man becoming the first and highest ranking chief we ever had carrying the chieftancy into the chief gens as well as among the warriors, a thing that was promised to us but which we never expected to see.
>
> The Owa-ka Katcina are those who make the black rock (coal &c) and who stir the fires in the mountains. They are usually harmless but when their anger is aroused (as it was many years ago) they pull down the high places and burn everything. Today they come in peace – bringing only a small gourd of water which was given to

---

BAE, NAA, SI.

86 Charles A. Taylor, Class of 1873, Alumni File and Reunion Books for 1873, Seeley G. Mudd Manuscript Library, Princeton University.

87 Reported in the "Personal" column of the *Madison Daily Courier* (Anon. 1881). Sullivan told Herman ten Kate his name was Oyiwisha, He Who Plants Corn (Kate 2004:249).

the chief Ka-tci-na who will use it in the dances. When my father's father was a boy these Ka-tci-na sent word they were coming but they came not on the appointed day, soon afterward smallpox broke out and killed many. This made the people so angry they took the Chief who had delivered the message out into the valley and killed him.

The Ka-tci-na carry on their heads two crossed feathers of the hawk or raven. Their necklace is of corn shucks but formerly it was made of withered fruit pods of the yucca. A girdle was also plaited from yucca leaves which was eagerly clutched after (grabbed or) by the women who made pottery as it made the fires very hot & gave out well baked vessels. [The half page following this text has been cut out of Stephen's notebook.][88]

On October 25 a form was sent to U. S. Indian Agent John H. Sullivan approving the [continuing] appointments of Edward S. Merritt, Clerk, and Jeremiah Sullivan, Physician, each at an annual salary of $720.[89] Throughout the year Rev. Taylor continued his campaign to have John H. Sullivan removed as agent, sending six letters to Rev. Jackson and one to the Secretary of the Interior.[90] Meanwhile Mrs. J. D. Perkins, a teacher in the Navajo boarding school at Fort Defiance, wrote to Rev. Jackson:

> ...It seems that the Moquis and the Navajos both like Mr. Sullivan as agent and feel hard towards Mr. Taylor for trying to urge his removal. Mr. Taylor having said he would have him removed. Now this thing hurts us all with these people. They say 'These church people make trouble. We like Mr. Sullivan...'[91]

In November Agent John H. Sullivan was demoted to "Farmer-in-

---

88 [Jeremiah Sullivan], Notebook No. 1, pp. 74-76, ECP, CUL.

89 E. S. Stevens, Acting Commissioner, to John H. Sullivan, October 25, 1881, MS 1144, NA-LN.

90 Taylor to Jackson, January 20, February 25, May 26, October 5, November 20 and December 1, 1881, SJC, PHS; Taylor to Samuel J. Kirkwood, Secretary of the Interior, April 22, 1881, Interior Department Appointment Papers: Arizona, NA..

91 Perkins to Jackson, March 26, 1881, SJC, PHS. See also her letter of November 6, 1881 defending Agent Sullivan's provision of school rooms.

Charge." On November 16, the Commissioner of Indian Affairs, Hiram Price, informed the Secretary of the Interior, Samuel J. Kirkwood, of the circumstances:

> ...John H. Sullivan—at present acting in the capacity of Farmer-in-Charge at the Moquis Pueblo Agency Arizona was on the 10th day of May last, appointed by the President and confirmed by the Senate to be Agent of the Indians in said Territory for four (4) years from the 5th of the same month, and ...since that time ...he has so far failed to render his official bond as Agent ... the employees... have received no pay for about twelve months, owing to the fact that no money can be placed to the credit of Mr. Sullivan until his official bond has been filled. ...serious charges have been made against ... Mr. Sullivan ...by Rev. Sheldon Jackson and Rev. Chas. A. Taylor ...I have the honor to recommend that he be suspended at once and that Mr. Jesse H. Fleming...be appointed in his stead.[92]

The Taylors—Rev. Charles Taylor, missionary, and his brother William, teacher—and their wives had now been in Keams Canyon for a year and had little success in accomplishing their evangelical and educational missions.[93] Rev. Taylor wrote to Rev. Jackson:

> Becoming almost desperate in the matter we determined to make an effort in the villages. My wife and I contemplate going up and spend the winter but after talking it over with Brother and his wife they decided that it was best for them to go on account of the exposure it would be to our little babe [their son, Alfred, born September 9] and one family must needs be here to care for our property.

---

92 CIA to Secretary of the Interior, November 16 1881, Interior Department Appointment Papers: Arizona, NA. It is not clear when John H. Sullivan was notified of his demotion. Rev. Jackson had no knowledge of John H. Sullivan except that provided by Rev. Taylor. Because his bond had been withdrawn, Sullivan had been demoted to Farmer-in-Charge on March 5, 1881 until his nomination of Agent was approved on May 10, 1881.

93 In his quarterly report in *Presbyterian Home Missions* (November 1881), Rev. Taylor stated, "Our work for the past quarter has been altogether manual labor" in an effort to complete building "the mission home" (Charles A. Taylor 1881c).

Accordingly we moved them up on [November] 8th securing them as comfortable as little [room] as the village afforded and also a room for the school in the middle village [Sichumovi] on first mesa. I had a little counsel with the chiefs but was obliged to use the Dr. for interpreter and it was rather unsatisfactory. The Dr. said that they would furnish wood and water for the school. I just received a note from Brother in which he says "The Moquis tell that the Dr. says that they must not give me wood unless I pay a dollar in silver per load." This means a burro load and whether it applies to the school wood as well as his private wood I do not know. The Dr. can fix his own price and pay for it in government goods, or haul his own in government teams and he will throw every obstacle possible in their way no doubt.[94]

As the year 1881 came to a close, the *Madison Daily Courier* reported Jeremiah Sullivan's initiation into the Warriors society on First Mesa giving the editor's version of his Hopi name—Oyiwisha (He Who Plants Corn):

Our friend Jere Sullivan has been made third chief of the Moquis Indians. He is vested with the authority of both "medicine man" and chief. His name, conferred by the tribe, is O-yi-wi-sha, which, being translated into English, is Sprouting Corn. Good for Jere!

When the corn begins to sprout,
And the tender buds we see,
May O-yi-wi-sha shout
"Wooh! Wooh! Big Indian me!"[95]

The year 1881 was "good for Jere." He had, after all, secured a position as Agency Physician, took up living in the village of Sichumovi where he began practicing medicine, learning Hopi, participating in the

---

94 Taylor to Jackson, November 20, 1881, SJC, PHS. "A dollar in silver per load" was the amount paid by Cosmos Mindeleff while surveying the Hopi villages in 1882 and seems to be the standard price.

95 *Madison Daily Courier*, December 19, 1881. As noted, Jeremiah Sullivan had a joking exchange with the editor who delighted in humorously revising Sullivan's letters.

social and ceremonial life of First Mesa, and had been accepted by many of the Hopi people in the other villages. And, important to him, his contributions to the Bureau of Ethnology were being acknowledged and encouraged by Powell. At the same time, it is clear the stage was set for a confrontation between Jeremiah Sullivan and Rev. Charles A. Taylor.

Evicting Jeremiah Sullivan -- "Capt. We seem to have blundered..."

With Agent John H. Sullivan's demotion to "Farmer-in-Charge" and the prospects of a new agent, Rev. Taylor now turned his attention to Jeremiah Sullivan "who claims to be a physician." In November he wrote to Rev. Jackson to report the establishment of a school on First Mesa. In doing so he claimed that the physician is "to be dreaded because his position offers him the great[est] opportunity for doing evil." He continued:

> The Dr. has taken up his abode in the Moqui village and above all, as many Americans 'money makes the mare go' and I am *morally certain* that the government goods are lavishly used to win the good will of the chiefs. The goods are certainly not equally distributed though doubtless they are otherwise reported.[96]

Less than a month after William E. Taylor and his wife established a classroom in Sichumovi, Jeremiah Sullivan wrote to Dr. Yarrow to complain of the "meddlesomeness" of Rev. Taylor who had accompanied his brother William as he moved to First Mesa.[97] At the same time he wrote a longer letter to Powell:

> If consistent with your ideas, I wish you would use your influence in having the Rev. Chas. A. Taylor and [his] brother Wm. E. Taylor removed. They are doing vast harm to the Study of Ethnology... I have before me the Petition of the Chiefs and head men asking that he [Rev. Charles Taylor] be taken away...[98]

James C. Pilling, Powell's Chief Clerk, responded to Jeremiah Sullivan's request for "advice and assistance":

---

96   Taylor to Jackson, November 20, 1881, SJC, PHS. Emphasis added.
97   Jeremiah Sullivan to Yarrow, December 6, 1881, LR-BAE, NAA.
98   Jeremiah Sullivan to Powell, December 6, 1881, LR-BAE, NAA. The petition was never submitted.

I am extremely sorry to hear of the obstacles put in your way by the missionary and regret that I see no way of remedying the difficulty. As you are aware the religious boards...[99]

Rev. Taylor resumed his attack on Jeremiah Sullivan in a letter to Rev. Jackson dated January 7, 1882:

You know something of the mongrel Zuni (Cushing) and his influence and we are likely to have a worse one here in the M.D. ... He lives in one of the villages and on their feast days and other occasions he dresses after their customs, etc. He is already a sub-chief.[100]

In early February Rev. Taylor drove a wagon to the railroad station at Holbrook, Arizona, to greet the new "U. S. Indian Agent for the Moquis Pueblo," Jesse H. Fleming, returning to Keams Canyon. Two days later the new agent signed a letter addressed to Commissioner of Indian Affairs that contained a list of charges against Jeremiah Sullivan, "coming from *a most reliable source*":

The following specific charges have been urged against Mr. J. Sullivan, your physician here, which, coming from a most reliable source, I deem it my duty to submit to you at once.

I[st]: That he is given to the use of profane & vulgar language in the presence of Indians.

IInd: That he has a violent temper over which he exercises no control.

IIIrd: He has been the means of keeping open if not starting a quarrel of words between the first & second villages.

IIIIth: That he has joined the tribe & is adopting their dress & customs, wearing moccasins, leggings & a pouch for his tobacco & corn husks; he also "attends & joins in their dances with no shirt on."

---

99   Pilling to Jeremiah Sullivan, January [date?] 1882, LS-BAE, NAA. Much of the text is indecipherable. Pilling appears to point out the independence of the religious boards in the nomination and supervision of its missionaries and teachers.

100 Taylor to Jackson, January 7, 1882, SJC, PHS.

...it seems evident that this man is degrading himself below the level of the Indians instead of endeavoring to elevate & civilize them... I would therefore recommend his early removal.[101]

While waiting for the commissioner's response, Agent Fleming dismissed Jeremiah Sullivan on February 7—to be effective March 7-- for "profanity, inciting quarrels, adopting Moqui habits & joining in their dances" and "invited [him] to leave the Moquis villages at once."[102] The following day, Jeremiah Sullivan received orders, delivered to him by his father, that all medicines and office furniture be packed and brought to the Agency and on February 11 he delivered the materials. Writing the Commissioner of Indian Affairs that same day, Jeremiah Sullivan noted, "I...am now, with the exception of a few minor remedies, unable to relieve any who may be suffering from sickness or injuries."[103] Fleming had acted without authority and it wasn't until March 2 that the Commissioner of Indian Affairs sent a letter directing Agent Fleming to "discharge the Physician to take effect on the 1st of April."

Having made all the necessary transfers of property to the new agent on February 10, John H. Sullivan left Keams Canyon on February 13. He returned to Madison, Indiana, on March 1 then traveled to Boston and Washington, D.C., before taking up residence in Albuquerque, New Mexico, in August.[104] On September 1, the *Albuquerque Morning Journal* reported:

---

101   Fleming to CIA, February 6, 1882, LR-OIA, NA. The content and formulation of the charges are clearly those of Rev. Charles A. Taylor; the handwriting is that of his wife, Elizabeth S. Taylor. The letter also requests the appointment of Mrs. Taylor as clerk at the agency. An attached note says: "Comm. Says have him discharge the Physician to take effect on the 1st of April."

102   See "Descriptive Statement of proposed changes in Employees" enclosed with Fleming to CIA, March 3, 1882, Moqui Agnecy Letterbook, Moqui Agency Records, Office of Indian Affairs, MS 1145, National Archives, Laguna Niguel. Cited hereafter as MS 1145, NA-LN.

103   Jeremiah Sullivan to CIA, February 11, 1882, LR-OIA, NA.

104   See John H. Sullivan to CIA, February 10, 1882, LR-OIA, NA; Fleming to CIA, March 16, 1882, MS 1145, NA-LN; *Madison Evening Courier*, March 1, *Madison Courier*, March 6, 25 and 29, 1882; *Albuquerque Morning Journal*, August 15 and 17, 1882. John H. Sullivan, Jr. had moved to Albuquerque in March to work in real estate. Mrs. C. E. Sullivan did not join her husband in Albuquerque until early in the summer of 1884.

> [A party of eleven Hopi men and women] arrived in Albuquerque on the Atlantic & Pacific passenger train yesterday and left soon after in a boxcar for the Pueblo of Santa Domingo. … On their arrival in Albuquerque they immediately hunted up J. H. Sullivan who was at one time their agent. …and expressed their great pleasure at meeting him again.[105]

On April 7 Jeremiah Sullivan wrote to the Commissioner of Indian Affairs to report the post master in Winslow had been ordered "not to put it [Sullivan's mail] in the Moqui sack anymore." Sullivan wrote, "I can see no reason but the personal spite of Mr. Taylor and Mr. Fleming for refusing to carry any of my letters or papers." On May 13 the Acting Commissioner of Indian Affairs informed Fleming there was "no impropriety…in allowing [Sullivan's mail] to pass through the Agency sack from Winslow and return."[106] On August 7, former Agent John H. Sullivan wrote to the Commissioner of Indian Affairs to report "Agent J. H. Fleming… still refuses to let the mail of Dr. Jer. Sullivan be carried in the sack with other mail…to and from the Moquis Agency." In an apparent reversal of position, the Commissioner of Indian Affairs replied:

> …the mail service at the [Moquis] Agency is performed by a messenger authorized and paid for by this office with a private mail bag and is in no manner a part of the U. S. Mail Service. It is performed for the benefit of the Indian service and is entirely under the control of the Indian Agent… You are further advised that Dr. J. Sullivan was dismissed from the Indian service at Moquis Pueblo on March 7th last.[107]

The mail of Rev. Taylor, Keam and Stephen was carried in the agency's mail bag on a weekly basis. The position of the Commissioner of Indian Affairs was not rescinded. It is not known how Jeremiah Sullivan resolved the problem of receiving and sending mail.[108]

---

105 "Moquis after Medicine," *Albuquerque Morning Journal*, September 1, 1882.

106 Jeremiah Sullivan to CIA, April 7, 1882, LR-OIA, NA; E. S. Stevens, Acting CIA to Fleming, May 13, 1882, MS 1145, NA-LA. John H. Sullivan to CIA, June 8, 1882, LR-OIA, NA; Edward S. Merritt, with enclosures, to Secretary of the Interior, May 23, 1882, LR-OIA, NA.

107 CIA to John H. Sullivan, August 13, 1882, LS-OIA. NA.

108 With the closure of the Moquis Pueblo Indian Agency in the spring of 1883, A.

In May Jeremiah Sullivan received the final $351.05 due him for services as Agency Physician.[109]

Contrary to expectations, Jeremiah Sullivan remained on First Mesa. He began building a two room house furnished with "a table, cook stove, a shelf or two with bottles, and a wooden bench," its ceiling "so low we could not stand upright without striking our heads against it."[110] He planted his crops, provided medical care for Hopis on all three mesas and continued writing accounts of Hopi religious practices.

Sullivan's notebook "6"—the only one to survive—describes katsinas he saw in the spring and early summer of 1882 and is illustrated with colored sketches of katsina masks drawn by his Hopi neighbors.[111] During the summer, Sullivan sent an article on the "Moqui Pueblo Indians" to Powell. It was not received, apparently as Fleming prohibited mail to and from Sullivan to be carried in the Agency's mail sack from Winslow.[112]

In mid-May Rev. Taylor, his wife and young son ("babe") took the train from Winslow to her family's home in Butler, Missouri. On his return Taylor explained to Rev. Jackson:

> As the rainy season approached—the time when we lost
> our dear little Hattie last season—and as we could not

M. Stephen was appointed post master and Sullivan's mail was carried in the mail bag from Keam's trading post.

109 Fleming to U. S. Assistant Treasurer, June 21, 1882, and Fleming to Second Auditor, June 27 1882, MS 1145, NA-LN.

110 Frederick S. Dellenbaugh, September 29, 1884, Diary, Dellenbaugh Manuscript Collection, MS 0215, Arizona Historical Society, Tucson. Cited hereafter as MS 0215, AHS. Dellenbaugh is describing Sullivan's house "just completed": "One door, two windows, a small hole. Inside very barren." Sullivan had purchased a cast iron stove from Keam when he first moved to Sichumovi. When he left First Mesa, Dellenbaugh gave his cook kit to Sullivan. For comparison with Cushing's rooms in Palawahtiwa's Zuni house, see Kate 2004: 274.

111 On June 10, 1921, anthropologist A. L. Kroeber sent Elsie Clews Parsons "a notebook compiled at Hopi in 1885 [1882-1883] by J. Sullivan that [he] was given by a former teaching fellow, Mrs. Lucile LaPrade, in the Department of Anthropology, University of California, Berkeley, who had received it from her father-in-law [Fernando T. "Ferd" LaPrade], a resident of [Winslow] Arizona, who had some way got it from Sullivan." Kroeber observed the small notebook was marked "number 6." Kroeber to Parsons, June 10, 1921, and [Jeremiah Sullivan], Notebook No. 31, ECP, CUL.

112 Jeremiah Sullivan to Powell, August 10, 1882, LR-BAE, NAA, SI.

get into our new house and did not deem the old one suitable to pass the season in, we came to feel it expedient to take baby elsewhere and especially as there is to be no lady in here.

In this letter of July 17, 1882, Rev. Taylor complained about the failure of the Board of Home Missions to provide him with an adequate salary or funds for books and stationery. "Would it not be fair, at least, for the Church to furnish such articles as will last, as stoves, tables, chairs, bedsteads, etc.?" he asked. He complained, too, that the Board had failed to pay the salary due to his brother, William. A day later Rev. Taylor received a telegram informing him that his son had died on July 16. He borrowed money from Keam to make the journey to be with his wife. On July 21, then in Trinidad, Colorado, Rev. Taylor wrote to Rev. Jackson, "Again we are childless!" and asked that his salary be sent to Butler, Missouri. On July 25, Agent Fleming recommended that the Indian Department purchase "a building now owned by Mr. W. E. Taylor...he built two years ago & as he contemplates leaving soon would sell cheaply." Three months later the *Albuquerque Morning Journal* of October 26 reported "Dr. Taylor, missionary to the Moquis, left this city for the agency yesterday morning."[113]

In the summer of 1882, U. S. Indian Inspector C. H. Howard visited Zuni Pueblo and the Moquis Pueblo Indian Agency. In reporting to Powell he reflected the content of rumors encouraged by Presbyterian missionaries among both the Zuni and the Hopi:

> From all I heard as to [Dr. Sullivan's] previous character and present conduct, and from what I saw of him myself, I could but conclude his presence there [among the Hopi] was a positive injury to that people. . . .
>
> I was exceedingly reluctant to credit some reports injurious to Cushing (with the Zunis), but they came from so many sources I felt obliged to take notice of them also. His shooting of horses of Navajos was brought officially to my attention. From the statements of the

---

113   Taylor to Jackson, July 17 and July 21, 1882, SJC, PHS. Fleming to CIA, July 25, 1882, LR-OIA. In a continuing effort to support Rev. Taylor and his wife, on December 4, 1882, Fleming proposed hiring Mrs. L. S. Taylor as a Post Mistress at the agency. CIA to Secretary of the Interior, December 15, 1882, LS-OIA.

Zunis themselves, it was at best but a reckless and lawless act and was in the line of the old barbarism rather than the civilization which Mr. Cushing ought to exemplify. Worse still is his reputation for licentiousness, which I found to be wide-spread in that country. . . .[114]

As an officer of the Smithsonian Institution, Cushing's salvage ethnography[115] of Zuni culture through participant observation was officially sanctioned and, for the most part, rumors of his inappropriate behavior were dismissed by Powell; as an employee of the Indian Bureau, however, Sullivan's active participation in Hopi social, economic, political and ceremonial life was taken—by Rev. Taylor and later by the Commissioner of Indian Affairs—as a direct challenge to the assimilationist goals of government Indian policy.

After he returned to Washington, D.C., Indian Inspector Howard wrote that "there is no power vested in the Agent, *under the present arrangement*, to expel him [Sullivan] from the village." However, because of illness Howard's "Report of Moqui Inspection"—in which he proposed an enlargement of the Navajo reservation to include the Hopi villages—was not submitted until December 19, 1882, three days after the creation of the Executive Order Moqui Pueblo Indian Reservation.[116] If Howard's recommendation had been accepted, it is possible a separate reservation

---

114 Green, ed., 1990:263. For a detailed and well documented account of the conflict between policies of Bureau of Indian Affairs and the Bureau of [American] Ethnology, see McCluskey 1980.

115 "Salvage ethnography" refers to any study carried out in order to document cultures or institutions which are disappearing or expected to in the near future. Most of the ethnological research carried out by the Bureau of Ethnology under John Wesley Powell had this rationale.

116 C. H. Howard to H. M. Teller, Secretary of the Interior, July 31, 1882, LR-OIA, NA. See Howard to Powell, December 26, 1882, LR-BAE, NAA, SI. G. P. Hammond argues that "Howard's earlier letters set forth clearly his recommendation for a different setup of agencies to serve the Moquis and Navajos, the heart of his idea being that there should be a new and combined Navajo-Moqui Agency that would serve the western Navajos as well as the Moquis." George Peter Hammond, Hopi-Navajo Relations, p. 105, George P. Hammond Collection, MSS 55 BC, Center for Southwest Research, University of New Mexico General Library. In the spring of 1884, two years after the closure of the Moquis Pueblo Indian Agency, a Congressional Act brought the Hopi under the supervision of the Navajo Agency in Fort Defiance.

for the Hopi would never have been created.

In August, shortly after Howard's inspection, the Commissioner of Indian Affairs wrote to Agent Fleming:

> You were directed to discharge Dr. Sullivan on the 7th of March last. ... He therefore has no business whatever at the Agency and has no right to remain on the reservation. You are directed to order him off the Reservation and prevent all intercourse between him and the Indians.[117]

On receipt of the commissioner's letter Fleming ordered Jeremiah Sullivan to leave. Sullivan immediately wrote the Commissioner of Indian Affairs:

> ...I would like to state to you first there is no reservation here, much less a treaty with these people, as the records of your office will show. ... I would also notice that there be several white men here [e.g., Keam and Stephen], who according to your order, 'have no business here.'[118]

Fleming also reported that Sullivan was not on a reservation; a note on Fleming's letter made in the commissioner's office states: "Capt. we seem to have blundered in ordering this man off the reservation."[119]

Meanwhile, the Bureau of Ethnology's James Stevenson returned to the Southwest for a fourth field season. His field party included the brothers Cosmos and Victor Mindeleff, who were to map the Hopi villages, as well as photographers, an artist and a journalist who would accompany Stevenson through parts of Canyon de Chelly.[120] On September 13, while Victor Mindeleff was exploring Canyon de Chelly with Stevenson's party, Cosmos Mindeleff, unaware of the antipathy of the Hopi Agent, hired Sullivan as an interpreter to assist him in mapping the village of Oraibi.[121] The result was a map enhanced with the clan

---

117   CIA to Fleming, August 16, 1882, LS-OIA, NA.
118   Jeremiah Sullivan to CIA, September 15, 1882, LR-OIA, NA. See Fleming to CIA, September 9, 1882, LR-OIA, NA. Sullivan's carefully written letter cites sections of the Revised Statutes in presenting his case. There is no record of a reply by the Commissioner of Indian Affairs.
119   Fleming to CIA, October 17, 1882, LR-OIA, NA.
120   See Hieb 2005.
121   Cosmos Mindeleff, Services, Invoice 41, Appropriation for Ethnologic Researches, Report 235,605, Records of the Accounting Officers of the Department of the Treasury, Office of the First Auditor, Settled Miscellaneous Treasury Accounts,

ownership of every house block carefully recorded – information about the social organization of house form that is now recognized as a significant contribution to the study of vernacular architecture. However, before starting work on the Second Mesa villages, Sullivan was arrested by Agent Fleming and ordered to leave.[122]

Sullivan was given four weeks to "secure his crops," after which he was expected "to leave permanently and to have no further communication with the Moquis." In his monthly report dated November 1, 1882, Agent Fleming wrote:

> Your order for the removal of Dr. Jer. Sullivan from the Moquis Pueblos has been executed, and I trust we are effectively rid of his presence and influence. On the whole I believe an advance is being made in the right direction. The future now looks brighter... I am sure much good will be accomplished.[123]

But on November 11 Agent Fleming reported to the Commissioner of Indian Affairs that Sullivan had returned to his "old quarters in the nearest village," says "he had come to stay" and claims "the Government has no power to cause his removal."[124] The commissioner responded immediately by telegram:

> Describe boundaries for reservation that will include Moquis villages and Agency and large enough to meet all needful purposes and no larger—forward same by mail immediately.[125]

NA. Under the date, October 16, 1882, Mindeleff lists, "Interpreter [Jeremiah Sullivan] at Oraibe six days @ 2.50 per day." Payment was not made until after November 4 when Sullivan had returned following his arrest. Mindeleff gives the names of each Hopi who carried water and wood during his survey but not the name of this "interpreter." Cosmos Mindeleff encouraged Sullivan to seek employment with the Bureau of Ethnology as on the same day, September 13, Sullivan wrote to Powell: "Have you any employment, in your department, at Moquis. I am very anxious to continue my studies here, and while I was drawing a salary from the Government I gave any and all information that I had, to you, willingly, but now as I have not connection with the Department I would like to work with you." Sullivan to Powell, September 13, 1882, LR-BAE, NAA.

122 Fleming, ibid.
123 Fleming to CIA, November 1, 1882, MS 1145, NA-LA.
124 Fleming to CIA, October 17, 1882 and November 11, 1882, LR-OIA NA.
125 CIA to Fleming, November 27, 1882 [Telegram], LS-OIA, NA. For Fleming's

Fleming complied with the request and on December 16, 1882, President Chester A. Arthur established the Executive Order Moqui Pueblo Indian Reservation, thus providing the legal basis to evict Jeremiah Sullivan.[126]

On the same day the executive order reservation was established, Jesse H. Fleming submitted his resignation as agent.[127] Ten days later, Fleming received a telegram informing him of the creation of the reservation and directing him to evict Sullivan. Fleming immediately wrote to the commanding officer at Fort Wingate, who responded that Arizona was not in his jurisdiction. No further effort was made to remove Sullivan.[128] On receiving Fleming's resignation, the Commissioner of Indian Affairs ordered him to close the Moquis Pueblo Indian Agency.[129]

---

response, see Fleming to CIA, December 4, 1882, MS 1145, NA-LN.

126 CIA to Henry M. Teller, Secretary of the Interior, December 13, 1882, LS-OIA, NA. See also CIA to Teller, December 13, 1882, LS-OIA, NA, enclosing a copy of the Executive Order as issued. The Executive Order Moqui Pueblo Indian Reservation was created on December 16, 1882, by President Chester A. Arthur. No Hopis were consulted; thus the religious concept of *Hopitutsqwa* (Hopi land) was ignored. More importantly, the lines drawn on the map were invisible on the landscape and neighboring Navajos continued to occupy lands surrounding the Hopi mesas, creating a conflict known in the twentieth century as the Navajo-Hopi land dispute.

127 Fleming to CIA, December 16, 1882, MS 1145, NA-LN.

128 CIA to Fleming, December 21, 1882, Land Division, Correspondence, vol. 53 (Letter books 105-106), 177-178 [copy of telegram], NA. See Fleming to CIA, December 26, 1882, MS 1145, NA-LN, in which Fleming reports contacting the commanding officer at Fort Wingate for assistance in removing Jeremiah Sullivan.

129 Closure of the Moqui Pueblo Indian Agency was both complex and controversial. Fleming was directed to make a "general issue of all surplus stores and goods of every kind to the Indians of the Moquis Pueblo Indian Agency." Fleming reported 3839 pounds in storage at the agency. In addition, medicines, school books, two office desks, a sewing machine, etc., were to be delivered to the Navajo Agent, D. M. Riordan. Fleming hired E. S. Merritt, former clerk and sometimes seen as a persona non grata, to assist him. On January 31 a claim was made that "One Fleming, the present Indian Agent for said Indians…did on or about the first of January, 1883, permit one Taylor a missionary teacher, to sell to one Keam an Indian trader, a certain house erected by the United States upon the public domain." The letter contained other charges and while sent by a "Henry T. Martin" of Holbrook, Arizona the style and content suggest it was written by Merritt. On April 5, another letter, this sent by a "Geo. Blake" of Williams, A.T.,

While these events were taking place Rev. Charles A. Taylor was transferred to Fort Defiance to be Superintendent of the Indian school at the Navajo Agency, bringing an end to the Presbyterian mission to the Hopi as well.[130] And, once again, Thomas V. Keam learned his trading post was located on land set aside by the government for an Indian reservation.[131]

In January 1883 Rev. Sheldon Jackson wrote to Rev. Charles H. Taylor and posed the question: "why is it that our ministers avoid Indian work?" Rev. Taylor replied:

---

explains, "The house referred to was constructed by Col. Sullivan and paid for in Government goods. Mr. Taylor had no right to sell it to Keam…" On March 16, Fleming's resignation was accepted and the charges ignored. Fleming to CIA, January 16, and Fleming to D. M. Riordan, January 23, 1883, MS1145 NA-LN. The letters of Martin and Blake are in Special Files of the Office of Indian Affairs, File 267, Charges Against Agent J. H. Fleming, Moqui Pueblo Agency, 1882-1883. CIA to Secretary of the Interior, March 16, 1883, LS-OIA, NA.

130   CIA to Fleming, December 30, 1882, LS-OIA, NA. With regard to Rev. Taylor's transfer to Fort Defiance, see Perkins to Jackson, January 6, 1883, SJC, PHS. Perkins expresses her disappointment with the appointment of Taylor as Superintendent of the Indian school at Fort Defiance. Fifteen years later, Taylor wrote of his appointment to be a missionary to the Hopi: "[We] made the journey to this Mission, in N. E. Arizona, overland in covered wagons, being seven weeks on the road. On arriving there [I found myself] 250 miles from any railroad, and 135 miles from any post office, and [my] wife the only American lady within 90 miles. [I] erected buildings and a home for myself and teachers' principally with [my] own hands. [I] continued here teaching and learning the language, waiting for the Interior Department to erect buildings, expecting to be recruited with teachers and other necessary assistants to run a successful Boarding and Industrial School. The Interior Department promised to furnish school buildings, clothing and provisions for such a school, but utterly failed to provide anything suitable and finally abandoned the Agency, leaving the Indians without any protection. Thus, after three years effort, and an expenditure of a large sum of money, the church was obliged to abandon a work that might have been rendered efficient, on account of the fickleness of the Indian Department and its failure to keep its promises. [I] was then transferred to the Navajo Agency, by the Board of [Home] Missions and put in full charge of that school, and mission, but in view of the fact that this work was also largely dependent upon the whims and prejudices of politicians, resigned without assuming charge." College of New Jersey (Princeton, N.J.), Class of 1873, *Biographical Record of the Class of 1873 … 1873-1883*; edited by the class secretary, Bridgeport: Bristol, 1883, p. 41.

131   Keam's trading post south of Fort Defiance was on land claimed for an expansion of the Navajo reservation in 1880.

If you make your question more personal, I will answer it… I am sorry to say that the greatest obstacle to the work has been placed there [by] the church. I cannot understand how it is but such are the facts in my experience. How such a drinking, profane man as agent Sullivan with the reputation he has at his own home could be recommended by the church is beyond my ken. But I know he could not have received an appointment but through the church. He was an effectual barrier to all missionary and school work while he remained, and he was there long enough to entrench his son so strongly that the repeated efforts of Commission Price to remove him have been in vain, and thus the whole cause of failure among the Moquis is traceable to sending out a wicked man by the church.[132]

The government's efforts to evict Jeremiah Sullivan and the creation of the Executive Order Moqui Pueblo Indian Reservation created a shadow that would hang over the work of subsequent anthropologists. For instance, as a member of the Hemenway Southwestern Archaeological Expedition A. M. Stephen would write his employer, J. Walter Fewkes, that Ralph P. Collins, the Superintendent of the Keams Canyon School and local representative of the Office of Indian Affairs, had sent "a note . . . saying that he had heard that I was opposing 'Govt Officials' and would like a report from me." Stephen met with Collins and received a warning:

[Collins] went on to say that while he, in a measure, recognized the value of our Ethnologic studies, yet he was convinced that when 'men of influence' such as Dr. Fewkes and myself, came among these people and showed so much deference for their ceremonials, it was prejudicial to the 'progress' of the Indian. It was opposed to the policy of the Govt in relation to his methods of civilizing these people and he said we—you and me— would have to give way![133]

In early December 1882—at the same time the reservation was being created—Cushing joined Powell, the Mindeleffs and others at a

132 Taylor to Jackson, February 1, 1883, SJC, PHS.
133 Stephen to Fewkes, August 10, 1892, MS 4408, NAA, SI.

United States Geological Survey camp near Holbrook, Arizona. Cushing was detailed to assist Victor Mindeleff in a collecting expedition to Oraibi. In route the party stopped at First Mesa where Willard Metcalf, a young artist accompanying Cushing, "made inquiries for Mr. Sullivan who was living here in much the same way as Cushing was at Zuni." Sullivan was found in a room where a ceremony with masked figures (*katsinum*) was taking place. Metcalf asked Sullivan if he could "house us for the night."

> "Why of course man" said he and returned an apology for having to stay in the *estufa* [kiva] and addressing a few words in Moqui to To-tchi,[134] bade us follow him as he would show us the way and for us to build up a fire and make ourselves at home.

The following day, after "rambles around the mesa," Metcalf returned to Sullivan's house where "I found Mr. Cushing seated before the fire smoking." Nothing more was recorded of this visit between Cushing and Sullivan.[135] Cushing went on to Third Mesa, having been instructed to "clean out Oraibi, ethnologically speaking."[136] Once there Cushing forced his way into a kiva (quite possibly the chief kiva during the Soyal or Winter Solstice ceremony) to trade and was met with considerable hostility from the leadership of one faction and forced to leave the village.[137]

Earlier in the fall of 1882 Sullivan had written to Powell seeking employment with the Bureau of Ethnology. Powell sent blank books on philology, geology, zoology, ornithology and ethnology and Sullivan believed he would be placed in the Smithsonian Institution as an ethnologist.[138] "I am dearly fond of researching into the old musty legends

---

134   To'tchi, Badger clan, was married to a Zuni woman. See Parsons, 1936, 1131.

135   See Green, ed., 1990:255-260. Green provides a useful overview of Cushing's visit to Oraibi, drawing on Willard L. Metcalf's "Journal from December 7th, 1882 to February 1st, 1883." Cushing's visit with Sullivan was omitted, however, from Green's edited version. See W. L. Metcalf, Journal, Willard Leroy Metcalf Papers, Thomas Gilcrease Institute, pp. 28, 30.

136   Joseph Stanley Brown writing to Cushing on October 30, 1882 in advance of the expedition to Oraibi. Green, ed., 1990:247. Brown was Powell's personal secretary.

137   Whiteley 1988a:42.

138   At the suggestion of the Mindeleffs, Jeremiah Sullivan wrote to Powell asking

and mysteries of these people," he said in a letter to the *Madison Daily Courier*.[139] On December 30, 1882, Sullivan completed the schedules in Powell's *Introduction to the Study of Indian Languages with Words, Phrases and Sentences to be Collected* (1880) for the "Moquis or Hopitu language" and was paid $50 for the "job."[140] In the early months of 1883 Powell sent stationery and an additional check for $25.[141] However, by the end of the summer articles sent went unacknowledged. Sullivan wrote a number of letters asking if his work had been received.[142] Clearly, the Commissioner of Indian Affairs was embarrassed by the circumstances leading to the establishment of the Executive Order Moquis Pueblo Indian Reservation and in due time Powell was apparently encouraged to have no further dealings with the doctor.

The Snake Dance of 1883 – Herman ten Kate

The Dutch physical anthropologist Herman F. C. ten Kate arrived for the Snake Dance at Walpi that summer (1883). At Walpi he met "Oyiwisha (He Who Plants Corn), alias Jeremiah Sullivan, M.D., an adopted son of the Moquis [who] places himself completely at my

---

if "there is any employment in your department at Moqui." Jeremiah Sullivan to Powell, September 13, 1882, LR-BAE, NAA, SI. The *Madison Evening Star* (Anon. 1882) reported, "Dr. Jere Sullivan, Government physician for the Moquis Indians, has been detailed by Maj. Powell, of the Smithsonian Institute, to compile their vocabulary, translate it into English, and catalogue their pottery and crockery. The work will be tedious and difficult, but very valuable, and is looked forward to with interest by the '*savants*' of the country." A week later, Sullivan wrote, "I have been taken from the Indian Department and placed in the Smithsonian as ethnologist" (Jeremiah Sullivan 1882).

139   Sullivan, Ibid.

140   Jeremiah Sullivan, Hopitu (Moqui Pueblo, November 1882), MS 792, NAA, SI. Like others gathering linguistic information for the Bureau of Ethnology, Sullivan used Powell 1880. For Sullivan's receipt of payment, see Appropriation for Ethnologic Researches, March 5, 1883, Report 237,177, Records of the Accounting Offices of the Department of the Treasury, Office of the First Auditor, Settled Miscellaneous Treasury Accounts, NA. Sullivan acknowledged receipt of $50.00 in Sullivan to Powell, March 26, 1883, LR-BAE, NAA, SI.

141   Jeremiah Sullivan to Powell, January 28, 1883, LR-BAE, NAA, SI.

142   Jeremiah Sullivan to Powell, February 4, 1883, February 23, 1883, March 11, 1883, March 26, 1883 and May 27 1883, LR-BAE, NAA, SI. Several letters are marked "Ans" but there is no indication Sullivan received the support requested.

disposal."[143] In the days following the Snake Dance, Sullivan provided ten Kate with a general introduction to Hopi language and culture and assisted him in recording information on Hopi physiology. In route to Second Mesa to observe a Snake Dance at Mishongnovi they passed a grave. Ten Kate, who had removed skeletal remains for study throughout his year-long tour of the Southwest, recalled:

> Although I was seized by the desire to remove a skull and even attempted to do this the following day, Oyiwisha urgently besought me to desist so as not to make his stay among the Indians untenable.[144]

After ten Kate's visit, Sullivan sent Powell a second description of the Snake Dance as well as an account of the Antelope society. His inquiries about whether they had been received went unacknowledged, as did his request for a supply of writing materials.[145]

In a letter to Powell of December 11, 1883, Sullivan reported:

> The book on Tewa language is still unfinished as I lack many things. I have expended the $50.00 some time ago, and as the Indians expect little gifts for talking I am compelled to stop and await developments; I really think I should be allowed a couple of rations, if nothing more, as you know an Indian judges a man by his gifts and while it is not best to lead them to think they will get pay for any of this assistance, yet 'a full stomach opens the heart.' I spoke to Col. [James] Stevenson about the matter, but as he was not authorized to do anything I have been compelled to rely upon your kindness for substantial assistance.[146]

On March 25, 1884 Sullivan sent the completed schedules for Tewa with a bill for $75.00. There is no record he was paid and this was Sullivan's last correspondence with the Bureau of Ethnology.[147]

---

143   Kate, 2004:249.

144   Op cit., 257.

145   See Jeremiah Sullivan to Powell, October 20, 1883, LR-BAE, NAA, SI. The manuscript has been lost.

146   Jeremiah Sullivan to Powell, December 11, 1883, LR-BAE, NAA, SI. Sullivan enclosed an account of the Snake Dance and a request for stationery. There is no indication ("Ans.") of an acknowledgement or reply.

147   Jeremiah Sullivan to Powell, March 25, 1884, LR-BAE, NAA, SI. Again, there is

Trading Songs and Narratives

Throughout 1883 Sullivan eked out a living by growing corn and other crops, and by bartering his medical knowledge for food, water, and wood from his Hopi neighbors. In addition, he began supplying Stephen with Hopi clan migration narratives and accounts of Hopi religion in trade for supplies at the trading post. Among these texts are several songs, including the following:

The Song of the Maidens at the Mealing Stones

 Corn, corn-planting; O my lover;
 Come, come, I am longing to see you.
 Come and I will set food before you.
 E-hem-a-a-i-ai-o-yum-o.
 O go forth strong love of my heart
 And swiftly tell this to him.

 Corn, corn-planting; O my lover;
 O musk-melon, O water melon;
 Hear them sing as they grow for our feasting.
 E-hem-a-a-i-ai-o-yum-o.
 Leap forth, love of my heart,
 Flash this to my lover.

 Corn, corn-planting; O my lover'
 Bean-plant, squash-plant, grow lustily;
 Come love, hasten to our gardens.
 E-hem-a-a-i-ai-o-yum-o.
 Go forth, go forth, strength of my heart;
 The rain has come.[148]

Song of the Maidens at the Feast of the Coming Harvest

 I
 O cloudy Rain-bringer come! Come thou

---

no indication ("Ans.") of an acknowledgement. Sullivan's account of the Arizona-Tewa language was received. See Jeremiah Sullivan, Tewa (Moquis Pueblo, April 1883), MS 1015, NAA, SI.

148 [Jeremiah Sullivan] Notebook 1, pp. 178-179, ECP, CUL.

And hang thy cool shadow wide o'er the land;
Come to our feast O Cloud-God Omaw,
And pour the life-giving rain from thy hand.
This way, this way, e-e-e
O-e-ya-ha-e-e-e.

II

O Father Sky God, give ear we implore thee,
Behold us in rapturous ecstasy dancing,
Hold the Cloud-Mask of Omaw in kindness before thee,
For Dawa's hot rays on our mesas are glancing.
This way, this way, e-e-e
O-e-ya-ha-e-e-e.

III

Big dropping showers Omaw now is planting;
We sound thanks to Sky-Father for hearing us;
Gladly we dance, in contentment we're chanting,
For this token that Harvest is nearing us.
This way, this way, etc.

IV

Musk-melon vines are running and trailing,
Water melon vines with blossoms are glowing,
Nowhere our planting prayer proved unavailing,
For all the land over, sweet verdure is blowing.
This way, this way, etc.

V

Listen O Lovers to our Priestesses greetings,
Tomorrow you feast from our baskets, partaking
Of buds of the melon, the squashes, the seedlings,
Plucked from their vines ere day began breaking.
This way, this way, etc.[149]

---

149   Op cit, pp. 180-181.

In early April 1883, Stephen copied Jeremiah Sullivan's "Legend of the Horn People" into a notebook, the first of a series provided by Sullivan over the course of the next two years.[150]

Notebook 1[151]

> Legend of the 'Horn People' told by Na-cin-uwe-be of the Antelope Gens, Horn Phratry, April 3, 1883.[152]
>
> From Montezuma to Oraibi, as told by Mu-au-wutaka, Eagle people, June 1883.[153]
>
> Legends related by the following old men of the Mokis— Mau-au-wu-taka, An-i-wi-ta, Si-kyau-is-ti-wa, Pau-i-ti-wa and Si-mo, August 1883.[154]
>
> An-a-wi-ta talks.[155]
>
> The Flood, as told by Pau-i-ti-wa, High Priest of the

---

150 Parsons, ed., 1929. The narratives on pages 35-50, 57-60, and 67-72 were recorded by Jeremiah Sullivan between 1883 and 1885 and attributed by Parsons, incorrectly, to A. M. Stephen. Parsons selected the "tales" from various narratives, omitting one alluding to Sullivan's initiation and another in which his name is given as the source. See Stephen, Notebooks Nos. 1 and 2, ECP, CU. These first two notebooks contain materials supplied by Sullivan as well as notes made by Stephen as he prepared a catalogue of Thomas Keam's pottery collection. Parsons was perplexed by the differences between the narratives recorded between 1883 and 1885 and those recorded—often by the same narrator—by Stephen in 1893 in Field Notebook No. 24, but did not consider Sullivan as the source.

151 Stephen copied narratives supplied by Sullivan in chronological order. The dates, in Stephen's hand, were added at a later date and probably indicate when Stephen obtained the narrative from Sullivan rather than when they were recorded.

152 There are many references to Nashin'weve in Stephen's notebooks (Parsons, ed., 1936:1113-1114) where he is identified as being a member of the Cedarwood or Coyote clan. Stephen recorded Si'mo's version of the Horn clan migration narrative (Parsons, ed., 1936:810-811).

153 Muau wutaka (old man) of the Eagle clan died in 1894. He could narrate only piecemeal and did not complete his clan migration narrative. See Parsons, ed. 1929:70.

154 Si'mo of the Horn clan. His mother and grandmother married Navajos. The Town chief of Sichumovi.

155 A'nawi'ta of the Patki clan and chief of the Agave society "owned" Sullivan's house in Sichumovi. Frequent reference is made to him Stephen's notebooks (Parsons, ed., 1936:1089).

Warriors.[156]

Legend by Mu-an-wu-taka (aged about 90 years).[157]

Bu-lin-i-ya-li—ki-ba, told by Nu-ku / Dance of the Maidens[158]

Pau-wu-mu / Po-wuni-u-w Growing Corn Dance, Story of Told by In-ti-wa.[159]

Masau, from conversations held in various estufas [kivas].[160]

Ye-ho-ho-ta Ka-tcina, told by Nu-ka, High Priest.[161]

Owaka Ka-tci-na, Pau-i-tiwa speaks.[162]

---

156   Pauwa'tiwa of the Eagle (Reed) clan. Sullivan amputated his mother's arm (Fewkes 1922:269). Stephen makes frequent reference to him (see Parsons, ed., 1936:1116-1117).

157   Parsons provides a title, "The Kachina Bring the Tiponi to the Rain Phratry," as well as important notes (Parsons, ed., 1929:60-63).

158   Na'ka of the Kachina (Parrot) clan, assistant to the chief of the Powamu society. The context in the notebook suggests it was recorded/written ca. August 1883, a time when Stephen was away from Keams Canyon. The "Butterfly dance" is usually performed in August. Although no date of composition is given, the title ('Dance of the Virgins') is included in Pilling 1885:744, No. 3775, where authorship is attributed to Dr. Jeremiah Sullivan. Pilling described the manuscript "in the Library of the Bureau of Ethnology" [apparently lost] as containing "a Moquis, or Ho-pi-tu, song, p. 6, and Indian terms throughout." It was reprinted from Notebook No. 1 by Parsons (Parsons, ed., 1936:147-148, n.2).

159   In'tiwa of the Kachina-Parrot clan played an important role in the ceremonial life on First Mesa (see Parsons, ed., 1936:1098-1099).

160   Sullivan to Powell, March 11, 1883, BAE-LR, NAA. Sullivan enclosed an account of Masau (now lost).

161   Parsons provides a title for this narrative: "Sun Punishes, then Sends his Kachina as Saviors." Sullivan to Powell, March 26, 1883, BAE-LR, NAA. Sullivan enclosed an article on Ye-ho-ho-ta Ka-tci-na (now lost).

162   Chief of the War society into which Sullivan was initiated.

Notebook 2[163]

> Popular Tradition, Tcua-ti-ki-bi Snake Dance, Wi-ki, High priest, Na-tci-wa Chief, June 6, 1885 [Added title: Legend of the Snake Order as told by 'outsiders'].[164]
> Legend of the Snake Order, as told by Na-sin-a-we-bi, January 16, 1884.
> Tcu-ku-wympka Song.[165]
> Salyko, January 9, 1884.[166]
> Ancient's Wings, Simo, July 1883.[167]
> The Song of the Maidens at the Mealing-Stones [transcribed above]
> Song of the Maidens at the Feast of the Coming Harvest [transcribed above]
> The Na-kui (Manna Kui) – Snake Rites [songs]

In a letter to Cushing dated December 15, 1883, Stephen mentions his work on Keam's pottery collection and continues, "I have been

---

163 Stephen began notes at both ends of the notebook as a consequence the materials are not in chronological order.

164 Wiki of the Snake clan and chief of the Antelope society. See Chapter 3 for a biography. As for Sullivan, Wiki was an important source for Stephen, especially from 1891-1894 (see Parsons, ed., 1936:1134 and Fewkes 1894b). Stephen shared his notebooks with visitors to Keams Canyon, including Washington Matthews and Archbishop Jean Baptiste Salpointe. Matthews copied this narrative and published it, attributing authorship to Stephen (Stephen 1888). Evidence that Sullivan was the recorder of the narrative is to be found in Sullivan 1940 where the narrative is presented as found in Stephen's notebook. Sullivan to Powell, December 11, 1883, LR-BAE, NAA, SI refers to a manuscript enclosed on "Antelope degree, Snake order, Tribe Ho-pi-tu" that may rely on Wiki.

165 Or Chuku'wimkya. The ritual clown engages in kahopi (bad, misbehaving, nonconforming, un-Hopi) behavior, most notably in the Chuku'lalwa (clown ceremony, a part of the spring and early summer Kachina "dances"). In this song the clowns poke fun at the appearance (mask and attire) of a kachina. See Hieb 2008 for an account of the Third Mesa ceremony.

166 Parsons found this a perplexing narrative. The Sha'lako ceremony is known as a Zuni ceremony although it is performed in the Hopi villages (see Parsons, ed., 1936:415ff). In the narrative recorded by Sullivan there are many elements that do not appear to correspond with what is known of the ceremony (see Parsons, ed., 1929:57).

167 Si'mo, Horn clan chief and Flute society chief, was an important figure in First Mesa ceremonial life. He died October 18, 1892.

trying to get some information from our friend 'Jere.'"[168] Stephen was critical of Sullivan's ideas on the development of Hopi pottery ("terrible rubbish") but soon incorporated verbatim Sullivan's translations and summations of Hopi religious thought into his "Catalog of the Keams Canon Collection of Relics of the Ancient Builders of the Southwestern Table Lands" ([1884].[169]

In August 1883 Sullivan wrote an account of the "Butterfly Dance" (his Bu-lin-ya-li—ki-ba):[170]

> Formerly none but young women who had passed the age of puberty took part, now, on account of the rapidly diminishing numbers of the Hopitus any girl from the age of seven dances [takes part] so as to make up the number necessary for the ceremony. Formerly at this dance the boys and girls were compelled to confess [disclose] to the assembled spectators the names of their sweethearts, which gave occasion to much rude mirth and jesting. This festival is not of the order of sacred feasts, but an auxiliary, occurring once in three years, but in common with all the Moki dances it bears a petition for rain & bounteous crops. Sometimes both sexes take part in it. Rehearsals take place regularly for a week or ten days before so that all can sing the songs and perform the necessary pantomime. The girl wears a towering headdress made of wood, painted in red, green, yellow and black with plumes of turkey feathers fastened to it. [As shown in a sketch, it has:] clouds at either side [and] in center is rude representation of growing food [vegetable]. Turquoise earrings, coral beads, fancy blankets and tunics are worn by the young women. Much ingenuity displayed in making these headdresses – tools consist of hunting knife and piece of sandstone to use as a

---

168   Stephen to Cushing, December 15, 1883, Frank Hamilton Cushing Manuscript Collection, MS.6, Braun Research Library, Autry Museum of the American West. Cited hereafter as MS 6, BRL, AMAW.

169   See Hieb 2004b.

170   The song was sent to the Bureau of Ethnology as indicated in Pilling 1885:744, No. 3775. The words supplied in brackets were added by Stephen.

plane. One of the songs sung to a drum accompaniment:
>Come here thunder and look
>Come here cloud and see it rain
>Thunder strike and makes it hot
>All seeds grow when it is hot.
>Corn is blossom,
>Beans in blossom,
>Your face on farms [gardens] looks
>Watermelon plant, musk-melon plant
>Your face on farms [gardens] looks
>Aha – aha- ehe – ihe &c &c

In the dance two lines are formed—one of young men, the other girls—headed by the best dancers and extending for twenty five or thirty couples. In a slow shuffling trot they approach each other, hands and arms swaying in gestures, they countermarch to right & left then pass down center—something similar to the figures in a reel [contra dance]. Two old men with long sticks pass up and down the line correcting all errors. The girl's partner must furnish her with the entire suit she wears at the dance.[171]

When the Moquis Pueblo Indian Agency was closed after the creation of the executive order reservation in 1882, no provision was made for supervision or services. Early in 1883 Sullivan approached the Navajo Agent, D. M. Riordan, with the request that "medical supplies and remedies be turned over to me as acting Physician" with no charge for his services.[172] Riordan resigned before a response was made.[173] In the spring of 1884 a Congressional Act combined the "Maquis Agency" with that of

---

171   Jeremiah Sullivan, Notebook 1, pp. 55-57, ECP, CUL.
172   Jeremiah Sullivan to D. M. Riordan, February 15, 1883, LR-OIA, NA. Sullivan's letter was forwarded to the CIA for instructions. The CIA responded that Dr. Charles Carter, hired by Fleming as Agency Physician, would remain there for the present. No mention is made that the Moqui Pueblo Indian Agency was in the process of being closed and that Carter would leave within a month. See CIA to Riordan, March 9, 1883, Accounts, LS-OIA, NA. There is no record of any communication between Riordan and Sullivan.
173   Riordan to CIA, July 3, 1883, LR-OIA, NA.

the Navajo. The newly appointed Navajo Agent John H. Bowman soon contacted Sullivan for assistance with an upcoming issue of implements to the Hopi and, in turn, Sullivan made an effort to get medical supplies through him.[174] In November 1884, Bowman proposed to employ Sullivan as interpreter and physician. The Commissioner of Indian Affairs responded immediately: "you are advised that the experience by employing Dr. Sullivan heretofore will prevent any further dealings with him."[175] Despite the odd construction, the meaning was clear.

At about this time Sullivan found a patron in Daniel Garrison Brinton, Professor of Ethnology at the Academy of Natural Sciences in Philadelphia and soon (1886) to become Professor of American Linguistics and Archaeology in the University of Pennsylvania. No correspondence between the two men survives; however, we may assume Sullivan received remuneration. During 1884 and 1885 he sent Brinton two speculative accounts of the Hopi luni-solar calendar, a brief history of the Hopi, as well as a lengthy, three-part description of the Hopi women's Mamzrau ceremony (parts one and two have been lost). The surviving manuscripts reveal Sullivan's interest in the thought world of the Hopi.[176] Taken together, Sullivan's surviving notebook, reports sent to Powell, and manuscripts offered to patrons reveal an unparalleled access to Hopi narratives, songs, and other oral traditions.

An interesting glimpse of Jeremiah Sullivan is given in two brief

---

174 See John H. Bowman to CIA, July 17, 1884, Bowman to Jeremiah Sullivan, August 2, 1884, and Bowman to CIA, August 25, 1884, Letters Sent, Fort Defiance Letter Book, Navajo Agency Records, Office of Indian Affairs, NA-LN. Cited hereafter as LS-NAR, NA-LN. The Hopi remained a sub-agency under the supervision of the Navajo Agency at Fort Defiance until 1899.

175 Bowman to CIA, November 6, 1884, LR-OIA, NA with a note attached, "Has not this man Sullivan been in the service & discharged?"; CIA to Bowman, November 20, 1884, and Bowman to Jeremiah Sullivan, November 27, 1884, Letters Sent, LS-NAR, NA-LN.

176 Jeremiah Sullivan, Hopitu Calendar, 913.72 Su53, Daniel Garrison Brinton Collection, Museum of Anthropology Library, University of Pennsylvania. Cited hereafter as DGBC, UP. The title is supplied from what appears to be the earliest of the essays. None are signed by Sullivan. The only surviving part of his account of the Mamzrau ceremony has a covering note: "Moki, Jan'y 11, 1886. My Kind friend, Dr. Brinton, Inclosed please find Part 3 Feast of Mu-in-wuh Hopituh. Yours truly, Jer: Sullivan." For modern analyses of the Hopi calendar, see McCluskey 1977 and 1981.

accounts by a Mormon settler who came to Keam's trading post for supplies. In his journal for March 12, 1884, Christian Lyngaa Christiansen reports going to "Hannoo [Hano] village to Poloca [Polacca's] house":

> Told him our Erond [errand] they sent to all the other villages for all the old men and Chiefs to come which they did. We preached the same Gospel to them... We all went to see Jeremiah Sulivan [sic] a Gentile a Government Employee. Bore our testimony to him about the Gospel and also about a true and living God to which He cussed and Swore and said He cared nothing for Religion, etc. We had a long chat... We told Him we were amongst the Indians our Friends to give them some good advice such as leaving off adultery and all means of Evil to which He Swore again.

Christiansen returned in October "on Business with T. V. Keam & Company." In his journal for October 17 he noted:

> ...in the afternoon Witnessed a Buffalo Dance at the Walpi village. A Gentile named Jeremiah Sillivan [sic], a doctor, took an active part with them. He was Painted Black.[177]

Another Visitor – Frederick S. Dellenbaugh

Also in September 1884, Colorado River explorer and artist Frederick S. Dellenbaugh arrived at Keams Canyon and immediately arranged to rent a room from Tom Polacka (Polacca) in Tewa on First Mesa with plans to paint Hopi subjects. Dellenbaugh kept a richly descriptive diary which begins with a note added later:

> Probably I would have progressed more as an artist if I had remained in Paris where I had a fine, comfortable studio, but I had an impelling urge to go and so fifteen days after leaving Paris I was in camp at Fort Wingate, New Mexico with the Geological Survey party under Prof. Thompson.[178]

---

177   Christian Lyngaa Christiansen, Journal, Ms fl70, History Department, The Church of Latter-Day Saints, Salt Lake City.

178   Diary of F. S. Dellenbaugh, June 21, 1884 to January 1, 1885. Dellenbaugh Collection, MS 0215, Arizona Historical Society, Tucson. Cited hereafter as MS 0215, AHS. In July of 1882, Almon Harris Thompson (1839-1906) was appointed

Dellenbaugh traveled by buckboard from Fort Wingate to Keams Canyon, reaching there on September 26.

On September 29 Keam took Dellenbaugh to First Mesa in a spring wagon to meet Polacca in Tewa and then tour the other villages:

> We [Keam and Dellenbaugh] passed through Cichomovi [Sichumovi] about half way [to Walpi]. It is a small town. Here we were greeted by Jerry Sullivan—called the "Doctor" and the "Governor" sometimes—a young man who has lived with the Moki's for three years. He showed us his house—just completed—not remarkable for its architecture or finish or strength. One door, two windows and a small hole. Inside very barren. A table, a cook stove, a shelf or two with bottles, and a wooden bench...[179]

They returned to Keams Canyon later that afternoon and the following day Dellenbaugh accompanied Keam to Fort Defiance. Three weeks passed before Dellenbaugh returned to First Mesa. His lengthy account of his first two days includes the fullest portrayal of Jeremiah Sullivan and his life among the Hopi written by any visitor during the seven years of the doctor's residence.

> Sunday [October] 19th afternoon Mr. Keam brought me over to the Moqui towns. He desired to stay overnight in order to collect some baskets, etc. We reached the peach orchard at foot of trail about 3:30 and found no burros awaiting us... Tom Polaki's brother came down [with a horse and mule]. Arrived at the Polaki house, we found the room I had engaged had not been prepared...
>
> Then we went up toward Cechuminavi [Sichumovi]... We entered Tochee's house and found Sullivan there, his red shirt outside his trousers and his whole air more that of a Moqui than [a] white man. They were all clustered

---

to take charge of the Wingate Division of the United States Geological Survey. "Professor" Thompson, as he was known, was the brother-in-law of John Wesley Powell, and had served as second-in-command in charge of geographical work during Powell's 1870-1878 explorations of the Colorado River. From 1871-1873 Frederick Samuel Dellenbaugh (1853-1935) was artist and assistant topographer with Thompson on Powell's second expedition down the Colorado River.

179   Op cit., September 29.

about the stove eating watermelon in their way—that is, scooping it out with the fingers and then drinking the juice...

Tuesday [October] 21. After breakfast... The "Doctor" (Sullivan) came and offered me a horse to ride with him to Mishongnavi, six miles distant on the other mesa [Second Mesa]. The horse was a sorry looking beast and the saddle still worse, the stirrups being very short with no way of lengthening them. It was rather amusing... We crossed the valley and at the foot of the other mesa stopped at a spring and ate some potted turkey and bread that I had brought along. When I had mentioned lunch to Sullivan before starting out, he said, "Why you can eat watermelon can't you." We went up on the cliff...

As it was a dance day everyone was at home and there were numerous visitors from the other villages. Sullivan went up into one of the houses to dress a wounded head—the result of a kick from a horse—and I was left to wander... Noticing the women in their festive toggery moving toward the dance place, I followed... [Dellenbaugh gives a partial description of the woman's ceremony of Mamzrau.]

An Indian came up, shook hands in a friendly way and asked me, as near as I could make out, to go with him to his house. [Dellenbaugh finds Sullivan.] ...the man was one whom Sullivan had cured of a bad arm, and his gratitude was great. He asked us to sit down to his feast. In every house we found watermelons, peaches, a huge bowl of soup (rabbit, corn & chili) and a large tray of their tissue paper bread [*piki*]. These were generally arranged together in the middle of the floor, and rolls of sheepskins placed about for seats. ... In one place Sullivan dressed the fingers of a boy of eighteen. The ends of thumb and two fingers appeared to have rotted away. After one or two more visits, we started back about 3:30. Sullivan said we would come back like the wind, but the poor old crow-baits were so tired that we walked them the whole distance...[180]

In a letter to his sister, Dellenbaugh described other aspects of Sullivan's life at Hopi:

> Last evening I went down to Tochee's in the next village having heard there would be a dance there. Heard singing in the "Doctor's" house so went in and found the room full of men singing. ... [Tochee] was beating a big drum in time with the singing and instructing the younger men in songs with which they were not familiar. A single candle on the floor gave light.[181]

Entries in his diary indicate Dellenbaugh became ill and increasing ill at ease on First Mesa and on November 13 he wrote, "Packed up and got ready to depart from Tewa. Many of my neighbors came to see what I had and pick up things cast off. Gave Sullivan my kitchen outfit."[182] For the next ten weeks Dellenbaugh stayed at Keam's trading post. He returned to First Mesa once, to observe a "dance" on November 26.

In a manuscript attached to his diary, dated January 26, 1885, Dellenbaugh describes a trip to Oraibi from Keams Canyon undertaken for the benefit of George H. Bendle, recently appointed Farmer-in-Charge for the Hopi.[183] Bendle had not been to Oraibi and suggested

---

180   Dellenbaugh, October 19 and 21, 1884, MS 0215, AHS. In an untitled and revised version of Sullivan's treatment of the boy of eighteen, p. 38, Dellenbaugh added: "The first two fingers of one hand had so decayed in a most repulsive manner and had been covered with pitch. After removing the pitch by means of warm water, the doctor dressed them with glycer[ol] till he could come again." Papers of Frederick Samuel Dellenbaugh, MS 407, Special Collections, The University of Arizona Library. Cited hereafter as MS 407, UAL.

181   Dellenbaugh to [his sister] Belle, November 2, 1884, MS 407, UAL. Dellenbaugh copied verbatim from his diary of November 2, 1882. MS25, AHS. In his diary he gives a brief description of the dance then adds: "The night was beautiful with a full moon. The doctor was gracious enough to walk as far as my house with me."

182   Dellenbaugh, November 13, 1884 MS 0215, AHS.

183   Dellenbaugh, "A Trip to Oraibi," January 26, 1885, MS 0215, AHS. When the Moquis Pueblo Indian Agency was closed in December 1882 no provision was made for the supervision of the 1882 Executive Order Moquis Pueblo Indian Reservation. The Executive Order was not published in the *Annual Report of the Commissioner of Indian Affairs* and while Dennis M. Riordan, the new Navajo Agent, and Thomas V. Keam, whose land was now included in the reservation, had heard a "rumor" that a reservation had been established for the Hopi no official communication was sent to affected parties. As noted above, in 1884

that Dellenbaugh join him. Dellenbaugh begins:

> We sent word to Doc. Sullivan…his company being quite necessary as neither Bendle nor myself could speak the Moki language or even a few words of it.[184]

The two men reached Sullivan's house at 1:30 in the afternoon and immediately set out for Oraibi, eighteen miles to the west. It was "about sunset and the keen winter wind swept the bleak mesa with unobstructed force" as they "discerned Oraibi through the settling gloom." Dellenbaugh continues:

> …we found ourselves before the town, lying silent as death in the moonlight, not a light visible and looking for all the world like deserted ruins. The dogs on this side had as yet not scented us, and it was not until we had fairly entered the village before a chorus of a thousand barks and howls greeted our ears. … At length Doc. stopped before a group of buildings and bidding us wait said he would 'see if the old folks were in.' They were some people he knew and who were friendly to the Americans.[185]

By the second half of the nineteenth century many seeds of change and conflict had been introduced through Spanish explorers, Mormon missionaries, and other contacts—direct and indirect—and the people of Oraibi were divided nearly equally into those who were "friendly to Americans" and those who were not ("Hostiles"). The Oraibis refused to have a census taken, to receive annuity goods and rations and to send their children to a boarding school established at various times at the Moquis Pueblo Indian Agency. Dellenbaugh, Bendle and Sullivan stayed overnight with a "Friendly" family, visited men in a kiva and "called

---

a Congressional Act combined the "Maquis Agency" with that of the Navajo under the over-all supervision of Navajo Agent John H. Bowman

184   In his diary and letters Dellenbaugh often spoke of his loneliness while living on First Mesa. Sullivan invited him to visit—Sullivan's house was little over 300 yards from Polacca's house—but he did so only occasionally. His sense of isolation was increased by his lack of a means of communication with the Hopis and Tewas who watched him paint.

185   The emergent factionalism in the Third Mesa village of Oraibi has been documented and analyzed by anthropologist Peter Whiteley. See his 1998a and 2008.

on the head chief"—Loololma, a "Friendly."[186] The men "inspected the whole village" and left at noon for First Mesa:

> We reached Doc's all right and remained there for the night. Doc. prepared some chili and mutton and tea for supper and we made our bed in his inner room while the Indians, his companions [not otherwise identified] slept in his outer room.[187]

What is most interesting about this visit to Oraibi is Sullivan's obvious rapport with the Hopis of the village they interacted with. Sullivan had chosen to let Hopis from other villages report about him and his work as a physician. There is no record of his medical work among the Oraibis. Be that as it may, Sullivan could assist Cosmos Mindeleff in mapping the house blocks and ten kivas in Oraibi in 1882 and introduce Bendle to Lololoma in 1885. At Oraibi, Sullivan was welcomed but others were not. In September 1881, the Oraibis abandoned their village "leaving only the aged and bed-ridden" at the approach of a Bureau of Ethnology expedition led by Stevenson. In December 1882, Cushing was forced to abandon his efforts to collect materials at Oraibi for the National Museum. And in November 1885, again during a collecting expedition, James and Matilda Stevenson were forced to leave the village when several Hopis seemed to threaten violence.[188]

The Snake Dance of 1885

During the time of Dellenbaugh's visit, Bourke's *The Snake Dance of the Moquis* appeared, and the subsequent sensation brought two

---

186 Loololoma became the village chief in the early 1870s. In 1878 Agent W. R. Mateer went to Oraibi and afterward reported "I found the chief, Lo-lulul-ah-my, friendly and willing...but a majority of his council were opposed and not being influential enough to control them we were compelled to return without performing our errand." W. R. Mateer to CIA, December 1, 1878, LR-OIA, NA. The factionalism at Oraibi led to a military confrontation in 1891 and to the break-up ("split") of the village in 1906. Again, see Whiteley 1998a and 2008.

187 Dellenbaugh, "A Trip to Oraibi," MS 0215, AHS.

188 See Chapter 4 for a discussion of the 1881 and 1882 confrontations. The incident in 1885 received national attention through an article and illustration in *Illustrated Police News* (see Miller 2007:68-69). The Stevensons' friend, Thomas V. Keam, took a small party to Oraibi and "arrested" two of the protesters and held them as prisoners until they "promised good behavior in the future."

dozen curious on-lookers to the 1885 observances at Walpi. Stationed at Whipple Barracks in northern Arizona, Bourke received an advance copy of *The Snake Dance of the Moquis of Arizona* on September 16, 1884. By late December and early January 1885 a number of favorable reviews appeared in the *New York Sun, New York Evening Post, Nation,* and other periodicals. In his journal of April 14, 1885, Adolph Bandelier noted he had lent his copy to a friend in Santa Fe. In Washington, D.C., the Stevensons, the Mindeleffs and H. C. Yarrow, acting assistant surgeon U. S. Army, began preparations to return to the Southwest. For Dr. Yarrow, whose specialties included reptilian fauna, the Snake Dances to be held at Walpi and Mishongnovi were of great interest. As the dates drew near, popular interest grew.

The first to arrive that summer were the Mindeleff brothers. From a main camp near Mishongnovi, Victor and Cosmos visited "each of the Moki villages in succession obtaining drawings and traditions bearing on the ruins in the vicinity," including a summary of Hopi traditions regarding Payupki from Sullivan.[189] On August 17, the Mindeleff party attended the Snake Dance at Mishongnovi, making a series of photographs during the Ceremony. Cosmos with a guest, Marion Warren, made notes. Victor noted there were "no whites present except our party." The following day, the Mindeleff party traveled east for the Snake Dance at Walpi.

Early in the summer, the photographer Ben Wittick traveled from Fort Wingate to Flagstaff where he joined another photographer, J. C. Burge. However, after "days and weeks" of being asked "Are you going to the Snake Dance?" the two photographers left Flagstaff on Tuesday, August 11, to take photographs of the Hopi villages and the "Snake Dance." Two days after the ceremony, on Thursday morning, August 19, "with our boxes well filled with negatives of the ancient Pueblos," they returned to Flagstaff where "the renowned photographers of the southwest, pitched their tent adjoining the CHAMPION [newspaper] office...for a few days." To promote the sale of photographs, Burge wrote an article on the "Dance of the Moquis" that appeared in the

---

189   See "Work of Messrs. Victor Mindeleff and Cosmos Mindeleff" in Powell 1891:xxvi, and Report of the Director, *Seventh Annual Report of the Bureau of Ethnology* (Washington: Government Printing Office, 1891): xxvi, and Sullivan 1891a. '

Arizona Champion on September 5.

W. Cal. Brown and [Stephen Poole?] Sanders, an Atlantic and Pacific Railroad photographer, "photographers of Albuquerque," also attended and Sanders made ten cyanotypes of First Mesa and the Snake Dance. Brown also was successful in taking photographs and his description of the ceremony, entitled "A Carnival of Horrors," was published in the *Albuquerque Morning Journal* on August 26.

From Burge's article we know "there were quite a number of visitors present." He lists "Dr. [H. C.] Yarrow, of Washington, Mr. [Douglas D.] Graham, [trader] of Zuni, Mr. [Edwards] Roberts of Santa Barbara, Cala., [and] Mr. [John Lorenzo] Hubbell [of St. Johns, then Sheriff of Apache County]. The *St. Johns Herald* reported "W. W. Hall, the pioneer stage man of Apache county" took a large party: "The excursionists consisted of the Misses Lynch, of Navajo; Miss Wall, Master Wall and the Misses McCormick, of St. Johns and Mr. Lew Lynch, of Navajo."[190] Brown, too, reported there were "quite a number of spectators." Four women in bonnets and full skirts are clearly visible in Wittick's photographs as well as a number of Anglo men. In addition to the "visitors" listed by Burge, the Mindeleffs, A. M. Stephen, and Jeremiah Sullivan were among attendees.[191]

Stephen's journal notes are the first he made regarding a Hopi ritual (Parsons, ed., 1936:580-586). After the ceremony, with Sullivan as interpreter, Dr. Yarrow interviewed Wiki, the chief priest of the Antelope Society, regarding the handling of the snakes used in the ceremony.[192] This was the third Snake Dance at Walpi Sullivan had observed.

At the end of August, Sullivan and Stephen went to Canyon de

---

190   Anon., August 27, 1885. The Great Register for Apache County lists "Lou Lynch."

191   For a list of photographers at the 1885 Snake Dances at Mishongnovi and Walpi, see Hieb 2011a:140. The accounts of the Snake Dances in 1885 include Brown 1885, Burge 1885, Kosmos Mindelieff [sic], i.e., C. Mindeleff 1886, Roberts 1886, Stephen in Parsons, ed., 1936:580-586; Sullivan 1940 [attributed to A. M. Stephen] "Hopi Indians of Arizona," *Southwest Museum Leaflets*, No. 14 (Los Angeles: Southwest Museum, 1940): 1-8, 22-46, and 67-72;. and H. C. Yarrow, "Remarks" [Presented before the Washington Anthropological Society following Cosmos Mindeleff's "An Indian Snake Dance"], MS 3794, National Anthropological Archives, Smithsonian Institution.

192   Yarrow, ibid. Yarrow's notes were taken verbatim from a work on the Snake Dance Sullivan was preparing.

Chelly with a party led by Victor Mindeleff where they explored the ancestral Hopi ruins, including the Puebloan tower structure in Canyon del Muerto's Mummy Cave. While in Mummy Cave, Sullivan left a note in a crevice on which he penciled, "Jer: Sullivan, M. D. / Alex. M. Stephen M.A. / September 2" [2nd] 1885 / Sketch, etc."[193] The following year Sullivan sent an account of their visit to the *Madison Courier*.[194]

Another Visitor – Charles R. Moffet

Later that September Charles R. Moffet[195] and his ranch partner, identified only as "Herbert L----," traveled from the railroad at Holbrook north to "Keem's Canon." There they met Keam who "annually collects great stores of wool and goat hides, baskets, blankets, pottery and antiquities brought in by these Indians" and "Stevens" who "has also collected, and with the greatest skill put together, much of the broken ancient pottery found in the extensive ruins [Sikyatki] lying to the north of Keem's, and has secured from some of the old burial crypts many very beautiful and unbroken pieces." After staying overnight with Keam, Moffet and his partner continued to the foot of First Mesa:

> Leaving L---- to look after our effects, I climbed the trail, to find if possible Dr. Jeremiah Sullivan, --the only white man living in the villages. I met two Indians coming down the trail . . . and when I asked for "*El Americano*" they pointed in the direction of Walpi. Making my way there, I found the Doctor in the act of putting his brand upon a fee that he had just been fortunate enough to

---

193 See Morris 1938:137 and Alexander M. Stephen, Hopi Notebooks No. 1, MS 1563, American Philosophical Society Library, Philadelphia. The narrative of the Sullivan-Stephen explorations in Canyon de Chelly from 31 August 31 to September 2, 1885 in the notebook and the line drawings are in Stephen's hand; sketches in a softer pencil are by Sullivan.

194 Jeremiah Sullivan 1886.

195 Charles R. Moffet may be an individual listed in the California Great Register for 1888. If so, he was then 31 years old (b. 1857?). The Charles R. Moffet who met Jeremiah Sullivan in 1885 (Moffat 1889b) also visited northern Arizona in the fall of 1884 (Moffat 1889a). "California Great Registers, 1866-1910," database, *FamilySearch* (https://familysearch.org/ark:/61903/1:1:VYD3-J9H: accessed 29 January 2016), Charles R Moffet, 27 Apr 1888; citing Voter Registration, Fourth Ward, Los Angeles, California, United States, county clerk offices, California; FHL microfilm 977,9. I have been unable to identify Moffet's "ranch partner."

collect. The fee was a very good two-year-old pony.

The Doctor returned with me to the foot of the mesa for L----, and from that time on had us under his care, and acted as interpreter. He took us to his quarters, in the house of Anniwita, the secretary of war, or war chief of the tribe, and the old chief, immediately offering fruit and melons, gave us a cordial invitation to make his house our home during our stay in the village.

A short time afterwards, Cimo, the head chief of the tribe, came to see us. ...

After a time the wife of Anniwita announced that dinner was ready, and many a man has sat down to a poorer one: a nice rabbit stew, *piki* (bread made of corn-meal), with green corn, green beans, muskmelons, watermelons, and peaches. ...

Seated upon sheepskins, our food on a rug upon the floor, we made a very hearty dinner in the hospitable house of Anniwita, a much more hearty dinner than we should have eaten had we known what was in store for us, for many times that afternoon were we called upon to repeat it.

After rising from our repast, the Doctor said: "Come with me; we will return the calls now, for it is expected." We visited every house in the village ... In each place, after the host had assured us that he was glad that we had come, sheepskin rugs were spread for us, and melons and peaches offered, and we ate, of course, some part of each, until had the village been any larger the Doctor would certainly have had two patients.

Moffet's account continues with a description of a "social dance" held in a kiva in Walpi. After the dance they returned to Aniwita's home where "we spread our blankets upon the smooth rock floor of the house … with our boots for a pillow." Nothing, Moffet thought, could "mar my restful slumbers:"

About four o'clock, however, I was awakened, and that quickly and thoroughly, by a loud grating together of rocks almost against my head, and by a song in the high voice of a woman.

"What, in the name of all that is unearthly, is that?" I asked the Doctor.

He laughed and replied: "It is dawn, and the daughter of the house is grinding the meal for the day, and you hear the song of 'the maid of the mill.' Listen, and presently you will hear some woman in every house in the village sing it."[196]

Throughout the fall of 1885 a petition was mounted to have Sullivan appointed "Physician to the Moquis." Among those signing or writing letters of support were Washington Matthews, James Stevenson, Navajo Agent Bowman, and H. C. Yarrow, who noted: "Practically, he has been their physician, without fee or award, for several years."[197] No action was taken by the Indian Bureau.

In October 1886, John H. Sullivan, Jeremiah's father and the former Hopi Agent, died in Albuquerque.[198] The senior Sullivan was involved in real estate and local politics as was Jeremiah's younger brother who, among other activities, was captain of the Albuquerque Browns baseball team. There is no record that Jeremiah ever visited his family in Albuquerque, or that any of them traveled to Hopi.[199] Had his father sent him money? In the four years since he was dismissed as Agency Physician, Jeremiah Sullivan had received less than $100 from the Bureau of Ethnology and unknown, but probably only token amounts, from patrons.

---

196 Moffet 1889b:245, 247-248.

197 Yarrow to John D. C. Atkins, CIA, December 14, 1885, with four enclosures, LR-OIA, NA.

198 A month before his death, the *Albuquerque Morning Democrat* carried the announcement "Mrs. C. E. Sullivan will open a Boarding Day School for young ladies…September 13th, 1886." On December 30, the *Democrat* noted, "The 'Mistletow Bough' performance [will] be given tonight at Grant's Opera by Mrs. C. E. Sullivan's select school…" However, she soon returned to Lexington, Kentucky, where other relatives lived. John H. Sullivan, Jr., moved to Los Angeles and apparently worked in the City Clerk's office.

199 See Anon 1886b and 1886c. The *Apache County Critic* (21 October 1886) noted the death of John H. Sullivan. There is no indication in Albuquerque newspapers that Jeremiah Sullivan attended his father's funeral. John H. Sullivan, Jr. signed the death certificate.

Documenting Hopi Architecture

In the fall of 1887 Victor and Cosmos Mindeleff returned to the Hopi villages to undertake a survey of ancestral Hopi ruins to the east and west of three mesas. Victor Mindeleff arranged for Stephen to carry out the field work as an employee of the Bureau of Ethnology. Stephen, in turn, then hired Sullivan to assist him with research in the Hopi villages on First and Second Mesas for $25.00 a month from November 1887 to April or May 1888.[200]

Terraced Houses in Walpi, 1876. Photograph by J. K. Hillers. Bibliotheque nationale de France/Societe de Geographie. Image: #Sg Wf 5(3).

By October 6, 1887 Stephen was in the field with the Mindeleff brothers[201] surveying ancestral Hopi sites from the Jeddito Valley in the

---

200   Stephen, Notebook No. 33, Field Notebooks, 1882-1894, ECP, CUL. Stephen notes "Jere Sullivan – paid him" followed by a list of dates and amounts.

201   Victor and Cosmos were joined by younger brother Charles for the field work in October and November. On October 31, "Charles killed a duck in four shots and by wringing its neck." Stephen, Notebook 32, ECP, CUL.

east to Moencopi in the west.[202] In early November the Mindeleffs left Stephen in charge of field work at the Hopi villages while they went on to Chaco Canyon and Jemez Pueblo in New Mexico before returning to Washington, D.C.

Two notebooks from the Hopi research survive with entries by Stephen and Sullivan as well as sketches of architectural features by Sullivan (signed "JS87," "JS88," and "JSullivan").[203] Some notes, usually those of Stephen, describe the "sticks and stones" of Hopi architecture:

> Ladders were of two kinds—a notched log, set on end, still in use; and two poles notched into the notches of which smaller sticks (rounds) were tied with yucca rope.[204]

Many other notes, mostly in Sullivan's hand, record Hopi narratives that give meaning to various architectural forms:

> When the roof is put on the house a stick with four feathers attached is stuck into the roof from the inside and a little of the native bread put in likewise; this is called feeding the house that no ill luck may attend the occupancy.
>
> A former practice among them was to leave a portion of the inside of a room un-plastered; a belief existing that a katcina would come and finish the room. Notwithstanding the barren spot, it was always considered as entirely plastered, even the barren place for it was covered by an invisible coat of mud.[205]

---

202   Stephen, October 28, 1887, Notebook 32, ECP, CUL. Pages 46-48 include descriptions of ruins in the Moencopi area with notes about the Mormon settlement and mill. In addition, Stephen noted, "Mr. E. D. Stone, who formerly lived at this place as a trader, made some excavations finding several valuable pieces of pottery of the black-line decorative series."

203   Notebooks 32 and 33, ECP, CUL. In Notebook 32, pages 11-56 are Stephen's entries for the period from October 6 to November 6, 1887 at Hopi ancestral sites. Notebook 32, pages 57-76 and all of Notebook 33 from November 17, 1887 to February 18, 1888 contain entries by Stephen and Sullivan. Notebooks 32 and 33 were added to ECP, CUL, after Parsons' death and bear a note "Not Stephen." In any case, none of the materials were included in Victor Mindeleff 1891 or in Elsie Clews Parsons, ed. 1936. Victor Mindeleff (1891) appears to be based entirely on his own field notes (now lost) and photographs by the Mindeleffs and J. K. Hillers, supplemented by reports submitted by Stephen (now lost).

204   Notebook 32, p. 72, ECP, CUL. The handwriting appears to be Stephen's.

205   Notebook 33, p. 38, ECP, CUL. The handwriting appears to be Sullivan's.

Feby 17 [1888] From the story of death, to die, the absence of life. Much can be gleaned to assist in ascertaining the Hopituh idea of that mystifying state. The house of Massau-wuh is really the grave, the place of the dead. When the people came up out of the earth, the child of the presiding chief died. Po-wa'kuh, a mysterious personage of some sort, came to the parents with an inquiry, saying who do you mourn? Come with me and I will show you that your child is not dead but has only gone home. So the parents followed this Po-wa'kuh to the opening in the ground when upon looking into the dark shaft, and at the bottom of it, they saw their child sitting there, drying its hair, dressed in the same kind of garments as used in this life. Then Po-wa'kuh said, remember that no Hopi dies, they only return to their home.[206]

Something of the nature of their research is conveyed in the following notebook entry written by Stephen:

Sunday – March 25th [1888]. Snowy gales last night & today wind howls with fierceness & coldness. It is impossible to do any plans on housetops today. Indeed it would be impossible to stand erect on the roofs. Have some talk with Jere today & we gather some few details as to occupancy of houses &c.

Noted occupancy & construction of house groups by phratry & gentile [clan] groups in Walpi, Tewa and Citcumovi [Sichumovi]. Wind still blowing pretty stiffly and very cold this evening. Will try and get over to Second Mesa tomorrow. But it looks [page missing]...

Stayed up at Jere's house last night. Found Tom's [Keam] old stove in one of the houses. It was sold by him to Jere Sullivan 6 years ago & it is still doing fair good service. Jere sold it to Tea-kwai-na [Tawai'yauma?] & from him

---

206   Notebook 33, p. 98. Then handwriting appears to be Sullivan's. Compare with Stephen's account (Parsons, ed., 1936: 151-152). A po-wa'kuh is a sorcerer or wizard. Sometimes glossed as "witch…demon, spirit more or less evil or mischievous" (see Parsons, ed., 1936:1283). The narrative quoted continues with a description of the burial cyst.

the present owner bot it.[207]

The results of their field work were published in Victor Mindeleff's "A Study of Pueblo Architecture, Tusayan and Cibola" (1891).[208] Although very little remains of the research materials used it appears much of was based on "memoranda" submitted by Stephen after the end of the field season. The opening chapter, "Traditional History of Tusayan," is credited to Cosmos Mindeleff and includes summaries and quotations from several clan migration narratives clearly derived—sometimes verbatim—from Sullivan's translations. A "Supplementary Legend" is appended regarding the ruins of Payupki. In a brief introduction Cosmos Mindeleff wrote:

> ...the only version that could be obtained is not regarded by the writer as being up to the standard of those incorporated in the "Summary" and is therefore given separately, as it has some suggestive value. It was obtained through Jeremiah Sullivan, then resident in Tusayan.[209]

Jeremiah Sullivan and Wiki

Following the Snake Dance at Walpi in 1885 Sullivan began completing an account of the Hopi Snake Dance based on his

207 Stephen, March 25, 1888, Notebook 7, ECP, CUL.
208 Victor Mindeleff 1891. Tusayan (Hopi) and Cibola (Zuni) were terms preferred by John Wesley Powell and like Powell, F. S. Dellenbaugh gave his location on First Mesa as "Ancient Province of Tusayan." In July 1540, Francisco Vasquez de Coronado dispatched Pedro de Tovar, Franciscan friar Juan de Padilla, and about twenty soldiers from Zuni to investigate the Hopi villages. Pedro de Castaneda, chronicler of the Coronado expedition, wrote, "This province is called [by their Navajo guides] Tusayan"—the isolated province. For the Navajo origin of the word "Tusayan," see Stephen to Fewkes, December 24, 1891, MS 4408, NAA, SI. See also Haile 1917. Sullivan concurs in suggesting the word "Tusayan" is Navajo in origin but differs as to its meaning: "Tucyan—or probably more correctly, Tok-si-ya (the place of water.)" Jeremiah Sullivan, "The Hopitu," DGBC, UP. The word Tusayan was used to refer to the Hopi (and Hopi-Tewa) villages collectively as well as to the immediate area around the three mesas.
209 Victor Mindeleff 1891:40-41. Sullivan may have given this narrative to Cosmos Mindeleff while the Mindeleffs were working on Second Mesa in the summer of 1885. Another narrative recorded by Sullivan, "A Genesis Myth of the Tusayan (Moki)," by Katc-ve, father of Polacca and Nampeyo and frequently referred to by Sullivan, was attributed to Stephen ("collected by Mr. A. M. Stephen"). MS 1310, NAA, SI.

conversations with Wiki, the chief of the Antelope Society, as well as notes compiled during the previous years on other areas of Hopi religious thought and practice. Sullivan begins with Wiki's narrative of the origin of the ceremony that ends with Wiki's words:

> Now this which I have told you is true, for the uncle of
> my uncles spoke with but one tongue, and to his children
> this story he told, which we were to tell to our children,
> and I have told to you.

This is followed by a detailed description of the ceremony, much of it in Wiki's words, with drawings of the altars and other ritual paraphernalia employed as well as its songs and prayers. As extraordinary as the account is, it is also troublesome. On the day of the public ceremony, all the members of the Snake Order assemble in their kiva. Sullivan wrote:

> They jealously preserve the secrecy of this noon-day
> ceremony, and all my efforts to induce any of them to
> disclose the details have been fruitless. Wiki did begin,
> one night, to tell me, but after he had spoken a few
> words, his conscience failed him; he actually grew pale
> through his brown skin with fear of his own temerity—
> and would talk no more that night on any subject.

Sullivan understood but did not always accept that this sacred knowledge and practice (*wiimi*) is the property of Hopi clans (living and extinct), and even within these groups *wiimi* is restricted to defined elders. In Sullivan's work among the Hopis there is a recognition of and respect for the privileged and stratified nature of Hopi sacred knowledge and practice. As a doctor, Sullivan had something to give. In return, Hopi elders shared much religious knowledge and practice with him. For Hopis, *wiimi* is only for the initiated and can even be harmful to the uninitiated. No one—certainly no one within the Hopi community at the time—could anticipate the implications of later publication. Stephen (who owed Sullivan money) created a clean copy of the manuscript in 1888 that was sent to the naturalist and historian George Bird Grinnell.[210]

---

210   Sullivan 1940:8, 39. The untitled manuscript, MS 5.291, that served as the basis of Sullivan 1939-1940 is a part of the George Bird Grinnell Manuscript Collection, MS 5, Braun Research Library, The Autry Museum of the American West. Cited hereafter as MS 5, BRL, AMAW. Frederick Webb Hodge, Director

It may be this work Sullivan was referring to when he told Cushing he had "a vast quantity of materials which is now being put in shape for publication."[211] Sullivan's masterpiece was not published until 1939-1940.

Leaving the Hopi – A Fire and Burning Words

During the fall of 1887 Sullivan decided to leave Hopi.[212] He sold the iron stove he had purchased from Keam in 1882 and early in 1888 began making arrangements to move to Holbrook, Arizona, where he hoped to establish himself as a physician.[213] Unfortunately for Sullivan, fire destroyed the Holbrook business district on June 26 – just ten days before the *St. John's* [Arizona] *Herald* announced his arrival.[214] Then, less than a week later, *The* [San Francisco] *Daily Examiner* published the last of a series of interviews with Cushing who had returned to the

---

of the Southwest Museum, supplied the title, "Hopi Indians of Arizona," and attributed authorship to "Alexander MacGregor Stephen." It was first published in *The Masterkey*, 1939-1940 and reissued as *Southwest Museum Leaflets*, no. 14 in 1940. The manuscript was completed following the Snake Dance of 1885 and includes materials previously submitted to the Bureau of Ethnology by Jeremiah Sullivan. See Hieb 2004b. The handwriting is clearly Stephen's, just as the content in clearly Sullivan's. Unfortunately the surviving papers of George Bird Grinnell provide no information regarding the provenience of the manuscript.

211 Sullivan to Cushing, July 20, 1888, Frank Hamilton Cushing Manuscript Collection, MS 6, BRL, AMAW.

212 What prompted his decision is not known. The death of his father and the end of his financial support—if there was any—might have been a factor. His correspondence with Daniel G. Brinton (and Brinton's patronage?) seemed to have ended in 1886. The opening of the Moqui Boarding School in Keams Canyon on October 1, 1887 might have seemed threatening. In a letter of May 10, 1891 J. G. Owens wrote "Dr. Sullivan...was a rake, and lived off the Indians until they drove him away"—perhaps repeating Cushing's slander or something Keam or Stephen said. In any case, there is nothing to support the assertion. See Hinsley, Hieb and Fash, eds., forthcoming.

213 See "Holbrook Items" (Anon. 1888) which reported "Dr. J. Sullivan, of the Moquis, was in town Saturday and Sunday" and an announcement and advertisement in *The Apache Review* 1/7 (St. Johns, Arizona, July 11, 1888): 3. Prior to his move to Holbrook, Jeremiah appears to have visited his brother John and sister Mary and her husband Clarence in the Los Angeles area. See Jeremiah Sullivan 1888.

214 Anon. 1888c and Banta 1888 give detailed accounts of the fire that destroyed the business district of Holbrook, Arizona. The fire started in wool owned by Keam and stored in a warehouse operated by H. H. Sorse

Southwest in charge of the Hemenway Southwestern Archaeological Expedition. In the interview he stated:

> The Moquis wanted me to live with them as I had among the Zunis, and a fellow has actually done it—the son of a former agent. He went into it with the avowed intention of studying the people, as I had done with the Zunis. He was a young fellow, quite bright and a good physician, but he has degenerated into a "squaw man." That is dangerous to him, dangerous to his purposes, and also to the people themselves. But they were so delighted with the idea of having something that the Zunis had, that they have done everything they could for him, and have put up with all kinds of things from him. His opportunities are unexampled.[215]

Sullivan wrote to Cushing, who had returned to Zuni, stating he had been "sadly misrepresented":

> None other I can assure you was ever farther away from becoming a "Squaw Man" than your humble servant. I never placed any indignities upon the Mokis nor did I ever admit of any familiarities. I received compensation for all my services while among them, and when the pay ceased, I left, and am now practicing my profession at this place [Holbrook], doing well, and will be pleased to entertain you at any time when at home.[216]

A month later Cushing sent a letter to Sullivan in which he denied writing the article, acknowledging only that he had given an interview in which he made "very plain mention" of Sullivan's name. However, he added: "But it is quite needless for me to deny, totally and unconditionally, having, during the interview called you ... a "Squaw-man.""[217] Cushing went on to provide a text of what he said in the interview which included the statement, "It was maliciously said of him [Sullivan], as it had been said of me, many times, that he turned squaw-man..."

---

215   Cushing 1888.
216   Sullivan to Cushing, July 20, 1888, MS 6, BRL, ACAW.
217   Cushing to Sullivan, August 15, 1888, Vol. 5, pp. 210-214, Letter Books of Frank Hamilton Cushing, 1886-1896, Hemenway Southwestern Archaeological Expedition, Huntington Free Library.

Sullivan immediately responded that Cushing's letter left "no doubts but what your article in the Examiner was a gross misrepresentation" and the "speech seemed ... particularly uncalled for."[218] Apologies aside, the damage was done. When he began field work among the Hopi in 1891, J. G. Owens was told Jeremiah Sullivan was a "rake." Hopis later recalled merely that "the doctor danced with us."[219]

Starting Over

In spite of the impairment to Holbrook's economy by the fire, Sullivan opened a drug store and ran advertisements offering his services as a physician in the *St. John's Herald* from October, 1888, through the final issue of the newspaper in January, 1889. By July, 1890, he had moved west to the more prosperous town of Winslow, Arizona.[220] In 1891 Sullivan gave interviews regarding the Snake Dance to be celebrated that August at Walpi but left Winslow soon afterwards, discarding his Hopi research materials.[221] In April 1894, the Medical Department of the University of Louisville announced the graduation of Jeremiah C. Sullivan of Arizona in allopathic medicine.[222] Sullivan moved to southeastern Idaho where he practiced medicine in several communities until his death in 1916.[223]

---

218 Sullivan to Cushing, August 22, 1888, MS 6, BRL, ACAW.

219 Parsons, ed., 1936:1117. Parsons wrote, "In 1920 I was told that 'the doctor danced with us.'"

220 *The Great Register of Apache County, Arizona* (St. Johns, Weekly Herald Print., 1890), lists "Sullivan, Jere, 40, Winslow, registered July 14." A handwritten note, "July List for the Year 1890—1/8/90," implies Sullivan registered in Winslow on July 14, 1889. He is not listed the 1892 edition.

221 Sullivan 1891b and 1891c are based on interviews with Sullivan in Winslow in advance of the 1891 Snake Dance.

222 *Fifty-Eighth Annual Announcement of the Medical Department of the University of Louisville...with Catalogue of the Matriculates and Graduates of the Session of 1893-1894* (Louisville: John P. Morton, 1894): 23. Jeremiah Sullivan received his M.D. degree in April the same month Stephen died at Keams Canyon. For Sullivan's career as a doctor see Hafner, Hunter and Tarpay 1993:1509.

223 Sullivan's name appears in the 1900 Census for Bannock County, Idaho where he is listed as a "physician & surgeon." In the *Register of Licensed Physicians of the State of Idaho* published in April 1905 by the Idaho State Medical Society and State Board of Medical Examiners, J. C. Sullivan is the only registered physician listed for American Falls, Oneida County, Idaho. Sullivan is listed in the Rockland Precinct in the 1910 Census. Medical records indicate he began practicing medicine in Rockland as early as January 1911. Settlement of the

A few years later Fewkes published these recollections of Sullivan:

One of the first Americans to live with the Hopi for purposes of study was Dr. Jeremiah Sullivan, or, as he was called by them, Urwica [Oyiwisha, He Who Plants Corn]. When the writer began work at Walpi, Urwica was remembered as the American who amputated the arm of the mother of Pautiwa [Pauwatiwa], the chief of the Bow priesthood [*Kaletakwimkya*, War Society]. He slept in the pueblo, ate Hopi food, and worked on the farms with the Hopi, but he left Walpi [Sichumovi] a few years before the writer began his Hopi studies. He published a few short notes on the Hopi but no elaborate work on this interesting people.[224]

In fact, several hundred pages of Sullivan's manuscripts survive, some attributed to Stephen while others remain unpublished. Still, ethnography is both process (fieldwork) and product (writings). As

---

Rockland Valley began in 1879. The town of Rockland, approximately 16 miles south of American Falls, was laid out in 1909 and in 1910 had a population of 800. *Northwest Medicine*, a journal published by the Washington Medical Library Association beginning in 1903, regularly included news on medical professional in southern Idaho. No mention is made of Jeremiah C. Sullivan from the first issue in 1903 until his death. For example, in 1907 he is not listed as a member of the Southern Idaho District Medical Association. Again in 1911 he is not listed as a member of the Idaho State Medical Association. By 1910 other physicians had settled in the Rockland Valley and undoubtedly had an impact on Sullivan's practice. In April 18, 1912 the 'Rockland Department' section of the *American Falls Press* is "conducted by J. C. Sullivan." The June 26, 1913 issue describes an Old Folks Party listing "J. C. Sullivan" as one of the guests. In his last column, January 6, 1914, he wrote, "Dr. Sullivan took a day off which he spent in the county seat." When Rockland Valley celebrated its centennial in 1970, Sullivan was thought to have been the first doctor in the area with his office "in a lean-to on the Jim Anderson saloon" in Rockland. He treated "wounds and fractures," delivered a number of babies in the valley and occasionally served as a veterinarian. James Anderson's daughter recalled, "He stayed in dad's pool hall until he passed away" (Rockland Centennial Book Committee 1979:94). Jeremiah Sullivan died on April 4, 1916 and was buried in American Falls, Idaho (Records, Davis Mortuary, American Falls). Special thanks to Margene K. Tomlinson of Rockland, Idaho, and Gertrude Gereats of Madison, Indiana, for their research in documenting the final years of Jeremiah Sullivan's life.

224   Fewkes 1922:269.

exemplary as Sullivan was as a participant observer, the politics and economics of the emerging discipline of anthropology denied him the recognition of his extraordinary, if problematic, authorship.

3. Wiki's World: The Hopi in 1880

Wiki

One of the most important Hopi leaders and intellectuals during the years Jeremiah Sullivan lived on First Mesa was Wiki. A brief sketch of his life is followed by an overview of Hopi culture in the latter part of the nineteenth century. This chapter concludes with a brief biography of Wiki's contemporary Polacca, whose life reflects many of the changes and conflicts in Hopi culture during the same period.

Known as Wiki to all who visited First Mesa, Wiki was Sa'miwi'ki, born into the Snake Clan, a matrilineal descent group, in the village of Walpi, ca. 1850. A. M. Stephen tells us the meaning of Sa'miwi'ki: "*Sami*, green corn, ear in husk; *sa'miwi'ki*, the ears selected by the women for their beauty and symmetry which are tied in a bunch and hung to dry, to be used ritually."[225]

At the time of Wiki's birth there were seven villages on three mesas—finger-like projections at the southern escarpment of Black Mesa. On the First or East Mesa were Walpi, Sichumovi, and Tewa (or Hano, a Tewa-speaking village); on the Second or Middle Mesa were Shungopavi, Mishongnovi, and Shipaulovi; on the Third Mesa was the single large village of Oraibi. A summer farming village on the Moencopi Wash, thirty miles further to the west, became a year-round settlement by 1880 as a result of factional disputes in Oraibi.

In 1853-1854, when Wiki was a child, a smallpox epidemic decimated the villages of First Mesa. Zuni guides, part of Lieutenant A. W. Whipple's Pacific Railroad Survey, reported "by the hundreds the Moquis were dying by smallpox; only 3 men could be found in health, and they were insufficient to throw the dead over the walls."[226]

---

225   Parsons, ed., 1936:1134.
226   Whipple, Amiel W. 1854-1855:75.

Like others of his age, when Wiki was about eight he was initiated into the Katsina society and soon participated in Katsina dances. When he was about twelve Wiki was initiated into the Antelope Society. As a young man, he was chosen to be chief priest of the Antelope Society and given responsibility for preserving the traditions relating to the Snake-Antelope ceremonies. When he was about sixteen Wiki was initiated into one of the Wuwutsim (Manhood) societies. He also was a participant in the ceremonies of the Mamzrau (Womanhood) and Flute societies. At some point he married a Horn clan woman named Mo'ko and Wiki then lived in her house in Walpi (in accord with rule of matrilocal residence).

Wiki, Antelope Chief, ca. 1897. Photograph by Maud and James. Plate L, *Nineteenth Annual Report of the Bureau of Ethnology*. Washington: Government Printing Office, 1898.

The 1880 census gave Wiki's age as 30 and that of Mo'ko as 26; the 1885 census lists a son, 18, and a daughter, 1 year old, and more accurately gives Wiki's age as 40 and that of his wife as 37. Wiki had a sister and two brothers, Wikya'tiwa and Mo'mi, all of whom lived in Walpi.

For Sullivan, and later for Stephen, Wiki was an important source of information regarding the Snake Dance. Wiki provided Sullivan detailed descriptions of the preparations made for the ceremony—information known only to initiates—as well as the traditions regarding origin of the ceremony.[227] Wiki also provided Sullivan with information regarding the Mamzrau ceremony.[228] As he had done for Sullivan, in 1891 Wiki told Stephen "his tradition" of the Snake Dance; Stephen noted that "owing to his deafness, Wikya'tiwa and Masaiyu'mtuwa assist him." Stephen's field notebooks and correspondence make frequent reference to Wiki's participation in the ceremonial life of First Mesa in the early 1890s.

Walter Hough, who met Wiki later in life, described Wiki as a "Hopi gentleman of the old school, a survivor of the best of the past generation," and a man whose brain contained "a vast stock of ancient lore, of legend, myth and song."[229] For Hough, one particular story summarized Wiki's character:

> Wiki . . . was in every fiber imbued with the usages and traditions of the past. . . . The leaven of the new was in Kopeli [ca. 1870-1899; chief priest of the Snake Society]. A wide-awake town in New Mexico [Albuquerque] wanted the Hopi Snake Dance reproduced at the fair held there in the autumn [1897], realizing that it would be a feature to attract many visitors. Kopeli was approached and offered what seemed to him a large sum of money for the performance. Though in some doubt as to the care and transportation of the snakes, Kopeli and the

---

227 [Sullivan, Jeremiah] Hopi Indians of Arizona. MS 5.291, George Bird Grinnell Manuscript Collection, Braun Research Library, Autry Museum of the American West. See Appendix X.

228 Sullivan, Jeremiah, Feast of Muinwuh, Hopituh, Part 3. Hopitu Calender, 913.72 Su53, Daniel Garrison Brinton Collection, University of Pennsylvania Museum Library. Only the third part of Sullivan's account of the Marau or Mamzrau ceremony has been preserved.

229 Hough 1915:233.

younger snake priests were tempted to favor the scheme, through his avaricious father, Supela. When Wiki, chief of the related society of the Antelopes, heard the proposal, he became very angry and put his foot down, reading the young men of lax morals a severe lecture on their duties to their religion.[230]

Wiki was witness to dramatic changes in Hopi culture, especially that of First Mesa, none more telling than the circumstances of his death on March 30, 1910. In 1881 tracks for the Atlantic and Pacific Railroad were laid across northern Arizona and new towns were established, including Holbrook, Winslow and Flagstaff. *The Winslow Mail* on Saturday, April 2, 1910, carried the headline, "Trian [sic] Kills Indian Chief," and the following report:

> Chief Wiekee [sic], an old and well known Moki Indian, head of the antilopes [sic] was killed instantly Wednesday morning by passenger train No. 7 at the west approach to the railroad bridge one mile east of the Winslow depot.
>
> Wiekee was on his way home to the Moqui reservation, about fifty miles northward. He had started across with his pack animals loaded with provisions on the previous day, intending to cross the Little Colorado River by fording as he had done when he came to town a few days before. The current proved too strong however and he returned to town, remaining until Wednesday morning. His presence at the railroad bridge is accounted for by the belief that he decided to pack his provisions across the bridge and repack them on the other side when he got the animals across the water.
>
> When Engineer Clark first saw the Indian, the latter was standing in the middle of the track between two of his burros and [although] there was ample time for him to get off after the whistle had sounded, he remained immovable apparently looking at the approaching train. Engineer Clark succeeded by applying the emergency brakes in bring [sic] his train almost to a stop before striking the Indian and it is thought the injury to the

---

230   Ibid, 220; see Fewkes 1899.

victims [sic] head that resulted in immediate death, was received by contact with a rock after he was pushed off the track. Neither of the burros that were thrown off with him sustained any injuries.

An even more tragic view of his death is provided by the artist Kate Cory who was visiting First Mesa at the time:

April 2 – News reached us of [Wiki's] death today. Wiki's wife was unkind to him. Their son had been away to [the Phoenix Indian] school many years & had married a Pima girl & did not come home. His mother would drive Wiki out because the boy did not come home. He used to have letters written to him once Snake dance time but the boy did not come. Finally she drove him out & told him to go down to Winslow & find the boy. So the poor old man took his 2 burros & started out, not knowing of course how he was to reach him. At Winslow he got on the track, & being deaf, did not hear the engine nor of course understood the motion & was killed...[231]

As an introduction to Hopi culture, what follows is a brief overview of "Wiki's world" with an emphasis on First Mesa and the various forces accelerating changes in Hopi life during the second half of the nineteenth century.

The Hopi in 1880
Language

The Hopi language is a member of the Uto-Aztecan language family, which also contains (among others): Comanche, Shoshone, Ute, Piman, Yaqui, and Nahuatl. Within this language family, however, Hopi has no close relatives. Nor is Hopi related, even distantly, to the languages of other "Pueblo Indians"—Zuni, Keresan, and Tanoan. These linguistic differences—among others—suggest an ancient and complex past. At the time Sullivan and Stephen lived with the Hopi there were seven villages with distinctive dialects. The dialect of Third Mesa was spoken in Oraibi, the largest of the Hopi villages.[232] Two dialects were

---

231   Hopi Notes, A Diary Written by Miss Kate Cory, 1909-1910, at First Mesa, pp. 88-89, MS 208-2-2, Museum of Northern Arizona.

232   See Hopi Dictionary Project 1998 for a description of the Third Mesa dialect.

spoken on Second Mesa: Shongopavi (also spoken in Shipaulovi) and Mishongnovi. The dialect of First Mesa was spoken in Walpi and Sichomovi. In the other First Mesa village, Hano (also called Tewa), the language spoken was Arizona Tewa, brought to First Mesa in the 1690s by refugees from the Spanish reconquest that followed the Pueblo Revolt of 1680.[233] This variety of Tewa was spoken by people who lived in the Galisteo Basin near Santa Fe and was (and is) distinct from the Rio Grande Tewa spoken in six villages in northern New Mexico. The culture as well as the language of the people of Hano differed in significant ways from that of the Hopis.

Wiki spoke Hopi and, like many men and women on First Mesa, he knew some Tewa of the variety spoken in the village of Hano and undoubtedly knew some English, Navajo and Zuni. Many Hopi men spoke some Navajo, enough for Stephen to carry out his initial field work in the 1890s using that language. Stephen wrote the following of "Toby":

> ...my next door neighbor Toby, so named by Capt. Palmer who was in charge of these folks many years ago [1869-1870], when Toby was a boy... in his own way [is] an excellent linguist, speaking his mother's tongue—Tewa, his father's Hopi, also Navajo, Zuni and a smattering of other tongues and a few words of English, which he was very keen to acquire.[234]

The 1890 census reported one individual in Hano spoke Spanish, probably Tom Polacca, who was also fluent in English and Zuni. The 1890 census indicated four people in Walpi could speak, read and write [some] English as well as six in Sichumovi and twelve in Hano. The people of First Mesa learned English from a variety of sources including the Keam brothers—William and Thomas, Stephen and other individuals working at Thomas Keam's trading post beginning in 1875; agency employees, including William H. H. Metzger, farmer and Spanish translator, who lived on First Mesa 1869-1873 and Edward S. Merritt, teacher and clerk, who worked at the agency 1876-1883;

---

233   See Stanislawski 1979 for the language, history and culture of this village.

234   A. M. Stephen, A Report on the Field Work of the Hemenway Expedition in the Autumn and Winter of 1892-1893," Hemenway Expedition Records, Peabody Museum Archives, Harvard University. In Sullivan's notebook of 1883, Toby drew a katsina mask and signed it "Toby."

Mormon missionaries, primarily at Oraibi; and Jeremiah Sullivan, although it appears he learned Hopi soon after his arrival and carried on daily interaction with Wiki and others using Hopi and, to a lesser extent, Tewa. The acquisition of English language skills accelerated with the establishment of the Keams Canyon Indian School in 1887. Intermarriage also was a factor in language skills. For example, a Sichumovi man, Naghevema, whose mother's family was Navajo, worked at the Hopi agency as a translator and mail rider. In the 1890 census, no one in the Second Mesa villages was reported as knowing English. However, due to Mormon influence that began in 1858,[235] twenty-eight individuals in Oraibi were said to speak English, twelve could read and three could write. Lyee (or "Lie"), a Mormon convert at Oraibi, often served as a translator.[236]

Population

Between 1869 and 1878 several estimates of the population of Hopi villages were made.[237] Three of these appear to be based, in part at least, on careful enumerations. In December 1869 U. S. Army Captain A. D. Palmer, serving as agent, reported the total of the Hopi villages to be 1,505. Two years later agent W. D. Crothers was successful in taking a census of the First and Second Mesa villages but not at Oraibi, "the chief utterly refusing me the privilege."[238] On June 1, 1878 agent W. R. Mateer submitted a census, probably compiled by his clerk, E. S. Merritt, noting "The inhabitants of the village of Oraibi (some 600) still decline to be enumerated."[239]

---

235 In 1859 a second Mormon mission was sent to Oraibi with one member, Marion Jackson Shelton, directed to learn the Hopi language and devise a writing system (orthography) with the aim to translate the Book of Mormon into Hopi and converting the Hopi to Mormonism. The phonetic alphabet used was the Deseret Alphabet which was abandoned by the Mormons in 1875. See Beesley and Elzinga 2015:19-41. See Peterson 1971 for an account of the Mormon missions to the Hopis, 1858-1873.

236 The photographer E. A. Beaman employed Lie as a guide and translator when he visited the villages on Second and First Mesa in 1872 (Beaman 1874:642-643). Jeremiah Sullivan mentioned Lie as a translator during a meeting on First Mesa in 1882.

237 There is no census information regarding the impact of the small-pox epidemic of 1853-1854. It appears the epidemic was limited to First Mesa.

238 Crothers 1872:704.

239 Mateer to Commissioner of Indian Affairs, June 1, 1878, Letters Received by

A census of the population of the First and Second Mesa villages was made on five occasions between 1880 and 1894. In March 1881 Jeremiah Sullivan, as "U. S. Indian Enumerator," completed census schedules for the "First Census of the United States Indian Division," probably for First Mesa only.[240] In 1880 and 1890 an enumeration was made for the United States Census. Navajo Agent John H. Bowman, officially in charge of the Hopi agency, made a census in 1885 of the First Mesa villages only, quite likely with the assistance of Sullivan. The most accurate census of First Mesa is that of Stephen made in December 1893.[241] Hostile leadership[242] in Oraibi prevented a census being taken until 1890. In that year the total population of the seven Hopi villages was 1,996.

	1869	1871	1878	1880	1885	1890	1893/4
First Mesa							
Walpi	312	333	277	270	239	232	248
Sichumovi	91	103	116	104	120	103	133
Hano (Tewa)	143	163	143	149	147	161	163
Total	546	599	536	523	506	496	544
Second Mesa							
Mishongnovi	221	238	267	244		244	
Shipaulovi	96	109	117	113		126	
Shungopavi	160	176	220	216		225	
Total	477	523	604	595			
Third Mesa							
Oraibi	482					905	

---

the Office of Indian Affairs, Records of the Bureau of Indian Affairs, National Archives, Washington, D.C.

240 Apparently lost. See J. W. Powell to Jeremiah Sullivan, April 7, 1881, MS 1144, National Archives, Laguna Naguel.

241 Fewkes 1894a and 1894b

242 Oraibi was divided into two factions, those "hostile" to anything perceived to be a threat to traditional Hopi life (e,g, annuity goods, census, education, etc.) and those who were "friendly" or open to these. See Whiteley 1988a for the development of factionalism at Oraibi in the second half of the 19th century.

In 1906, a factional dispute that had been developing for over a quarter of a century culminated in the disintegration of the Third Mesa village of Oraibi. By the time of Wiki's death four years later several new villages had formed on Third Mesa: Hotevilla, Bacabi and Kikotsmovi.

Kinship and Social Organization

The Hopi population in 1880 had a distinctive Pueblo life-style and language, although there were slight but identifiable dialect and other differences between the communities. Tribal "unity" was created only through the Indian Reorganization Act of 1934. It is more accurate, following anthropologist John C. Connelly, to see Hopi social structure in 1880 as

> ...contain[ing] a number of significant interlocking social groupings, named and unnamed. The (village) residence sites, the clans, and the societies are named groups. The households, lineages, and phratries are unnamed groups or named only by reference.[243]

During Wiki's lifetime, the Hopi and Hopi-Tewa of First Mesa were what anthropologists sometime characterize as a 'kinship based society.' Virtually every relationship between individuals was defined by the categories of kinship and social organization. Simply put, Hopi social structure was "based upon matrilineal exogamous clans, matrilocal households, and a Crow or matrilineal type of kinship system"[244] and by the 1880's Hopi-Tewa had largely "rearranged" themselves to conform to the Hopi model.[245] Individuals found themselves having a multiplicity of relatives by virtue of birth, marriage or marriages, and membership in religious societies. These relationships shaped Hopi daily life.

Sullivan recognized individuals belonged to a clan (or "gente") and Stephen clearly understood the matrilineal and matrilocal character of Hopi social organization, that clan ownership of the land, including the residency sites and the houses, belong to the women and that a man who

---

243 Connelly 1979:539.

244 Eggan 1983:724; see Eggan 1950. Crow and Omaha terminologies correspond to matrilineal and patrilineal types respectively. They are named after the North American Indian peoples with whom they were first identified.

245 Dozier 1954. In general, Eastern Pueblo (Tewa) social structure was based on dual organization and a bilateral kinship system.

marries comes to live in his wife's house.[246] Stephen also recognized the unnamed groupings of clans into phratries.[247]

As a result of studies on the Hopi Third Mesa in the 1930s, anthropologists Mischa Titiev and Fred Eggan added to our understanding of Hopi social organization. Eggan concluded "marriage is not permitted, in Hopi theory, within one's own, one's father's, or one's mother's father's phratry," leaving only a limited number of potential marriage partners within the small population of especially the first and second mesa villages. The logical implications of Eggan's understanding has been questioned.[248]

It is clear from Stephen's census of 1893 that most marriages, while following the rules of exogamy (to some degree), were endogamous within the village or the mesa. For example, in Walpi of the 133 adult men resident in the village, only twenty-two were born elsewhere. Of these, eighteen were from the First Mesa villages of Sichumovi (10) and Hano (8). Stephen also noted that of thirty-three men born in Walpi but living elsewhere, twenty-five were living in either Sichumovi (13) or Hano (12). Of course, it cannot be assumed all of the adult men were married; however, the general conclusions of village or mesa endogamy appear valid.[249]

Architecture/Settlement Patterns

The Spanish called the Hopi and their cultural relatives in New Mexico "town" (Pueblo) Indians because they lived in villages. For most of Wiki's life, a Hopi village consisted of a series of multi-storied, terraced structures, each containing a number of living units arranged in long rows or irregularly around a central plaza (*kisoni*). The *kihu*, the individual matrilineal/matrilocal residence, was a rectangular structure constructed of sandstone and adobe mortar, with a roof built up of layers

---

246 One of the consequences of the rules of matrilineality and matrilocality is that few women or men ever relocated to a village on second or third mesas. The consequences of this 'inbreeding' is an unusually high rate of albinism. See Woolf and Dukepoo 1969.

247 Fewkes 1894a and 1894b.

248 Whiteley 2012:95.

249 One man married (it is assumed) to a Walpi woman was born in Shipaulovi on Second Mesa, two were from Zuni and one from Jemez. Fewkes 1894b:398.

of timbers, cedar bark and adobe mud.[250] The *kiva*, an underground or partially underground ceremonial chamber constructed of similar materials and built in the form of a rectangular keyhole, was located in the plaza, in the broad streets, at the ends of the house-blocks. A significant architectural feature of the *kiva* was/is the *sipapu* (*sipaapuni*), the hatchway from whence the Hopis believe they emerged to the Fourth World. The structure and function of the kiva symbolizes this passageway but it is symbolized in other ways as well. More importantly, it is a channel of communication and exchange between the Upper World of the living and the Lower World of the spirits. While doing research in 1887-1888 for Victor Mindeleff's classic, *A Study of Pueblo Architecture in Tusayan and Cibola*, Sullivan or Stephen recorded the following:

> When a new village site is chosen, first of all a temporary si'papu is constructed, in some fissure or cavity. Then the chief selects a place for the permanent si'papu and around this the houses are built, on three or four sides of the square. The si'papu should be as near the centre of the village as possible. The si'papu may not be marked by other than a flat stone…but from the si'papu come the kachinas, and at it they perform their first ceremonies when they "return"… The ancients knew all about choosing a village site and about si'papus, they knew how to make them. That is why you see so many ruins. People then could go anywhere and build villages anywhere because they knew how to make si'papus. *They did not choose sites for beauty or for abundance of water, these and all other blessings would come from the si'papu.* Now should we leave this mesa, we could have no si'papu, and in a year, within the cycle of our feasts, all would die, the gods would be angered.[251]

Elsewhere Stephen notes: "At the si'papu beside the water in the west, after four days they came up and reached the surface of this world; the sand on the kiva roofs is *tuwa'mkya*, i.e., reached this earth, *tuwa'nuquka*."[252] Thus, not only is the opening in the floor of the kiva

---

250 See Whiteley's discussion of "Orayvi's Houses" in 2008:195-239.
251 Parsons, op cit., 1295. Emphasis added.
252 Ibid, 691.

a si'papu, so (in another sense) is the hatchway from the kiva. It is important to note, "during the kiva rites in virtually every ceremony, communication with the other world is carried on by means of the sipapu."[253]

By the early 1880s changes were taking place in the Hopi settlement pattern as well as in the form and material of individual dwellings. Writing in 1895 J. Walter Fewkes noted:

> Between the years 1880 and 1890 a beginning of a new distribution of Hopi families began. ... A large number of [First Mesa] families have built houses in the foothills of the Mesa and in the plain beyond the "wash." ... This movement is shared to a lesser extent by the Middle Mesa and Oraibi people. ... I believe that if this exodus of Hopi families from the old pueblo to the plain continues during the next two decades as it has in the past ten years, there are children now living in Walpi who will someday see it uninhabited.[254]

Material Culture

While the Hopi were, in large part, dependent on their immediate environment for subsistence, they were involved in a wide network of exchange with neighboring groups. Trade involved both food and non-food items. The Hopis offered blankets, ceremonial textiles and knit leggings, yarn, bridles and saddles, foods of all kinds—especially corn, beans, and peaches—and, by the 1880s, surplus government issue axes and hoes. From the Navajos they obtained meat (mutton), blankets, saddles and bridles; from the Coconina buckskin, baskets, cactus bread, agave fruit, and paints—red and green—used on katsina masks; from the Apaches buckskin and cow-hides, bows and arrows, hats, and agave fruit; from the Paiutes wicker water bottles; and from the Rio Grande Pueblos beads and turquoise.[255]

---

253 Titiev 1944:172.

254 Fewkes 1895:280. McIntire 1971 and 1982 provide insightful and well-documented accounts of the changing settlement patterns.

255 J. G. Owens, "Exchange – Hur-huh," [J. G. Owens Field Notes], Folder 287—Hopi, Series 17: Division of Ethnology, Manuscript and Pamphlet File, Records of the Department of Anthropology, NAA, SI.

Several other sources of cultural exchange were introduced when Wiki was a young man. In 1869, the first agent assigned to the Hopi (and the only agent to live in one of the villages), U. S. Army Captain A. D. Palmer distributed "to the seven villages *per capita*: 48 camp kettles, 300 axes and helves, 60 extra helves, 100 pickaxes, 300 spades, and an assortment of garden seeds, &c" and, at a later visit "issued to them twenty S. B. [smoothbore] muskets, caliber 69, and two thousand rounds of ammunition."[256] Although they were "extremely jealous of innovation," especially at Oraibi, Palmer also reported:

> they [the Hopis] have a tradition . . . that the Americans were to come some day and give them horses, oxen, wagons, clothing, rifles, teachers, farmers, in fact all they could wish for, which they say they have but to receive and live in ease and plenty.[257]

The next agent, W. D. Crothers, reported issuing unspecified "goods" carried on sixty donkeys that were issued "to all the Moquis, apart from the Oreybes, who, at that time, refused to accept anything from the Government."[258] "Government goods" were issued again in 1872 and, with some exceptions, "issue day" became part of agents' annual calendar.

Another form of exchange took place between Hopis and the trader Thomas V. Keam. Hopis received script good only at Keam's trading post in exchange for kachina dolls, coil and wicker baskets, prehistoric and heirloom historic pottery and some ceremonial paraphernalia. Sometime before 1882 Keam began encouraging two potters (possibly Nampeyo as well as a berdache, a transsexual male, from Walpi named "Morphy" by Americans) to make rectangular and triangular tiles for a potential commercial market.[259] Between 1881 and 1883 Keam sold over 4,000 pieces of prehistoric and historic pottery to the Smithsonian Institution. In 1891 a collection of over 2,000 was purchased by J. Walter Fewkes for the Hemenway Southwestern Archaeological Expedition.[260] This collection included 1,146 "modern

---

256   Palmer 1870:133-134.
257   Ibid, 135.
258   Crothers 1872:704, reporting for 1871.
259   See Fewkes 1892:11 for his description of "Morphy."
260   Hieb 2009.

productions," evidence of Keam's growing interest in the work of contemporary potters. During the summer of 1891 Fewkes made notes on "Clay used by Wolpi Potter" ("Morphy"?) and "Clay used by Nampio" suggesting her skill as a potter had been brought to his attention.[261] However, it is not until ca. 1895 that Nampeyo's distinctive designs began to achieve commercial interest.[262]

Remembering the Past / Informing the Present

In 1850 no Hopi could read or write. By 1880 a few individuals, e.g., Polacca (see below), may have been able to read and write a few words in English. However, for the period under consideration in this book, Hopi was an oral culture, a preliterate culture.

An oral culture is one in which the technologies of literacy (especially writing and print) are unfamiliar to most, if not all, of the population. Over the years I have worked on this book I have wondered what it must have been like for Wiki, whose meaningful world was largely one of sounds spoken or sung, to become increasingly deaf.

Soon after Jeremiah Sullivan took up residence on First Mesa he heard a narrative of destruction of the nearby village of Sikyatki. Shortly thereafter he began collecting other Hopi narratives of the past, primarily the migration narratives of various clans represented in the

---

261   [J. Walter Fewkes] "Clay used by Wolpi Potter [1891]," Folder 287—Hopi, Series 17: Division of Ethnology, Manuscript and Pamphlet File, Records of the Department of Anthropology, NAA, SI. It is an undated and unsigned three page manuscript in Fewkes's hand and on paper of a type he used during the summer of 1891. Fewkes notes that among "Nampio's" clays are two from "Sikiatki." With two exceptions, I have been unable to find any other documentation of Nampeyo's pottery written before 1900. In 1893, without naming her, Stephen wrote "the exceptional best potter is a Tewa woman who reproduced many of the beautiful early forms and decorative designs [i.e., those purchased by Fewkes] but most of which, unfortunately, seems to have lost their meaning to the modern Hopi." A. M. Stephen, A Report on the Field Work of the Hemenway Expedition in the Autumn and Winter of 1892-1893, Hemenway Expedition Records, Peabody Museum Archives, Harvard University. Two years later Fewkes wrote, "The best potter of the East mesa, an intelligent woman from Hano, named Nampio, acknowledged that her productions were far inferior to those of the women of Sikyatki, and she begged permission to copy some of the decorations for future inspiration." Fewkes 1896c:577.

262   See Blair and Blair 1999.

three villages. In these narratives Hopis (and Hopi-Tewas) made no reference to a specific date when something happened; there was no chronology or chronological framework in which to locate events, no "history" in the Euro-American meaning of the word. Sullivan learned it was not so much when something happened, but where. The landscape became a kind of archive in which meaningful mementos marked where the people of a clan had been during their migration. As Fewkes noted, "So sacred are these places to the Hopi ... proprietorship in them is not abandoned even when clans in their migrations seek new building sites."[263] A chain of memories linked the present to the past grounded not in written documents but to a sacred landscape.

In the first pages of his journal for 1883, Jeremiah Sullivan wrote,

The [Hopis] cannot keep dates. When the old ancient of the tribe passes away to the land of his fathers, [it] is said that when ... the old man was yet alive, he told of these things as his father had told them before.[264]

Still, as the world historian Ashis Nandy reminds us:

However odd this might sound ... millions of people still live outside "history." They *do* have theories of the past; they *do* believe that the past is important and shapes the present and future, but they also recognize, confront, and live with a past different from that constructed by historians and historical consciousness.[265]

Sullivan worked closely with Wiki (as did Stephen in the early 1890s) to record the migration narrative of Wiki's Snake Clan. As a reconstruction and representation of the past, Wiki's version begins, in translation, "Many years ago." But taken as a narrative, the texts shows the huge importance given to place and space, and to a question about water (the blessing most often sought through prayer and prayer offerings). Note, too, how very different this narrative is from the chronologically structured narratives of Euro-American histories.

Many years ago the fathers came up out of the west. Turtle-dove led them to the Colorado River, and they returned

263   Fewkes 1906b:346-347.
264   Jeremiah Sullivan, Notebook 31, Elsie Clews Parsons Field Notebooks, Columbia University Library.
265   Nandy 1995:44.

and brought the others. Close to Navajo Mountain (at the junction of the San Juan and Colorado Rivers) was this early dwelling place. They built houses of stone but their garments were of yucca, and their shoes and their ropes. From the rock they made their hoes and axes. There was but little rain, only fogs. They had four kinds of corn, yellow, blue, white, and speckled (blue and white), but the stalks grew only about the length of the hand, and the ears were only a finger's length. For reasons that are now forgotten, dissensions arose among the people, so the elder ones gathered together and consulting, said, "Let us seek a chief." They sought a certain woman who had a son, and when they found him he had become a youth. He has no name with us, we speak of him as *Tiyo* (the youth). He was constantly thinking, "To what place does the water of this river flow," and he was told, "Its feet-marks carry it to the south." The youth said to his father, 'You are fond of this water; do you never long to know where it comes from and whither it goes?" The father said, "It is true, my son: I long to know, and in four days you shall go and explore."[266]

There follows an account of Tiyo's travels and his final return with the knowledge of how to bring life-sustaining rain through prayers and prayer offerings made during the Snake/Antelope ceremony.

The techniques employed for remembering and representing the past are very different for a culture without writing. For the Hopi, social memory and sacred knowledge was (and continues to be) embodied and represented in significant places in the built and natural landscape, in the architectural forms of their villages, in the bodily memory of ritual performance, and in a variety of unwritten but memorized songs and narratives that were (and are) the property of Hopi clans and societies. Within these clans and societies this sacred knowledge (*wiimi*) was (and is) the privileged property and responsibility of various priests, producing a hierarchy of knowledge. Thus, Sullivan

---

266   [Jeremiah Sullivan, The Hopi Indians of the Arizona], MS 5.291, George Bird
        Grinnell Manuscript Collection, Braun Research Library, Autry Museum of the
        American West.

observed about the Snake/Antelope ceremonies:

> There are three legends concerning this feast. One, which may be called the popular legend, as it is generally familiar to the people of all the villages; another is told by the "Keeper of the West Gate" (one of the Antelope priests), which is known only to the members of the two religious fraternities—the Snake, and the Antelope; and one known only to the chief priests of these orders.[267]

Wiki was not alone in telling Sullivan his clan's migration narrative as it contained the answers to questions of origin, identity and destiny. Maurice Bloch asks,

> If people act within their own history, constructed within their own narratives, any other history is irrelevant to their action, and who are we... to understand their actions and their past in any other way than in the terms of these narratives.[268]

Hopis recognize two major categories of traditional narrative: *navoti* (teachings, traditional knowledge) and *tuutuwutsi* (stories, legends). *Navoti* means, literally, "knowledge gained from hearing, i.e., not from seeing or experience [or reading]." While there is no established way of referring to these narrative genres, Emory Sekaquaptewa suggests the following possible Hopi glosses and translations:[269] (1) the emergence narrative (*qatsiyamakiwqat navoti* = "traditional knowledge relating to the emergence of life"); (2) clan migration narratives (*qatsihepnumyaqat navoti* = traditional knowledge relating to their search for a settlement, a place to make life"); (3) ruin narratives (*kiiqova hiniwtiput tuutuwutsi* = "stories about what happened along the ruins"); and (4) prophetic narratives (*yuumoq qatsi hiniwmaniqat tuutuwutsi* = "stories about happenings, that which will happen in the life of the future"). Sullivan recorded a number of clan migration narratives, including several versions of the snake clan narrative as told by Wiki, as well as stories, songs, prayers and other forms of narrative.

---

267   Ibid.

268   Bloch 1998:101.

269   Emory Sekaquaptewa, 7/17/1997. Hopi words are given in the Third Mesa dialect.

Hopi Thought

Hopi thought consists of systematic conceptions of order (e.g., orientations in space and time), evaluative ideas (e.g., *hopi/qahopi*, Hopi/unHopi), various categories of person (e.g., kinship, religious specialists), theories as to their origin and destiny (emergence and clan migration narratives as well as prophecy), assumptions about the nature of humans and their relations to one another and their place in the natural order, etc.

Stephen in a letter to his employer J. Walter Fewkes, reported a "simple fact" central to many areas of Hopi thought and religious practice:

> The Hopi orientation bears no relation to [Euro-American concepts of] North and South, but to the points on the horizon which mark the places of sunrise and sunset at the summer and winter solstices. He invariably begins his ceremonial circuit by pointing (1) to the place of sunset at summer solstice, next to (2) the place of sunset at winter solstice, then to (3) the place of sunrise at winter solstice, and (4) the place of sunrise at summer solstice, &c. &c.
>
> Doesn't that please you? ... As soon as it flashed upon me, I hastened in to apply the key to some of the old fellows' knowledge boxes. And then they one and all declared how glad they were that I now understood, how sorry they had been that I could not understand this simple fact before.[270]

In an article written the next month Stephen added "(5) the above, and (6) the below." He goes on to give the names of these directions and "their emblematic colors":

> Kwi-ni-wi; yellow, because the anthropomorphic deity who sits there is yellow, wearing a yellow cloud as a mask which covers his head and rests upon his shoulders; a multitude of yellow butterflies constantly flutter before the cloud, and yellow corn grows continually in that yellow land.

---

270   A. M. Stephen to J. Walter Fewkes, June 29, 1893, Correspondence, MS 4408, NAA, SI.

Similar phenomena are manifest at all the other directions, only of different colors, thus:

Te-vyun-a, Blue.

Ta-tyuk-a, Red.

Ho-po-ko, White

O-mi, Black.

At-kya-mi, all colors, and here sits the deity regarded as the maker of all life germs. He sits upon a flowery mound on which grows all vegetation; he is speckled with all the colors, as also is his cloud mask, and before it flutter all the butterflies, and all the sacred birds.[271]

Hopi cardinal directions are the empirically observable ones defined by observations of sunrise and sunset at the winter and summer solstices. Points on the horizon serve as the basis for a solar calendar used, in part, for determining the beginning of ritual observances throughout the year. Hopis also employ a lunar calendar. For example, at the Powamu ("Bean dance") ceremony in February 1883, Sullivan recorded this statement by Intiwa, the Powamu chief at Walpi:

> When my people had learned to build houses and men had grown accustomed to life in the [kivas], Masau came and taught them many things concerning the growth of plants and trees and instructed them about planting beans when the moon should be at a certain age and after the sun had come a certain distance on his way back to the north. Many, many days this has been the custom and we have no right to forsake the ways of our fathers.[272]

Sullivan attempted to intercalate the lunar and solar calendars.[273] That various incongruities and inconsistencies are revealed in any attempt to mesh the two ignores the fact that while Hopis made exact observations, their use of this information was also shaped by their

271   Stephen 1898:261-261.

272   [Jeremiah Sullivan], Notebook No. 1, pp. 60-61, Elsie Clews Parsons Field Notebooks, Columbia University Library.

273   Sullivan sent two essays to Daniel G. Brinton in which he attempts to explain the intercalation of the lunar and solar calendars. See his "Hopitu Calendar," Daniel Garrison Brinton Collection, University of Pennsylvania Museum Library.

knowledge of agriculture and meteorology, as well as the requirements
of ritual observances.

As Stephen's discussion of the use of color in Hopi ritual suggests,
the cosmological framework also serves as the basis for a vast system
of correspondences including not only direction and color but places,
corn, beans, flowers, trees, animals and various fauna associated with
water, e.g., frogs, tadpole, duck, snipe, etc., as well.

In addition to the unified system relating concepts of space, time,
color and number (or sequence), another important aspect of Hopi
thought and life is metaphor. As anthropologist Mary Black documented
in her insightful essay "Maidens and Mothers: An Analysis of Hopi Corn
Metaphors" (1984) corn is not only a food, it is the central metaphor
of Hopi life. Black explores the Hopi statement, "People are corn," a
metaphor seen in the developmental cycles of corn plants and humans:

> [First]… As humans are believed to have emerged from
> below to gain access to this world, so do corn sprouts
> emerge from their point of origin in the ground.
> [Second]… Humans are said to nurse on the mother…
> So, too, young corn plants take juice/moisture/
> sustenance…from…the earth mother.
> [Third]… "To see is to live." Humans are said to be
> fully alive if their eyes…can see… The plant is also
> said to become mature when it has…"eyes" which
> are also kernels or the seed grains that will ensure the
> continuation of life.
> [Fourth]… When a person dies, it is said that he goes
> home…but that his body is left here as a lifeless, useless
> thing, qatungwu, the corpse, or "that which held life."
> Qatungwu also applies to the corn plant that has been
> harvested of ears, and so is without life…[274]

Thus, there is in Hopi thought "a series of conventionalized, shared
metaphors that recognize the life stages of birth, growth, reproduction,
and death based on the comparable life cycle of corn."[275] As a figure
of speech, metaphor compares two essentially unlike objects—here,
people and corn—suggesting the essence of the first by identifying it

---

274   Black 1984:280.
275   Sekaquaptewa and Washburn 2004:467.

with certain qualities of the second. Without using "like" (as in simile) metaphor implies a "likeness." In Hopi thought and, more importantly, in Hopi experience the relationship between people and corn is more than "like," it is essential. Fewkes noted, "Corn appears in virtually every Hopi ceremony either as corn meal, or as an actual ear of corn or as a symbolic painting" as well as in song and prayer.[276] In his study of Hopi agriculture and other food resources, J. G. Owens wrote, "at least ninety per cent of the vegetable food eaten…is made of corn."[277] Corn, corn agriculture, made Hopi life possible. For Wiki and other Hopi men and women, "People are corn" experientially. "People are corn" is figurative or metaphorical only from an outsider's analytic point of view.

The Ritual Calendar

The elaborate performances of the Hopi ritual calendar may be divided into the Katsina season—roughly from the winter solstice to the summer solstice—and a season of ceremonies performed by religious societies—from August until December. The latter include the Snake/ Antelope, Flute, Wuwuchim (manhood) and Maraw (womanhood) societies, Lakon and Owaqol (women's "basket dance" societies), and the Soyal society ceremony in midwinter. Two "social dances," the Butterfly dance of late summer and the Buffalo dance of early winter, celebrate agriculture and hunting. Other ritual observances occur throughout the year. On First Mesa the ritual calendar of the Hopi village of Walpi was based on the solstices while that of the Tewa village of Hano, in part, on the equinoxes. In addition, there were ritual exchanges between First Mesa and Zuni with the Shalako ceremony performed at Hopi at least once during a period of extreme drought.[278]

The annual cycle of ritual performances was well-known to outsiders by the 1880s. However, the conceptual framework or logical structure of the ceremonial calendar was not understood until the

---

276   Fewkes 1901:214 quoted in Black op. cit. 279.

277   Owens 1892:163.

278   See Parsons, ed., 1936:415-442 for Stephen's account of the Shalako ceremony performed on First Mesa in July 1893. At Zuni, the Shalako ceremony celebrates the annual coming of the Kachinas to the village. It takes place at the end of the ritual year, in late November or early December before the winter solstice ceremonies. The Zuni ceremony is best known for the arrival of the Shalakos (six tall birdlike figures) in a procession into the village.

appearance of anthropologist Mischa Titiev's classic account of Hopi religion, *Old Oraibi: A Study of the Hopi Indians of Third Mesa*, published in 1944. In it he wrote there is:

> ...a dual division of time and space between an upper world of the living and the lower world of the dead. This is expressed in the description of the sun's journey on its daily rounds. The Hopi believe that the sun has two entrances, variously referred to as houses, homes or kivas, situated at each extremity of its course. In the morning the sun is supposed to emerge from its eastern home, and in the evening it is said to descend into its western home. During the night the sun must travel underground from west to east in order to arise at its accustomed place the next day. Hence day and night are reversed in the upper and lower "worlds."[279]

The "upper world of the living and the lower world of the dead," or, better, of life and life after this life, are involved in a system of alternation and continuity. As historian of religion John Loftin has more recently written:

> The spiritual source of all life and forms issues from the land of the dead, the underworld, where it appears as life-giving water. Indeed, the Hopi petition their own departed ancestors to visit their villages in the form of clouds to bless them with the sacred gift of rain. Thus death is understood by the Hopi as the return to the spiritual world from which comes life.[280]

This world and the world of the spirits are transformations of each other and yet are of the same essential substance. At death a cotton mask, a "white cloud mask," is placed on the face of the dead person.[281] At burial it is said, "You are no longer a Hopi; you are changed (*nik'ti*, grown into) a kachina, you are Cloud (*O'mauuh*)." After death, Stephen wrote, "the breath body, *hi'ksi ah'paa*, goes from the grave along the trail to the sipapu in the west."[282] Both the sun and the spirits of the departed

279   Titiev 1944:173.
280   Loftin 1991:11-12.
281   Parsons, ed., 1936:825.
282   Op cit., 826.

descend to the lower world through the sipapu. From there the spirits of the dead return to this world as katsinas. All katsinas take on cloud form, to be "cloud people," and their substance is manifested as rainfall. The katsinas do not bring rain, they *are* rain. The Hopi people pray for rain and, indeed, the ritual calendar consists of practices that bring the rains that nurture the corn and the Hopi people.

Titiev also recognized the sipapu to be a channel of communication and exchange, of prayers and prayer offerings, between the upper world of the living and the lower world of the spirits. The prayers and prayer offerings—the practices that bring the rains—involve a reciprocal relationship. Reciprocity, according to anthropologist Claude Levi-Strauss, involves the unconscious principle of the obligation to give, the obligation to receive and the obligation to give in return.[283] The counter-gift, it has been noted, must be deferred and different.[284] As Sekaquaptewa and Washburn put it:

> Hopi life is sustained by reciprocal relationships between individuals and groups in the human world, as well as between the human and spiritual and the human and natural world.[285]

In Hopi thought, a *katsina* (*katsinum*, pl.) is a spirit being who has control over the rains.[286] When a Hopi dies he or she becomes a katsina,

---

283 Levi-Strauss 1987:38, 40-41.

284 Bourdieu 1977:5.

285 Sekaquaptewa and Washburn, ibid.

286 In Hopi, the term *tihu* (*tithu*, pl.) or *katsintihu* refers primarily to small, flat, carved and painted representations of Katsinas given to young girls and then hung on the walls of the family room. *Tihus* are carved by the Katsinas in the village kivas and more elaborate forms are distributed to girls and sometimes to Hopi women at the *Powamuya* and *Nimaniw* ceremonies. *Tihus* are carved from cottonwood root and painted the colors of the cardinal directions. The English term Kachina is often used to refer to dolls made for sale to non-Hopis since the latter part of the nineteenth century. The commodification of these sacred objects may have had its origin in government sponsored collecting expeditions in the 1870s. In the early 1880s the trader Thomas V. Keam encouraged the use of katsina imagery on pottery and the development of more elaborate Kachina dolls. By the beginning of the twentieth century commercial paints replaced traditional mineral and vegetable based colors. Cloth, feathers, and beads were often incorporated. New tools have aided in the development of more realistic figures, often intentionally created so as not to portray the katsinas represented in traditional *tihus*. Modern carvings also include Snake, Butterfly and Buffalo

a cloud that returns as rain to the villages in answer to the Hopis' prayers. Katsinas are also personated spirits who appear in ceremonies.[287] In their song performances the katsinas give advice and admonitions since they have observed that the Hopi have deviated from the practices, *natwani*, that will lead them to a fulfilled life.[288] Other song performances appear to be prayers or petitions for rain as well as expressions of thanksgiving for blessings received.[289] At the same time the katsinas are messengers who receive the prayers and prayer offerings of the Hopi people and reciprocate with the gift of rain. Hopi life is based on corn agriculture and it is sustained by a cycle of reciprocal relationships between persons

---

dancers and other figures that are not Katsinas.

287   The representation of a spirit—the *katsina*—in performance and in material object has provided the basis for two theories as to the "origin" of the Katsinas among the Hopi. In the first, the appearance of Katsina iconography in kiva murals and rock art as well as on ceramics in the fourteenth century at ancestral Hopi and other puebloan sites has led to the argument that the "Katsina cult" was introduced at that time to cope with the social complexity of increasing village size. The source of Katsina ceremonialism is thought to lie in northern Mexico. It is suggested that once accepted, a number of Katsina-inspired social changes took place including the creation of plaza space for large ceremonial performances and changes in burial practices consistent with ancestor-oriented rituals (Adams 1991). In the second theory, it is argued that the fundamental conceptual elements of Hopi cosmology—the reciprocities between spirits, humans, and the natural world—have remained unchanged over the past two millennia. Rather, the symbolic expression of this cosmology has evolved, becoming more complex. The *sipaapuni*—symbol of the place of emergence and a channel of communication and exchange between the world of the spirits (Katsinas) and the human world—appears in the earliest ancestral puebloan pithouses. The kiva—itself an evolving architectural form—is a development around (if not of) the *sipaapuni*. Evidence of prayer sticks offerings to the spirits is present in kivas and near the *sipaapuni* in pit structures between A.D. 725 and A.D. 900. Katsina iconography appears by the beginning of the fourteenth century giving visual and ritual representation to centuries of verbal images of the spirits. The ritual personation of these spiritual beings in kivas and plazas may well have preceded their appearance in art forms in the fourteenth century and continued to develop and change into the historic period (Hieb 1994b).

288   See, for example, the 150 song performances analyzed in Sekaquaptewa, Hill and Washburn 2015. While collected from all three mesas, this emphasis is more consistent with the apocalyptic world view of Third Mesa than the few songs collected by Sullivan on First Mesa.

289   Washburn contends "Katsina songs are not prayers" (Sekaquaptewa, Hill and Washburn 2015:20) although those recorded by Sullivan appear to be prayers.

and groups in the human world as well as between the human and spiritual world. Thus, while one purpose of ritual in this world involves a contribution to the well-being of the spirit world, the spirit world is obligated to contribute to the well-being of this world by providing rain that is essential to the crops and hence, to the health of the Hopis (and all living things of this world). Rain is the most common request in Hopi prayer, however the "gift," "blessing," or "benefit" (*nahmanqwu*) may take other forms as well.[290]

Katsina ceremonies take place inside kivas at night in the months immediately following the *Qooqlo* Katsinas' appearance at the winter solstice and in the plazas in the daytime in the spring and early summer. Katsinas may appear in groups, sometimes singly or in pairs. Some katsinas appear only in specific ceremonies, while others may appear throughout the Katsina season. Important ceremonies include the *Powamuya* (Bean Dance) in February and the *Nimaniw* (home-going or Home Dance) in July when the Katsinas depart for their cloud dwelling places in the four cardinal directions around *Hopitutsqwa* (Hopi land).[291]

Sullivan recorded a Hopi account of the origin of the katsinas:

> There was a time when these supernatural messengers actually came directly from the gods, delivering their decrees and returning with the petitions of the people. But at a very early day their visits ceased, though not until they had imparted to certain good men the mysteries of the peculiar rites and ceremonies by which they might acquire the power of communicating with the deities. ... [The masked impersonators] are the initiated who thus represent the original Katcinas and are supposed to lose their human identity and to become endowed with his supernatural attributes upon assuming their masks.[292]

The other half of the ritual calendar consists of ceremonies performed by religious societies. These unmasked ceremonies consist in large part of prayers and prayer offerings to the spirit world made

---

290 Voth 1901:146, n.4).

291 There are many accounts of Hopi katsinas. Of particular note are Fewkes (1903), Earle and Kennard (1938), Hieb (1994a) and Sekaquaptewa, Hill and Washburn (2015), especially Washburn's introductory essay.

292 Sullivan 1940:103-104.

on behalf of the people of the village. Here, for example, the priests of the Snake society—in elaborate attire and painted faces—employ snakes as messengers who can descend through the cracks and crevices in the earth's surface.

In Hopi thought each clan and each religious society was welcomed to become a part of a village only on the assurance it would make a contribution to sustaining the life and common good of the community. Fewkes, who began his research among the Hopi shortly after Jeremiah Sullivan left, learned this about the introduction of the Flute Ceremony:

> As the Flute chief and his followers approached [the edge of the village], the Bear chief challenged him, demanding 'Who are you? Whence have you come?' The Flute chief responded that they were kindred and knew the songs necessary to bring rain.

Fewkes goes on to comment, "the dramatic reception… symbolizes a historic event [and/or precedent] in the growth [and continued existence] of Walpi."[293] The performances of the ritual calendar were documented in rich detail by Stephen primarily on First Mesa in the early 1890s.[294] A synthesis of accounts from all three mesas is to be found in anthropologist Richard Maitland Bradfield's *An Interpretation of Hopi Culture* (1995).

The Keams Canyon Community

Keams Canyon, ten miles east of the Hopi First Mesa villages, was the location of a trading post owned and operated by Thomas V. Keam, the Moqui [Hopi] Pueblo Indian Agency, and the Presbyterian mission to the Hopi established in the fall of 1880.

In *The Indian Traders*, historian Frank McNitt states it "is said" a trading post was established in Keams Canyon—then known as Peach Orchard Spring— in the late 1860s by H. W. "Billy" Dodd, brother of the Navajo Agent, Major Theodore Dodd.[295] It was an attractive location. There were springs, and Hopis had orchards and wheat fields in the canyon.

Welshman Thomas Varker "Tom" Keam came to New Mexico in

---

293   Fewkes 1900:592.
294   Parsons, ed., 1936.
295   McNitt 1962:46. There is no documentation in support of this statement.

1862 as a member of the First California Cavalry, and in 1865 he joined the New Mexico Volunteer Cavalry. On August 13, 1863, during Col. "Kit" Carson's Navajo campaign,[296] Private Thomas V. Keam, Company C, California Volunteers, carved his name on a sandstone cliff in the canyon. While in the New Mexico Volunteer Cavalry, he spent time among the Navajos who were held at the Bosque Redondo Reservation near Fort Sumner, New Mexico, from 1864 until 1868. Following the Treaty of Bosque Redondo on June 1, 1868, the Navajos made the "long walk" to a newly established reservation in northeastern Arizona. In February 1869, Keam was hired an interpreter the Navajo Indian Agency at Fort Defiance, Arizona.

By January 1870, Tom Keam was joined by his younger brother, William "Billy" Keam, who was also employed as an interpreter at the Navajo Agency. Like his brother, Billy Keam soon married a Navajo woman. In August 1872, when Tom Keam was officially appointed Special Agent for the Navajos, Billy Keam became the agency clerk. In less than a year, as a result of various political pressures and accusations of their being "squaw men," both Keams were fired under order of the Commissioner of Indian Affairs. A year later, Tom Keam established his Fair View trading post south of the Navajo Treaty Reservation, near Fort Defiance. Tom Keam boasted an excellent knowledge of the Navajo language and culture, and the trust and confidence of many important Navajo leaders. In spite of his years of experience working with the Navajo people as an interpreter, trader, and advocate, his many applications for the position of agent to the Navajo in the 1870s were denied.[297]

As discussed below, it was not until 1874 that Tom Kean established a trading post at Peach Orchard Spring.

---

296   On July 7, 1863, Col. "Kit" Carson, under orders from Major James Henry Carleton, began a "round up" of Navajos living in northeastern Arizona. By 1865 9,000 Navajos had been sent to the Bosque Redondo Reservation on the Pecos River in eastern New Mexico. The internment was a failure, Carleton was fired, a congressional investigation ensued, and on July 1, 1868 a treaty was signed. Before the end of the month, the Navajos began the "long walk" to their newly established reservation.

297   Graves 1998:27-138; McNitt 1962:124-199. Nothing came of Keam's application to be the agent for the Hopi in 1879.

Thomas V. Keam, ca. 1884. Frederick Dellenbaugh Papers, Ms 407, Special Collections, The University of Arizona Library.

The Moqui Pueblo Indian Agency, as it was called when Stephen arrived at Keams Canyon, came into existence in a less than orderly fashion. In his annual report for the Superintendency of Arizona, dated September 30, 1864, Charles D. Poston[298] recommended the appointment of agents for tribes located in Arizona Territory, including "John Moss, agent for the Moquis, [effective] August 1, 1864 [at an

---

298   Referred to as the "Father of Arizona," Charles D. Poston (1825-1902) was appointed Superintendent of Indian Affairs for the Territory of Arizona in 1863. In 1864 he was elected as a Delegate to the U. S. House of Representatives and during his term of service Poston submitted bills to establish Indian reservations along the Colorado River.

annual salary of] $1,000."[299] It was Poston's suggestion that "these lost and forgotten people…ought to excite an interest in their favor in the Indian Bureau."[300] Nothing came of Poston's recommendation or that of Michael Steck, Superintendent of Indian Affairs in New Mexico, who wrote the following year:

> Steps should be taken to remove these inoffensive people [the Hopi] to a more favorable locality; and as they belong properly to the Arizona superintendency, I would respectfully ask that the proper superintendent be instructed to inquire into their condition, and to adopt some plan by which their immediate wants can be supplied and their future prospects improved.[301]

The recommendation that the Hopis be "removed" to a "more favorable locality" would be echoed in correspondence with Hopi Agents and Indian Inspectors throughout the following decade. Steck's brief statement also revealed the apparent uncertainly in the Office of Indian Affairs as to where exactly the Hopi were located.

In 1869, U. S. Army Captain A. D. Palmer was appointed "United States Special Agent for Moquis Pueblo Indians." Arriving at the Hopi First Mesa villages on December 9, Palmer made a census, then prepared "an estimate for such implements and seeds as I deemed most necessary for the purpose of assisting the Moquis in planting and raising their crops for the present season." As noted above, Palmer returned the following spring and on May 13, 1870,

> [he] distributed to the seven villages…: 48 camp kettles, 300 axes and helves [handles], 60 extra helves, 100 pickaxes, 300 spades, and an assortment of garden seeds, &c. The carpenters' tools were retained in Se-cho-ma-we [Sichumovi], where I remained during my stay.[302]

Palmer returned in August, accompanied by Dr. Jules Le Carpentier, Assistant Surgeon, United States Army, for the purpose of "vaccinating such of the Indians as would desire it." A smallpox epidemic in the fall of

---

299   For a biography of John Moss, see Secrest 1975. See Chapter 3 for Moss's relationship with Polacca.

300   Poston 1865:158, 155.

301   Steck 1865:171.

302   Palmer 1870:133.

1853 had taken a heavy toll on the Hopi. Their openness to vaccination was shaped by cautious uncertainty and fear, as well as by factionalism, especially at the village of Oraibi, where apocalyptic versions of some Third Mesa emergence narratives formed the basis for rejection of non-Hopi materials and practices. Palmer reported:

> They were at first inclined not to receive vaccination, as some of their chiefs said that it would "propagate the smallpox among them, and the whole purpose of my coming was to kill them off." I was about to leave when several of the chiefs came to me and expressed their willingness to be vaccinated. In order to give them confidence I was vaccinated in their presence, after which they came willingly, not only for vaccination, but to consult the doctor as to diseases which were prevalent among them... When I arrived at O-rey-be [Oraibi], the head chief was anxious to have all the children vaccinated, and we had finished some fifty cases, large and small, when a sub-chief arose and made a speech to the people who had assembled to the number of three hundred or more. Immediately the children stopped coming and we were forced to leave the work unfinished. ... The next day after my return to Se-cho-ma-we, I was informed that the speaker had said we were their enemies and wished to kill them all, and urged the people to kill us rather than let the vaccination go on.[303]

Palmer's periods of residence among the Hopi were brief, nevertheless he was the only agent to ever live in one of their villages.

Although appointed for four years, there was a constant turnover of Hopi agents in the nineteenth century. W. D. Crothers replaced Capt. Palmer at the beginning of January 1871, having been nominated by the Board of Foreign Missions of the Presbyterian Church.[304] From Fort Defiance, by then the headquarters for the Hopi agent, Crothers visited the Hopi on several occasions. He reported the "Orebyes ... manifested much hostility to me, the chief utterly refusing me the privilege" of taking a census of the village. Initially the Oraibis refused all annuity goods,

---

303   Palmer 1870:134.
304   See Chapter 1 for a summary of Federal Indian Policy in the 1870s.

and although some "gladly accepted their portion, the chief refused to accept anything."[305] At the end of his first year, Crothers recommended that the Hopi be removed to Old Fort Wingate, New Mexico.[306] His suggestion was rejected; Crothers then proposed building schools at each of the villages, and the house for an agent at one of the villages. In October 1872, a party including Walter Clement Powell, cousin of John Wesley Powell, reported Oren C. Crothers, the agent's son, was living on First Mesa where a school had been established by the agency farmer, William H. H. Metzger.[307]

On July 10, 1873 Agent Crothers was replaced by William S. Defrees, who repeated the recommendation to remove the Hopis to "a more suitable place for farming and grazing," and in October proposed locating an agency at Moencopi, an Oraibi summer farming village located forty miles west of Third Mesa. Defrees was staying at Fort Defiance, still the headquarters for the Moqui Pueblo Indian Agency. William F. M. Arny, the Navajo Agent, objected to his presence there, and the situation became increasingly acrimonious. At the same time, a conflict also raged between Tom Keam and Agent Arny.[308]

In his annual report to the Commissioner of Indian Affairs, written at Fort Defiance on December 30, Defrees acknowledged:

> I have received $1,500 for the purpose of erecting an agency building and one school-house; I have also received permission from the honorable Commissioner to build at the place to which I will remove the Moquis;

---

305   Crothers 1871:704.

306   [Old] Fort Wingate, a post established in 1862 at Ojo del Gallo (Chicken Springs) near present day San Rafael, New Mexico. Following the Treaty of 1868, and the return of the Navajos to northeastern Arizona, Fort Fauntleroy (established in 1860 at Bear Springs, south of present day Gallup, New Mexico) was renamed Fort Wingate and the earlier post, abandoned in 1863, was then called Old Fort Wingate.

307   William H. H. Metzger, farmer and interpreter accompanying Palmer in 1869, stayed on First Mesa for four years, building roads, lining springs with rock walls, and constructing the "Government House" at the edge of Sichumovi on First Mesa.

308   See Graves 1998: 69-91 for a detailed account of the conflict. Arny refused Tom Keam's application for a trader's license, as Keam had undercut Arny's efforts to convince the Navajos to trade the San Juan River gold fields and Carrizo Mountain areas for land south of the agency (Ibid, p. 72).

I have already commenced operations preparatory to building.[309]

In the months following submission of his annual report, Defrees abandoned the idea of locating the agency at Moencopi, and on April 8, 1874, he reported:

I have ... commenced building an Agency eighteen [ten] miles east from the present Moqui Villages; in a canyon; quite a pretty place, and sufficiently extensive for an Agency; and near enough to be among my Indians.[310]

And, adjacent to the agency, the first buildings for Keam's trading post were being constructed. Prior to this letter, Defrees had made no mention of Peach Orchard Spring or Carriso Canyon (as Keams Canyon was also known) as a location for the Moqui Pueblo Indian Agency. Meanwhile, Agent Arny reported the Hopi agency was located at Trout Spring, west of Canyon de Chelly and forty miles northeast of the First Mesa villages.[311] Apparently the exact location of the new agency was not revealed to Arny or the Commissioner of Indian Affairs until it was a fait accompli. Did Tom Keam and Defrees secretly work together to establish the trading post and agency at the same location? The evidence of collusion by the two men is indisputable on the basis of existing correspondence. In any case, by the late spring of 1874 the Moqui Pueblo Indian Agency and Keam's trading post had been established ten miles east of the Hopi First Mesa villages. Not surprisingly, Tom Keam had chosen the site near the best spring in the canyon. The opportunistic Keam brothers turned to trading with the Navajo and the Hopi, and catering to the needs and interests of government expeditions in the area.[312]

In August 1874, U. S. Indian Inspector J. W. Daniels visited the newly established Moqui Pueblo Indian Agency. Agent Defrees was away but Mrs. Defrees supplied the fiscal reports for the previous three

---

309 Defrees 1874:286.

310 Defrees to Commissioner of Indian Affairs, April 8, 1874, Letters Received by the Office of Indian Affairs, Records of the Bureau of Indian Affairs, National Archives. Cited hereafter as LR-OIA, NA. Commissioner of Indian Affairs is abbreviated hereafter as CIA.

311 Arny to CIA, July 24, 1875, LR-OIA, NA.

312 See Chapters 3 and 4. Keam's trading post was a base camp for expeditions led by James Stevenson, Victor Mindeleff, and Cosmos Mindeleff.

124

quarters; Daniels found them to be in order. William H. H. Metzger, now employed as a teamster, reported an average of twelve students in attendance at the school on First Mesa between August 1873 and March 1874. In his annual report written just six weeks later, Agent Defrees stated:

> Heretofore the agent for these Indians has lived in Fort Defiance, [Fort] Wingate, or Santa Fe, making visits about every three months. Within the past year I have erected a good agency-house, with funds provided by the Department, near the Indians, and have been living among them with my family for more than two months. This residence of the agent among them will tend to good results.[313]

Inspector Daniels recommended that an agency be built nearer the Hopi villages,[314] that in the meantime the Navajo Agent take over the "Moqui duties," and that the Moqui Pueblo Indian Agency as such should be abandoned. Daniels also recommended a reservation be created to "protect them from the encroachment of the Mormons," whose settlements near Moencopi to the west and along the Little Colorado River to the south were seen as a threat.

But by the end of the year, Defrees had given up hope of accomplishing anything of substance for the Hopi, and recommended that the agency be greatly curtailed. He now recommended the agency building be occupied by the teamster and a teacher and, at the discretion of the Department of Interior, the agency be withdrawn. In the meantime, Defrees asked that he, as agent, be permitted to establish his office at Santa Fe or Las Vegas, New Mexico, where he could keep in touch with the teacher at the agency by mail. Less than two months later, on February 25, 1875, Defrees resigned as agent, giving the following reason: "that it is the duty [of] the Agent [to] live among the Indians. I cannot consent to take my wife back to that place."[315]

As the turnover in agents continued, the Keam brothers expanded

---

313 Defrees 1874:290.
314 Daniels to CIA, August 16, 1884, LR-OIA, NA. Keams Canyon is approximately ten miles east of First Mesa—an "inconvenient location" in the words of a later U. S. Indian Inspector.
315 Defress to CIA, February 25, 1875, LR-OIA, NA.

their trade, especially with the increasing number of Navajos living west of the 1868 Treaty Reservation.

On March 11, Rev. John C. Lowrie, Secretary of the Board of Foreign Missions of the Presbyterian Church, nominated William B. Truax of Chicago to replace Defrees. It was Truax's perspective[316] that:

> These Indians, living in permanent abodes, far removed from all disturbing causes, and to some extent civilized, furnish a most hopeful field for missionary and educational effort. The Bible and the common school must be given them, if they would ever rise to the true position of citizens. I believe that no nation or people ever did or ever will, by their own unaided efforts, lift themselves out of a state of degradation and barbarism into a permanent civilization. If this be so, how important, then, that those in ignorance and superstition should be afforded the means to bring them to the light of civilization and Christianity.[317]

Truax arrived in Santa Fe while waiting Senate confirmation, and completed arrangements for the bond required of agents.[318] Truax

---

316 Truax's ethnocentric perspective was widely accepted in the nineteenth century. It was one of the assumptions of progressive evolutionary thought that similarities and differences could be measured against American (western) standards, qualitatively or morally. The West was seen as the culmination of progress. Charles Darwin's *The Descent of Man* (1871) made the implications of evolution and natural selection explicit for the human species; Herbert Spencer's *System of Synthetic Philosophy* (1862-1896) developed the idea of "Social Darwinism" into a major theory of social evolution; Lewis Henry Morgan's *Ancient Society* (1877) fashioned an evolutionary schema for mankind's intellectual and material progress; and Edward Burnett Tylor's *Primitive Culture* (1871) extended evolutionary thought to religion. Truax (and Stephen) reflects an unsophisticated, popular knowledge and use of the notions that the human family has or can progress through stages—from savagery through barbarism to civilization—and Truax (as well as Stephen) freely used words like "savage" and "semi-civilized" in this sense. At the same time, evolutionists accepted the concept of the 'psychic unity of mankind' which assumed all humans were equal in rational intelligence, if different in knowledge. Morgan's *Ancient Society* was "required reading" for Powell's staff and Stephen had read it as well.

317 Truax 1875:212.

318 A bond of $15,000 was required as surety in order for agents to distribute funds for salaries, supplies, etc.

relieved Defrees in Santa Fe, on June 4. Truax immediately wrote the Commissioner of Indian Affairs to request funding:

> ...absolutely necessary for use at my agency. The estimate for incidental expenses is for corn & hay for the animals & also to pay teamster [Wallace] & for traveling expenses, until the commencement of the new fiscal year. There is not one cent on hand for these purposes. If you can possibly furnish the small amount called for you will prevent the suffering of the Government animals & much embarrassment on my part.

Truax added:

> Capt. Defrees, my predecessor, requests me to say to you that the corn & hay asked for...may be provided with money still in his hands, belonging to [i.e., owed by] the party [William Keam] that used the Government forage at the Agency to feed private animals.[319]

Four days later Truax sent a request for a teacher and a matron—"absolutely indispensable to the success of the school"—as the children "must be boarded at their Agency & also clothed." Moreover, because of the great expense of living at that isolated place, Truax argued the salary "should be at least one thousand dollars each,"[320] an increase from the seventy dollars per month currently paid. It was assumed that the Agent's wife would serve, unpaid, as a teacher. Unfortunately, as Truax explained, "the deplorable condition of my dear unfortunate wife" who was "upon the very verge of insanity," made it impossible for her to join him.[321]

Arriving at the agency in early August, Truax soon requested funds for "a cheap but comfortable building" to accommodate the expected children and employees, and a month later he requested funds to employ two additional teachers, at nine hundred dollars per annum.[322] In all, Truax requested funds for six employees: three teachers, a matron,

---

319 Truax to CIA, June 12, 1875, LR-OIA, NA. A statement that reveals something of the close relationship between the agency and the trading post.

320 Truax to CIA, June 16, 1875, LR-OIA, NA.

321 Truax to CIA, August 28, 1875, LR-OIA, NA.

322 Truax to CIA, August 9 and September 3, 1875, LR-OIA, NA.

a teamster, and an interpreter.[323] An exasperated Edward P. Smith, Commissioner of Indian Affairs, wrote to the Rev. James C. Lowrie, Secretary of the Board of Foreign Missions:

> I have not yet been able to get Mr. Truax to comprehend the fact that the only object I have had in continuing the agency among the Moquis Pueblos was to secure the establishment of a school among them, and the only function that an agent for those Indians could have, was the establishment and teaching of a manual labor school. For this purpose I wanted a man and his wife who would go as two missionaries would go to India, simply to work; and that work exclusively educational. For this service they would receive $1500 a year with rent and rations in the school, which I suppose would be a full salary for a missionary *and* his wife.[324]

Meanwhile there had been a continuous turnover of persons hired to be teacher or matron. In September, the commissioner informed Truax his appointment of a teacher was not approved and that of a matron "will stand suspended."[325]

A frustrated Truax replied:

> Is it possible for one man to cook, and wash, and care for, and teach a boarding school, and also teach schools in seven villages from fifteen to thirty miles distant? And at the same time perform the duties necessarily pertaining to an Indian Agency? I need only refer to this matter to show its utter impossibility.[326]

He closed his letter by asking the appointment of Charles [sic] S. Merritt, as an Assistant Teacher at $50 per month, from October 1, be approved. As the Monthly School Report for October 1875 shows, it was Edward S. Merritt who Truax wished to hire, a jack-of-all-trades who later served as Clerk and, briefly, as Acting Agent before the Moquis Pueblo Indian Agency was closed in the spring of 1883.

---

323   Truax to CIA, September 9, 1875, LR-OIA, NA.
324   CIA to Lowie, Letters Sent, Office of Indian Affairs, RG75, NA. Cited hereafter as LS-OIA, NA. Emphasis added.
325   CIA to Truax, September 7, 1875, LS-OIA, NA.
326   Truax to CIA, October 23, 1875, LR-OIA, NA.

In the meantime, in August 1875, a party from F. V. Hayden's U. S. Geological and Geographical Survey of the Territories reached Keams Canyon. William Henry Jackson, who was on his way to make photographs on First and Second Mesa, speaks of William "Billy" Keam as the "Agency Trader." Before the end of August, Truax granted Thomas V. Keam a license to trade with the Hopi.[327]

In his first annual report from the Moquis Pueblo Indian Agency, dated August 31, Truax wrote, "the Indians are so strongly attached to this poor and forbidding place that they cannot be induced to entertain any proposition for changing to a better one." Options he had presented as "a more promising section of the country," included Indian Territory [Oklahoma].[328] Truax was pressed by the commissioner to propose to the Hopis that they relocate where there would be better lands. Two months later, Truax reported:

> I very much regret to inform you that I have not been able to induce them to entertain the proposition for their removal to a better and more promising country. They are so much attached to their present locality, that they become angry when they are asked to consider any overtures for an exchange of locality—they cannot be moved at present except by force, which is not desirable.[329]

Truax's wife was ill in Santa Fe, and unable to join him at the Moqui Pueblo Indian Agency. Near the end of March, he asked for a leave of absence for sixty days, beginning July 1. He was granted a leave; however, Congress did not appropriate funds to continue the Moquis Pueblo Indian Agency during the ensuring fiscal year which forced the Commissioner to suspend its functions.[330] As a consequence, Truax had to discharge his employees and dispose of the property in his charge at public auction.[331] Truax served until the closure of the

---

327 Under pressure from former Navajo agent W. F. M. Arny, the license was denied by the Commissioner of Indian Affairs on November 13. Truax appealed on Keam's behalf and his license was reinstated on January 31, 1876. See Truax to CIA, December 10, 1875 and January 6, 1876, LR-OIA, NA.

328 Truax 1876:5.

329 Truax to CIA, December 10, 1875, LR-OIA, NA.

330 CIA to Truax, September 28, October 9, and October 24, 1876, LS-OIA, NA.

331 There is no record of the proceeds of this auction. However, the Keam brothers purchased the agency furniture which they were able to sell to the next agent,

Moqui Pueblo Indian Agency on September 30, 1876.

Keam's trading post at Peach Orchard Spring, soon widely known as Keam's/Keams Canyon, proved to be profitable. Here the brothers developed a virtual monopoly on trade with the Hopi and the western Navajos—because of location and Keam's use of script, redeemable only at his trading post.[332] Tom Keam continued to use the Fair View trading post as a center of operations, while Billy Keam worked at Keams Canyon.

William H. R. Keam, Hopi Trader and Interpreter, 1875. Photograph by William H. Jackson. U. S. Geological Survey Denver Library. Image: Hillers #1003. "Billy" Keam is seated on a roof-top in Tewa (Hano). The villages of Sichumovi and Walpi are visible in the distance.

In March 1876, John K. "Jack" Hillers, the photographer, and Olin D. Wheeler, a topographer, passed through Keams Canyon on their way to the Hopi First Mesa villages to collect materials for the International Exhibition of Arts, Manufactures, and Products of the Soil

---

William R. Mateer, when the agency reopened.

332 Other traders issued their own coins which were accepted at many trading posts.

and Mine, popularly known as Centennial Exhibition, that was to open in Philadelphia just two months later. They had been sent to the Hopi by J. W. Powell as one of several expeditions assigned to gather "tangible tokens" representing "past and present conditions" of American Indians for an exhibit to be mounted by the Smithsonian Institution on behalf of the Office of Indian Affairs. Both men were members of Powell's United States Geological and Geographical Survey of the Rocky Mountains and Hillers had visited the Hopi in 1872. Hillers and Wheeler spent over three weeks taking photographs and bartering for over 600 items of Hopi material culture. Billy Keam served as their interpreter, and when their supply of trade goods—46 pounds of beads, 11 dozen earrings, one bundle of peacock feathers, yard goods, and a 400 pound bale of raw cotton—was exhausted, he was able to sell them 100 yards of calico and 50 yards of Columbia sheeting from his brother's supplies.[333]

From Wheeler and Hillers, Billy Keam undoubtedly learned of Powell's insistence that the materials collected reflect Indian cultures "before contact with the white man," and realized the potential profit of ancestral Hopi pottery and other antiquities to be found at ruins near Keams Canyon and in Canyon de Chelly.

In addition to his employment at the Fair View and Keams Canyon trading posts, Billy Keam often served as a guide into Canyon de Chelly. In April 1877, for instance, he led a party that included William H. Jackson, the photographer, and John Vance Lauderdale, Assistanat Surgeon, U. S. Army, stationed at Fort Wingate, from Fort Defiance into the canyon as far as White House ruin.

For the sixteen months following the closure of the Moqui Pueblo Indian Agency on September 30, 1876, the Hopis were served by the Navajo Agent at Fort Defiance, Alex. G. Irvine. Irvine first visited the Hopi villages in November, and on his return sent a recommendation to the Commissioner of Indian Affairs that "a reservation of fifty (50) miles square be set apart for them and that it be made to include the agency buildings."[334] Irvine returned during May 1877, for "an issue of goods for clothing…to six villages and one family of the Oraibies." In his Annual Report submitted in September, Irvine noted:

[the Hopis] are much attached to their homes and dislike

---

333   Hieb 2011b.
334   Irvine to CIA, November 14, 1876, LR-OIA, NA.

the idea of removal. They, however, are not ignorant of the advantages of other locations, several of their number last year going as far as San Bernardino and Santa Barbara, California.[335]

He made two recommendations: that they be furnished with a teacher and that "a reservation be surveyed and set apart for their use."[336]

Irvine resigned as Navajo Agent, to take effect September 30, and William R. Mateer was appointed to serve as the agent for the Hopi.[337] Mateer reached Fort Defiance at the beginning of February 1878, and met with Irvine and Billy Keam, "who has been their [Moqui] interpreter and been in charge of the Agency buildings until recently."[338]

Later in February, with the re-establishment of the Moqui Pueblo Indian Agency,[339] Mateer went to First Mesa where he held "a council of all the chiefs, except the Oraibi." The agent found them "all friendly towards the Government, expressed their willingness to carry out the wishes of the Government and seemed desirous of having their schools started." Mateer went on to Oraibi, accompanied by Billy Keam and two chiefs who had participated in the council on First Mesa. The agent's plan was to make a census of Oraibi. Mateer reported:

> This village trades altogether with the Mormons and we soon found the difference in the Indians after getting amongst them. After explain[ing] the object of my visit to the chief, Lo-lu-lul-a-my,[340] the only reply he made was "That it was a lie and he didn't believe a word of it." .

---

335   See Chapter 3 for the biography of Polacca, one of the Hopis who traveled to California.

336   Irvine 1877:160.

337   Mateer was probably the most capable, and certainly the most conscientious agent during the decade. His extensive correspondence with the Commissioner of Indian Affairs provides a rich portrait of the activities at the agency. See, for example, Mateer 1878. After leaving the agency, he published the first account of a Snake Dance (Mateer 1879a).

338   Mateer to CIA, February 1, 1878, LR-OIA, NA. William Keam was not officially "in charge."

339   The agency consisted of one six-room adobe house, badly in need of repair, and an uncompleted stone stable. There was no government property as all had been sold by Truax [to Keam].

340   Looloma, village chief (*kikmongwi*) and member of the Bear Clan, was a leader of the "Friendly" faction at Oraibi (see Whiteley 1988a).

. . [H]e went on to tell what the Mormons had said, that they must not have anything to do with the Government that they only want their names so that they can again carry off their wives and their stock. We finally talked the chief into terms the first night but when his council got together the next morning they all opposed our taking the census . . .[341]

The agent noted "this is the fifth time they have resisted the taking of their census." In November, Mateer returned to Oraibi, having been informed they were willing to be enrolled. He arrived at the beginning of the *Wuwutsim* (manhood initiation ceremony) and found the trail into the village blocked. After being delayed overnight, Mateer wrote:

I found the chief, Lo-lulul-ah-my, friendly and willing that I should enroll them but a majority of his council were opposed and not being influential enough to control them we were compelled to return without performing our errand.[342]

Mateer saw that the land near the agency, where Hopis grew wheat, had been damaged by flash floods and overrun by Navajo sheep and horses. With Hopi labor, he had a stone wall built to enclose the agency building, springs, and eleven acres for fields and agency gardens. A stone building with school rooms, a stable, a granary, a carriage shed, and two reservoirs were also constructed. Throughout these efforts, Mateer recognized the importance for the Hopi men to return to their villages to participate in ceremonies and tend to their crops.

Soon after Mateer took up residence in Keams Canyon, the commissioner informed the agent that it had long been the desire of the Department of Indian Affairs to obtain the consent of the Hopi for moving them to the Indian Territory. The proposition had been submitted to the Hopi in 1876 but, the commissioner noted, they had refused to entertain the idea, seeming adverse to any change.[343]

A few months later, Mateer met with village leaders to again discuss the possibility of relocating to Indian Territory or to the Little Colorado River, a location Mateer knew had been occupied at some time in the

---

341 Mateer to CIA, February 24, 1878, LR-OIA, NA.
342 Mateer to CIA, November 28, 1878, LR-OIA, NA.
343 CIA to Mateer, May 2, 1878, LS-OIA, NA.

past by ancestral Hopi people.[344] He concluded:

> These Indians…have been driven to their present location for defense against the more powerful tribes who have surrounded them.[345]

They could only be convinced to move if they were assured of adequate protection.

In his monthly report for April 1878, Mateer again raised the question of a reservation:

> Tu-bee,[346] formerly a chief of the Oraibi Village, is here and complains that the Mormons are intruding upon their farm lands at Moen Kappi and interfering with their planting. He states that his father planted there when he was a boy, as well as many other Oraibis, and that it is their ground.
>
> I would respectfully inquire whether there is not some law by which the Indians can be protected in their rights to lands which they have cultivated for a century or more?[347]

On August 14, the commissioner responded:

> As the Moqui Indians occupy the public lands without any authority of law, the provisions of the statutes enacted by Congress for the protection of Indians in their lands within a reservation, cannot be invoked to protect the Moquis, and remove and punish white settlers. With the

---

344   Mateer visited Lot Smith, leader of the Mormon settlement of Sunset, located on the Little Colorado River. The ruins of Homolovi, occupied by ancestors of the Hopi from ca. 1260-1400 A.D., were located nearby. The Mormons, like the people of the Homolovi settlements, farmed on the flood plain of the Little Colorado River.

345   Mateer 1878:9-10.

346   Tuuvi, an Oraibi man and early convert to Mormonism, welcomed the Mormon settlers in the Moencopi area as protection against Navajos who raided their orchards, fields, and gardens. Ironically, the Mormon settlement of Tuba City, established in 1876, was named for Tuuvi. See Peterson 1971:192-193.

347   An Oraibi farming village located forty miles west of Third Mesa. On March 30, 1880, Navajo Agent, Galen Eastman, submitted a proposal, with map, for a Moquis Pueblo Indian Reservation "believing that the Mormons are about to settle on last" that ought to be enclosed in such a reservation. See Eastman to CIA, March 20, 1880, LR-OIA, NA.

view of establishing a suitable reservation for the Moquis Indians, and to prevent further encroachments upon the lands which they occupy and cultivate…[348]

This was followed by a list of twelve questions to determine what would be necessary and sufficient for a reservation, again including the possibility of relocating the Hopi to an area on the Little Colorado River. To this possibility, the commissioner indicated the need to find out "whether the Moquis are willing to remove to the location designated."[349]

Owing to the illness of his wife, Mateer resigned at the end of the month, and a response to the letter fell to the clerk, Edward S. Merritt. Merritt recommended four reservations, one for each of the three Hopi mesas and a fourth, a timber reservation some distance away.[350]

Mateer's abrupt resignation was followed by a series of agents and acting agents and, except for Merritt's recommendations, the issue of a reservation was set aside for the time being.

Merritt became "acting agent" on August 31, although not officially until November.[351] On November 14, the Navajo Agent, Galen Eastman, was put in charge of the Moquis Pueblo Indian Agency. As he was unable to stay at Keams Canyon, he put his son, Edward, at the agency as Farmer-in-Charge. On December 26, Merritt was again requested to serve as Acting Agent.[352] Less than a month later, on January 21, 1880, agent Eastman discharged Merritt,[353] and appointed Rev. Alexander

---

348 CIA to Mateer, August 14, 1879, LS-OIA, NA.

349 Ibid.

350 Merritt to CIA, February 23, 1880, LR-OIA, NA.

351 Due to delays in mail from the Moqui Pueblo Indian Agency, via Fort Defiance, to Washington, Merritt was—on paper--Acting Agent from November 2 to 20, 1879.

352 CIA to Merritt, December 26, 1879, LS-OIA, NA. and Merritt to CIA, January 20, 1880, LR-OIA, NA. Merritt noted he had not be paid for seven months.

353 Merritt documented Eastman's embezzlement of goods intended to be distributed to the Navajos and collusion with others, including Thomas V. Keam (Merritt to CIA, January 1, 1880, LR-OIA, NA). In a letter to the Solicitor, U. S. Treasury, February 20, 1880, Merritt said, "I have never seen an honest Ind. Agent in 20 years on the frontier." Merritt also being replaced by a "boy," Eastman's teenage son—"a perfect burlesque on Indian Service: (Merritt to CIA, January 20, 1888, LR-OIA, NA). Even after he was dismissed, Merritt prepared fiscal estimates that were then signed by Eastman, see for example, Eastman [i.e., Merritt] to CIA, Feburary 10, 1880, LR-OIA, NA. An "estimate of medical

H. Donaldson as clerk and teacher.[354] Donaldson became ill and died suddenly at Fort Defiance on April 30.[355] Eastman immediately assumed the responsibilities of Agent-in-Charge.[356]

Meanwhile in February, Milo C. Boynton, a young lawyer from Grand Haven, Michigan, was nominated by the Board of Foreign Missions of the Presbyterian Church and appointed agent. Arriving at Fort Defiance on April 13, Donaldson reported, "[Boynton] has become so terrified by the rumors of Indian troubles that he is going to leave the country tomorrow & resign his position at once."[357] Boynton immediately returned to Michigan and resigned on May 14.[358] Captain Frank T. Bennett,[359] stationed at Fort Wingate, was made Acting Agent until the arrival of John H. Sullivan at Fort Wingate on October 1.[360]

---

supplies" was submitted by W[illiam] Keam, Acting Physician, on February 10, 1880, LR-OIA, NA. It, too, was prepared by Merritt.

354 Donaldson, Presbyterian missionary to the Navajo, was sent to the Moquis Pueblo Indian Agency on January 5, 1880. See his report to CIA, January 30, 1880, LR-OIA, NA, with detailed criticisms of Merritt. Eastman accused Merritt of "cohabiting with a squaw concubine" and theft of agency supplies as justification for his removal (Eastman to CIA, January 21, 1880), LR-OIA, NA.

355 Several obituaries for Rev. Donaldson (1849-1880) appear in the Sheldon Jackson Correspondence, Vol. 58, pp. 48-49, Presbyterian Historical Society.

356 See Eastman to CIA, May 24, 1880, LR-OIA, NA.

357 Donaldson to CIA, April 14, 1880, LR-OIA, NA. The incident was reported in a Santa Fe newspaper under the headline "Naughty Navajos." Vol. 54, pp. 58-59, Sheldon Jackson Correspondence, Presbyterian Historical Society. Cited hereafter as SJC, PHS. For another perspective, see H. R. Boynton to John C. Lowrie, June 15, 1880, American Indian Correspondence, Presbyterian Historical Society. Cited hereafter as AIC, PHS. H. R. Boynton was Milo's brother.

358 Boynton to CIA, May 14, 1880, LR-OIA, NA. Meanwhile John H. Sullivan submitted his application for a position as Indian Agent. Sullivan to CIA, March 8, 1880, LR-OIA, NA.

359 Frank Tracy Bennett, 9th Cavalry, was appointed June 22, 1880, Special Orders 73, Fort Wingate, New Mexico. Moqui Indian Correspondence, Moqui Agency Records, National Archives, Laguna Naguel. Bennett, the Navajo Agent at Fort Defiance in 1868, hired Thomas V. Keam to be the Spanish interpreter at the agency. Bennett returned to military duty in 1871. On June 12, 1880, Bennett was again appointed to be acting agent at Fort Defiance, following the removal of Galen Eastman. McNitt 1962:80, 125-126, and 167.

360 See Chapter 2 for a history of the Moqui Pueblo Indian Agency from 1880 to its closure in 1883.

Polacca

Wiki's world was undergoing rapid change. For Walter Hough, as noted above, Wiki was a "Hopi gentleman of the old school, a survivor of the best of the past generation." Polaccaca (various spellings)—Tom Polacca as he was known for much of his life—represented much that was changing. A contemporary of Wiki's, Polacca (ca. 1849-1912) was born in the First Mesa village of Tewa. His father, Ko'icheve (various spellings), a Snake clan man, married a Corn clan woman in Tewa, and they had several children including Nampeyo, the famous potter. Polacca was an early convert to Mormonism, a supporter of education for the Hopis and the first to build a house in the valley below First Mesa.

In 1875 newspaperman E. A. Barber described "Captain Tom" as "a bright, fine looking young fellow, dressed in full American costume, with a cocked hat and red feather, who took off his hat, shook hands, and in broken English, interspersed with Spanish, bade us [Barber and photographer W. H. Jackson] welcome."[361]

In 1880 "Polacco Chiquito" was employed as an interpreter at the Moquis Pueblo Agency.

Polacca accompanied Frank Hamilton Cushing to Havasupai in 1881 and Cushing made note of Polacca's exposure to American culture:

[In the] evening Pu-la-ka-ka gives long account of his wanderings to California. The ocean, people, steamboats, porpoises, *and* dolphins, sea shells, printing, book stores, street cars, wheat and fruits, etc. etc. [Several days later Cushing added:]

Pu-la-ka-kai tells of printing, distribution of mail, fountains, his dancing … a museum, graftings, Chinese store, silk, ribbands, lacquer-ware, houses of prostitution. Talk with captain of steamer, landing of passengers. His minuteness of observation unsurpassed…[362]

Polacca may have accompanied the explorer John Moss (nominated in 1864 by Arizona territorial governor Charles D. Poston to be the first "agent for the Moquis") who visited the Hopi in 1873 as he traveled to and from San Francisco where he obtained financial support for mines he was developing in southwestern Colorado. In December

---

361   Barber 1875.
362   Green, ed., 1990:168-169.

1882 Polacca served as Cushing's guide and translator during the ill-fated "Oraibi Expedition." The artist Willard L. Metcalf, a member of Cushing's party in 1882, met Polacca as they prepared to go to Oraibi:

> We [Cushing and Metcalf] went over to Te-wa, the most eastern of the three towns on this mesa. … There we were hospitably received by Pulakaki, or Tom as we heard Mr. C. speak of him. He is an old friend of F's, having accompanied him to "Huava-su-pai" in '81. He had a very good-natured face and did everything to make us comfortable. He is a believer in Americans, has very advanced and common sense ideas in certain matters, wore American clothes and was quite wealthy. He was, I found, a great linguist, speaking no less than six or seven Indian languages, most of them perfectly, and also Spanish and English. We had supper there and he made us down some fine beds and gave me plenty of blankets when he found out what a time I had had the night before [at Jeremiah Sullivan's house]. He had lived in Zuni some years before and spoke the language very fluently and it seemed good to hear C. and him talking together.[363]

Following the failure to obtain substantial collections at Oraibi, the expedition moved to Second Mesa. Victor Mindeleff, in charge of the expedition at the Hopi villages, wrote in a report to Powell:

> On Jan. 3rd [1883] we rec'd information from our interpreter "Tom" of a deposit of bowls &c as offerings on graves [near the Second Mesa villages], so Mr. Cushing & I went on a little exploring trip. We found the point described and saw a number of Moqui graves with specimens of the modern pottery and basket-work laid on them.
> The locality appeared to be the site of quite an extensive ruin. We found also a sacrificial shrine—recently used as evidenced by the newly painted images deposited on the rocks—the contents of which we propose to add

---

363   W. L. Metcalf, Journal from December 2, 1882 to February 1, 1883, Willard Leroy Metcalf Papers, Thomas Gilcrease Institute of American History and Art.

to the present collection. We shall not venture to take possession however until the trading is finished in order to avoid any bad results to our work that might follow in case of discovery.[364]

In drawing attention to these "grave goods," was it Polacca's supposition, if not intention, that the pottery, basketry and "new painted images" would be added to the collection being made by Cushing and Mindeleff?

Tom Polacca, 1890. National Anthropological Archives, Smithsonian Institution. Image: Neg. #1803A.

---

364   Victor Mindeleff to J. W. Powell, January 15 1883, Records of the Bureau of American Ethnology, Correspondence, Letters Received, NAA, SI.

In 1887 a boarding school was opened in Keams Canyon and about this time Polacca, by now a prosperous rancher, built a commodious house, fifty-six feet long and nearly as wide, at the base of First Mesa. Over the next decade his house served as a base camp or way station for many visitors and passers-by including Fewkes and his assistant, J. G. Owens, in 1891. In the early 1890s, a number of government funded, peak-roofed and dressed stone houses were built nearby, forming the nucleus a settlement soon to be known as Polacca. As Peter Whiteley has pointed out, Hopis refer to these houses as *palakiki*, "red houses," on account of their rusted tin roofs, a playful reference to Polacca.

From the beginning attendance at the boarding school was poor, with the conservative faction at Oraibi refusing to send any children. In 1890 a delegation was sent to Washington, to discuss the problem of school attendance with the Commissioner of Indian Affairs. The delegation was headed by C. E. Vandever, the Navajo agent, with Thomas V. Keam as interpreter and included leading men from Oraibi, Shungopavi and First Mesa, including Tom Polacca, a strong supporter of the government's education program. During the same year E. S. Clark, Special Enumerator with the Eleventh Census of the United States, directed the census of the Hopi. Clark experienced resistance to his efforts, especially at Oraibi where the final number (estimate) of 905 was "confirmed and partially enumerated by Special Agents in 1890 and 1891."[365] At the close of his brief narrative report, Clark wrote:

> It would be an injustice to a good and worthy man should I fail to make favorable mention of the Indian or Tewa who devoted his time so generously in the height of the harvest season to our interests, who has forsaken the home of his fathers and many of their ways by moving his home down from the mesa and breaking away from many of the customs and superstitions of his tribe, thereby invoking the anathemas of this people; a man whose highest ambition is to learn and adopt the ways of the white man in all things (excepting possibly the vices). It is with profound respect and admiration of a good, true, and brave man that I commend to the fostering care and generous treatment of those who have

---

365   E. S. Clark, Report on the Moqui Pueblos of Arizona, Donaldson 1893:49.

charge of the nation's wards the big, kindhearted Tom Polacca.[366]

Julian Scott, a Special Agent with the Eleventh Census, reported that Polacca was an agency policeman, a position he held until 1910, and added a pen and ink sketch of Polacca and his house that were published in the final report of the census.[367]

Polacca also served as a guide for Gustaf Nordenskiold in 1891, following the latter's explorations of the cliff dwellings at Mesa Verde and again, 1901, he was an interpreter for Stewart Culin during his visit to First Mesa.[368]

Although prominent and prosperous, there was much about Polacca's life, even as a young man, that was at odds with the lives of his contemporaries. Edward Dozier, a Tewa from Santa Clara Pueblo in New Mexico and an anthropologist by training, did his dissertation on Polacca's home village of Hano (or Tewa). He reported "only one case of social ostracism and exile were related to me":

> During the greater part of his life Polacca was highly respected and esteemed but in later years he lost the good will of his community. [Well] before his death Polacca departed from the traditional pattern of life and was converted to Mormonism. The ire of Hano was aroused, however, when the Tewa leared that Polacca had sold his house and land below the mesa to the Baptist Mission— land to which he had only use right. Polacca and his family were exiled to Sand Dunes [Wepo Gardens], five miles from First Mesa and he was forever prohibited from participating and viewing Tewa ceremonies.[369]

Other, more generous, explanations of Polacca's move to his Sand

---

366   Ibid, note.

367   Donaldson 1893:52. The two unnumbered plates follow this page.

368   Stewart Culin (1858-1929) was an ethnographer and collector with a particular interest in games. At the time he visited First Mesa with Polacca he was employed by the University of Pennsylvania. In 1903 he was appointed Curator of the Brooklyn Museum's newly established Department of Ethnology. About this time he purchased A. M. Stephen's notebooks and papers from Thomas V. Keam, later selling them to E. C. Parsons.

369   Dozier 1966:67.

Dunes ranch have been put forward by individuals who knew him.[370] Polacca died of pneumonia on May 11, 1912. In 1940 the Church of Jesus Christ of Latter-Day Saints erected a monument at the Sand Dunes ranch to "Tom Polacca, linguist, trader, rancher, social and religious advocate."[371]

370   Blair and Blair 1999:55.
371   Quoted in Kramer 1996:107.

4. Frank Hamilton Cushing and the Bureau of Ethnology Expeditions – 1879-1888

"F. H. Cushing, 1st War Chief of Zuni, U. S. Ass't Ethnologist," Tenetsali, Cushie… Frank Hamilton Cushing had many names and, arguably, many identities.

In many histories of anthropology—certainly histories of American anthropology—Frank Hamilton Cushing was "the first professional anthropologist to 'go to the field' and function as a 'participant observer.'"[372] Of contemporaries considered in this book, Jeremiah Sullivan was more the participant and A. M. Stephen more the observer, but Cushing was recognized by the Washington establishment as a *the* model *par excellence* of the most basic technique of anthropological fieldwork—later termed "participant observation."[373] His participation in daily activities, his ability to work in the language of the Zuni people, and his observation of events in their everyday context, as exemplified in his writing and publicized by his admirers, made him, more than the others, a pioneer in the emerging discipline of anthropology. There were and are very different portraits of Cushing; a man, at once, brilliant, charismatic, creative, a gifted writer but also ego-centric, arrogant, irresponsible, and, on occasion, clearly dishonest. As his Zuni correspondence reveals, he was often sick and frequently paranoid. To some he was a genius, to others he was a fraud; to some, a collector, to others, a looter. He was, and continues to be, a controversial figure.[374] My emphasis here is on his

---

372   Fowler 2000:118.

373   For an insightful analysis of Cushing's ethnographic method, see Murray 1987. The Zuni anthropologist, Edmund J. Ladd, found much of Cushing's participant observation questionable, from his knowledge of the Zuni language to his role in the 'council of the bow priests.' See Ladd 1994

374   Ladd, ibid, p. 32 gives his Zuni perspective on Cushing: "He was tolerated and allowed to enter into the religious activities because of his intrusive and abrasive

years at Zuni, from 1879 to 1884. There remains the need for a biography of Cushing—a careful accounting of the man, as well as the myths that surround him and his accomplishments.

Cushing went to Zuni as a member of the first expedition organized under the auspices of the newly established Bureau of Ethnology. As a context for understanding his work as well as that of others discussed in the book, this chapter includes accounts of the expeditions under the leadership of James Stevenson, from 1879 until his death in 1888. From 1883 until 1890, another series of expeditions was carried out under the leadership of Victor Mindeleff. These were continued by his younger brother, Cosmos, until 1895, when appropriations to the Bureau were cut, forcing the termination of a number of projects, including the work of Cosmos Mindeleff. In general, the Stevenson led parties were concerned with building collections; those led by the Mindeleffs documented architecture as the basis for creating scale models, and is the subject of Chapter 5. Cushing's participant observation and narrative accounts of Zuni culture constituted a third area of research.

In assembling this description of Cushing's life at Zuni, I have drawn on many sources, but primarily his own writings. It is an illusion to imagine one could ever actually reconstruct the past. This is particularly the case with Cushing's professional career. His letters to his superiors—sometimes drafted and redrafted before they were sent—are clearly strategic, charged with premeditation and intention. If his daily journals appear to consist of a matter-of-fact descriptions of places, persons and events, the articles he wrote for some of the elite literary magazines of the day—the *Atlantic Monthly*, *Harper's Monthly*, and the *Century Illustrated Monthly Magazine*—reveal a style historian Curtis Hinsley has termed "ethnopoetic."[375] As well as anyone at the time, Cushing convinced his readers through the "miracle" of writing that he "actually penetrated … another form of life," in the words of anthropologist Clifford Geertz, "of having, one way or another, truly 'been there.'"[376]

---

manners. He was probably not fully accepted, however. And, he was there at Zuni at the pleasure of the 'Washington people' whom he used like a whip. The Zuni people, in general, are prone not to embarrass strangers and they avoid unpleasantness at all cost, traits of which Cushing took full advantage."

375   Hinsley 1999a.

376   Geertz 1988:4-5.

Frank H. Cushing, 1882. Engraving based on an image by Willard Metcalf. Sylvester Baxter, An Aboriginal Pilgrimage, *Century*, 24: 528.

Frank Hamilton Cushing was born in the village of North East, Erie County, Pennsylvania on July 22, 1857, the son of Thomas Cushing, a physician, and Sarah Harding Cushing. He was three years old when the family moved to a farm outside Barre Center, New York. It was here that Cushing became interested in Indian artifacts and subsequently in the techniques used to create them. A neighbor, aware of Cushing's interests and abilities, encouraged him to write Joseph Henry and Spencer F. Baird, the officers of the Smithsonian Institution.[377] His first published work, "Antiquities of Orleans County, New York," appeared before he was eighteen years old in the *Annual Report of the Board of Regents of the Smithsonian Institution, 1874*. Cushing enrolled briefly in Cornell University in the spring of 1875, intending to study geology, but that November, he accepted an appointment in the Smithsonian Institution as an assistant in ethnology to Dr. Charles Rau, and began the arrangement of Indian collections in the U. S. National Museum for display at the Centennial Exhibition opening the following spring in Philadelphia. Two years later, during the summer of 1878, Cushing engaged in archaeological research in Virginia as a member of the Woodruff Expedition. A year later, Baird asked Cushing if he would like to join a Smithsonian expedition to the Southwest.

Between 1879 and 1888, James Stevenson led annual expeditions to the Southwest for the newly established Bureau of Ethnology. Cushing was a member of the first expedition in 1879, and assisted with the collecting efforts of the third and fourth expeditions in 1881 and 1882.

The First Bureau of Ethnology Expedition - 1879

The first Bureau of Ethnology expedition began its trek to the Southwest on August 5, 1879. The day before, John Wesley Powell, newly appointed director of the Bureau, gave Stevenson these orders:

> You are hereby placed in charge of the party organized to make ethnological and archaeological explorations in south-western New Mexico and contiguous territory. Mr. J. K. Hillers has been instructed to report to you as photographer and Mr. F. H. Cushing of the Smithsonian Institution will assist you in making collections and in other ethnologic work.[378]

---

377 Joseph Henry (1797-1878) was the first Secretary of the Smithsonian Institution. Spencer F. Baird (1823-1887) was the first Curator of the Smithsonian Institution. Later he served as Assistant Secretary before succeeding Joseph Henry to become Secretary from 1878 to 1887.

378 J. W. Powell to James Stevenson, August 5, 1879, quoted in Fowler 2000:107.

A fourth member of the party—unnamed and unpaid—was Stevenson's wife Matilda.[379]

Their destination would be the pueblo of Zuni in western New Mexico.

James Stevenson, ca. 1885. National Anthropological Archives, Smithsonian Institution, Image: Neg. #76-15187.

Stevenson, his wife Matilda, and Cushing left Washington by railroad in August. They were joined in St. Louis by Hillers. They traveled on to Las Vegas, New Mexico, the railhead of the Atchison, Topeka and Santa Fe Railway, and from there the party followed the stage road to

---

379   For a biography of Matilda Coxe Stevenson, see Miller 2007.

Santa Fe. While the Stevensons and Hillers traveled by wagon, Cushing rode ahead on a mule "as this enabled me to make short trips to either side of our train for the purpose of exploring any ancient remains which might be along the way."[380]

From the outset, Cushing chose to operate independently from the others.

Cushing had been on the staff of the National Museum since 1875, and was the protégé of Spencer F. Baird, Secretary of the Smithsonian Institution. Powell, Stevenson, and Hillers had joined the staff of the Smithsonian with the creation of the Bureau of Ethnology, only two months before the expedition began. Of course, Baird knew these men. He had worked closely with Powell in developing the Indian exhibit for the Centennial Exhibition.[381] Stevenson had been the executive officer in the field and a lobbyist for the Hayden survey since 1869; Powell and Hillers had worked together for nearly a decade, beginning with Powell's explorations of the Colorado River. Cushing was very much their junior in age and field experience.[382] Once in the field, Stevenson (and Hillers) reported to Powell; Cushing reported directly to Baird—with continual complaints about Stevenson (and his wife).[383] Over time, the gulf between the Stevensons and Cushing widened and served as a gathering point for a growing number of people who were either Cushing's admirers or were critical of him.

For the expedition, Stevenson carried a number of letters of introduction, including one from Baird:

> Mr. Stevenson is authorized to make use of all facilities granted to the Smithsonian Institution by railroad companies and the War Department in the transportation

---

380   Green 1990:32. Wherever possible I have quoted from the transcriptions in *Cushing at Zuni: The Correspondence and Journals of Frank Hamilton Cushing, 1879-1884*, edited by Jesse Green (Albuquerque: University of New Mexico Press, 1990).

381   See Hieb 2011b.

382   Cushing (1857-1900) was 22; Hillers (1843-1925), 36; James Stevenson (1840-1888), 39; Matilda Stevenson (1849-1915), 30. Cushing had some archaeological experience in New York and Virginia. Hillers and the Stevensons had extensive field experience in the West. Hillers had been to the Hopi villages in 1876.

383   Cushing was on the staff and budget of the National Museum; Powell, Stevenson and Hillers were all on the staff and budget of the Bureau of Ethnology.

of collections made or otherwise obtained by him.[384]

In Santa Fe, at Fort Marcy, Military Headquarters of New Mexico, Stevenson gathered supplies and equipment, and arranged for transportation to Fort Wingate.

Writing to Powell from Fort Wingate on September 16, Stevenson reported that "two six mule teams left [for Zuni] yesterday with our materials." He continued:

> We have made arrangements with a gentleman to have a
> large collection made for us at the Navajo settlement &
> at the Moquis by the time we return from Zuni.[385]

The "gentleman" was Thomas Varker Keam, a trader with posts south of Fort Defiance, Arizona, and ten miles east of the Hopi villages, in a canyon known by then as "Keams Canyon." The simplicity of Stevenson's statement is hardly more than a clue to the complex relationship that would develop between the two men over the years between 1879 and James Stevenson's death in 1888, or to Keam's role in developing collections for the National Museum.

The Stevensons, Hillers, and Cushing reached Zuni on September 19. At this point, two very different stories emerge: Cushing's, as told two years later in "My Adventures in Zuni," and that of the expedition leader, James Stevenson.[386] Within a few days of their arrival, Cushing moved from the expedition camp into the house of Patricio Pino, the Zuni governor, and began his "participant-observation" of Zuni social and ceremonial life. Writing to Baird on October 15, Cushing said, "I withdrew, upon our arrival at Zuni, entirely from such work [collecting], busying myself with measurements, sketching, and note-taking."[387] For all intents, Cushing was no longer a member of the Bureau of Ethnology expedition.[388]

---

384   Baird 1880:42.

385   James Stevenson to J. W. Powell, September 16, 1879, Records of the Bureau of Ethnology, Correspondence, Letters Received, 1879-1888, National Anthropological Archives, Smithsonian Institution. Cited hereafter as LR-BE, NAA, SI.

386   Cushing 1882-1883. Stevenson's perspective is represented in his correspondence with Powell, LR-BE, NAA, SI.

387   Green, ibid, p. 43.

388   See Parezo 1985 for a portrait of Cushing as 'part of the team.'

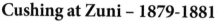

Cushing at Zuni – 1879-1881

At the time of Cushing's arrival, Zuni Pueblo had a population of ca. 1,500, concentrated in a single village, though the Zunis had begun to spread out into farming communities—Ojo Caliente, Nutria and Pescada—during the summer. As an Anglo, Cushing was not alone at the pueblo. Rev. Taylor F. Ealy, the government teacher, and his wife Mary, arrived at Zuni in October 1878, with their two small daughters, and their assistant, Susan Gates. The Ealys secured a place to live as well as a school room from Pedro Pino (Lai-iu-ah-tsai-lu), long time governor of the pueblo (1830-1878), and father of current governor Patricio Pino (Ba:lawahdiwa; Cushing's Palowahtiwa).[389] Also present were traders, William Burgess, who had been granted a license to trade at Zuni in 1877 and Douglas Dher Graham, who arrived to trade on September 1, 1879 and would remain at Zuni for the next two decades.[390] Cushing was often a dinner guest at the Ealy's home, and he found food and friendship at Graham's store. Increasingly over the next several years, Cushing was joined by family and friends. As the journalist Sylvester Baxter would remark, "there was now [fall 1882] at Zuni a considerable little American community."[391]

Cushing arrived at Zuni on September 19, 1879 and left the pueblo on April 29, 1884, a period of over four and a half years. However, the continuity of Cushing's residence at Zuni was interrupted by a three month long expedition to the Havasupai (1881), and one of two months to Hopi (1882-1883), as well as a seven month tour of the East (February 22–September 22, 1882). Intermittent illness, financial difficulties, and political conflicts created other interruptions and distractions that overlap seemingly discrete periods of fieldwork activity at Zuni.

By October 12, while Cushing was "hard at work securing the dialect and making a diagram of the town," Stevenson reported from Fort Wingate that he had filled "two large wagon loads [with] ... 1,400 specimens [that] ... filled 42 large boxes" ready for shipment east.[392] While the collection was catalogued by Cushing, and prepared for

---

389   For an account of the Ealy's stay at Zuni, see Bender 1984. For a biography of Pedro Pino, see Hart 2003.

390   See McNitt 1962:240.

391   Baxter 1883:124.

392   James Stevenson to James C. Pilling, October 12, 1879, LR-BE, NAA, SI.

shipping, Hillers completed a photographic survey of Zuni architecture in seventy 11 x 14 inch photographs, many of which were duplicated in stereographic form for use in promoting the work of the Bureau of Ethnology. On October 12, the date of Stevenson's report, Hillers went to Fort Defiance, where he made stereographic views of Navajos on an "Issue Day," and proceeded to Canyon de Chelly, where he made photographs using a huge 20 x 24 inch camera.

A week later, Stevenson reported to Pilling, "I go to Moqui & Navajo Agency where I have a six mule team load of specimens from the Navajo & Moqui Indians." Stevenson joined Hillers at Fort Defiance, and the two men continued west to Keam's trading post. Unfortunately, Stevenson's reports of October 27 and November 7 have been lost so we have no record of his transactions with Keam. However, it is important to note that Stevenson does not mention the cost of items "collected" at Hopi, nor did he submit invoices for payment. Then, and over the years to follow, Keam sent materials east on the promise or speculation he would be paid.

Meanwhile Cushing remained at Zuni observing and acquiring knowledge of the language. He would later recall, "I wandered about day by day making notes and sketches of everything I saw." On October 15, Cushing wrote to Stevenson of his desire, if not his duty, to remain at Zuni, "a solitary sojourn among these people [even though] living as I have to is not pleasant."[393] On the same date Cushing wrote to Baird,

> I regret that Col. Stevenson and I have started out with such entirely different impressions regarding my position on the Expedition. He has seen fit to regard me as a boy..." [Cushing then complained, in detail, about what little Stevenson had left for him:] "...no tent, barely half a camp kit, half a pound of sugar, a little coffee, *no* cloth, four coffee mills ... no trading material or money."[394]

More complaints regarding Stevenson's "thoughtlessness" followed.[395]

Nevertheless, Cushing went about his self-defined task of observing

393   Green, ibid, p. 43.

394   Ibid, p. 44.

395   For example, see Cushing's letters to Baird, November 24 and November 24, 1879 in Green, ibid, pp. 60-62 and 64-65.

and describing Zuni social and ceremonial life. His daily journal contains matter-of-fact accounts, e.g., the "Ho-ma-tchi" dance, October 20, 1879; his later reminiscences reveal the dramatic point of view adopted in his published accounts. More importantly we see, even in his earliest writing, the emergence of the methodology associated with his name: participant observation. On October 29, Cushing wrote to Baird:

> I do not count myself a man of as much ability as those possessed who have preceded me; but my *method* must succeed. I live among the Indians, I eat their food, and sleep in their houses. Because I will unhesitatingly plunge my hand in common with their dusty ones and dirtier children's into a great kind of hot, miscellaneous food; will sit close to [those] having neither vermin nor disease, will fondle and talk sweet Indian to their bright eyed little babies; will wear the blanket and tie the *pania* around my long hair, will look with unfeigned reverence on their beautiful and ancient ceremonies, never laughing at any absurd observance, they love me, and I learn. On account of this, the women name me *Cushi K'ok shi, Cushi Tihi Nima* (the good Cushing, the sweet Cushing) and the speakers of the dance call me (in Zuni of course) the little Capitan Cacique.[396]

Stevenson left Zuni on November 19, and at Fort Wingate he wrote to James Pilling, Powell's chief clerk, to report:

> ...I have just returned from Zuni ... & brought with me nearly a wagon load more of collections not previously obtained. I secured from the Old Church of Zuni two large images 4' high, carved out of one block of wood & the center piece of the altar representing a crown with a large heart carved on it below. Got them in the dead of night.

As to Cushing, Stevenson gives quite a different report:

> I have left Cushing at Zuni with provisions & transportation for a stay of two months, provided the Major [Powell] approves of it, if not he can come immediately.[397]

---

396   Ibid, p. 60.
397   Stevenson to Pilling, November 19, 1879, LR-BE, NAA, SI.

Stevenson's reports from the field are invariably positive; no inkling of a conflict with Cushing is ever suggested—at least not in writing. As noted above, Stevenson carried letters of introduction and General Edward Hatch, Commanding, District of New Mexico authorizing him to draw from military commissaries, at favorable government rates, food as well as materials intended for trading. The military also provided transportation for the Stevensons and for the collections assembled. Clearly Cushing's "provisions" were far from adequate and, as he would soon discover, he lacked letters of introduction.

On November 19, Stevenson also wrote to E. A. Hayt, Commission of Indian Affairs, to recommend the appointment of Keam as Indian Agent at the Moqui Pueblo Indian Agency—the first of a number of efforts on the part of the Stevensons to reciprocate for Keam's assistance and hospitality.[398]

Stevenson's departure from Fort Wingate was delayed by illness. In Santa Fe on December 11, he wrote Powell:

> I arrived here last evening not very well, but will leave for N.Y. this evening, where I will remain for a short time to consult with Dr. Hammond. I forwarded to Prof. Baird from here a list of the Moqui collection, the additional list from Zuni, & invoices for our freight from Fort Wingate to Santa Fe. I think all our things will reach W[ashington] in 10 or 15 days. The total weight of our collection is 10,512 lbs.[399]

In March 1880, U. S. Army Surgeon John Vance Lauderdale, who had been stationed at Fort Wingate from October 1874 to October 1878, was invited by Stevenson,

> to visit his collection, temporarily stored in the old U. S. Arsenal… [where] shelving has been erected on one side … enclosing a space probably 25 feet long by 15 feet wide. The shelves are placed one above the other to the height of 7 or 8 feet, and are completely filled with pottery, the

---

398   James Stevenson to E. A. Hayt, November 19, 1879, Letters Received by the Office of Indian Affairs, Records of the Bureau of Indian Affairs, National Archives. Cited hereafter as LR-OIA, NA. For Keam's efforts to attain the position of Navajo Agent, see Graves 1998:45-138.

399   Stevenson to Powell, December 11, 1879, LR-BE, NAA, SI.

smaller articles nested into the larger ones, like crockery in a crockery store. ... The collection will go into the National Museum, where it will remain as long as our nation exists, to illustrate the manners, customs, habits and arts, of a people who "have sadly passed away."

Ten days after Lauderdale's article appeared in the Hamilton, NY *Freeman,* a similar article summarizing the work of the first expedition appeared in the Washington *Evening Star.* It announced "ANOTHER EXPEDITION TO NEW MEXICO":

Major Powell contemplates an extensive exploration of this region during the coming season. As settlers pour into our country, relics of inestimable value to the scientist are destroyed or ploughed under. Foreign governments are sending American antiquities by the ship-load from our shores. Time must be taken by the forelock, or we shall have foreigners describing to us strange peoples, who once lived within our borders, of whose products they alone possess satisfactory exhibits.[400]

Cushing had no direct contact with the Stevensons until the fall of 1881 when the third Bureau of Ethnology expedition returned to Zuni. The story of Cushing's life at Zuni continues here.

On November 24, 1879, as the Stevensons returned to Santa Fe, Cushing wrote to Baird that he planned to write "a long letter detailing my journey here, and some of the more interesting features in the life of these people ... design[ed] for publication..." He felt "inclined to thus popularly publish something since I learn that two at least, if not several, letters have appeared in the East from the pen of Mrs. Stevenson."[401] In fact, there is no record of publication in any form by Matilda Stevenson that might have preempted Cushing's efforts. In the same letter, Cushing reported James Stevenson had left him with only twenty dollars, given a large part of Cushing's rations to Ealy, and failed to pay the rent on the

---

400   James [i.e., Matilda] Stevenson Scrapbook, Archive 91 JSS 000, Laboratory of Anthropology, Museum of New Mexico.

401   Green op. cit., p. 64. Matilda Stevenson collected newspaper articles regarding the first four Bureau of Ethnology expeditions. None of the articles are by her. A pamphlet, "Zuni and the Zunians, by Tilly E. Stevenson," was privately published in 1881.

large room he had taken for the season. Nevertheless, Cushing closed his letter by saying, "I neither murmur, nor do I complain of Colonel Stevenson…"[402]

Three days later, Cushing received the news from Baird that he would be "enabled to remain here a couple of months longer." In his reply to Baird, Cushing wrote:

> While nothing short of an absolutely perfect knowledge of the Zuni language will enable me to make an exhaustive monograph of the people *internally*, the entire amount of time which you kindly see fit to permit me to spend here will enable me to make a complete *descriptive* report and a passable one on their institutions, political, religious and other…[403]

It is all too easy to see Cushing's distinction between internal vs. descriptive as comparable to the twentieth century debates over emic (explanations of the behavior or ideology of members of a culture according to indigenous definitions, the "native's model") vs. etic (descriptions based on external, universal models rather than those that are culture specific). Be that as it may, there is in Cushing's work a pioneering effort to describe the world of the Zuni from the inside.

Soon after writing Baird, Cushing made two trips into the Zuni Mountains, east and north of Zuni. As he would later report to Powell,

> During the month of December [1879] I explored, with the loss of my mule and consequent great *suffering*, the Zuni Mountains, in search of the ancient green-stone and turquoise mines of which the Indians had told me, but the location of which they refused to reveal to me. These were found, sketches and plans made of them, and a brief epistolary report concerning them was forwarded to Professor Baird.[404]

In his report of January 11, 1880 to Baird, following the expedition, Cushing concluded,

> The sole material result of this trip was the acquisition of some ancient wooden picks, samples of the paint and

---

402   Ibid, pp. 64-65. Emphasis added.
403   Ibid, p. 65. Emphasis added.
404   Ibid, p. 66.

accompanying materials, and one or two of the stones referred to. I was compelled from want of transportation to leave other specimens behind.[405]

As will become increasingly evident, the Zunis' secrecy, Cushing's suffering, and the lack of trading materials and transportation are frequent topics of his letters and reports. By the end of the month, he again wrote to Baird this time suggesting Stevenson had "designed" to provide no more aid than was officially necessary, adding to his expenses by not furnishing "the proper papers for identifying me with the Expedition of which I once believed myself to be a member."[406] In reply Baird wrote he would talk to Powell about "your troubles."

In a long letter to Baird, December 24, 1879, Cushing outlined plans for travel to "Oraibi in the Province of Tusayan," requested shells and other materials for trade and revealed more of his method of participant observation:

> With the partial acquisition of the Zuni language, and the entire adoption of their costume and habits of life, I have not only opened an easy way to their more obscure relations but also have overcome that superstitious prejudice with which all observers of savage life have most to contend.[407]

His admirer, the Dutch anthropologist Herman ten Kate, described Cushing's "costume" as "part Indian, part fantasy."[408] Far more important for the success of his field work was the "conversational knowledge of the language of the Zunis" he was acquiring.[409]

In February 1880, Cushing wrote to a friend, "You do not know how much I have suffered this winter," apparently in reference to an attack of pneumonia that continued to leave him "very much prostrated" until April, and there is a break in his correspondence, at least with Baird and Powell. On May 5, Cushing wrote to Baird to again request materials appropriate for trading: shells and "*blue* (turquoise shade) and

---

405   Ibid, p. 89.

406   Ibid, p. 85.

407   Ibid, pp 85-86.

408   Kate 2000: 277. Ten Kate visited Cushing in 1883. See Ladd 1994:31-31 for a Zuni's view of Cushing's costume.

409   According to Zuni anthropologist Edmund J. Ladd, "Cushing's rendition of the Zuni language is terrible." Ibid, pp. 31 and 35, n. 8.

green stone material, imitation or the genuine." As he explained, "Little would get *much* of the kind of material which Mrs. and Col. Stevenson collected…" And in the same letter, he wrote:

> I have always made my paramount duty here in Zuni that of collecting not material but data, yet always, when the opportunity presented, have gotten together what I could toward filling up some of the gaps in our collection.[410]

Although there is little correspondence from Cushing during the early months of 1880, in the draft of a lengthy report to Baird and Powell, composed between February 18 and April 13, he outlined fifteen areas "which appear to me open for research to a future student in Zuni." At this date Cushing assumes he would soon be returning to Washington, and is outlining all he would seek to accomplish during a return visit. His research proposal begins:

> First, then, among the objects of extended residence among the Zunis would be the acquisition of the language, as essential to all the following:
>
> Second, the recording, in the original language and with faithful translation, of the industrial and art formulae;
>
> Third, [the recording] of the "Ancient Talks" (*i-no-ti pe-ie-we*) or religious instructions for ceremonies, dances, etc. and of prayers and songs;
>
> Fourth, the collecting of a vast amount of material (costumes, altars, masks, wands, etc. etc.) illustrative of this study;
>
> Fifth, study of the plume sticks with collecting of a series…[411]

In the spring of 1880, the government teacher, Rev. Taylor F. Ealy, wrote several letters concerning the 1877 Executive Order Zuni Indian Reservation to his immediate supervisor, Ben Thomas, United States Indian Agent for the Pueblos in New Mexico. On February 28, 1877—before either the Ealys or Cushing arrived at Zuni—Thomas had written to the Commissioner of Indian Affairs of the need for a reservation:

> The Pueblos of Zuni, like the other eighteen Pueblos

---

410   Green, ibid, pp. 93, 92.
411   Ibid, p. 104.

of this Agency, have a land-grant from the Spanish Government, but unlike those of most of the other Pueblos, the Zuni grant is nearly worthless, and if the Zuni Indians were restricted to their grant, they could not possibly maintain themselves nor their stock, consisting as it does of a sand-bed two leagues square. These Indians have hitherto supported themselves by farming outlying arable lands at or near … "Nutrias," "Ojo Pescado," and "Ojo Caliente," and many small patches of land on the course of the stream [i.e., the Zuni River]. … The Indians have held and farmed it from time immemorial and have firmly believed, and still believe, that it belongs to them; but now as the country settles up, they are being crowded more and more, year by year, and if some protection is not guaranteed them, they will soon lose their only means of subsistence.[412]

Zuni land use extended far beyond Thomas's portrayal.[413] On March 16, 1877, "a reservation for the use and occupation of the Zuni Pueblo Indians," was established by order of President R. B. Hayes. It had immediate and far-ranging consequences for the Zuni. Thomas at once informed Pedro Pino, the Zuni Governor, that the tribe no longer could control their sacred salt lake as they had since aboriginal times. Two years later, soon after his arrival at the pueblo, Ealy (who Cushing acknowledged as the "local Ag't of Zuni") was approached by Pino who expressed a number of concerns regarding their lands.[414] On February 21, Ealy wrote to agent Thomas, and requested a survey of the Zuni reservation to determine the exact location of its boundaries. On March 6, Ealy wrote again, this time recommending "the extension of the Zuni grant to cover the salt lake on the south side thereof as desired by the Indians." Ten days later, Thomas informed Ealy there were no funds available for a survey of the Zuni reservation. On April 20, undoubtedly at Pino's insistence, Ealy wrote another letter this time recommending the annexation of "a certain tract of land [the location of a spring and the Zuni farming village at Nutria] to the Zuni reserve" and enclosed the names of "officers…desiring the

---

412   Hart 2003:105.
413   See Ferguson and Hart 1985 for maps of traditional Zuni land use.
414   Green, ibid, p. 92.

additional territory as described." One of the officers was Major William F. Tucker, son-in-law of powerful Senator John A. Logan of Illinois and friend of James Stevenson, who was part owner of a cattle ranch adjacent to Nutria. In the spring of 1880, Cushing was not involved in the Nutria land claim controversy, a controversy that would play a role in bringing his fieldwork at Zuni to an end.

Although Cushing was undoubtedly aware of Pino's concerns, there is, with one exception, nothing in his surviving correspondence to suggest he took an active role in addressing the problems created by the boundaries drawn for the 1877 reservation until several years later. Writing as "an officer of the Int[erior] Dept., Washington, D.C., and as a vindicator of the legal rights of the Zuni Nation," Cushing did become involved in land claims of two Zuni individuals in April 1880, at the same time Ealy was addressing the larger issues.[415] Needless to say, Cushing was not an officer of the Interior Department, as the bravado of his letter would suggest. However, as "a vindicator of the legal rights of the Zuni Nation," nothing could have had more immediate importance than control of the sacred salt lake to the south or the lands around Nutria, concerns Pino took to Ealy, not Cushing.

Throughout the spring and early summer of 1880, Cushing's letters, reports and diary describe his continued observation and participation in Zuni daily life, as well as his explorations in the surrounding area. In a report to Powell, written two years later, Cushing said,

> During [this time] I continued my investigations into the mythology, traditions, and ecclesiastical as well as governmental institutions of the Indians and explored many of the traditional ruins within a radius of fifty miles of Zuni. Before the close of the year, I had so far acquired knowledge of the Zuni language as to take an important position in the councils and was made Chief Councilor of the nation. This increased knowledge also enabled me to learn traditions bearing on historic matters.[416]

But underneath the surface, Cushing continued to voice various complaints to Baird and others. For example, in a letter to Baird written on June 18:

---

415   Ibid, pp. 91-92.
416   Ibid, p. 110.

[Were it not] for the ethnologic interest which it still has for me, my exile here, [owing to] the superstitious character of the natives, the desert character of the country, and absence of all vegetable substance from my diet, as well as the stale character of the flesh and utter flatulency of most Zuni cereal preparations, [would be] absolutely unbearable.

He goes on to express his gratitude for Baird and Powell's approval of his remaining at Zuni. A month later, he would again write of "the isolated and at times intensely suffering life which I lead here."[417] Nevertheless, Cushing's diaries make frequent mention of his friend Graham and the hospitality of the Ealys, of Zuni ceremonial life and of his continuing exploration of ruins in the area.

On July 12, the Pueblo Indian Agent, Ben Thomas, came to Zuni to pick up four children who, with Cushing's assistance, were being sent to the recently established Carlisle Indian Training School in Pennsylvania. Because Indian names were not used at Carlisle, the children were given the names Taylor F. Ealy, Mary E. Ealy, Jennie Hammaker, and Frank Cushing.[418]

At Fort Wingate, on October 2, Cushing met John H. Sullivan, Jeremiah Sullivan's father, who was on his way to assume the duties of agent for the Hopis.

While at the fort, Cushing wrote in his diary:

Quartermaster sergeant called my attention to a letter from General Sherman entitling me to commissaries. It was received on the 19th of May. How much I have *suffered* for want of knowledge of this. I learned that Col. Stafford had *designedly* kept me from a knowledge of this.[419]

Three weeks later, on October 28, Capt. Washington Matthews, Assistant Surgeon, United States Army, arrived at Fort Wingate.[420] By

---

417 William Jones Rhees to Cushing, July 24, 1880; quoted in Green, ibid, p. 118.

418 Bender 1984:140:140-141, 212 n.18. Education was a key part of the Grant "peace policy." See Chapter 1 for the early history of Federal Indian policy It was Cushing's hope that his name-sake, the Zuni Frank Cushing, would return and assist him in his research.

419 Green, ibid, p. 128. Emphasis added.

420 See below, The Stevensons and Washington Matthews, for a brief account of his career.

February of the following year Cushing would describe him as "an esteemed friend and collaborator."[421] Matthews became one of Cushing's strongest supporters and, perhaps only coincidentally, he was recalled to Washington within weeks of Cushing in 1884.

At about the same time, Cushing became involved in a series of incidents involving Navajos, whose horses were threatening Zuni wheat fields near Nutria. In an undated note, Cushing wrote:

> ...I have constantly warned them ... in council and out, that should they persist I would shoot their sheep, horses or oxen. I therefore, in the hope of luring the herd away, cut off by a pistol shot some of the tail of one of the horses in this band, as the Navajos had sent word I was a liar and had told the Zunis I was afraid to do anything with them or their stock.[422]

As will become clear below, if Cushing was successful in deterring Navajo incursions into Zuni farmlands on this occasion, on another his actions resulted in an investigation ultimately involving the office of the Commissioner of Indian Affairs.

Throughout the fall of 1880, Cushing continued his observations of Zuni life as evidenced by brief notes in his daily journal regarding an annual Shalako ceremony. In December, he complied with a request from Powell to make a census of Zuni. At this point, he had been at Zuni for a full year, purposefully engaging in a new form of ethnology. He took an opportunity in writing to L. W. Ledyard, an early admirer and supporter in Medina, New York, to reflect on his experience:

> It has been months since I left Washington to enter into researches among the Pueblo Indians of Zuni and to investigate the archaeology both of traditional and prehistoric connections in this paradise of ethnography, the great Southwest.
>
> ... For many months my suffering and loneliness were dreadful. ... The Indians were all my masters... By policy and patience I won, in long months, their confidence, respect and esteem, gained authority over them, and

---

421   Ibid, p. 148.
422   Ibid, p. 129.

with the acquisition of their language, became their chief councilor, so that at present the table is turned and I am *their master*... I am on the eve of departure for the exploration of some very interesting caves in Arizona, in which I hope to discover the rarest treasures of ancient art...[423]

Soon after writing to Ledyard, Cushing left for Arizona for three weeks, the last week of December 1880 and the first two weeks of January 1881. He made the trip with burros with the intent of visiting a series of ruins, sites the Zunis referred to in some of their traditions, and collect pottery and other materials. Some fifteen miles south of the town of St. Johns, Arizona, Cushing reported finding caverns "which had been used by the ancestors of the Zunis as sacrificial depositories."[424] In the caves he found numerous well-preserved sacred objects. After returning to Zuni, he went directly to Fort Wingate with a portion of the materials, which he catalogued there and prepared for shipment. In a letter to Baird and Powell, dated January 13, Cushing gave a detailed account of this expedition, with descriptions of many of the sacred objects he found. In all, he gathered "two large coffee-sacks full of relics."

Many years later, perhaps in the late 1890s, Cushing added some recollections to his "Catalogue of Prehistoric Zuni and Cave Remains":

Collected in the Spring of 1880 [1881] and later forwarded to Professor Spencer F. Baird in two lots, the first lot comprising a selected dozen objects sent by hand of Mr. Charles Kirchner, the second lot sent by freight in two 3 x 4 boxes, from Fort Wingate—catalogue and descriptive letters accompanying—with various other ancient and a few choice modern specimens.

After describing where he had located the materials, Cushing continued:

It may be imagined that the dear-bought relics I brought up were precious to me, aside from their unique archaeologic valuation. But if precious then, they were rendered doubly so when, discovered by Zunis, I was

---

423   Ibid, pp. 136-137; emphasis in the original. It was Ledyard who introduced Cushing to Baird.

424   Ibid, p. 140.

compelled to take them to their pueblo, lay them out to the east in a council chamber and undergo a trial as for sorcery by the tribunal of the entire secret priesthood of the tribe—saved only by the uninjured condition of the specimens—by the evidence therein of my "gentle and reverential handling" of them.

In the course of the trial, each particular object was minutely examined and commented upon... The object of this careful examination was the identification of such of the sacred objects as could on no account leave the custody of the priests. About a dozen of these objects were thus selected to serve as tribal relics, and were taken away from me, alas! The remainder, however, were ultimately yielded up to me in recognition less of my pleadings than in "token of the will of the Beloved gods as manifest in my escape alive from the "Hole of Descent" and in my loving care of the relics.[425]

With the exception of these two lots of materials sent during the spring of 1880 [i.e., 1881], there is little information regarding what—*if anything*—Cushing collected and forwarded for the National Museum. Fiscal records, for example, indicate all materials collected at Zuni between 1879 and 1884 were acquired by purchase from Thomas V. Keam or through trade with materials Stevenson brought. In spite of his on-going fiscal difficulties, there were no vouchers submitted by Cushing for collections or for shipping materials. As will become evident below, Cushing did continue to "collect" during his years at Zuni but much of this material he intended to sell as his debts to local traders continued to grow.

In the *Second Annual Report of the Bureau of Ethnology* Powell reported that sometime during the spring of 1881:

> [Cushing] again set out for the cave country, with one soldier and a citizen, re-exploring not only the caverns before visited but also other important grottos on the Rio Concho, and the caves still used for sacrificial depositories by the Zunis, near La Laguna del Colorado Chiquito, north of San Juan [St. Johns]. The collections,

---

425   Ibid, p. 344.

the greater portions of which were cached, aggregated over two thousand specimens.[426]

More details are provided by Cushing in a letter to Baird dated March 12:

> With regard to collections, I have on hand…five or six hundred ancient pieces which I have brought home, at the expense of walking, on our burros. … I am supplied with no transportation, nor with authority for commanding such as Mr. Stevenson had at his disposal…
>
> [As a consequence] I have cached at one of the caves more than a thousand specimens, at another five hundred, and at a third a trifle more than the later.[427]

Cushing acknowledged he could take advantage of transportation provided by the War Department. However, he added,

> I might secure the boxes and lumber (entirely lacking here of course) for packing such collections, from the Post [Wingate], had I the proper papers, but it still would be necessary to have transportation from the latter place to this, as well as from here to there. … It is not only expensive but very dangerous to transport such things on horse-back, and it would be quite impossible thus to carry the collecting and investigations at these places [e.g., shrines] much further.

Cushing continued,

> The Indians have only within the past ten days consented to my collecting any of the paraphernalia of their sacred dances, or of the ancient trophies of their tribe.[428]

For whatever reason, Cushing delayed shipment of the materials he had cached. A year and a half later, on November 10, 1883, the weekly newspaper, *Orion Era* (St. Johns, Arizona), reported the discovery by J. S. Harris of "crockery-wear, beads, ear rings and other curiosities" in a cave, and their purchase by the traders J. L. Hubbell of St. Johns and W. B. Leonard from near Navajo Station, Arizona. Cushing wrote immediately to Keam, reporting the loss of the cached materials. Keam shared the letter

---

426   Powell 1883:xxviii; Green, ibid, p. 140.
427   Green, ibid, p. 150.
428   Ibid.

with A. M. Stephen, who replied, suggesting the newspaper might have used more vivid headlines: "The Ravishment of Cushing's Cave" or "The Vandals Raid on Cushing's Treasure." Stephen said the report "was very funny—but at the same time, to tell you the truth, it was very mortifying." Keam had offered to market the pottery and other materials Cushing had cached, a point Stephen emphasized in saying, "May the mortified *manes* of the pre-Columbian potters haunt you and destroy your slumber for—until you come over here and reach absolution."[429] The fate of the materials Cushing cached in other caves is not known. Anthropologist Nancy Parezo gives no documentation for her claim that Victor Mindeleff came to Zuni with packing materials to send the materials Cushing had looted to the National Museum.[430] Neither Mindeleff's correspondence nor the annual reports of the Bureau of Ethnology and the Smithsonian Institution provide any information regarding the cached materials, except to note that at a later date Victor Mindeleff made photographs of the materials purchased by J. L. Hubbell.

On his return from the expedition to Arizona, Cushing sent a piece of pottery to Matthews, acknowledged in a letter to Cushing:

> I have got your sacred pot and will take the best care of it. Is it one of the sacred pots you found in the cave, or is it the promised facsimile thereof?[431]

The question Matthews posed is interesting, as throughout his career Cushing's ability to create facsimiles of various artifacts led to praise as well as repeated accusations of fraud.[432]

At Fort Wingate six weeks later, on March 24, Matthews reported an event that, over the months and years to follow, would bring extraordinary changes to western New Mexico and across northern Arizona:

> For the 1st time a locomotive–at the head of a construction train–comes in sight from the post, and is seen from the porches of the officers' quarters.[433]

---

429 Stephen to Cushing, December 15, 1883. Ibid, p. 312. Keam had offered to include Cushing's collection with the material he was preparing to offer to the Smithsonian Institution. See Chapter 6 for more details.
430 Parezo 1985:767.
431 Matthews to Cushing, December 14, 1881. Green, ibid, p. 148.
432 Wilcox 2003 defends Cushing's "veracity."
433 Washington Matthews, March 24, 1881, Fort Wingate, 1880-1884, vol. 820, Medical Histories of Posts, RG 94, National Archives.

By the fall of 1882, the Atlantic and Pacific Railroad had laid tracks across northern Arizona, and a series of towns were established including Holbrook, Winslow, and Flagstaff.

Throughout the early months of 1881 Cushing continued work on the census of Zuni designed by Powell. However, in a long letter of March 12 he assured Baird,

> By night I am as busy with my more proper pursuits. I am making more rapid progress in the study of the *inner life* of these wonderful savages…[434]

In the same letter, Cushing mentions an invitation "directly from this people (the *Kuh'-ni-kwe*) [Havasupai] to visit them," an adventure that would take Cushing away from Zuni from late June until the middle of September. However, other events of importance took place in the meantime.

On April 27, Lieutenant John Gregory Bourke met Cushing at Fort Wingate. Bourke had been aide-de-camp to Brigadier General George Cook during the Apache wars of the 1870s. Earlier in 1881, he had met with Powell and other staff with the Bureau of Ethnology in Washington, but decided to get U. S. Army support for his research projects among various American Indian groups, including the Pine Ridge Sioux in South Dakota, who he visited during their Sun Dance ceremony, and the Hopi, at the time of the Snake Dance both later in 1881. In April, he was on his way to Fort Defiance to continue research among the Navajo. Bourke recorded in his diary,

> During our brief tarry at Fort Wingate, I had the great pleasure of making the acquaintance of Mr. Cushing, of the Smithsonian Institute, who has been living among the Zuni Indians since last summer. … Cushing is a man of intelligence, persistency and enthusiasm, just the character to carry to a successful conclusion the mission he has undertaken.[435]

A month later, Bourke returned to Fort Wingate and found Cushing at Matthews's residence. Over the course of two days, the two men discussed "our S. W. Indians and their customs." Bourke found Cushing "to be the most intelligent ethnologist I have ever encountered." In his diary, he added, "we have arranged to go together to the Moqui

---

434   Green, ibid, p. 151, emphasis in the original.
435   Bloom 1937:94.

[Hopi] villages, to witness the 'rattle-snake dance' which comes off in August."[436]

During his return to the east, Bourke wrote articles praising Cushing published in the *Omaha Herald* and the *Chicago Times*.[437] Also at Fort Wingate during Bourke's visit were Sylvester Baxter, special correspondent for the *Boston Herald,* and Willard Metcalf, an artist on the staff of *Harper's Magazine,* both on assignment to the West. Baxter soon published an article on the "wonderful achievements of Frank H. Cushing" in the *Boston Herald*.[438] A year later in "The Father of the Pueblos," an article published in *Harper's New Monthly Magazine,* Baxter wrote a description of Cushing:

> At Fort Wingate … while sitting in the officers' club-room one warm afternoon, we saw a striking figure walking across the parade ground: a slender young man in a picturesque costume; a high-crowned and broad-brimmed felt hat above long blonde hair and prominent features; face, figure, and general aspect looked as if he might have stepped out of the frame of a cavalier's portrait of the time of King Charles.[439]

Metcalf would become Cushing's admirer; Baxter became his promoter and supporter.

In May, Cushing received a scalp from Dr. H. C. Yarrow of the Surgeon General's Office, a prerequisite to his initiation into the "Priesthood of the Bow" that would take place in the fall.

In the meantime, Cushing was making preparations for his expedition to the Havasupai. A letter to Baird, written from "Camp Waterless, Mesa Prieta, Arizona" on May 12, indicated Cushing was not only "devoid…of that melancholy spirit which has heretofore haunted me so much," he felt "greatly encouraged" by the recognition and support he had recently received from Baird and Powell, as well as the military at Fort Wingate, notably "Dr. Matthews and General [Luther P.]

---

436 Bourke attended the Snake Dance at Walpi, as reported in Bourke 1884. Cushing did not attend as he was on his return to Zuni from his expedition to the Havasupai.

437 Robinson 2013:50-54.

438 Baxter 1881.

439 Hinsley and Wlcox 1996:66.

Bradley," in command at the fort. Bradley had provided Cushing with a soldier who "accompanies me as assistant without pay."[440] In addition, Cushing had met Lieutenant W. W. Wotherspoon, post adjutant and quartermaster at Fort Whipple, Arizona, who suggested a letter from Baird to General O. B. Wilcox, post commander, would assure Cushing of transportation and other support during his visit to the Havasupai. Elsewhere in his letter to Baird, Cushing continued his critical allusions to the Stevensons:

> Harry [Biddle, a young staff member at the Smithsonian Institution, who had expressed an interest in joining Cushing] is an *honest* boy, and it requires more honesty than has qualified those who have hitherto entered this field to do...
>
> I am glad to say that I am popular with all the officers and their ladies at Fort Wingate, save only one [W. F. Tucker, son-in-law of Senator Logan, long-time friend of the Stevensons, who was involved in the conflict over Zuni lands at Nutria]. ... It is an unwise policy in a scientific expedition to be accompanied by supernumeraries [Matilda Coxe Stevenson]—especially when these develop malicious influences toward any of the proper officers of such expedition [i.e., Cushing himself].[441]

Before turning to Cushing's expedition to the Havasupai, brief mention is to be made of several events that took place while he was away. Shortly before leaving his position at Zuni, Ealy wrote to Thomas complaining that Cushing was interfering with the school. How he was interfering was not explained. Rev. Samuel A. Bentley replaced Ealy as government teacher, arriving at Zuni on July 18. Matthews met Bentley and immediately wrote to Cushing calling Ealy's successor "one of those cadaverous sky-pilots who wear a stereotyped smile on their faces."[442] On July 22, the Zuni boy given the name "Frank Cushing" died at Carlisle Indian School. It fell to Bentley to inform the parents, a task he postponed for nearly two months.

---

440   Green, ibid, p. 153.
441   Ibid.
442   Ibid, p. 174.

Cushing's Expedition to the Havasupai - 1881

Cushing left Zuni in mid-June accompanied by Titskematse, an acculturated Cheyenne Indian, and Tsai-iu-tsaih-ti-wa, a Zuni guide. Titskematse had attended Hampton Institute in Virginia and had assisted Cushing during the summer of 1879 as an informant on Cheyenne sign language. In May, when Baird sent Titskematse west to assist Cushing, he was on the staff of the Carlisle Indian School.

The party traveled the well-established trail to the northwest reaching the Hopi First Mesa villages on June 22. Cushing stayed in Hano (Tewa) for five days. He met with Agent John H. Sullivan and his son Jeremiah at the Moqui Pueblo Indian Agency, and was joined on First Mesa by the younger Sullivan for a "long talk" and tour of Walpi. Cushing asked his host, the Hopi-Tewa Pulakakai (Polacca), to join him for the trip to Havasupai.[443] The party, now four in number, visited Oraibi then continued west before descending Cataract Canyon, to the fields and homes of the Kuh'ni (Havasupai) which they reached on July 4. Cushing stayed in the canyon for six days, much of the time spent in the company of a miner, Harvey Sample. At the time of Cushing's visit, the Yuman-speaking Havasupai had a population of 214. Because ranchers and miners were beginning to encroach on traditional Havasupai hunting-gathering and agricultural areas, a reservation had been established in 1880. Nevertheless, the Havasupai were still living essentially under aboriginal conditions.[444] In his daily journal, Cushing often records "busy with writing," "spent day in writing," etc., the results of which would be published a year later in the *Atlantic Monthly* magazine as "The Nation of the Willows."[445] Cushing's notes and published account of his expedition represent the only detailed account of the Havasupai before rapid cultural changes began to take place only a few years later. Cushing made collections and sketches (apparently lost) but acknowledged "Inner life not to be investigated without study of language."[446]

On July 8, Pulakakai and Tsaiiutsaitiwa left for the Hopi villages and Zuni while Cushing and Titskematse, now accompanied by Sample,

---

443   See Chapter 3 for a biography of Polacca.
444   Euler in Cushing 1965:5.
445   Cushing 1882b.
446   Green, ibid, p. 171. Note: Cushing spent less than a week with the Havasupai.

began their trip south. On July 16 they reached Rogers Ranch, an Atlantic and Pacific Railroad construction camp, where they learned of the attempted assassination of President Garfield on July 2. Cushing wrote in his daily journal:

> Shocking. I wish I could see Joe [Joseph Stanley Brown], as he is now the President's private secretary.[447]

Three days later, Cushing reached Fort Whipple, near Prescott, Arizona. In his correspondence with Baird and Matthews, nothing is reported regarding his lengthy stay at Fort Whipple which was extended until the end of August. Cushing returned to Zuni on September 16—a three month absence from the pueblo.

In the meantime, Matthews wrote to Cushing to report the return of James Stevenson to Fort Wingate on August 2. Stevenson was on his way to Zuni with Victor Mindeleff, who would make maps and sketches for a model of Zuni pueblo.[448] Stevenson's party of Bureau of Ethnology and USGS employees had taken the Atlantic and Pacific Railroad, as did Bourke who returned to Fort Wingate three days later. Bourke, with the artist Peter Moran, were on their way to the Hopi villages to witness the Snake Dance at Walpi. In his diary Bourke wrote:

> We remained at Fort Wingate all day, laid in subsistence supplies to last us for fifteen days, and sent an ambulance and four mules ahead… Met my friend, Tom Keam [who accompanied Bourke to the Snake Dance].[449]

Bourke and Moran returned to Fort Wingate on September 4. On September 22, news of President Garfield's death reached Fort Wingate.

In a letter to Baird, written on September 24, Cushing announced the beginning of what he would later call "the most interesting chapter of my Zuni life."[450] Cushing reported on his return from Fort Whipple,

> …after a severe journey—four days of it through country raided by Apaches… This…enabled me to secure a scalp, which, with the ones furnished by my father and

---

447 Ibid, p. 173. Daily journal for July 18, 1882.
448 See Chapter 5 for biographies of the Mindeleffs and accounts of their field work with the Bureau of Ethnology expeditions.
449 Bourke 2013:240.
450 Cushing 1882-1883:(26): 29.

Dr. Yarrow, enabled me ... entrance into the Order of the *Apithlan Shiwani*, or Priests of the Bow...[451]

For Cushing this meant he could progress "further with the study of the secret religious institutions which, without membership, are barred even from the Zunis."[452] In his autobiographical "My Adventures in Zuni" Cushing provides a detailed and dramatic account of his initiation as a Bow Priest but leaves a number of questions without answers. In going through "country raided by Apaches," did Cushing kill an Apache Indian and take a scalp? Cushing explains why he wanted to become a Bow Priest, but what interest did the Zunis have in making him a Bow Priest? In "The Zuni Social, Mythic, and Religious Systems," a lecture Cushing gave in the spring of 1882, he described the Zuni religious organization as having sacred and secular components. Supreme over all was the priest, "cacique of the sun or Pekwina," who was concerned with sacred, internal religious aspects of Zuni life. The Bow Priests appointed the secular leaders of the village, the governor and his council, and concerned themselves with the external secular problems facing the pueblo. It is not surprising that Zunis saw in Cushing an intermediary who could protect the sacred and secular interests of the community. As "1st War Chief of Zuni" and "Commander of the Zuni People," Cushing was soon in conflict with missionaries (Ealy and Bentley), other anthropologists (the Stevensons), army officers and politicians (the "Logan affair")[453] as well as Navajos, Mormons, Hispanics, etc. For now, Cushing could tell Baxter,

> ...it is not an American who writes to you now. It is a *Zuni* by right of his 'clanship with the Parrots,' his 'sonship of the Eagles,' his 'birth from the Sun' and the *Kiapin-a-bai*, his membership in the 'Order of the Bow,' and his sacred position as 'Junior Priest of the Bow,' and secular status as Commander of the *A-shi-wi*. Surely the gods have favored me [draft of an undated letter but

---

451   Green, ibid, p. 178.

452   Ibid, pp. 178-179; see also Cushing's letter to Baxter, ibid, p. 181. Ladd 1994:32 offers a Zuni's perspective on Cushing's initiation, suggesting it was much less than Cushing claimed.

453   Discussed below.

undoubtedly written in October 1881][454]

Cushing's initiation into the Priesthood of the Bow occupied sixteen days, beginning shortly after his return from Havasupai.

While at Fort Whipple, Cushing began preparations for a trip to the East as is evident from his letter of October 12 to Baird:

> I have decided to ask your permission for my return in January [1882] with four or five Indians to Washington, and with this in view, I have begun negotiations for securing free passage for myself and my party via Omaha and Chicago. ... Some of my enthusiastic friends in the two cities mentioned will aid me strongly; and the ladies of Boston have extended cordial invitations to me, to bring my party on, if not to Boston, as far East as New York and Washington, promising their aid, etc.[455]

Cushing saw this as an opportunity to advance his work at Zuni. Moreover, "through the promised aid of Col. Stevenson[!] ... this scheme ... would aid immensely in popularizing—not more mine than his own part of the ethnographic work."[456]

The Second Bureau of Ethnology Expedition - 1880

The second Bureau of Ethnology expedition under James Stevenson was delayed by the illness of Matilda Stevenson ("my wife's misfortune"). Stevenson used the time to lobby, and letters supporting the work of the Bureau were received from Representative James W. Singleton as well as from General John A. Logan, Senator, both from Illinois. He also purchased trade goods: imitation coral for Cushing, and "$103 worth" for Thomas V. Keam "in part payment of our last year's indebtedness to him."[457]

It was not until the first of September that the party arrived in Santa Fe. Accompanying James Stevenson were J. K. Hillers, photographer; F. G. Galbraith and F. W. Morancy, "ethnologic assistants;" and his wife,

---

454   Ibid, p. 182.
455   Ibid, p. 180. Cushing does not identify the "ladies of Boston"; Mary Hemenway, later his benefactor, is not mentioned in any of his correspondence during his years at Zuni, 1879-1884.
456   Ibid, pp. 180-181.
457   Stevenson to Powell, September 18, 1880, LR-BE, NAA, SI.

Matilda. They reached Santa Fe by the Atchinson, Topeka and Santa Fe Railroad which had completed rail construction to the territorial capital in February 1880. The Exchange Hotel on the plaza served as a base of operations over the next several months as Stevenson's party visited sixteen Rio Grande Pueblos, from north to south, from Taos to Isleta.

Powell budgeted $4,000 for the 1880 expedition to the Southwest. By October 22, $1,400 of the $2,000 budgeted for the Pueblo expedition had been expended. A week earlier, Stevenson sent a telegram to James C. Pilling, Chief Clerk and now Disbursing Agent for the Bureau, to report "am seriously delayed for want of money." Meanwhile Stevenson wired his father-in-law who sent funds. Elaborate paperwork requirements and salaries in arrears were often the subject of Stevenson's letters east.[458] As historian Michael J. Lawson has carefully documented, although Stevenson brought "trade goods" to barter, most of Stevenson's acquisitions were purchases made with "bags of silver" he had obtained on his arrival in Santa Fe in September.[459] Adolph Bandelier, who Stevenson first met at Cochiti and later visited in Santa Fe, wrote in his journal, "I find that Stevenson has bought nearly all the stone axes in town [Santa Fe]. Easy manner of collecting for the Smithsonian Institution."[460]

Other areas of field work were less problematic. Stevenson carried letters of introduction and, as in 1879, General Edward Hatch, Commanding, District of New Mexico, authorized him to draw from military commissaries, at favorable government rates, food and other materials intended as gifts for pueblo leaders (soap, candles, tea, coffee, tobacco) as well as providing transportation.[461]

Stevenson, Morancy, and Galbraith reached Taos Pueblo on September 2. For transportation, "General Hatch kindly furnished us with two spring wagons and a six mule team and two men, with an order for forage." He added, "Also tents, axes and other camp equipage."[462] Stevenson was disappointed in the material acquired at

---

458 Lawson, ibid, pp. 75-76.
459 Lawson's discovery of the fiscal records of the Bureau of Ethnology for the second through the sixth field seasons has greatly enriched our understanding of the economics of the Bureau's field research as well as the movement of field parties.
460 Lange and Riley, eds, 1966:181.
461 Lawson, ibid, p. 61.
462 Stevenson to Powell, September 2, 1880, LR-BE, NAA, SI.

Taos: "comparatively nothing in the way of aboriginal production is to be found amongst them."[463] Meanwhile, Hillers made photographs of the village, including a panoramic view, a triptych of three 11 x 14 inch images. He also made photographs of prominent individuals, often paying one dollar per pose, a procedure he would follow in many of the sixteen Rio Grande villages the party visited.

In early October they moved on to San Juan Pueblo, then Santa Clara, where Stevenson acquired "two or three hundred" polishing stones used in pottery making as well as "a number of interesting stone implements, nearly all of an older kind than any made by the people at the present day."[464] In a lengthy report to Powell, Stevenson wrote an account of the process of making Santa Clara black pottery.[465] He then turned to the highlight of the field season:

> Almost 12 miles from Santa Clara we discovered what I
> believe to be one of the most important and extensive cliff
> habitations in the South-west—it is not only extensive,
> but peculiar in character, and essentially different from
> any yet known.

The "discovery" was the cave dwellings and ruins at Puye, which the Santa Clara Indians had long considered the home of their ancestors:

> In the faces of these cliffs [composed of a yellowish
> volcanic tufa], we found an immense number of cavate
> dwellings, cut out by the hand of man. We made no
> attempt to count the number of these curious dwellings,
> dug like hermit cells out of the rock, but they may be
> estimated with safety among the thousands. ... They
> are excavated with rude stone implements resembling
> adzes, numbers of which were found here, and which
> were probably used by fastening one end to a handle.
> ... Upon the top of the mesa of which these cliffs are
> the exposed sides we found the ruins of large circular
> buildings made of square stones 8 by 12 inches in size. ...

---

463 Quoted in Lawson, ibid, p. 63.

464 Stevenson to Powell, October 10, 1880, LR-BE, NAA, SI. It is hard to imagine the research or exhibition value of "two or three hundred" polishing stones.

465 Stevenson to Powell, October 27, 1880, LR-BE, NAA, SI.

From four to five hundred people can find room within such an enclosure.[466]

To Pilling, Stevenson wrote, "These Cliff Ruins surpass any I have ever learn[ed] of in this country & a knowledge of them will excite great interest." Another eight years would pass before Richard Wetherill first saw Cliff Palace and other large ruins in the Mesa Verde.

From the northern Pueblos, Stevenson returned to Santa Fe with two loads of "specimens" and over the next few days visited San Ildefonso, Nambe and Tesuque where additional purchases were made of pottery and stone implements.

Two weeks later, on November 9, Stevenson wrote Pilling, "I came in here [i.e., to Santa Fe] yesterday from a journey down the Jemez River in a bad snow storm." He continued, "I shall make a trip down to Isleta [by train] then return to Santa Fe, pack up & vamoose for home." The expedition to the Southwest was finished in less than three months. Nearing the end of this field season, Stevenson felt "Our success in many ways surpasses that of last season though the collections [2,800 items] will not be as bulky." He continued, "The photos are superb":

> We have secured an 11 x 14 plate of the Pueblos of Taos, San Juan, Santa Clara, San Ildefonso, Nambe Tesuque, Cochiti, Jemez, Jemez Ruins [Giusewa Pueblo and San Jose de los Jemez Mission], Silla [Zia], Santa Ana, Sandia, Santo Domingo, San Felipe & will make one of Isleta...[467]

Back in Washington, Hillers would add photographs made at Hopi in 1876 and 1881, and at Zuni in 1879, to the photographs of the Rio Grande Pueblos (22 images in all) and include them in a portfolio used by Powell, Stevenson, and others in lobbying for congressional support of the work of the Bureau: *Photographic Illustrations of the Puebla [sic] Indian Villages in New Mexico & Arizona.* Hillers's "landscapes," as Powell termed them, are an unparalleled documentation of the settlement patterns and architecture of the Rio Grande and Western Pueblos.[468]

---

466   Stevenson 1883:430-432; see Miller 2007:51.

467   Stevenson to Pulling, November 9, 1880, LR-BE, NAA, SI.

468   For an account of Hillers's expeditionary photography, see Hieb 2011a.

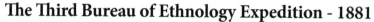

The Third Bureau of Ethnology Expedition - 1881

Prior to Stevenson's third expedition to the Southwest, Clarence King retired as head of the USGS, and on March 18, 1881, Powell was appointed his successor. Seizing the opportunity, anthropologist Don Fowler notes, "[Powell] restructured the Survey, combined the administration of both agencies in one office, with James Pilling as chief clerk and disbursing officer of both."[469] Stevenson, Pilling, Hillers, and Powell were all put on the payroll of the USGS, thus giving Powell the flexibility to pursue his anthropological interests with the Bureau's budget. In addition, several contributors to the Bureau's publications were put on the payroll of the Census Office. The salaries of Washington Matthews and H. C. Yarrow continued to be paid by the U. S. Army and the Army Medical Museum. USGS historian Mary Rabbit concludes, "In effect, the Geological Survey appropriation was being used to supplement that of the Bureau of Ethnology."[470] Powell's creative accounting allowed him to shuffle personnel and expenditures between departments and their budgets. By the end of the year, Powell's efforts to control all areas of government sponsored anthropological research would also include Cushing.

Stevenson left for the Southwest on July 25. Prior to his departure, Powell laid out the objectives of the expedition:

> To make collections representing the arts and industries of these people—said collections to be deposition in the National Museum.
>
> To make photographs and drawings, for illustrative purposes of the Indians, their houses, ground plans of the villages and scenes representative of daily life.
>
> To make investigations into their languages, customs and mythology, government, architecture, etc.—such material to be deposited in this office for publication.[471]

Stevenson's party included Victor Mindeleff, an assistant topographer on the USGS payroll, H. J. Biddle and Howard F. Chappell, "voluntary assistants," and (unofficially) Matilda Stevenson. Hillers, also on the USGS payroll, joined Stevenson at Fort Wingate after first going

---

469   Fowler 2000:94.
470   Rabbit 1980:59; Hieb 2011a.
471   Powell to Stevenson, July 20, 1882, LR-BE, NAA, SI.

to Utah on assignment. Field work was carried out at Zuni, Hopi, and at the ancestral Hopi ruins at Awatovi.

Before leaving the east, Stevenson purchased $1,460 worth of trade goods, including beads, mirrors, shirts, various tools, 200 pounds of leather and over 5000 yards of cloth, e.g., lawn, gingham, various prints, ticking, flannel and brown sheeting.[472] It is likely that a significant amount of these "Articles for Indian Distribution" were given to Keam in partial payment for the pottery and other material acquired in 1879.

Once again, letters of introduction provided military transportation in the field as well as government rates for commissary goods at Fort Wingate. En route to the Southwest, as Lawson has documented, Stevenson detoured to Topeka, Kansas, to obtain rail passes on the Atlantic and Pacific Railroad and its subsidiary, the Atchinson, Topeka and Santa Fe Railroad, a practice already in use by Powell during his surveys in the 1870s.[473] The Atlantic and Pacific Railroad had already reached Fort Wingate, months before Stevenson's arrival there on August 2, 1881.

Within days of their arrival at Fort Wingate, Mindeleff left for Zuni and began mapping the pueblo with a party that included Cushing's brother, Dr. Enos L. Cushing. In a report published at the end of the field season, Mindeleff was described as an "architectural artist, whose duty it was to make plans, sketches and measurements [of Zuni] from which to construct [a model] for exhibition in the National Museum."[474]

On September 13, Stevenson, Hillers, Albert L. Webster, and party left for Hopi, returning to Fort Wingate one month later. Webster, an assistant topographer with the USGS, was assigned to "map the Moki towns," producing a detailed topographical map of the three mesas, showing the location of the villages, farming lands, trails, wagon roads, springs, and ruins. Hillers completed his photographic survey of the Pueblos by making 11 x 14 images of the Hopi villages on all three mesas. In a scrapbook assembled by Matilda Stevenson, an article clipped from

---

472   Lawson, ibid, pp. 116-120.
473   Lawson, ibid, pp. 119-120.
474   *New York Tribune*, January 1, 1882. See Chapter 5 for more on Victor Mindeleff's career with the Bureau of Ethnology.

THE DOCTOR DANCED WITH US ◦◈◦

The Tribune (New York) of January 1, 1882 reported:

> [Oraibi's] inhabitants are so exclusive that they do not
> even visit the Government agency nor have they ever
> received any annuities. The people of this village are
> subject to influences from some source which induce
> them to object to any communication with whites. When
> the inhabitants discovered the approach of the exploring
> party they became so much alarmed that they abandoned
> their homes, leaving only the aged and bed-ridden. The
> opportunity was thus presented to the party to make
> their investigations in the homes of the people at their
> leisure. A series of fine photographic views of exteriors
> and interiors were obtained, but it was thought best not
> to carry away any of the utensils or curious objects of
> furniture with which the village homes were filled. Mr.
> Hillers, the photographer, had once before visited this
> village [1872] with Major Powell [i.e., Powell's party led
> by W. C. Powell], and had secured a few photographic
> negatives but the result of the last visit was much more
> complete and satisfactory.[475]

While Webster and Hillers were engaged in their work, Stevenson
was at Keams Canyon where "a very large and fine collection of Indian
objects was made ... number[ing] about 4000 specimens." In his report
to Powell, Stevenson added,

> Since I left here Mr. Keam writes me he has secured
> many additional and interesting objects. I shall return
> to Moqui to pack and ship these specimens as soon as
> the collection at Zuni is completed. I have sent 2000
> feet of lumber and many boxes to Moqui for that
> purpose.[476]

During his stay at Keam's trading post, Stevenson made a hasty
survey of the ruins of the ancestral Hopi village and Franciscan mission
church at Awatovi.

475   James [Matilda] Stevenson, Scrapbook, Archive 91 JSS 000, Laboratory of
      Anthropology, Museum of New Mexico.
476   Stevenson to Powell, November 3, 1881, LR-BE, NAA, SI.

Cushing and the Third Bureau of Ethnology Expedition - 1881

While Stevenson was at Keam's trading post, Cushing returned to Zuni from his expedition to the Havasupai on September 16. In an odd coincidence, a month later Stevenson returned to Fort Wingate on October 12, the same day Cushing's initiation into the Priesthood of the Bow was completed.

Back at Zuni a few days later, Stevenson, with the assistance of Cushing and Mindeleff, was collecting pottery and other materials, and planned to hire "a competent Indian to assist us in our catalogue, from whom we will secure the Indian name and use and history of each object." Eventually, Stevenson reported the collection at Zuni to be "in the neighborhood of 7000 specimens." He added, "When the work at Zuni and Moqui is finished I shall proceed to Santa Fe & secure transportation from the Q. M. [Quarter Master] for the purpose of securing a stone house from ruins near Pena Blanca."[477]

The material "secured" at Hopi weighed about 12,000 pounds, and from Zuni about 21,000 pounds. Stevenson's letters give no information regarding the acquisition of these collections, except for $1,539.16 spent on material for "distribution to Indians." Vouchers submitted by Stevenson for the expedition record $450.29 paid to Keam for 2,405 "Ethnological Specimens" acquired between September 10 and October 13, 1881, and $88.00 paid to John Menaul, Presbyterian missionary at Laguna Pueblo, for 155 specimens in three lots, three packing boxes, 100 pounds of wool for packing pottery and other items and freight from Laguna to Albuquerque.[478] Apparently no payment was made for the huge collection from Zuni. Stevenson makes no mention of Douglas D. Graham, trader at Zuni, nor is Cushing ever reimbursed for acquisitions or acknowledged for any of the materials collected there. In his reports, vouchers and correspondence, Keam was the "sole source" for all of the materials acquired during the 1881 expedition at Hopi. It *appears* all the collections made at Zuni were acquired by trade, using materials Stevenson purchased in New York

---

477   Stevenson to Powell, November 3, 1881, LR-BE, NAA, SI. No other information regarding the "stone house" has been located.

478   Lawson, ibid, pp. 129, 132.

and at the U. S. Army Subsistence Department at Fort Wingate.[479]

In his letter of transmittal accompanying the catalogue of materials collected at Hopi and Zuni in 1881, Stevenson acknowledged Cushing:

> ...I am indebted to Mr. Frank H. Cushing for his preparation of the field catalogue for the collection from Zuni. His thorough knowledge of the Zuni language enabled him to obtain the Indian name of most of the articles procured, which names are given in this catalogue. I have also to thank him for valuable assistance in making the collection [as well as] Mr. Victor Mindeleff for his aid in making the collection, in which labor he rendered faithful assistance[480]

There is no day-to-day account of Cushing's work in his published letters or in his daily journal. However, in his letter to Baird written December 4, Cushing gives this account of his role in the collecting done at Zuni:

> During Col. Stevenson's presence ... [I gave] him my personal assistance in the collecting and turning over to him much, both ancient and modern, which I had collected.[481] ... I also prepared for the Colonel a catalogue in both English and Zuni. ... This catalogue might have been far more complete ... had I not been compelled to keep pace with the packers. ...

Cushing continued:

> On account of ... my work on the catalogue (more than two hundred pages), I have been unable to complete my notes on the Ha-va-su-pai. ... Much time is liable to elapse ere I can publish anything regarding my Zuni work ... with reference to the news that may be from time to time published about Zuni: *all* is either a direct or indirect emanation from my researches here.[482]

---

479 Ibid, p. 126.
480 Stevenson 1884:517.
481 Apparently by looting, not by trade or purchase.
482 Green, ibid, pp. 196, 200, and 201. Cushing makes no mention of Matilda Stevenson's thirty page *Zuni and Zunians*, privately published in early 1881, and cited at length by Morgan 1881:137-140 (preface dated June 1881).

Although Cushing then adds, "I have been unable to complete my notes on the Ha-va-su-pai," it is appears likely that he completed "The Nation of the Willows" as well as some of his more famous "My Life at Zuni" before he left for his trip to East less than two months later.[483] His January 3, 1882 statement to Baird, "I have never responded to the many tempting and liberal offers I have received…" seems disingenuous at best for in a letter to Baird, written on July 8 while he was in the midst of his busy tour to Washington and Boston, Cushing says these articles were "already written for and accepted by these magazines"—the *Atlantic Monthly* and the *Century Illustrated Monthly Magazine*.[484]

For Cushing, the last months of 1881, from September 16 onwards, had been very busy. He had been initiated into the Order of the Bow Priests, assisted with Stevenson's collecting efforts, writing, and continued in making arrangements for his trip to the east coast.

In November, Bourke returned to Zuni to observe the colorful Shalako, an annual house blessing ceremony. At the end of the ceremonies, the kachinas left the village, crossing the river to the south. Matilda Stevenson and the recently appointed Presbyterian missionary, Rev. Samuel A. Bentley, followed them, intruding into Zuni sacred space as well as the procession. Patricio Pino, the governor of Zuni, confronted Bentley, who didn't understand what was said to him. In Bourke's account, Patricio came to Cushing who, in turn, explained to Bentley, "he simply didn't want you to stand up so close to the Sacred Dancers." Bentley responded,

> "…tell Patricio from me that if he ever again … orders me away from anyplace, I'll knock the stuffings out of him. [He continued:] I am master here and propose to go where I please and see what I please and if any man

---

483   Cushing 1882b and 1882-1883. Much of his article on the Havasupai may have been written during Cushing's stay at Fort Whipple during July and August 1881.

484   Green, ibid, p. 213; Cushing to Spencer Baird, July 8, 1882, RU28, Smithsonian Institution Archives. Cited hereafter as SIA. Cushing continued to work on "My Adventures in Zuni" during his trip to the East, arranging illustrations and making revisions. A letter to R. H. Johnson, editor of The Century, indicates Cushing had planned a series of six articles and had not yet settled on a title. Cushing to Johnson, July 1and July 18, 1882, Zuni 1.32, MS.6, AMAW.

attempts to interfere, I'll knock his head off."[485]

Bourke was critical of Bentley's "many indiscretions." For Cushing, there were additional concerns. As he wrote to Baird in his letter of December 4:

> ...[Bentley] is here as "U. S. Indian Teacher," although he claims to be Agent and supreme master of the Zunis, with the privilege of turning me or any of my party— without reference to their moral standing or scientific purpose—out of the Pueblo and off the Reservation. ... Col. Stevenson urged me to have a conference with the irate, bull-dozing representative of the [Presbyterian] Home Missions, promising to be present, and I accepted the invitation. ... [Cushing told Bentley]
> I had a right to command in Zuni as a chief of native choice, a right sanctioned by the Treaty of Guadaloupe and a treaty now in Zuni securing to Zunis the right to personal property, government, and religious protection from the United States...
> [Bentley responded:] ...he [would] *ruin* me, turn the Indians against me so that they would drive me out. He should simply and entirely "crush" me and "inform the scientific world how unreliable were my investigations."[486]

Soon after the Stevensons left Zuni, Cushing wrote to Baird, Powell and others about "the Bentley matter... proposing in the future to avoid all trouble with our Missionary Agent by having nothing whatsoever to do with him."[487] Rev. Bentley left Zuni early in 1882 and Cushing's friend, Graham, was asked to take charge at Zuni[488] and served as teacher from April until October 1882. More importantly, it appears James Stevenson and Cushing parted on good terms.

---

485   Bourke in Green, ibid, pp. 190, 191.

486   Ibid, pp. 198-200. On behalf of Baird and Powell, Pilling wrote to assume Cushing "of your rights on the reservation and both the Smithsonian Institution and Bureau of Ethnology will be glad to help you maintain them." Pilling to Cushing, December 17, 1881, Zuni 1.45, MS 6, AMAW.

487   Cushing to Pilling, December 24, 1881; Ibid, p. 209.

488   The teachers were regarded as the Government's representatives.

Cushing's Transfer to the Bureau of Ethnology – 1882

As Cushing made preparations for his trip to the East, he arranged for Douglas D. Graham, the trader at Zuni, and L. N. Hopkins, Jr., post trader at Fort Wingate, to submit statements of his accounts to the Smithsonian Institution and the Bureau of Ethnology for payment.[489] Towards the end of December 1881, Cushing's "bill contracted with Mr. Graham" for $344.29 was submitted to Baird; at about the same time Hopkins's bill for $168.71 was submitted to Powell as well as another bill for $40, submitted by a Mr. Smillie of Washington. Baird forwarded Graham's bill to Powell, who responded on January 14, 1882:

> …Mr. Cushing has made no request for authority to make such purchases, and no authority, direct or indirect, has been given him by myself to incur such expenses.
>
> … I have from time to time assisted Mr. Cushing in various ways, but have not considered him to be under my instructions and have in no way given him orders or controlled his work.[490]

Powell emphasized that the aggregate of the three bills, $553.00, would be impossible to pay with funds allocated to the Bureau of Ethnology for the fiscal year, without cutting off some other work in progress. However, on January 23 the opportunistic Powell wrote to Baird, reporting that he had made arrangements with the Census Office to "free a certain amount of funds that can be used during the remainder of the fiscal year [by the Bureau of Ethnology]." He continued:

> Under these circumstances I have the honor to suggest that the work of Mr. Cushing now immediately under the direction of the Secretary of the Smithsonian Institution be placed in charge of the Director of the Bureau of Ethnology and that his salary and expenses be paid from the appropriation for the support of this office.[491]

On February 8, Pilling wrote Cushing to inform him:

> [As of the] date of January 1ˢᵗ Prof. Baird has formally transferred you and your work to the Bureau of

---

489   Cushing acted on his own initiative, not wanting to leave Zuni for six months with outstanding debts.

490   Ibid, p. 213.

491   Ibid, p. 216.

Ethnology, and I am instructed by the Director to say that from that date your salary will [continue to] be at the rate of $100 per month.

In addition … this office will pay the expenses of your own subsistence when in the field and transportation by rail when such mode of travel is necessary for the successful prosecution of your work, but expenses other than these above mentioned must be borne by yourself.

Apparently in response to a request made by Cushing, Pilling's letter continued with instructions regarding his travel by train to Washington with a party to include five "Zunians…well versed in the beliefs and customs of their people and one … thoroughly instructed in the government of the tribe" and a sixth, "a Moki [Hopi.]"[492]

Before leaving Zuni, Cushing sent to T. B. Aldrich, Editor of the *Atlantic Monthly*, "a couple examples of Zuni folk lore" for publication in the magazine or a book.[493] Nothing came of the proposal. Many years later, in 1901, Cushing's *Zuni Folk Tales* would be published posthumously.

During his first year at Zuni, Baird had made few demands on Cushing. As Jesse Green observes, Cushing's transfer to the Bureau of Ethnology, and Powell's supervision, meant "from this time forward, he would be subject to much more stringent (though still not altogether undodgeable) rules."[494]

Cushing's Visit to the East Coast - 1882

Cushing and his party left Zuni on February 22, stopping for a day at Fort Wingate, where Cushing "exchanged his picturesque Zuni costume

---

492   Pilling to Cushing, February 2, 1882. Ibid, pp. 216-217. In 1882, Victor Mindeleff's salary was $50 per month, Cosmos Mindeleff, $25. In addition to his salary from the Smithsonian Institution, Cushing's salary was supplemented by patrons and commercial interests.

493   Cushing to Aldrich, August 16, 1883, Zuni 1.1, MS.6, AMAW.

494   Green, ibid, p. 212. On the back side of a photograph of a painting by Thomas Hovenden, Matilda Stevenson wrote "Frank Hamilton Cushing in his fantastic dress worn while among the Zuni Indians. This man was the biggest fool and charlatan I ever knew. He even put up his hair in curl papers every night. How could a man walk weighed down with so much toggery?" Brandes 1965:36, n. 27.

...for the dress of civilization" and on their arrival in Washington, on March 4, the Zuni consented to Cushing cutting his hair on "the promise ...he would have it made up, so that he could wear it beneath his head-band when back at Zuni...."[495] On the trip east, the Indians were introduced to travel by rail, and in Chicago, to a hotel, blocks of buildings, carriages, and a park where they saw sea-lions. In Washington, they met President Chester A. Arthur and other dignitaries. Pedro Pino, the aged, former governor of Zuni, stayed with the Stevensons in Washington, while Cushing and the rest of the party continued to Boston where they met the Governor of Massachusetts, John Davis Long, and Boston's Mayor, Samuel Abbott Green. The Zunis joined Cushing by singing and dancing at social events and at lectures given at the Paint-and-Clay Club, the "Old South" Meeting-house and Wellesley College, before traveling on to Salem, Massachusetts.[496] Back in Boston, called by the Zunis "the City of Perpetual Mists," they went to Deer Island. There, on the shore of the Atlantic Ocean, the Zunis collected sacred water to take back to the pueblo, and Cushing underwent a part of his initiation into "the order of the Ka Ka" (the Society of Masked Dancers).[497] The events of the tour during March were reported in the June issue of *Wide Awake* and the August issue of *Century Magazine*.[498] Following the visit to Boston, Pedro Pino and three others returned to Zuni, while two remained with Cushing in Washington for linguistic work.[499]

For Cushing, the time between February 22, when he left Zuni, and his return to the pueblo seven months later, was filled with successes. On April 22, Cushing presented a lecture, "The Zuni Social, Mythic and

---

495   Baxter 1882: 527, 529.

496   See Ober 1882 and Baxter 1882a for images of these gatherings.

497   Because he was recalled to Washington in 1884, Cushing was not able to complete this initiation. As Zuni anthropologist Edmund J. Ladd points out, the initiation into the *kokko* was required of all males and was a prerequisite for membership in the bow priesthood. Ladd, ibid, p. 30.

498   Ibid. The well-known portrait of Cushing (Baxter 1882a:528) was by Metcalf. See Metcalf to Cushing, October 24, 1881, Zuni 1.41, Frank Hamilton Cushing Manuscript Collection, MS.6, Autry Museum of the American West. Cited hereafter as AMAW.

499   Matthews wrote to assume Cushing "Your Indians got home all right and your brother [Enos Cushing] is at work again in the hospital [Fort Wingate] digging away at the teeth of this wretched community." Matthews to Cushing, May 13, 1882, Zuni 1.39, MS.6, AMAW.

Religious Systems," to the National Academy of Sciences in Washington, that was immediately published in the June issue of *Popular Science Monthly*.[500] A week later, Sylvester Baxter's article, "Some Results of Mr. Cushing's Visit [to Zuni]" appeared in *American Architect and Building News*.[501] Throughout the summer, Baxter wrote other articles about Cushing for the *Boston Herald* and *Harper's Magazine* in June, and the *Century Magazine* in August.[502] In Boston, Cushing was joined by his elite Boston friends, notably Sylvester Baxter, and met the philanthropist Mary Tileston Hemenway who would, four years later, sponsor an archaeological expedition to the southwest directed by Cushing.[503]

In May, Cushing gave a paper entitled "Life in Zuni" at a meeting of the Anthropological Society of Washington. Here, as elsewhere, the Indians sang and danced in costume. Under pressure from Baird and Powell, Cushing spent much of the month of June at the Smithsonian Institution where he completed an essay on "Zuni Fetiches," published that fall in the *Second Annual Report of the Bureau of Ethnology*.[504] During his employment with the Bureau of Ethnology, from 1879 until 1885, Cushing produced only two publications for the Smithsonian Institution, the source of the funds and other forms of support for his research.[505]

On July 10, Cushing married Emma Tennison Magill,[506] eldest daughter of John Whitehead and Catharine Cecilia Magill, of Washington. Emma's father was associated with the banking house of Lewis Johnson & Co. before his death in 1879. Although Cushing and

---

500   Cushing 1882a.
501   Baxter 1882c.
502   See Hinsley and Wilcox, eds. 1996 for the texts of these articles.
503   Ibid. Hinsley and Wilcox provide a chronology, review of Cushing work and his relationship with Hemenway, as well as a selection of Cushing's unpublished writings from the Hemenway Southwestern Archaeological Expedition.
504   "Zuni Fetiches" provides the religious contexts for these material objects, as well as a summary account of the Zuni creation narrative and the texts of prayers related to their use.
505   "A Study of Pueblo Pottery as Illustrative of Zuni Cultural Growth" (1886) was the other title. It, too, was produced under pressure after Cushing's return to Washington.
506   Although frequently called "Emily," her name was Emma. Cushing, following Zuni preferences, often called her "Emalie." Personal communication from Curtis M. Hinsley, August 25, 2016.

Emma were engaged [?] prior to his departure for Zuni in 1879, there is little about her in Cushing's letters and journals. A single draft fragment to [Emma Magill], written from Zuni in October 1879, concludes, "Good night, dear Love… Your loving Frank," and in his daily journal for June 27, 1881, while Cushing was at the Hopi agency en route to Havasupai, Cushing noted, "wrote Father and Emma."[507] During his visit to Zuni in November, Bourke recorded in his diary that following Cushing's initiation into the Bow Priesthood:

> …the heads of the Zuni people … have communicated their views to Cushing … as he is now a Zuni—a full member of the tribe—it is his duty to marry without further delay and become the father of children who shall grow up among their people.

However, Bourke writes, Cushing "has been forcibly impressed with the necessity of avoiding all entanglements which would impede his investigations." Still, two days later, there was another confrontation. Bourke again:

> Cushing, before breakfast, had a great wrangle with a party of Zunis, who were hoping to change his resolution about deferring his marriage. … Cushing is … determined to fight them off by all sorts of excuses until he can no longer evade the issue, when he will sever his connection with the Pueblo and return to Washington.[508]

At no time—at least in Bourke's journals—is Cushing's "engagement" to Emma Magill given as an "excuse" not to marry a Zuni girl. However, we have only Bourke's account of these events, as there is a break in Cushing's daily journal. According to William Eleroy Curtis, who visited the Cushings at Zuni in April of the following year, soon after Bourke left Zuni,

> …Cushing told the Indians of his engagement to a young lady in Washington, and of his intention to marry her and bring her to live with them… While the party of Indians were [sic] in Washington, Mr. Cushing presented them to his fiancée … the Governor [Patricio Pino] told him he must not go back to Zuni without taking his

---

507 Green, ibid, pp. 42, 168.
508 November 24 and 26, 1881. Quoted in Green, ibid, pp. 188, 189.

bride. She cheerfully consented to accompany him to his pueblo home, and to share his novel experiences.[509]

After the wedding, Cushing immediately returned to his office at the Smithsonian to complete work on "Zuni Fetiches," and attend to other matters. Cushing was also asked to provide a list of his manuscripts on linguistic material from Zuni, and on July 22, "after fresh attacks of my illness," he sent Pilling a list, that included a dictionary of the Zuni language, collections of prayers, songs, poetry, and speeches with interlinear and free translations. Meanwhile, Cushing received a letter from Matthews, alerting him that his brother Enos "has [not] done anything towards fixing up a house in Zuni for 'the bride.'"[510]

Late in July, Cushing decided to take Emma and the two Zunis who had remained in Washington to visit the Seneca Indians in western New York. After making arrangements for funding, the Cushings left on August 30 for the Seneca Reserve. Two weeks later, the party, that now included Emma's sister Margaret Whitehead Magill and the family cook, Abram, left by train for Chicago.

Cushing's Return to Zuni – Late Summer 1882

While Cushing was in the east, clouds of controversy began to form in the west: a report that Cushing had killed Navajo horses reached the Office of the Commissioner of Indian Affairs, and a report reached Powell's desk from U. S. Indian Inspector C. H. Howard saying he heard "complaints...so often repeated" of Cushing's "licentiousness... lawlessness of conduct...falsification to the Zunis and the public, and exerting an almost unqualifiedly pernicious influence upon these Indians."[511] More would soon follow.

The affair involving Navajo horses had its beginning while Cushing was in the East. In a letter to Cushing written on July 20, Navajo Agent Galen Eastman stated:

> My Navajos complain to me that you did at two different times fire with a pistol into their horses, that in consequence thereof they found two horses dead and a third one they trailed by the blood a long ways but failed

---

509   Curtis 1883:40-41.
510   Matthews to Cushing, June 29, 1882, Zuni 1.39, MS.6, AMAW.
511   Green, ibid, p. 263.

to find him, and not seeing him since believe him to be dead also. They desire me to present their claim and collect $100.00 as pay for the animals. I also respectfully request an explanation of the matter and the reasons why you did it.[512]

Eastman's letter was held at Fort Wingate in Cushing's absence, and it was not until October 11 that he replied. Cushing readily admitted shooting at the horses:

It is quite true that I fired, not twice, but three times into two different bands of horses belonging to the Navajo Indians. It is possible that, *as I intended*, I killed one or two of them, although of this I cannot be certain.[513]

Cushing detailed a history of Navajo incursions onto Zuni lands, and his various efforts—including:

application[s] both personally and through our Agent, Major Thomas, to the "Agent of the Navajos"—to keep them away from "*our* territory at and near Nutria... warn[ing] them that if they did not grant our request we should either take up their stock and claim damage to our pasture lands or fields, or else shoot any of their horses which we have found in the Nutria valley.[514]

He closed his letter to Eastman by saying, "I have acted according to my authority as one of the Native mandators of the [laws of my tribe]." He signed his letter, "F. H. Cushing, 1st War Chief of Zuni, U. S. Ass't Ethnologist."

Eastman responded immediately to Cushing's letter:

[I] am astonished at its contents, and that you have done what you now confess, viz., taken the law into your own hands ... and have pursued a lawless course toward the neighboring Navajos. ... I have never before received any communication from you...except in this case, of your willfully shooting the Navajos' horses...[515]

Eastman countered that he, too, had worked with Agent Thomas

---

512   Ibid, p. 402, n.23.
513   Ibid, p. 246; emphasis added.
514   Ibid.
515   Ibid, pp. 246-247.

in moving about thirty Navajos and their families from the "old 'Homestead' of theirs at 'Nutria Springs'" to lands included within the Navajo Reservation. He added that the Navajos also claimed the horses Cushing shot at were off the Zuni Reservation. Eastman insisted on "the settlement by you of their claim of $100.00 for the property value of their horses shot by you..."[516]

Eastman forwarded copies of the exchange of letters with Cushing to the Commissioner of Indian Affairs, and indicated he had asked Agent Thomas, who was on his way to Zuni, to "confer with Mr. Cushing in this matter."[517] Over the next several months, there was correspondence between Thomas and the Commissioner of Indian Affairs; Thomas and D. M. Riordan, who had replaced Eastman as Navajo agent; and Pedro Sanchez, who had replaced Thomas as Pueblo agent with Riordan and Cushing. In May 1883, over a year after the shooting of or at the Navajo horses took place, Agent Sanchez met with Cushing at Zuni. Cushing had changed his story. On May 22, Sanchez reported to the Commissioner of Indian Affairs:

> Mr. Cushing says the Indian whose horses were reported to have been killed is one of his best friends and that he has lost but one horse and that died of influenza. Mr. Cushing absolutely refuses to pay the claim of $100...[518]

Sanchez also wrote to Riordan and Cushing, and urged all parties to "settle [the matter] in a way that does the greatest good..." The matter was closed. It appears incredible (if we accept Cushing's account) that one of his best Navajo friends had approached Agent Eastman with the false claim that Cushing had shot and killed two, maybe three, of his horses and made a fraudulent claim for $100.

The Fourth Bureau of Ethnology Expedition - 1882

For the Bureau of Ethnology, the field season of 1882 was filled

---

516   Ibid, p. 247. See also T. S. Mumford, Regimental Quartermaster, Fort Wingate to Cushing, May 13, 1883, concurring the payment of $100 "or its equivalent perhaps in ponies is a just one." Zuni 1.42, MS.6, AMAW.

517   Green, ibid, p. 247.

518   Pedro Sanchez to Hiram Price, May 22, 1883, Miscellaneous Letters Sent by the Pueblo Indian Agency, 1874-1891, Records of the Bureau of Indian Affairs, RG 75, National Archives.

with adventure, accomplishment, and conflict. On August 29, eighteen men—employed by or affiliated with—the USGS and/or the Bureau of Ethnology arrived at Fort Wingate.[519] Over the next four months, they formed a number of parties carrying out geographical and anthropological work at several locations in New Mexico and Arizona. No other field season is as well documented. As in previous years, the activities of the USGS and the Bureau of Ethnology were summarized in the *Annual Report(s) of the United States Geological Survey* and the *Annual Report(s) of the Bureau of Ethnology*.[520] Interested readers learned the names of the individuals in charge of field operations, their instructions, dates of departure and return to Washington, the "field of operations," and details of their accomplishments. Surviving letters sent and received, monthly reports, and fiscal records, convey additional information regarding the logistics and economics of field work, and reveal Powell's masterly allocation of resources from the more generous USGS budget to allow the continuation of ethnological research. In addition to the official record, rich accounts of day-to-day operations, and the feeling of the adventure experienced, were written in letters and diaries by other participants in the Bureau of Ethnology's fall and winter expeditions into Canyon de Chelly and to the Hopi village of Oraibi, most notably those of the artist Willard Metcalf and the journalist H. C. Rizer.[521]

In July 1882, Almon Harris ("A. H.") Thompson was appointed to take charge of the Wingate Division of the USGS, and continue topographic work in New Mexico and Arizona begun the previous year by Gilbert Thompson (apparently no relation). "Professor" Thompson, as he was known, was the brother-in-law of John Wesley Powell, and had served as second-in-command in charge of geographical work during

---

519   For a more detailed account of the Bureau of Ethnology expedition, see Hieb 2005.

520   J. W. Powell, *Fourth Annual Report of the United States Geological Survey...1882-1883* (Washington: Government Printing Office, 1884) and Powell 1886.

521   Willard Leroy Metcalf, Journal from December 2, 1882 to February 1, 1883, Metcalf Papers, Thomas Gilcrease Institute of American History and Art; R. C. Rizer, a series of letters to the editor in the *Eureka* (Kansas) *Herald* from September 7, 1882 to February 1, 1883, and the *New York Tribune* (see Hieb 2005). Lawyer and journalist, Rizer later became head of the USGS.

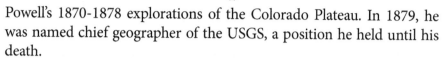

Powell's 1870-1878 explorations of the Colorado Plateau. In 1879, he was named chief geographer of the USGS, a position he held until his death.

While in Washington, on August 16, Thompson received his instructions:

> You are hereby placed in charge of the Wingate division of the Survey with headquarters at Ft. Wingate, N.M. This division will consist of one party for carrying on triangulation and two parties for topographic work besides the necessary barometric observers for base stations...[522]

Hillers arrived at Eureka, Kansas, on August 23, to visit Thompson, who had a ranch west of the town. The August 24 issue of the *Eureka Herald* noted that Joseph Stanley Brown, Powell's secretary, would also visit Eureka briefly as his brother, Benjamin, owned a sheep ranch adjacent to that of Thompson. The article closed with the announcement that the newspaper's young publisher and editor, H. C. Rizer, would join Thompson's party. The train from Kansas City, Missouri, arrived at Fort Wingate on August 29. By September 1, the combined USGS and Bureau of Ethnology party established "Camp Brown" near the military post, named in honor of Joseph Stanley Brown.

Stevenson was in New York City on August 23 when a telegram notified him of his appointment "to duty with the Director [Powell] at Fort Wingate." Stevenson also received instructions "to direct his work to an exploration and study of that class of ancient remains in Arizona and New Mexico commonly known as 'cave and cliff dwellings,'" beginning in Canyon de Chelly, and later moving on to the "Rito de los Frijoles" in New Mexico, the area west of Santa Clara Pueblo he had surveyed in 1880. Clearly James and Matilda Stevenson were prepared to leave on a moment's notice. They reached Fort Wingate by September 1, having in the meantime made arrangements with Gen. Ranald S. Mackenzie, the new District Commander in Santa Fe, and Gen. Luther P. Bradley at Fort Wingate, for "transportation, supplies, escort &c."

Besides the Stevensons, the Bureau of Ethnology personnel included Maj. A. J. Gustin, artist; J. K. Hillers, photographer; and Ben Wittick, who

---

522   Powell to Thompson, August 21, 1882, Letters Sent by the USGS, 1869-1895, National Archives.

joined the party in Albuquerque, assistant photographer. Also attached to the Stevenson's survey were Victor Mindeleff's ethnographic party that included Victor's younger brother, Cosmos, John L. Burnett, and U. S. Navy Ensign Charles C. Marsh. For budgetary reasons, Stevenson and Hillers were paid out of USGS funds, and for logistical purposes various personnel were reassigned, as needed, between the USGS and the Bureau of Ethnology groups. Thus, Hillers, Wittick, and Gustin were "temporarily assigned" to the USGS during November, and at the beginning of October, Thompson assigned E. A. Oyster, Topographical Assistant, to duty with Stevenson's party. Eventually, three projects were carried out under the auspices of the Bureau of Ethnology: the Mindeleff survey of Hopi architecture,[523] Stevenson's exploration of Canyon de Chelly, and a collecting expedition to Oraibi under the direction of Victor Mindeleff.

The separate assignments of Thompson and Stevenson were delayed at Camp Brown for much of September waiting the "arrival of materials, instruments, provisions, horses, &c." During the first week, Thompson and Brown[524] traveled to Santa Fe to secure camp supplies and saddlery. During the second week of September, the Stevensons and several other members of the Bureau of Ethnology expedition, accompanied the Stevensons' long-time friend, General John A. Logan, and his party to Zuni. Logan's visit became part of a series of events discussed below as "the Logan affair." Finally, during the last week of September, Thompson and Rizer traveled to the end of the Atlantic and Pacific Railroad as it was being constructed across northern Arizona, staying overnight at Williams Station, west of Flagstaff.

The expedition to Canyon de Chelly got underway from Fort Wingate on October 3, with James and Matilda Stevenson riding in an army ambulance with a military escort followed by a freight wagon filled with supplies.[525] Rizer accompanied the Stevensons and wrote a detailed account of the exploration of Canyon de Chelly for his newspaper, the *Eureka Herald*, thus providing us with the most detailed account of any of the Bureau of Ethnology expeditions during the decade. Three days

---

523   See Chapter 5 for a separate account of the Mindeleff's work.

524   Brown served as disbursing agent for the USGS and the Bureau of Ethnology in the field.

525   See Hieb 2005 for a detailed account of the expedition to Canyon de Chelly.

later, the Stevensons and Rizer reached Keam's ranch where they met the Navajo headman Ganado Mucho, who told them of a canyon "never before explored by white men."[526]

The party that left Keams Canyon the following day consisted of: James Stevenson, in charge; Matilda Stevenson; Thomas V. Keam and Keam's friend, Thomas A. McElmell;[527] J. K. Hillers, photographer; Ben Wittick, assistant photographer; Major A. J. Gustin, artist; Victor Mindeleff, "draughtsman"; Edward A. Oyster, "of the Survey"; four soldiers from the Thirteenth Infantry; two teamsters and their teams; two Navajo Indians, George and Charlie; Joseph Stanley Brown, disbursing agent; and H. C. Rizer, "volunteer assistant" and "correspondent to the *New York Daily Tribune.*"

The expedition reached the mouth of Canyon de Chelly on October 9, and moved three miles into the canyon before establishing camp. The following day, they reached a large side canyon Stevenson later designated as Canyon del Muerto ("of the dead"). The name was suggested by McElmell because of the burials visible in some of the ancestral Hopi surface dwellings, evidence "pot-hunting" had already taken place.

The party camped at "Royal Arch" and, over the course of three and half days, explored several of the cliff dwellings in the vicinity. However, as Stevenson reported, "the most interesting discovery of all awaited our search, two miles further up the canyon," where "we found an immense double cave containing the well-preserved remains of a village."[528] To reach the site, they had to climb "a steep bank of sand and broken stones," which had fallen from above. Once there, Brown discovered an open burial crypt containing two skeletons, which appeared to have been buried "in a sitting or rather a squatting [posture]."[529]

Victor Mindeleff's field notes and architectural drawings from the Canyon de Chelly expedition have been lost. However, his survey

---

526 Canyon del Muerto, a side canyon of Canyon de Chelly. It had been explored earlier by Col. Edward R. S. Canby in 1860 and Col. Christopher "Kit" Carson in 1864.

527 McElmo Creek, in southwestern Colorado and southern Utah, was named for Thomas McElmell, who had a trading post near its confluence with the San Juan River.

528 Mummy Cave ruin.

529 Anon [Brown], ibid.

provided the basis for an 8 x 3½ foot model of "Mummy Cave Cliff Ruin" created by his brother, Cosmos, and exhibited at the 1884 World's Industrial and Cotton Exposition in New Orleans. Hillers's photographs show the interior of the dwelling and include a view from the cave, looking down Canyon del Muerto. Hillers and Wittick seem to have worked side by side often creating virtually identical images of the cultural and natural wonders of the canyons.

Although Ganado Mucho assured Stevenson that this was a canyon "never explored before by white men," the Mummy Cave ruin had been "discovered" earlier. During Col. "Kit" Carson's 1863-1864 campaign against the Navajo, a detachment of troops under Col. A. W. Pheiffer marched down from the Tsaile area and through Canyon del Muerto. Pheiffer's report contains a brief description of Mummy Cave ruin which he called "Carey's Castle," in honor of the expedition's quartermaster, Asa B. Carey. That aside, it is likely that the extensive "pot-hunting" encountered throughout Canyon del Muerto was the work of William "Billy" Keam, who was often a guide for parties visiting Canyon de Chelly in the late 1870s.

The explorers broke camp and retraced their trail down Canyon del Muerto to the junction with Canyon de Chelly. From there they moved up canyon past White House ruin before a sandstorm forced them to make camp. The following day they moved three miles further up the canyon, and camped in Monument Canyon, a side branch of Canyon de Chelly, near "Explorer's Rock"—known today as "Spider Rock." The following two days were spent exploring the main and side canyons, and Mindeleff made a survey of White House ruin. The party left the canyon on October 17, and returned to Keams Canyon.

By today's standards, the Bureau of Ethnology expedition constituted little more than a reconnaissance. Not a single complete piece of pottery was reported, surely a disappointment to Stevenson who, nonetheless, regarded their efforts a success. In less than ten days, the explorers visited a total of forty-six sites—twenty-nine in Canyon de Chelly and seventeen in Canyon del Muerto. They made notes, drew sketches, drafted ground plans, and took photographs. Back in Washington at the end of the field season, the need to justify as well as to promote the Bureau of Ethnology expeditions resulted in an article that appeared in the *New York Daily Tribune*, probably written by Brown:

> The archaeological and ethnological explorations in the Southwestern territory … have continued with success under the direction of Professor Powell during the season which has just ended.
>
> The wisdom of Congress in making provision for this work three or four years ago is becoming strikingly apparent as the railroads extend their lines into this, the most interesting region to the archaeologist within the borders of the Republic. Private collectors and specimen hunters are now overrunning the places which are thus made accessible, and all that remains of scientific interest which is movable becomes their spoil. The already abundant collection in possession of the National Museum will become priceless as the opportunity for their duplication passes away.
>
> Some criticism has been passed upon the policy of adding to the store of specimens material of the character of that already on hand; but this policy is adopted in order to have the material for exchange with other scientific institutions. … There yet remains, however, a great field of exploration, which has not yet been entered upon, and which is still too remote from any of the present lines of public travel to be in danger of early invasion by the tourist and amateur relic-hunter. The incompleteness of the work of exploration may be inferred from…

The author goes on to note:

> The collections made from New Mexico and Arizona already number somewhere between twenty-five and thirty-five thousand specimens of pottery, stone implements … and a thousand and one things that appertain to, and illustrate the daily life of, the people who made them and used them.[530]

The Stevensons returned to Keams Canyon on October 21, and left for Fort Wingate four days later. Shortly thereafter, in early November, they visited Acoma to collect pottery and other materials. Finding the pueblo "full of small-pox," they abandoned their plans and went instead

---

530   Anon [Brown], ibid.

to examine the "remarkable cliff dwellings" at "El Rito de los Frijoles." By mid-December, the Stevensons were back in Washington.

The Mindeleff brothers completed their architectural survey of the Hopi villages on November 2, and moved to the winter camp of the USGS near Holbrook, Arizona. Meanwhile, on October 23, Powell arrived at Fort Wingate, and two days later Matthews accompanied him to Zuni. They returned to the fort and on October 29, Matthews noted, "Major Powell left for the Grand Canyon." The following day, in a letter to Cushing marked "Personal Confidential," Brown wrote:

> ...before [Powell] left we talked the Oraibi matter over fully, and he has instructed me to secure your cooperation and that of the Mindeleff's party and "clean out" Oraibi—ethnologically speaking.[531]

Brown added a cautionary note:

> Now my dear fellow, we don't want any "flair" about this. You and I will quietly go ... to Oraibi... But remember, the less we have to say about it, the fewer annoying questions we will have to answer and the less criticism we will provoke from "certain" sources.[532]

It is by no means clear who the "certain" sources might be. However, Cushing's "flair" was a matter of criticism and sarcasm from a number of quarters.[533]

Circles of Friends and the Logan Affair – 1882-1886

The story told in this book is, in part, the story of circles of friends and colleagues, of insiders and outsiders, and the consequences these relationships for an early chapter in the history of anthropological and geological research in the American Southwest. In the fall of 1882 two friendships, parts of larger circles, came into conflict with potentially disastrous consequences for the Bureau of Ethnology. One friendship was that of James Stevenson with Illinois Senator, General John A. Logan; the other, Frank Hamilton Cushing with journalist Sylvester Baxter.

In the course of his explorations of the Colorado River from 1869

---

531   Green, ibid, p. 247.
532   Ibid, pp. 247-248. Brown went to Keams Canyon but did not accompany Cushing to Oraibi.
533   The "Oraibi Expedition" is described below.

to 1872, Powell assembled a group of men, many of whom would be close associates for years to come. The group included Thompson, his brother-in-law and second-in-command, who would later become the chief geographer for the United States Geological Survey, and Hillers, photographer, whose work for Powell would include the explorations of the Colorado River, an expedition to the Hopi for the 1876 Centennial Exhibition in Philadelphia and various assignments for the Bureau of Ethnology until his retirement in 1900.

Early in the 1870s, Powell met Stevenson, who was in charge of field operations for F. V. Hayden's U. S. Geological and Geographical Survey of the Territories. Of the relationship between Hayden and Stevenson, Hiram M. Chittenden wrote:

> It rarely happens that a master is so far indebted to a servant for his success, as was true of the relationship of Dr. Hayden and James Stevenson. Stevenson's great talent lay in the organization and management of men. … His extraordinary influence with Congressmen was a vital element in [the survey's] early growth.[534]

With the consolidation of the four "Great Surveys" into the USGS in 1879, and the establishment of the Bureau of Ethnology with Powell as Director, Stevenson was chosen to be the executive officer in charge of expeditions to the Southwest. At the same time, Powell counted on Stevenson's experience as a lobbyist in securing the support of several influential members of Congress, in sustaining and increasing the Bureau of Ethnology's funding.

In 1872, James Stevenson married Matilda Coxe Evans, who joined him as a member of F. V. Hayden's expeditions in Colorado, Idaho, Wyoming, and Utah for at least three field seasons between 1872 and 1878. In 1870 Logan, Stevenson, and Hayden had lived in the same boarding house in Washington.[535] Historian Darlis Miller suggested the Stevensons may have been introduced by their mutual friend, then Illinois Congressman John A. Logan, an ardent supporter of Hayden's work. Hayden's field crews included Cyrus Thomas, Logan's former brother-in-law, and William B. Logan, Logan's nephew.

In the meantime another circle was forming. Joseph Stanley Brown

---

534 Quoted in Miller 2007:17.
535 Miller, ibid, p. 239, n. 36.

became Powell's secretary in 1876, at a time when Powell was seeking the support of Ohio congressman James A. Garfield to consolidate the independent geological surveys funded by the federal government. Powell offered Garfield secretarial assistance. As a result, Brown served as Garfield's secretary, without pay, in addition to his regular duties in Powell's office. After Garfield's presidential nomination, Brown became the Republican candidate's private secretary, serving in that capacity until President Garfield's assassination in 1881, when he returned to work for Powell at the USGS until 1885. Brown then attended Yale University, where he graduated in 1888. In that year, he changed his name to Stanley-Brown and married Garfield's daughter, Mary.

With the consolidation of the Great Surveys in 1879, Stevenson encouraged Logan's support of the Bureau of Ethnology. On March 12, 1881, President Garfield accepted the resignation of Clarence King, director of the USGS since 1879, and nominated Powell to be the second director of the USGS. On March 18, several nominations, including the President's, were forwarded to the Senate where, on the motion of Senator Logan, Powell was chosen and took the oath of office the following day.

For many years the Logans and the Stevensons shared the same circle of friends in Washington. The Stevensons learned Logans' daughter Mary ("Dottie") had married William F. Tucker, a West Point graduate and paymaster for the Military District of New Mexico, stationed in Santa Fe. In 1881, the Stevensons and Logans met in Santa Fe where they were joined by Tucker and a fellow officer, Captain Henry W. Lawton.

It will be recalled that in the spring of 1881, the government teacher at Zuni, Thomas F. Ealy, wrote to the U. S. Agent for the Pueblo Indians, Ben Thomas, on behalf of the former governor of Zuni Pueblo, Pedro Pino, to report that officers at Fort Wingate desired the land around the Zuni farming village of Nutria as a part of a ranch. The land had not been included in the 1877 Executive Order Zuni Pueblo Indian Reservation and, so the officers argued, it was in the public domain. The officers were Major Tucker and Captain Lawton, who were often seen at Fort Wingate in their capacities as paymaster and inspector.

In 1882, the Stevensons and Logans agreed to meet in Santa Fe, and from there visit Fort Wingate and Zuni. With the addition of several members of Senator Logan's family and friends, they left Santa Fe together on September 10, and traveled on a special train to the end of the Atlantic and Pacific Railway line at Williams, Arizona. En route, Captain Lawton and three others were dropped off at Fort Wingate to arrange supplies and transportation to Zuni. The Senator's party returned to Fort Wingate, and left on September 13 to visit Zuni Pueblo and the surrounding area. H. C. Rizer, editor of the *Eureka Herald*, who also wrote articles for the *New York Daily Tribune*, published in the latter a list of those in the party:

> Senator Logan and wife, Mrs. Tucker, their daughter, Miss Cunningham, sister of Mrs. Logan, the Senator's son, Manning, Colonel Stevenson and wife, Captains McKibben and Lawton and their wives, Miss McKenzie and Miss Smith, of Santa Fe, Lieutenant Parker, of the 4th Cavalry, Major Gusten, artist, and Mr. Wittick, photographer.[536]

Rizer added, in a letter to the *Eureka Herald* :

> The Senator and ladies went in ambulances kindly furnished by [post commander] Gen. [Luther] Bradley, while the rest of us went by buckboard and mule or horseback. It is a forty-mile ride through a pleasant country of varied scenery.[537]

In another article, written for the *New York Daily Tribune*, Rizer described their route, including the following:

> The trail to Zuni from Fort Wingate leads directly over a mountain… over a rough road [where] the narrow but beautiful valley of Nutria (Beaver) breaks upon the view, with the thread-like creek of Nutria stretching away with unusual directness for a distance of ten miles to the southeast. Near the head of this valley is the Pueblo of Nutria, where some half dozen families of Zunis dwell, ranging their flocks of sheep and goats in the valley and along the hillsides.[538]

The party arrived at Zuni Pueblo on September 14, and returned to

---

536   Rizer 1882b.
537   H. C. Rizer, Editorial Correpondence, *Eureka Herald*, October 12, 1882.
538   Rizer 1882b.

Fort Wingate three days later. While Mrs. Logan and other members of the Logan party returned to Santa Fe, Senator Logan, James Stevenson, and two officers went to Keams Canyon.[539]

If James Stevenson submitted a written report of their visit to Keams Canyon, it has been lost. Remarkably, fiscal records show he purchased from Keam 4,643 "specimens of Moqui [Hopi] pottery" for $1,857.20. As Keam was also paid for packing boxes and freight for hauling over 6,900 pounds of "Ethnologic Specimens" to the railroad at Holbrook, these appear to be new acquisitions, not payment for the collections acquired, but not paid for, in 1879.[540]

While Stevenson and Logan were away, Cushing returned from his long trip to the east coast, bringing with him his new wife. As he was gathering supplies at Fort Wingate, Cushing noted in his daily journal of September 19:

> Learned that Mrs. S[tevenson] was there. Had accompanied an expedition of Gen'l Logan's to Zuni, the whole thing boding me no good. Lies triumph temporarily![541]

On September 21, the Cushings left for Zuni, and three days later Stevenson, Senator Logan, and their party returned from Keams Canyon.

Shortly after Senator Logan's visit to Zuni, "two army officers and a citizen located claims of 800 acres each, upon the valley of Las Nutrias, 640 acres under the Desert Land Act, and 160 acres under the Homestead Act" entered at the government land office in Santa Fe.[542] The claims made by Major Tucker and Captain Lawton were hardly a secret.[543] In early December, Matthews noted that two other officers at Fort Wingate, Lieutenants Torrance and Mumford, had gone to Nutria to investigate the possibilities of locating a ranch there as well.

While these events were taking place, Cushing's friend Sylvester Baxter arrived in New Mexico. Baxter had attended universities in Leipzig and Berlin in the 1870s before returning to Boston, where he became a writer for the *Boston Herald*. In the spring of 1881, he traveled to the

---

539   The officers were not identified but they were not Tucker and Lawton.
540   Lawson, ibid, p. 162.
541   Green, ibid, p. 240.
542   Curtis 1883:46.
543   Ibid, p. 57.

Southwest, and on May 28 Baxter met Cushing at Fort Wingate. The following evening Baxter, Willard Metcalf, an artist who accompanied Baxter, Matthews, and Bourke were among guests who met at the home of General Luther Bradley, commandant of Fort Wingate, to hear Cushing discuss Zuni song prayers. On June 10, Baxter sent an article, "Solved at Last … Wonderful Achievements of Frank H. Cushing," to the *Boston Herald*.[544]

A year later, Baxter accompanied Cushing during his visit to Boston. At some point, Cushing and Baxter had agreed to meet again. In early November 1882, Baxter arrived at Fort Wingate

> …with the intention of paying a second visit to Mr. Cushing at Zuni. … but he [Cushing] arrived at Fort Wingate unexpectedly one evening [while Baxter was there], having received directions from Major Powell to visit Oraibe … and make a collection of pottery, etc., for the National Museum.[545]

Baxter says nothing more about their brief visit.[546]

On December 1, "S. B." [Sylvester Baxter], a correspondent of the *Boston Herald*, writing from Santa Fe, reported that Senator Logan, "in association with others," had taken steps to secure possession of the spring at Nutria in order to establish a ranch around it. The lengthy and detailed article entitled "Logan's Land?" was published in the *Boston Herald* on December 11. In it "Our Special Correspondent" wrote:

> …Sometimes it seems as if it were the deliberate policy of the government to do its best to discourage Indians in their efforts for improvement and to reduce self-supporting tribes to pauperism [and] vagrancy and to drive them into hostility.
>
> I have never heard Senator Logan's personal integrity questioned. But is it fair to deprive a small and helpless people of what is morally and actually their right and

---

544 Baxter 1881. Published June 16 or 21?
545 Quoted in Hinsley and Wilcox, eds. 1996:97, 99.
546 On November 9, Matthews noted that Baxter had arrived "in my absence" and would leave for Zuni on November 11. Baxter returned to Fort Wingate two days later and planned to leave for Chihuahua on the 16th.

thus to snatch the very bread from their mouths?[547]

Logan was furious. Two days later, a reporter for the *New York Times* asked Logan for a response, and the Senator said:

...he had not taken the land in question. If it was public land, however, he saw no reason why it should not be pre-empted. He said he had looked at the land and said that he would take it if he could get it.[548]

Within a week after the appearance of "Logan's Land?" in the *Boston Herald*, Senator Logan had a conversation with Stevenson regarding the article. On December 22, Stevenson wrote to Baird:

The Senator stated that he believed this was written or instigated by F. H. Cushing of the Bureau of Ethnology. Senator Logan seemed to be so incensed that I have deemed it proper to call your attention to the matter.[549]

Given the obvious threat to the Bureau of Ethnology's funding, Baird immediately wrote to Cushing:

...I shall be glad to have from you an authoritative denial of this, so that I may show it to the General, should the matter come to the case that I think it is likely to attain, namely, his opposition to the appropriations for the Bureau of Ethnology.[550]

Baird's letter was forwarded to Cushing who was then camped near the Hopi Second Mesa, following an aborted effort to collect materials at Oraibi. On January 3, 1883, Cushing replied:

Far from having been either the author or instigator of an article in the *Boston Herald* reflecting on General Logan or his visit to this country, I not only have had ... no knowledge either of the contemplated or actual appearance of such an article, but sincerely regret that anything of the kind should have been published.[551]

Jesse Green, editor of Cushing's Zuni correspondence and journals, says "it is barely possible that he was telling the truth...but it is hard

---

547 Green, ibid, p. 334.
548 *New York Times*, December 13, 1882.
549 Ibid, p. 263.
550 Ibid.
551 Ibid, p. 264.

to believe that Cushing was really as uninvolved as he claimed in his response to Baird."[552]

Baird was certain Baxter had written the article but, at the same time, he was not fully convinced of the veracity of Cushing's denial of involvement. In early February Baird wrote to Baxter saying he would

> take great pleasure in informing Gen. Logan that Mr. Cushing has had nothing whatever to do with the article to which he took exception...[553]

Baxter, in turn, wrote to Cushing to inform him of Baird's request and, in the same letter, said he had also received one from Brown, Powell's secretary, saying:

> I think you need give yourself no concern about any harm that might come to Cushing through Senator Logan. ... Major Powell told me a few days ago that he proposed to stand by Cushing.[554]

If nothing more on the affair appeared after Baxter's article, the matter might have faded away, but this is not what happened.

In his daily medical record for Fort Wingate of April 10, Matthews noted the arrival of William Eleroy Curtis, and a party from Chicago en route to Zuni and their return to the east three days later. After graduation from Western Reserve College in 1871, Curtis joined the staff of *The Inter-Ocean* from 1873-1887, and was the managing editor at the time of Cushing's visit to Chicago the previous spring. However, it was the Logan affair that led to his visit to Zuni, the publication of an article, "General Logan's Ranch," in *The Inter-Ocean* on May 2, followed by a book, *Children of the Sun*, on August 1, 1883.[555] The full title of the article, written from Santa Fe on April 21, provided a summary of the affair as it was perceived by Cushing's supporters:

> GENERAL LOGAN'S RANCH: A Charge That He Has Despoiled the Zuni Indians of Their Lands. His Son-in-Law and Friends Locate Upon the Indian Farm and

---

552 Ibid, p. 261. I concur. As noted, it appears Cushing met Baxter at Fort Wingate in early November.

553 Quoted in Baxter to Cushing, February 19, 1883; Green, ibid, p. 275.

554 Ibid.

555 Curtis 1883a and 1883b. The date of publication of *Children of the Sun* is from the copyright copy submitted to the Library of Congress.

Springs. Excitement and Anxiety Among the Indians. Logan's Attacks Upon Frank Cushing. A Mistake in the Description of the Reservation Gives Tucker and Company a Chance.[556]

Curtis ascribed to Cushing an earlier and far more active role in the conflict:

> The Indians became alarmed at the rumors of encroachment upon their reservation and pleaded with Mr. Cushing [as they had with Ealy by April 1880], with the officers at Fort Wingate, and with Mr. Graham, the trader... These gentlemen were of course powerless to do anything and could only apply to the authorities of the Land Office in Santa Fe and to the Indian Agent there for information and relief...[557]

The center piece of the book is a chapter entitled "A Senatorial Episode" in which Curtis reproduces a number of documents, including the entire texts of President Chester A. Arthur's executive order of May 1, 1883 extending the Zuni reservation to include "Nutrias Springs" and adjacent lands; Senator Logan's detailed criticism of the order and defense of Captain Lawton on the floor of congress; Nai-iu-tchi's grateful response (recorded by Cushing and sent to Curtis); and Metcalf's response to Logan, including a rejoinder to the Senator's published "denunciation" of Cushing. Curtis emphasizes,

> Mr. Cushing carefully avoids taking any part in the discussion with General Logan, and has maintained a dignified silence under the latter's attacks upon him.[558]

In a letter to Baird written on May 9, immediately after President Arthur's executive order, Curtis defended Cushing saying "the facts contained in my letter relating to the Tucker Ranch were not obtained from Mr. Cushing, but were gathered in the most part before I saw him [in April] at the officers' [clubroom] at Fort Wingate."[559]

However, on the same day, Baxter wrote to Cushing:

My dear Tenatsali [Cushing]:

---

556   Green, ibid, pp. 282-283.
557   Ibid, p .282.
558   Curtis 1883:57.
559   Green, ibid, p. 287.

> Has all Zuni celebrated a day of thanksgiving? And
> does not Nai-iu-tchi[560] think that Thliakwa [Baxter] is
> his loyal son? All of which refers to *our* triumph in the
> Nutria spring matter.[561]

In spite of the denials by Baxter and Curtis it is, to repeat Green's
words, "hard to believe that Cushing was really as uninvolved as he [and
his friends] claimed." Indeed, in a fictional interview with himself, dated
June 9, 1883, Cushing noted he had met with Secretary of the Interior
H. M. Teller, during his visit to Washington in the spring of 1882, to
press for an enlargement of the Zuni reservation—many months before
Baxter's "Logan's Land?"[562]

President Arthur's executive order did not put an end to the
matter. In a published letter, Logan intimated his intention to appeal the
decision of the President. Among other things, the Senator suggested:

> If a civilized white man can now get only 160 acres of
> land as a homestead by paying for it, and an Indian can
> get over 1,000 acres without paying for it, had not the
> white man better adopt the Cushing plan and become
> one of the Indians?[563]

On May 6, 1883, only a few days after President Arthur's executive
order, Matthews noted, "Senator Logan of Illinois and Captain Lawton,
4th Cav. arrive and depart on private business." On the strength of Logan's
support, Lawton chose to disregard the executive order, and in October
attempted to take up land near Nutria. The Land Office in Santa Fe
denied his entry. Lawton appealed but the issue was not resolved. Two
years later, on March 3, 1885, President Arthur's last day in office, a new
executive order was issued amending the prior one by excluding:

> …from the addition made to [the Zuni] reservation …
> all lands [e.g., lands claimed by Lawton and Tucker]
> which were at the date of said order [May 1, 1883] settled
> upon and occupied in good faith under the public-land
> laws of the United States.[564]

---

560   Naiiutchi, Elder Priest of the Bow, and Cushing's mentor.
561   Green, ibid, p. 287.
562   Ibid, p. 299.
563   Quoted in Curtis, ibid, p. 52.
564   Quoted in Brandes 1965:105.

The Zunis protested and in November 1885, the Commissioner of the General Land Office ordered the cancellation of all claims and entries on the Zuni reservation. By then Lawton was in Arizona in command of B Troop, 4th Cavalry, and was selected by General Nelson A. Miles to lead the expedition that captured Geronimo.

Before these events took place, Cushing received a letter from Curtis regarding his efforts against Logan on behalf of the Zuni:

> …The newspapers of the country, east and west, are keeping up the agitation…and the leading dailies… The madder I can get him [Logan] the worse it will be for him…and he is beginning to realize that his Presidential schemes are already knocked in the head. … My letters have been copied in almost every paper in the land, and I have the ears not only of our subscribers [The Inter Ocean] but of those of a hundred other papers.[565]

Nothing more is recorded in the extant correspondence of

---

565   Curtis to Cushing, June 12, 1883, Zuni 1.41, MS.6, AMAW. Two months after Cushing's return to Washington, June 3-6, 1884, the Republican National Convention was held in Chicago. Logan was a far distant fourth among those nominated to be the Republican candidate for President; however, he was a near unanimous choice for Vice President on the ticket with James G. Blaine. Although Republicans had won six consecutive presidential elections since 1856, they had lost 33 congressional seats in the 1882 mid-term elections, a backlash against political patronage and Republican corruption. By the time of the 1884 nominating convention the Republican party had split into three factions: the regulars, machine politicians who supported the spoils system; the moderates, including Blaine, who pushed for some reforms; and the reformers, soon to be labeled Mugwumps, who were appalled by what the party had become and were willing to bolt. The Democrats met in Chicago a month later, July 8-11, and nominated Grover Cleveland, Governor of New York, as their candidate for President, with Thomas A. Hendricks as his running mate. The personal character of the candidates became a central issue in the campaigns. Cleveland was accused of fathering a child out of wedlock. Although uncertain, Cleveland chose to acknowledge responsibility and "Tell the Truth" and "Grover the Good" became campaign slogans. Blaine was accused of attempting to cover up being paid for Congressional favors for railroad companies which he had acknowledged in a letter closed with the phrase "burn this letter." The turning point in the election came when a Blaine supporter slurred Catholics, and the Irish vote in New York shifted to Cleveland who won the state by a thousand votes out of the million cast, and the presidential election. Upon his death, December 26, 1886, Logan was laid in state in the United States Capitol rotunda.

Cushing, Baird, and Powell regarding the Logan affair. Many years later, on April 3, 1946, Frederick Webb Hodge, Cushing's brother in law and field secretary for Cushing's Hemenway Southwestern Archaeological Expedition, wrote:

> [Cushing] returned to Washington not by reason of his health but because Senator John A. Logan demanded his return under threat of 'killing' the Bureau of Ethnology's appropriation.[566]

Cushing and the Oraibi Expedition – 1882

In early November, Cushing left for Hopi[567] and met Brown, as well as some Hopi men from Oraibi, at Keams Canyon. Cushing wrote Baird that he succeeded "in winning the Oraibians over and confidently expect to make at their Pueblo—the finest collecting point left—a rich and extensive gathering."[568] On his way to Oraibi, Cushing was detained at First Mesa by a snow storm. He returned to Zuni to observe the "annual Sun Ceremonial." Brown stayed at Keam's trading post where, with Stephen's assistance, he compiled an illustrated catalogue of Hopi pottery types, with Hopi names for shapes and designs.[569]

On December 5, Cushing left Zuni again, this time with the artist Willard Metcalf, whose journal "of a winter's exploration trip to Oraibi" provides insight into Cushing's character.[570] Four day later, they reached the USGS camp near Holbrook where Cushing met with Powell, who had just returned from the Grand Canyon. Cushing received orders detailing him to serve as an assistant to Victor Mindeleff, who was

---

566 Quoted in Green 1979:27, n. 19 Metcalf also thought Cushing's recall was due to Logan ("this vile scoundrel"). "Will not the fact of Logan's defeat in the election be apt to change affairs somewhat?" Metcalf to Cushing, July 11 and September 7, 1884, Zuni 1.41, MS.6, AMAW. Edwin A. Curley also saw Logan as the cause. Curley to Cushing, July 18, 1884, Zuni 1.21, MS.6, AMAW.

567 It was during his trip to Keams Canyon he would have met Baxter at Fort Wingate. Green 1979:255-260 provides accounts by Cushing, Metcalf and Mindeleff of the ill-fated "Oraibi expedition," as well as an insightful introduction and notes.

568 Green, 1990:251.

569 Brown, J. Stanley, Hopi Names for Pottery and Pottery Designs, MS 1141, National Anthropological Archives, Smithsonian Institution.

570 Metcalf, ibid. Metcalf, a devoted friend, was distressed by Cushing's mistreatment of his horses.

placed in charge of the collecting expedition to Oraibi.

The party, with three wagons, got under way on December 13, and reached Walpi five days later. In Tewa village Cushing met Pulakaki (Polacca),[571] his guide to Havasupai the previous summer. Polacca agreed to serve as guide and translator. Leaving First Mesa in a snowstorm on December 20, the party reached Oraibi the following day. The trade goods—sugar, flour, cloth, blankets, beads, etc.—were unloaded at the house Cosmos Mindeleff and Jeremiah Sullivan had occupied earlier in the fall while mapping the village. Victor Mindeleff returned to Keams Canyon for boxing materials, leaving Cushing with Polacca, Metcalf, and a teamster. Metcalf recalled,

> Frank [Cushing] soon went out to attend a council and see what could be done in the prospects of a collection. … It must have been about 3 o'clock [in the morning] when I was awakened by a shake and saw or heard F. say "Come get up, quick! quick! We have got to get out of here before morning."[572]

Cushing had boldly entered a kiva—anthropologist Peter Whiteley suggests, "quite possibly the chief kiva during the *Soyalangw* ceremony"— and was met with much hostility.[573] What Cushing encountered was a village divided, a faction led by Loololma, the *Kikmongwi* (village chief), and another led by the "Chief Priest of the tribe and a *Wizard*." Cushing returned to the kiva for further talk. The next morning, he sent an urgent message to Mindeleff at Keams Canyon, recounting the discussions in the kiva:

> … I made no threats. I just simply said that we were under orders, and that we must carry out those orders. Their reply was that we could carry them out only over their dead bodies; that, furthermore, they would give us between this and daylight to leave. That we *must* get out of their pueblo before the sun rose or it would not be well for us. … I told them I should remain and send for

---

571 See Chapter 3 for a biography of Polacca.
572 Metcalf, ibid, p. 40
573 Ibid, p. 41; Whiteley 1988a:42. Whiteley's work is a thorough account of the historical and cultural contexts of the factionalism at Oraibi. See also Chapter 6 for additional historical background.

my wagons. They replied I should not, and informing them once more of the same intention, I left them. ... What the Oraibis propose to do about it, I know not. Probably they will, when they see our determination to stay, do nothing.[574]

After a brief discussion, Cushing's party agreed to stay until their freight wagons could return. Meanwhile, Mindeleff sent a telegram to Powell who had returned to Washington: "Oraibe extremely hostile no collections possible at present awaiting further orders shall collect at other towns."[575] Five days after his arrival, as Cushing later reported, "the wagons arrived and we bade farewell to foolish, bull-dozed Oraibi."[576]

Cushing's party left Oraibi with "a small collection ... numbering about a hundred and fifty pieces ... acquired principally among the members of the family in whose house we were stopping."[577] They relocated to Second Mesa and carried on trade near Mishongnovi where twelve hundred items, primarily pottery, were acquired. The collection was boxed and freighted to Holbrook.

By mid-February, Victor Mindeleff returned to Washington where, with his brother Cosmos, he resumed making models, this time models of the Hopi villages for the Louisville Exposition in the fall of 1883. Meanwhile, Cushing returned to Zuni by the first of February where he was confronted with more controversy and ill health.

It will be recalled that in the previous fall and winter Rizer accompanied a USGS party to Fort Wingate. As a voluntary assistant, Rizer soon accepted an invitation from James Stevenson to join the Bureau of Ethnology expedition to Canyon de Chelly. Throughout the three months Rizer spent in the Southwest, he sent weekly accounts to the *Eureka Herald*. At the conclusion of the expedition to Canyon de Chelly, Rizer spent several days at Keam's trading post, and on October 29 he accompanied Stephen to witness a part of a Navajo Mountainway ceremony. Rizer's account, "Hosh-Kon: Description of a Great Navajo Festival," was published in the *Topeka Capital* on January 14, 1883 and

---

574   Green, ibid, p. 260.
575   V. Mindeleff to Powell, December 26, 1882, LR-BE, NAA, SI.
576   Green, ibid, p. 403, n. 39.
577   Victor Mindeleff to Powell, January 1, 1883, LR-BE, NAA, SI.

reprinted in Rizer's *Eureka Herald*.

In an editorial column entitled "Reality vs. Romance," Henry King, editor of the *Topeka Capital*, praised Rizer for his "intelligent, straightforward and unsensational" account, which King regarded:

> [to be] very much at variance with the dime-novel newspaper letters and magazine articles on this topic [specifically the Zuni] during the last year by certain ambitious young scribes [specifically Cushing, but also Sylvester Baxter] evidently more anxious to 'work the racket,' as the boys say, than to contribute accurate and useful information.[578]

Capt. King, a civil war veteran, lawyer and journalist, would become editor of the *St. Louis Globe-Democrat* later in the year. He had made a number of trips west, including one to Fort Wingate during 1876, where he had met Stevenson, Keam, and others.

Back in Boston, Baxter saw King's editorial and sent clippings to Cushing. Cushing immediately rode to Fort Wingate to seek the advice and support of Washington Matthews. Within days Matthews's "The Zuni Dispute: An Army Officer's Defense of Mr. Cushing" was published in the *Topeka Capital*.[579] Matthews had read Cushing's articles, had many conversations with him at Fort Wingate over the previous two years but, if his official daily record is correct, he had never visited Zuni or observed Cushing in the field. From King's editorial, Matthews assumed Rizer was behind King's critical commentary on Cushing's articles. However, when Cushing wrote to King asking for the names of the sources for his editorial, King replied saying, while given in confidence, "in fairness to myself as to you," he named James Stevenson, Cushing's friend Douglas D. Graham and Thomas V. Keam.[580] Cushing was undoubtedly puzzled by this list. Certainly Matilda Stevenson was hostile to Cushing, but there is nothing in James Stevenson's public record to suggest he would agree with King's conclusion:

> [Cushing] has been pushing his Zuni investigations ostensibly in the interest of science, under the patronage

---

578   Green, ibid, p. 265.
579   Green, ibid, pp. 272-273.
580   Ibid, p. 274.

of the Smithsonian Institution, and he should be truthful if nothing else. He seems, however, to prefer the role of the sensationalist, and to invite attention to himself instead of the facts by embellishing his "scientific" remarks with cheap yarns of personal exploits that occurred only in his dreams or his imagination. ... The Smithsonian owes it to itself, we think, to dispense with the services of this elaborate young inflater of the facts...[581]

Although King compares Cushing's work with Rizer's, there is nothing in style or content of Rizer's articles to support Matthews's conclusion that Rizer was the source of the editor's criticisms. Capt. King's father, Col. Selah W. King, was a friend of Abraham Lincoln, Senator John W. Logan, and other prominent political leaders in Illinois, and it is likely Henry King was as well. If so, his editorial against Cushing may be seen as part of Logan's attack on the young ethnologist's advocacy of Zuni land claims.

Matthews seems to be aware of this possible motivation. In the conclusion of his letter to the *Topeka Capital*, he wrote:

I regret to say that Mr. Cushing has made many enemies in this country, not because there is anything in his amiable character which should engender hatred in the bosom of another, but because the champion of the oppressed is never in favor with the oppressors, and because there is nothing in the world more intolerant than self-satisfied ignorance.[582]

Cushing at the Tertio-Millennial Celebration – July 1883

On June 29, Cushing and thirty-seven Zuni Indians passed through Fort Wingate on their way to The Santa Fe Tertio-Millennial Anniversary Celebration and Grand Mining and Industrial Exposition.[583] The "Tertio" opened on July 2, and closed on August 3, "the 33rd day in the 333rd year since its settlement," 1500 having been arbitrarily chosen

---

581 Ibid, p. 266.
582 Ibid, p. 273.
583 Also called "The Santa Fe Tertio-Millennial Anniversary, Character Celebration and Industrial Exposition."

by civic leaders as the date of Santa Fe's establishment.[584]

The exposition officially began at 9 a.m. on July 2 with an artillery salute, a parade and addresses by various speakers, including Governor L. A. Sheldon. Exhibitions of the "three distinct civilizations"—the Pueblo or Village Indians, the Spaniards, the Americans—were included in a show of "Royal splendor and barbaric magnificence." Advance newspaper publicity, reduced rate fares on the Santa Fe Railroad, and letters of invitation brought an estimated ten to twelve thousand people to the opening. The featured event of the fourth day, July 5, was "An ambuscade and sham fight by the Zuni Indians, with an exhibition of their peculiar rites and ceremonies under the direction of Mr. Frank Cushing." On July 10, there were "Zuni war dances," followed on succeeding days by "the Zuni Indian game of hidden ball," and "a foot-race of three miles, for a prize, between the fleetest warriors of the Apaches and the swift footed Zunis." July 18, the first of three days "devoted to a presentation of historic scenes ... each day to represent a century of history and progress," was described in the following day's issue of the *New Mexican Review*:

> [The first day began with a parade led by] the Thirteenth United States Infantry band, playing its most thrilling airs [followed] in unique confusion [by] those splendid specimens of physical manhood, the Apache chiefs, warrior and hunters, with their gleaming spears and buckskin robes adorned with beads of many hues; the Oriental and innocent looking Zunis of the sixteenth century, with bows and arrows, ...and [several companies of] richly robed knights, ... a full quota of court officers, and a brilliant guard.

The climactic event, in which Cushing's party of Zunis played a prominent part, was a reenactment of Coronado's attack on the chief of the "Cities of Cibola," ending with the surrender of the Indians.[585] This spectacle was followed by a series of speeches portraying the three centuries of New Mexico's history. One of the speakers was Palowahtiwa

---

584 Santa Fe (La Villa Real de la Santa Fe de San Francisco de Asis) was founded in 1607 by New Mexico's Spanish governor, Don Pedro de Peralta.

585 Green, ibid, p. 301; see Ellis 1958:133. Ellis provides the only full account of the event.

(Patricio Pino, governor of Zuni) whose address was translated by Cushing and published in the same issue of the *New Mexican Review*.[586] Like his father, Palowahtiwa was, in Green's view, a practical politician who used the occasion to build a bridge of understanding and support for his people. For example:

> My brother and your child (here he referred to Mr. Cushing) has told me that these who sit around me in council are dressed as were Coronado and his warriors. "If so," I say to myself, "Why did our grandfathers receive them with arrows and stones, instead of with warm hands and good breaths, for they are dressed as by magic."[587]

Bandelier met Cushing during the exposition and reported "he is well, somewhat exercised over the Logan affair, but otherwise pleased and hopeful."[588]

Attendance at the Tertio-Centennial Celebration was far less than hoped for and destined to be a financial failure. Construction of the main exhibit building, a structure 60 by 480 feet, and a race track, purses totaling $5,000 for the entire race program, and other expenses continued to mount. On July 24, it was announced that the celebration, instead of ending on August 3, would be extended to August 15. Fares on the railroad were reduced still further, and efforts were made to organize mass train excursions from eastern states. Heavy rains during the last days of July forced the cancellation of a number of performances, and on the night of August 2, "a cloudburst sent floods raging through the city, destroying bridges and roads. Further east, the same storm severely damaged railroad trackage".[589]

Cushing and the Zunis left Santa Fe on July 21. Meanwhile the Dutch anthropologist Herman ten Kate learned Cushing was in Santa Fe for the Tertio-Millennial exposition. Ten Kate had planned to visit Zuni but realized "I could accomplish little among the Indians without the assistance" of Cushing. He decided to go to Albuquerque to see the

---

586   The account was reprinted elsewhere. Metcalf reported reading it in the *New York Herald*. Metcalf to Cushing, July 21, 1883, Zuni 1.41. MS.6, AMAW.

587   Green, ibid, pp. 301-302.

588   Bandelier to Mrs. Lewis Henry Morgan, July 18, 1883, quoted in Green, ibid, p. 301.

589   Ellis ibid, p. 133.

newly established Indian school, and then continue on to Santa Fe. The train arrived in Albuquerque at 4:30 a.m. and, after a brief rest at the Hotel Armijo, ten Kate went out to "view the city." He wrote:

> Arriving at the station, I find a number of Indians... With them is a Negro [Abram]; an Indian of lavender countenance with blond locks, clearly an albino; and a white man with long curly hair, who speaks the Indian language and directs them with gestures. From the bystanders I learn that he is Frank Cushing, who is returning from Santa Fe with his Zuni Indians [as well as his wife and sister-in-law].[590]

The following day the *Albuquerque Morning Journal* noted, "The Zunis took Frank Cushing back to Zuni last night. They thought he had exhibited himself enough for one trip." Ten Kate continued his travels, visiting Cushing at Zuni from August 28 to September 6. Ten Kate was impressed:

> ...I have been able to observe Cushing and know him through his work. Two things I have particularly gained from this acquaintance: a profound admiration for a man who has suffered for the sake of science alone and the conviction that his method of studying the ethnology of a people is the only authentic one.[591]

The Fifth Bureau of Ethnology Expedition - 1883

For the field season beginning in the summer of 1883, James Stevenson and Victor Mindeleff led separate, comparatively uneventful, expeditions to the Southwest. Stevenson's party left Washington on August 1, "for the purpose of making further studies among the pueblos and ruins of the Southwestern portion of the United States." Three weeks later the Stevensons arrived at Fort Defiance, where James Stevenson outfitted for archaeological research at Canyon de Chelly and at the ancestral Hopi village of Awatobi. In his annual report for 1883, Powell gave only a brief summary of the work of his executive officer as Stevenson had "continued the explorations ... prosecuted as reported in previous years":

---

590   Kate 2004:226. Abram was Cushing's cook.
591   Kate, ibid, p. 278.

He explored several large and important ruins in Northeastern Arizona, where he made some valuable collections, including skeletons, skulls, ancient pottery, and bone and stone implements. At the ruins of Tally-Hogan [Awatobi] the party discovered the ancient burial ground of the inhabitants. ... Mr. Stevenson subsequently visited the seven Moki villages... [Followed by] the examination of two distinct classes of ruins [near] Flagstaff, Arizona.[592]

Between September 2 and October 10, Stevenson paid Keam a total of $229.96 for food and other supplies. Other expenditures included reimbursements for payments (@ $1.00/day) for a messenger, two herders, and ten laborers for "excavating for specimens."[593]

Cushing at Zuni – Fall 1883

Cushing returned to Zuni at the end of July, refreshed and encouraged by the reception given his participation in the Tertio-Millennial Celebration. His surviving correspondence, reports, and accounts by others make no mention of Senator Logan, who was involved in a contentious and scandal plagued presidential campaign. Logan's political aspirations ended with Grover Cleveland's narrow defeat of James G. Blaine on November 25.

With the "Logan affair" seemingly behind him, Cushing turned to other matters. He had been authorized to establish a militia to respond to the theft of livestock and increasing incursions onto traditional Zuni lands. In his "Annual Report for 1884," Cushing reported the militia was called into action almost immediately by renewed raiding on Zuni stock. He led his warriors, "mostly unarmed," in an attack resulting in the death of two of the desperados (an American and a Mexican) and the suppression of outside difficulties for several months.[594] According to his annual report, this success influenced him to build a spacious

---

592   Powell 1883:xxiii.
593   Quarterly Report 239,597, Voucher 83, Records of the Accounting Offices of the Department of the Treasury, Office of the First Auditor, Settled Miscellaneous Treasury Accounts, RG 217, National Archives. The excavations were carried out on September 18 and 19 and on October 9 and 10.
594   I follow Green's summary, ibid, p. 304.

residence for his family on the outskirts of the village.[595]

At intervals during the fall and winter of 1883, Powell reported:

[Cushing] carried out systematic explorations of the sacrificial grottoes and native shrines of the Zuni in the main and tributary valleys of the pueblo. ... As, however, he was forced to visit these places either in company with Indians or by stealth, the objects could not be disturbed.[596]

However, other "burial places yielded perfect crania and well preserved vessels of pottery." To the end, Cushing persisted in removing grave goods and other sacred objects in spite of the confrontation he had had with tribal leaders in 1880.[597]

In February and early March, Bandelier spent fifteen days with Cushing at Zuni and, as noted above, visited him in Santa Fe during the Tertio-Millennial Celebration. Bandelier was experiencing financial difficulties, including the approaching failure of his father's bank in Highland, Illinois. Throughout the fall of 1883, he pressed Cushing to spend some of his time moonlighting as a private collector for the Museum für Völkerkunde in Berlin and the Missouri Historical Society. Cushing did not accept either proposal. Then, as discussed above, Cushing's cache of pottery and other artifacts was looted in November. However, Cushing responded to Bandelier's desperate need for money by sending him a check for $100.[598]

In November, in what appears to have been a coordinated effort, E. N. Horsford, a former professor of chemistry at Harvard, and Rev. Edward E. Hale, a well-known Boston clergyman, wrote letters to Powell to express their concern regarding Cushing's health and, in Horsford's letter, to request Cushing's return to Washington so "the immense amount of material Cushing has accumulated" can be preserved.[599] In

---

595   Ibid. However, the reasons given to "build an addition to the small room" he purchased the previous autumn (1882), were: (1) the space Cushing currently occupied was needed by the Zuni owners, and (2) "the unhealthfulness of my quarters." Cushing to Powell, August 20, 1883, in Green, ibid, p, 307. Cushing did not receive a reply from Powell and proceeded to build his own residence.

596   Ibid, xxvi.

597   Green, ibid, p. 344.

598   Green, ibid, pp. 410-411, notes 3 and 10. Given Cushing's own on-going financial difficulties, this gift is quite remarkable.

599   Ibid, pp. 309-310.

reply, Powell expressed the opinion:

> It would be better, however, for these suggestions to come from Mr. Cushing, for I fear that such an intimation on my part would be construed by him to mean a recall by reason of dissatisfaction with his work.[600]

Nevertheless, Cushing would soon be recalled to Washington.

Meanwhile Cushing was taking steps to publish the material he had collected and, in doing so, to address his on-going money troubles.

Cushing and *The Millstone* – 1884 - 1885

On January 19, 1884, James C. Pilling, Chief Clerk of the Bureau of Ethnology, wrote Cushing to inform him of his recall to Washington:

> It is thought best that the valuable ethnologic material collected by you at the Pueblo of Zuni should be put in shape for publication at as early a day as practicable and that progress to this end would be facilitated by your presence, for a time, in the East. As soon, therefore, as you can settle your affairs in Zuni…you will proceed to Washington and report to the Director.[601]

Just five days later, on January 24, David H. Ranck, publisher of *The Millstone*, "a monthly journal devoted to the milling and mechanical arts," wrote Cushing to tell him the first installment of "Zuni Breadstuff" had been published, and that one copy "under your frank" would be sent the following day. Cushing's "valuable ethnologic material" would be published not by the Bureau of Ethnology but by a commercial firm at the rate of 10 cents per typeset line. Indeed, Cushing's most comprehensive study of Zuni life would be published serially in nineteen issues of *The Millstone* from January 1884 through August 1885. It was not until the fall of 1885, after the completion of "Zuni Breadstuff," that Cushing responded to the terms of his recall by writing "A Study of Pueblo Pottery as Illustrative of Zuni Cultural Growth."[602]

Ranck's letters to Cushing tell us some, but not all, of the story of the origin and development of "Zuni Breadstuff." Sometime during the fall of 1882, Cushing corresponded with the editors of the *Century*

---

600   Ibid, p. 310.
601   Ibid, p. 316.
602   Cushing 1896.

magazine, publishers of his "My Life in Zuni," to propose a further series of articles on Zuni. In January 1883, while he was staying at Keam's ranch, following the expedition to Oraibi, Cushing wrote to Ranck. In a letter of response to Cushing, Ranck said:

> ...anticipating the favor of *The Century* folks to my proposition...I desire you shall take as wide a range with it as you as deem necessary to make the matter complete.[603]

Apparently the "it" is described in a letter from Cushing and included "the illustration and description of utensils, the composition and method of preparation of the various bread products, the legends and the folk-lore..." "Enough," Ranck continued, "to cover our issues for the greater part of a year." Ranck proposed to "set apart not more than three pages each month," and this would require "at least 2,500 words with...illustrations." With regard to payment, Ranck said, "I am willing to pay liberally," but not at the rate he assumes Cushing received from The Century Company. Make me a fair price," he asked.

Cushing returned to Zuni in February 1883. On April 19, he wrote agreeing to the length of the articles. Gently pressing to move ahead with the project, on September 18 Ranck wrote to suggest the series begin with the November issue. Cushing did not write until November 6. In response, Ranck proposed to pay Cushing at the rate of 10 cents per line of type or about $25 per page, a rate higher than that paid to any other contributor to *The Millstone*. On December 7, the first installment of Cushing's series reached the offices of *The Millstone* in Indianapolis. Cushing proposed "Zuni Breadstuff" as the title for the series. "Zuni Breadstuff" brought new subscribers to *The Millstone*, and the January 1884 issue was quickly sold out, with a continuing demand for back copies. Ranck was pleased, and at the conclusion of the series in March 1885, Ranck suggested Cushing might continue to contribute short pieces for future issues. Nothing came of this, or of Ranck's suggestion of making "Zuni Breadstuff" into a book.[604]

---

603   Ranck to Cushing, February 26, 1883, Frank Hamilton Cushing Manuscript Collection, MS.6, Autry Museum of the American West. Cited hereafter as FHCMC.

604   "Zuni Breadstuff" was published in book format in 1920 as Vol. 8, Indian Notes and Monographs, Museum of the American Indian, Heye Foundation, New

As with his publications in the *Atlantic Monthly* and the *Century Illustrated Monthly Magazine*, Cushing's motivations were monetary. There is little record of Cushing's finances during his years at Zuni. His monthly salary of $100 exceeded that of most Bureau employees in the Southwest. Unlike James Stevenson, for example, who submitted vouchers for purchase of collections, shipping and transportation, etc., Cushing sent no vouchers for reimbursement during his fieldwork. At the time of Cushing's transfer from the National Museum to the payroll of the Bureau of Ethnology in January 1882, Powell paid Cushing's outstanding debts of $513 to Graham and Hopkins for food, tobacco, and trade goods. Baxter suggested Cushing would receive $100 for each of the articles in the *Atlantic Monthly*, and $100 for an address in Boston during his tour of the East.[605] It is by no means clear how Cushing was able to support his family following his marriage in July 1882. In January 1884, he informed Powell he had expended $697 dollars in money and stock on the construction of his new house, and owed an additional $412 for freight, materials and labor.[606] In his letter responding to Powell's order that he return to Washington, Cushing asked for time, not financial assistance, in meeting these debts:

> I cannot, from the nature of my obligation, leave Zuni before these debts are discharged. I therefore beg that you shall allow me from four to six months more in the field for the payment of them.

He continues with a disingenuous, if not dishonest, request:

> I shall be able to make these payments much more expeditiously if...I am allowed by you to enter into literary engagements, which heretofore I have, for considerations of honor, held in abeyance.[607]

Cushing had, by this date, made "literary engagements" with the *Atlantic Monthly*, *Century Illustrated Monthly Magazine*, as well as *The*

York.

605   Green, ibid, pp. 215-216.

606   Powell had not approved construction of the house and Cushing did not seek reimbursement. Cushing moved into the new house, two weeks before receiving notice of his recall.

607   Green, ibid, p. 317. Cushing's draft response to Powell does not include this proposal. Cushing to Powell, January 29, 1884, Zuni 1.45, MS.6, AMAW.

Millstone. With the exception of "Zuni Fetiches," he had held nothing "in abeyance."[608]

Cushing received $1248.40 from Ranck for his manuscripts, and an additional $127.75 for his illustrations, equaling the amount he continued to receive as a salaried employee of the Bureau of Ethnology. Cushing asked Ranck to send $100 to Malone & MacIntosh, owed for construction of his house, and $222.80 to Graham. The balance sent to Cushing was $1053.35. It appears Cushing had no remaining debts from his field work at Zuni.[609]

Cushing's Recall to Washington

Cushing was recalled to Washington, "not later than Feb'y 15th, if possible"—actually not leaving Zuni until April 26.

Shortly before Cushing's departure, a story "From our Special Correspondent" was sent to the *Boston Herald* with the dateline, "Santa Fe, N.M., April 16, 1884." It was signed "H." The headline provides a summary of its contents:

> INDIAN FOLK-LORE: Why Mr. Cushing Has to Stay
> So Long in Zuni. His Persecution by Senator Logan.
> Expected Results from His Self-Denying Mission.

The author accurately describes Cushing's official position within the Smithsonian, his accomplishments at Zuni, including "a possible result of ethnological researches in wearing away race barriers and benefitting the Indian." Cushing "has wanted to stay longer at Zuni," and "H" concludes:

> I have only tried to convey an idea of his objects in remaining at Zuni and to give some reasons for the length of time required to round off his great work with success.

However, much of the article is an attack on Senator Logan:

> ...it is almost incomprehensible that a man who calls himself a statesman and who aspires to be President of the United States, should stoop to assail this self-

---

608 Cushing made no mention of the Bureau of Ethnology in his commercial publications.

609 In a letter to Powell, March 20, 1884, Cushing wrote "For [*The Millstone*] series...I received liberal aid toward the discharge of my debts." Green, ibid, p. 320.

sacrificing young scientist and endeavor not only to injure him socially here and in Washington but to procure his removal under threat of withholding funds for the Smithsonian Institute.

[The Bureau of Ethnology's annual appropriations] are made in the sundry civil bill, usually the last to come up for discussion in Congress. When this bill reaches the Senate, it is stated that Logan will refuse to consent to the appropriation of any money for the Smithsonian so long as Mr. Cushing remains connected with it.[610]

The style and content, the evidence of his authorship of the earlier so-called "interview" regarding the Nutria controversy, and Cushing's concern for his public image are among factors that lead Jesse Green, the editor of Cushing's correspondence and journals, to conclude "here too is a case of self-service journalism and that 'H.' stands for Hamilton, Cushing's own middle name."[611] Even "S. B.," Sylvester Baxter, would not have had access to the detailed information provided in the letter. In many ways, the letter can be seen as a bitter farewell to Zuni and to the work Cushing felt was left undone.

The stated purpose of his recall was the supposition that his presence in the East would facilitate the publication of "the valuable ethnographic material collected by you at the Pueblo of Zuni"—it may have been assumed—by the Bureau of Ethnology. However, once back in the nation's capital, Cushing continued to write articles for *The Millstone* through to the following spring. In spite of illness, he began writing "A Study of Pueblo Pottery as Illustrative of Zuni Cultural Growth,"[612] eventually published by the Bureau of Ethnology. On January 15, 1885 Cushing delivered a paper on the "Ancient Province of Cibola and the Seven Lost Cities" at a meeting of the American Geographical Society. Powell acknowledged these two papers in his annual report. Continuing his summary of Cushing's work, Powell wrote:

Early in 1885, Mr. Cushing furnished the Director with

---

610   Ibid, pp. 321-322.

611   Ibid, p. 320.

612   Cushing 1886. Because publication of the *Annual Report(s) of the Bureau of Ethnology* were behind schedule, Cushing's essay was included in the annual report for 1882/1883.

a schedule of his manuscripts, notes, and sketches, and from an examination of this it was deemed advisable that he should continue putting his linguistic material into permanent shape... This work had progressed but little, however, when a severe illness necessitated his temporary abandonment.[613]

Cushing's employment with the Bureau of Ethnology ended during the 1885-1886 fiscal year. Once again, Powell reported:

Mr. Frank H. Cushing was engaged in the preparation, from the large amount of Zuni material collected by him during several years, of papers upon the language, mythology and institutions of that people.[614]

However, Cushing returned to his home in Barre Center, New York, in June 1885, and appears to have spent the year recuperating from illness.

It is beyond the scope of this book to document Cushing's life beyond his employment with the Bureau of Ethnology to this date. In February 1892 he accepted a position, again, as an assistant ethnologist in the Bureau, and the work he produced that year, "Outlines of Zuni Creation Myths," was his third and final publication for the Bureau of Ethnology.[615]

The Sixth Bureau of Ethnology Expedition - 1884

James Stevenson was again placed in charge of explorations in the Southwest in the summer and fall of 1884. Stevenson's party was divided into three sections. F. T. Bickford, a newspaper man with the Associated Press in New York City and a friend of Stevenson, was in charge of one section. In his annual report, Powell simply lists the sites visited by Bickford's party: Chaco Canyon, Canyon de Chelly, the ruins in Walnut Canyon and "another group of interesting cave dwellings" near Flagstaff. He adds:

---

613   Powell 1888:xlvii

614   Powell 1891a:xxi.

615   Cushing 1896. Cushing assisted with the installation of the Bureau of Ethnology's exhibit at the World Columbian Exposition in Chicago, 1893. He was the Director of the Hemenway Southwestern Archaeological Expedition from 1886 to 1889. In 1895 and 1896 he led expeditions to the Florida Keys with support from Dr. William Pepper and Mrs. Phoebe Hearst. He died in April 1900 at the age of 43.

All these were carefully examined. Full and extensive notes, as well as sketches and photographic illustrations, were made of these ruins.[616]

However, a more detailed account of Bickford's explorations, illustrated throughout with engravings based on photographs, was published in the *Century* magazine in October 1890. Bickford spent eight days in Chaco Canyon in September, shortly after a second survey of the "great houses" in August by Victor Mindeleff. Navajo Charley, a guide during Stevenson's explorations in Canyon de Chelly two years earlier, accompanied Bickford. Like H. C. Rizer's accounts of the 1882 exploration of Canyon de Chelly, Bickford's "Prehistoric Cave-Dwellings" was a rich description of the areas he was assigned.[617]

C. A. Garlick, who had accompanied Stevenson to New Mexico in 1880, was in charge of another section, stationed at Acoma Pueblo. His party assembled a collection of about thirty-five hundred examples of pottery and other materials "illustrating the arts of the people of Acoma."

A third section, under Stevenson's supervision, and "with the important assistance of Mrs. Stevenson," engaged in making collections and studies at Zuni, less than six months after Cushing's departure. The collection was said to be "larger than any heretofore obtained," and included materials on Zuni ceremonial life "secured from sacred springs, caves, and shrines" by James Stevenson.[618] A far less charitable perspective of the Stevensons' efforts was offered by Matthews in a sarcastic letter to Cushing:

> He [Graham] assured me that Mrs. Stevenson had learned to talk both Zuni and Spanish fluently and was obtaining no end of valuable information on all points from the Indians. From the way she is working I think she will get all that is worth getting before long. The Indians are unbosoming themselves to her. Col. S. too has explored a number of caves around Zuni and made wonderful discoveries. He has found images that

---

616   Powell, ibid, p. xxviii.
617   Bickford 1890.
618   Powell, ibid, p. xxix.

apparently have beards.[619]

The collections made by the parties under the direction of Bickford, Garlick, and Stevenson were sent to Washington to enhance the Bureau of Ethnology's exhibits at World's Industrial and Cotton Centennial Exposition, that would open in New Orleans on December 16, 1884.

The Seventh Bureau of Ethnology Expedition - 1885

During the field season of 1885, the Bureau of Ethnology sent two expeditions to the Southwest, one under James Stevenson, the other with Victor Mindeleff in charge. Stevenson's expedition had the appearance of a social outing with Director Powell joining his long-time friend on a tour of archaeological sites in the vicinity of Flagstaff, Arizona, followed by a visit to the cavate (hand carved cave) dwellings near Santa Clara Pueblo in New Mexico. An article in the *Albuquerque Morning Journal*, August 30, 1885, gave the excursion a scientific tone, reporting that photographs, sketches and measurements as the basis for scale models were made. Leaving Powell at Santa Fe, the Stevensons traveled to Keams Canyon for a leisurely visit with Keam, and brief trips to the Second Mesa villages and Oraibi to collect materials.[620] Like Cushing, the Stevensons encountered resistance to their efforts to collect materials at Oraibi by leaders of the hostile faction. A rescue party, organized by Keam, went to Oraibi and returned with two head men, including "the hunchbacked chief," who were confined briefly at Keams Canyon. Meanwhile, members of the friendly faction sought out the Stevensons at Second Mesa, and engaged in trading. The story of this event was sensationalized by the eastern press. The headline of an account in the *Illustrated Police News* read: "Cowed by a Woman [Matilda Stevenson], A Craven Red Devil Weakens in the Face of a Resolute White Heroine – Exciting Adventure in an Indian Village in Arizona."[621]

During this field season James Stevenson was stricken with an attack

---

619   Matthews to Cushing, November 4, 1884, Zuni 1.39, MS.6, AMAW.

620   James Stevenson, Catalogue of Ethnological and Archaeological Collections from the Hopi Pueblos, October-November, 1885, MS 775, National Anthropological Archives, Smithsonian Institution.

621   Anon., 1886a.

of "mountain fever."[622] Meanwhile, the Stevensons became involved in a conflict with greater consequences for the Bureau of Ethnology.

The Stevensons and Washington Matthews

U. S. Army Surgeon Washington Matthews had a long, if unofficial, relationship with the Smithsonian Institution.[623] After joining the army in 1864, Matthews was stationed at various military posts on the Upper Missouri River. In 1865, at Fort Berthold, he came in contact with Arikaras, Hidatsas, and Mandans who lived in a village nearby. In 1867, he wrote Spencer Baird requesting vocabulary blanks and grammars to help in his study of their languages. His *Ethnography and Philology of the Hidatsa Indians* was issued in 1877 as a publication of the U. S. Geological and Geographical Survey. Between 1872 and 1880, while he served at various posts in Maine and later in California, he maintained a correspondence with Powell. It opened the opportunity for his transfer to Fort Wingate, and his work with the Navajo.

Captain Washington Matthews, Assistant Surgeon, U. S. A., arrived at Fort Wingate on October 29, 1880, and on April 9, 1884, he left for duty in the office of the Surgeon General where he was employed the Army Medical Museum in Washington.

As noted earlier, Matthews was required to keep monthly reports that became a part of "The Medical History of Fort Wingate" and while primarily concerned with the health of the garrison, Matthews reported the arrival of visitors, notable events, and his leaves of absence. However, on the matter of his research among the Navajo, his daily entries in his reports are silent with one exception. On November 2, 1882, he wrote:

> I obtain a seven days' leave from the Post commander and in the evening leave on the westward-bound train for Winslow, A.T. whence I am to proceed on horseback to Keams Canyon, A.T. to witness [a part of] the great annual ceremony [the Mountain Chant] of the Navajos.

---

622   Probably Rocky Mountain spotted fever. It may have been a contributing factor in Stevenson's premature death in 1888.

623   For a biographical sketch of Washington Matthews (1843-1905), see Halpern 1997.

[On November 9:] I return from Keam's in the morning.

Nevertheless, his interest in the Navajo led to two publications in the *Bureau of Ethnology Annual Report[s]*, "Navajo Silversmiths," and "Navajo Weavers."[624] Before leaving Fort Wingate in the spring of 1884, Matthews was reported to have "continued ... his collection of materials for a grammar and dictionary of the Navajo language, and also obtained materials, for future publication, regarding the ceremonies, myths, and folk lore of that tribe."[625] More importantly, before leaving New Mexico, he had:

> ...secured the friendship and confidence of some of the leading medicine men and obtained their promise to admit him to their most sacred rites during their entire performance whenever he should be able to avail himself of the privilege. He was also promised complete instruction in the mythology and symbolism of these rites.[626]

Matthews returned to New Mexico in the autumn of 1884, his three month expedition sponsored jointly by the Bureau of Ethnology and USGS. Powell used his influence to have Christian Barthelmess,[627] who had worked as Matthews's assistant previously, detailed to accompany him. After visiting a group of Navajos living near San Mateo,[628] he returned to Fort Wingate, where he learned the Mountain Chant[629] would be performed at Niqotlizi (Hard Earth) about twenty-five miles north of the post on the Navajo Reservation. Matthews left at once, arriving there on October 19. The importance of this opportunity was underscored by Powell:

> Dr. Matthews remained ten days in the Indian camp at Niqotlizi, during which time the shamans admitted him into their medicine lodge and allowed him to observe their rites and practices. His most interesting discovery

---

624 Matthews 1883b and 1884a.
625 Powell 1887:xxx.
626 Powell, ibid, pp. xxxviii-xxxix.
627 A soldier in the 13th Infantry stationed at Fort Wingate.
628 During his visit to San Mateo, Matthews climbed Mount Taylor, a mountain held sacred by the Navajo and the location of various events mentioned in Navajo mythology.
629 A Holyway chantway, a major Navajo curing ceremony. See Wyman 1983.

on this occasion was that of their system of mythic dry paintings...[630]

Matthews's account, "The Mountain Chant: A Navajo Ceremony," was published by the Bureau of Ethnology in 1887.[631]

In November, Matthews attended a Night Chant, or Yebitcai ceremony, held near a rock formation known as "The Haystacks," north of Fort Defiance. Immediately after, he wrote to Cushing of his discovery of dry paintings (sand paintings):

> Got into the medicine lodge and saw things I had never dreamt of. Would you imagine that the rascals, who have neither ornamental robes, skins or pottery, or carven idols, have nevertheless a complete system of pictographic mythic symbolism? They draw immense hieratic figures in powdered colors on the sanded floor of the medicine lodge & when done erase them and carry the very sand out of the lodge. Each day a separate design of really artistic appearance. Did you ever hear of such an art? .... Please tell me what you know about the "sand pictures."[632]

Again, from Powell's annual report for 1884-1885:

> Dr. Matthews was permitted to witness the whole performance and to take as many notes and sketches as were necessary. [Then, at Fort Defiance, from a Navajo priest] ...he obtained full explanations of all these rites and of the symbolism of the pictures and masked characters, with a complete recital of the long and elaborate myths on which the ceremonies depend, and the texts and translations of the very numerous songs which form the ritual of the ceremonies.[633]

The following spring (1885), Matthews gave a two-part lantern slide lecture on the "Mythic Dry-paintings of the Navajos" to

---

630   Powell 1888:xxxix-xl; see also Parezo 1997:54.

631   Matthews 1887. "A Night with the Navajos," by Zay Elini [pseudonym] was published by Matthews in *Forest and Stream* 23:15 (Novermber 6, 1884): 282-283 perhaps to establish his claim to this subject.

632   Matthews to Cushing, November 4, 1884, Zuni 1.39, MS.6, AMAW.

633   Powell, ibid, p. xl.

Philosophical Society of Washington, in which he summarized his investigations regarding the Nightway ceremony.[634] James (and possibly Matilda) Stevenson attended these lectures and later in the year he gave an illustrated talk on Zuni sand paintings at a meeting of the Anthropological Society of Washington.

That fall, as noted above, the Stevensons went to Keams Canyon where they were guests of Thomas Keam for the next two months. It was their "good fortune to arrive ... a few days before the commencement of a Navajo healing ceremony," the Nightway, that began on October 12. With the assistance of an interpreter, known variously as John Navajo or Navajo John, the Stevensons observed and documented the entire nine day ceremony. In his annual report of the "Work of Mr. James Stevenson," Powell was clear in pointing out:

> Mrs. Stevenson was ... enabled to obtain a minute description of the celebrated dance, or medicine ceremony, of the Navajos, called the Yeibit-cai [Nightway]. She made complete sketches of the sand altars, masks, and other objects employed in this ceremonial.[635]

Neither Stevenson knew Navajo. John Navajo had been employed as an interpreter at Fort Defiance, however his knowledge of English was limited. As a consequence, Matilda's account is little more than a description of what she observed. The "Ceremonial of Hasjelti Dailjis and Mythical Sand Painting of the Navajo Indians," was published in 1891, with James Stevenson as author.[636] When it was issued, Stephen remarked in a letter to Fewkes:

> Tilly's contribution—viewed as a votive offering to the manes of Colonel Jim—is highly laudable—otherwise I should call it a fragmentary tissue of absurd blunders.[637]

According to his notebook, Stephen attended the final night of the ceremony with the Stevensons, and he was undoubtedly the source of the list of "foods brought into the lodge," the song and prayer given on

---

634 Parezo, ibid.

635 Powell 1891a:xxv.

636 J. Stevenson 1891. To be bibliographically correct, I have cited James Stevenson as author. To be historically correct, Matilda Coxe Stevenson should be credited with authorship.

637 Stephen to Fewkes, October 11, 1893, MS 4408, NAA, SI. James Stevenson had died three years earlier.

the ninth day of the ceremony, as well as the texts of the "myths of the Navajo" appended at the end.[638] In a letter to H. C. Yarrow, less than a year after the ceremony Matilda Stevenson observed, Stephen clearly expected the result to be a collaborative effort, "an elaborate report to the Bureau of Ethnology by Dr. Matthews and Mr. [sic] Stevenson."[639]

However, Powell was confronted with the dilemma—both scientific and political. Two accounts of the Nightway ceremony were being prepared by two individuals affiliated with the Bureau of Ethnology: one by an acknowledged student of the Navajo (Matthews), the other by a long-time friend and colleague (James Stevenson [sic]).

Matthews resented the Stevensons' encroachment into his area of research. In a letter to Cushing, Matthews expressed his bitterness:

> I suppose that you have heard that the Stevensons poached on my preserve last fall. They went there to duplicate my work, with a stenographer [there is nothing to support this claim the Bureau's fiscal reports] and far more means and materials than had ever been placed in my disposal.[640]

Matthews made no further contributions to the Bureau of Ethnology. He was still bitter many years later as he drafted a preface (not published) to his own account, "The Night Chant: A Navaho Ceremony," published in 1902 by the American Museum of Natural History. In it Matthews wrote:

> He [i.e., Matilda Stevenson] fails, in [her] work, to mention my previous labors and also [her] indebtedness to Mr. A. M. Stephen of Keam's Canyon, who rendered [her] much assistance in his [sic] researches. ... [She] had precious little previous knowledge of the Navahoes, understood nothing of their language and had an incompetent interpreter, Navajo John.[641]

As anthropologist Nancy Parezo has underscored, "This incident reflects the intellectual and personal rivalries and factionalism of the

---

638 J. Stevenson 1891:256-257, 272, and 275-285.
639 Yarrow 1887:105, based on a letter from Stephen to Yarrow, dated September 16, 1886.
640 Quoted in Miller 2007:68. Matthews to Cushing, August 1886.
641 Quoted in Parezo ibid, p. 72, n.8.

Washington scientific community."[642] It also reflects the divided loyalties of others. Stephen, for example, was Keam's employee and, as such, assisted Keam with the sale of his trading post and a large collection of prehistoric puebloan pottery. In both instances, James Stevenson lobbied members of Congress to make these purchases, and Matilda Stevenson wrote an article, "An Arizona School Site," in support of the purchase of the trading post.[643] In turn, it appears Stephen supplied Matilda Stevenson with materials for her account of the Nightway ceremony.[644] At the same time, Stephen assisted Matthews in his study of Navajo religion.

When Matthews visited Keams Canyon in November 1882, Stephen joined him in observing the performance of the Mountain Chant. A few days before Matthews's visit, Stephen wrote in his notebook:

> Tsin-a-ga-hi tells me he represented the Hunter's wife in the Comedy occurring in the Hosh-Kawn [Mountain Chant] celebrated yesterday at Kai-itso-dez-nily-bi-to.

Stephen recorded the risqué dialog of the skit and sent a copy to Matthews. Matthews account of "The Mountain Chant: A Navajo Ceremony" was based on the observations of the performance Matthews had seen in October 1884, supplemented with information from Tall Chanter (*Hatali Nez*), a Navajo singer, who he brought east in the fall of 1885. When Matthews's account of the Mountainway appeared in 1887, it included the following statement:

> Many facts concerning not only the *hackan inca*, but other parts of the mountain chant, have not been allowed to appear in this essay. Recognized scientists may learn of them by addressing the author through the Director of the Bureau of Ethnology.[645]

It was Stephen's account of the "Comedy" that was omitted. The expurgation met with sharp criticism in Washington's intellectual community. For example, Katherine Spencer Halpern and Susan Brown McGreevy note,

> In a letter dated March 16, 1889, Louis Henri Ayme,

---

642   Ibid.
643   M. C. Stevenson 1886.
644   Stephen's contribution was not acknowledged.
645   Matthews 1887:35.

a career diplomat and amateur ethnologist, to W. H. Holmes of the Bureau of Ethnology comments, '...such evidence of ridiculous prudery as is here displayed is supremely stupid.'[646]

Matthews's response was the publication of *The Suppressed Part of the Mountain Chant*" printed on an army field press at Fort Wingate in 1892. In it, Matthews states:

> The dialogue was obtained for me by Mr. A. M. Stephen of Keam's Canyon, Arizona, who witnessed with me the night ceremonies of November 5th, 1882, and the next day learned the words of the play from the man who enacted the part of the woman. I have since heard other versions of the dialog, but none superior to this.

Dr. Washington Matthews, now Major and Surgeon, U.S.A., returned to Fort Wingate in 1890, and on May 3 took command of the post hospital. If his monthly reports are at all an indication, Matthews's focus was on Navajo religion, often at the expense of his official duties. His "sanitary report" for November 1891 indicates he was on "detached service" at Fort Defiance from November 4 to 18; his field notebooks contain detailed notes on another major nine-day ceremony, the Night Chant. In January 1893, he was reprimanded by the post commander for "neglect of duty" in failing to report a number of instances of drunkenness following pay days at the post. In fact, during much of December 1892 and January 1893, Matthews was making an account, sometimes hour by hour, of another Night Chant. Over time he developed a close working relationship with two medicine men, Tall Chanter and Laughing Singer, and towards the end of his stay he obtained a phonograph to record ceremonial songs.[647]

During his first tour of duty at Fort Wingate Matthews complained of neuralgia and insomnia. Early in his second field assignment he began to suffer other physical difficulties (deafness, vertigo, and muscular

---

646   Halpern and McGreevy 1997:36.

647   Halpern, ibid, p. 6; Washington Matthews, Fort Wingate, 1890-1894, Medical Histories of Posts. Vol. 821, RG 94, National Archives. See Matthews 1902 for the published results of his research on the Night Chant. Matthews brought Tall Chanter (*Hatali Nez*), a Navajo singer, to Washington in 1885 to assist him in writing an account of "The Mountain Chant."

incoordination).[648] Illness finally forced him to return to Washington. He left Fort Wingate in May, 1894.[649]

The Eighth Bureau of Ethnology Expedition - 1886

The series of Bureau of Ethnology expeditions to the Southwest that began in 1879 continued during the summer of 1886, although in abbreviated form. The Mindeleff brothers were engaged in "office work," completing "A Study of Pueblo Architecture in Tusayan and Cibola."[650] Curiously, Powell's published annual report for the fiscal year 1886-1887 makes no mention of James Stevenson. However, historian Darlis Miller, in her biography of Matilda Stevenson, cites an unpublished annual report for that fiscal year, written by James Stevenson. Miller summarizes:

> In the fall of 1886, the Stevensons returned to the Southwest to carry out Powell's orders to Jim to investigate Indian ruins in Arizona ... north of the San Francisco Mountains. From there, they traveled to San Diego, where ... Jim inquired into the possibilities for conducting a geological survey of southern California. While in the region, they visited several tribes of Mission Indians, from whom they obtained 'much valuable ethnologic data ... including portions of dialects of two of the Mission tribes.'[651]

End of an Era: The Ninth Bureau of Ethnology Expedition - 1887

The work marking the end of a remarkable period of expeditionary research sponsored by the Bureau of Ethnology began in the summer of 1887 and continued into the fall of 1888.

Towards the end of July 1887, Powell, the Stevensons, and William Henry Holmes, traveled together to Santa Fe. Powell's "Report of the Director" for the year begins by giving a brief account of

---

648   Halpern, ibid.
649   A month after Stephen's death in April. Matthews published his colleague's account of a Hopi medicine man's efforts to cure him (Stephen 1894b).
650   V. Mindeleff 1891.
651   Powell 1891b; Miller, ibid, pp, 82-83.

a geological [and archaeological] reconnaissance of the Tewan Mountains … a district of country [in north central New Mexico] drained by the Chama and Jemez and other tributaries of the Rio Grande del Norte [carried out in August and September].[652]

Powell was accompanied by the Stevensons in a survey of the cavate ruins in Frijoles Canyon and other prehistoric structures on the Pajarito Plateau. Later they were joined by Samuel P. Langley, who had become Secretary of the Smithsonian Institution following Spencer Baird's retirement because of ill-health in May. Meanwhile, Holmes was engaged in similar work in the Jemez Valley where he visited fifteen prehistoric village sites.

The Stevensons left Powell's party near the end of September, and spent ten days at Jemez Pueblo. From there they went to Zia Pueblo, eight miles to the southeast, for "six remarkably successful weeks in making a collection [of 864 'specimens'] and studying the customs, sociology, and mythology of the people."[653] James Stevenson was given access to ("permitted to inspect') the "ceremonial chambers," shrines and caves where sacred objects were stored and sketches were made of masks and other ritual paraphernalia.

From Zia, the Stevensons returned to Zuni for two weeks, where James Stevenson "closed his field season by obtaining from the Zuni priest-doctors additional detailed accounts of their secret 'Medicine Order.'"[654] However, by the time the Stevensons reached Washington in December, James "was literally prostrated," apparently by a second attack of "mountain fever." His health continued to decline throughout the spring and he died on July 25, 1888, in New York City. In May of the following year, Powell hired Matilda Stevenson to complete the unfinished manuscript on the Nightway ceremony and to organize James Stevenson's notes on the Zia. On March 15, 1890, this temporary appointment was made permanent, thus making her "the first and only professional woman permanently employed as a staff ethnology by the Bureau of Ethnology."[655]

---

652   Powell 1892:xxvii.
653   Ibid, p. xxviii.
654   Ibid, p. xxix.
655   Miller, ibid, p. 89.

Anthropologist Don Fowler writes:

> The years 1879-91 were halcyon ones for the Bureau of Ethnology and the National Museum in the Southwest. By various means, Powell had as many as eight researchers in the Southwest during most of the 1880s. During this time, the National Museum acquired tens of thousands of ethnographic and archaeological specimens from the region; major ethnographic studies were undertaken, and the concept of an interdisciplinary anthropological research project was brought into existence.[656]

This chapter ends with the ninth Bureau of Ethnology expedition to the Southwest. James Stevenson, who led the Bureau of Ethnology expeditions from 1879 to 1888, died and Spencer Baird, the long-time Secretary of the Smithsonian Institution, retired. The Mindeleffs completed their field research on Zuni and Hopi architecture. Frank Hamilton Cushing's years at Zuni had ended and while he had not "monographed Zuni," he had written what he was destined to write about his life among them. Cosmos Mindeleff continued the surveys of prehistoric architecture begun by his brother, and Matilda Stevenson carried forward the research at Zuni and Zia begun with James Stevenson. Washington Matthews continued his study of Navajo religion but would publish nothing more with the Bureau of Ethnology. And, in time, new names would carry on the work, most notably that of Jesse Walter Fewkes.[657] It was a remarkable decade—whether it is defined as 1879 to 1888 or 1879 to 1891.

---

656   Fowler, ibid, p. 106.
657   The first years of Fewkes's work in the Southwest is described in Chapter 6.

5. Creating Architectural Models of the Puebloan Southwest: The Work of Cosmos and Victor Mindeleff

An Introductory Appreciation

Between 1875 and 1893, the work of the Hayden, Powell, Wheeler, and Bureau of [American] Ethnology Surveys placed a major emphasis on the visual representation of the Pueblos.[658] This representation took the form of photographs and three-dimensional architectural models, supplemented with relief maps and artwork. Photographs were distributed as stereographs, included in publications, and gathered into portfolios. Scale models created for the U. S. National Museum were featured at regional, national, and international exhibitions. Eventually, significant narrative reports were written, most notably Victor Mindeleff's classic account of Zuni and Hopi architecture.[659] While clearly a part of the competition for influence and financial support,[660] the photographs of J. K. Hillers and the models of William Henry Holmes, William H. Jackson, W. J. Hoffman and the Mindeleff brothers are of lasting value as representations and documentations of prehistoric

---

658 Between 1867 and 1879 four independent expeditions sponsored by the U. S. Government explored, surveyed and mapped a large part of the geographical region west of the Mississippi. The first, Clarence King's U. S. Geological Exploration of the Fortieth Parallel (1867-1872), did not work in the Southwest and had completed its work before the Centennial Exhibition in Philadelphia in 1876. The others were the U. S. Geological and Geographical Survey of the Territories, led by Ferdinand Vandeveer Hayden (1867-1878); the U. S. Geological Survey West of the 100th Meridian, led by Lt. George Montague Wheeler (1869-1879); and the U. S. Geological and Geographical Survey of the Rocky Mountain Region, led by John Wesley Powell (1869-1879).

659 V. Mindeleff 1891.

660 Brunet 2007.

and historic Puebloan architecture at the end of the nineteenth century. More importantly, the work of the Mindeleffs—Victor and his younger brother Cosmos—marks the beginning of the scientific study of vernacular architecture in the Southwest.

Narratives and photographs are the primary means of representing other cultures; yet for the Pueblos, in museums and at exhibitions in the latter part of the nineteenth century, models were second only to artifacts. Holmes and Jackson prepared the first models for use in F. V. Hayden's Geological and Geographical Survey of the Territories exhibit at the Centennial Exhibition in Philadelphia, which opened on May 10, 1876.[661] Given the popular success of the models at the Centennial Exhibition, Jackson made others and a number of these models were soon placed in "several of the most famous museums in Europe."

An act of Congress on March 3, 1879 consolidated the four "Great Surveys" to form the United States Geological Survey (USGS). Ethnological research was transferred to the Smithsonian Institution and in June John Wesley Powell became Director of its newly established Bureau of [American] Ethnology. The following year, Powell's friend Lewis Henry Morgan published "A Study of the Houses of the American Aborigines with a Scheme of Exploration of the Ruins in New Mexico and Elsewhere," which "reset the anthropological research agenda in the American Southwest from 1880 to about 1910" through a specific program of research focused on architectural forms.[662] To carry out the actual exploration and investigation set out by Morgan, as well as to promote the work of the Bureau in the new National Museum, Powell hired young Victor and Cosmos Mindeleff, self-taught as architect and cartographer respectively, to prepare scale models of historic and prehistoric structures in the Southwest. Looking back on the first decade of archaeological investigations undertaken by the Bureau of Ethnology, Holmes reminded Powell:

> The work was commenced with two leading ideas in view:
> First, it was your desire to secure material for models of
> all the leading pueblos in Arizona and New Mexico, and
> in 1881 Mr. Victor Mindeleff, as the best qualified person

---

661   Anon. 1878:111-114. The article gives a detailed description of the models and their construction.

662   Fowler 2000:97.

within your reach, was placed in charge of the work; in 1882 his brother, Cosmos Mindeleff, became associated with him. In a few years a series of unrivaled models was produced. . . . The second subject to which you directed attention was the history of pueblo architecture...[663]

Between 1881 and 1894 the Mindeleffs mapped, sketched and photographed Zuni, the Hopi villages, Acoma, Taos, ruins in Canyon de Chelly, and Chaco Canyon, creating over thirty models of Pueblo architecture exhibited in the National Museum and at regional and world expositions: [664]

> Southern Exposition, Louisville, 1883
> Eleventh Cincinnati Industrial Exposition, 1883
> World's Industrial and Cotton Centennial Exhibition,
>   New Orleans, 1884
> Milwaukee Industrial Exposition, 1885
> Centennial Exposition of the Ohio Valley and Central
>   States, Cincinnati, 1888
> Exposition Universelle, Paris, 1889
> Exposicion Historico-Americana, Madrid, 1892
> World's Columbian Exposition, Chicago, 1893[665]

Made of clay and later of *papier mache* created from "macerated greenbacks from the Treasury Department," the first models were large and heavy; the model of Zuni, for example, was 10 x 20 feet in size and weighed nearly 2000 pounds.[666] A plaster model of Walpi, "considerably damaged in transit to New Orleans," in 1884 weighed over 1500 pounds; its replacement made of *papier mache* weighed less than 500 pounds.[667] The

663 Holmes to Powell, February 25, 1890, MS.6CM.1.1, Braun Research Library, Autry Museum of the American West. The letter contains a list of all the models, including duplicates, prepared between 1881 and 1889.

664 Models of other archaeological sites were also produced, including the so-called Great Elephant Mound in Wisconsin and the Etowah Mound in Georgia in support of the mound-builders work by Cyrus Thomas.

665 The models continued to be used in later exhibitions and examples of models by Holmes, Jackson, Hoffman, and the Mindeleff brothers are located in Peabody Museum, Harvard University.

666 On the use of macerated greenbacks, see Anon. 1884b:375.

667 C. Mindeleff to Powell, May 7, 1890, Records of the Bureau of Ethnology, Correspondence, Letters Received, National Anthropological Archives, Smithsonian Institution. Cited hereafter as LR-BE, NAA, SI.

models were carefully colored in solid oil paints to convey a fuller sense of the original architectural forms and surrounding natural environment.

The Mindeleffs' work included more than the creation of models. While making maps of the Hopi villages in 1882, Cosmos Mindeleff, with Jeremiah Sullivan as interpreter, noted the clan distributions in each of the house blocks. Later, A. M. Stephen and Sullivan assisted the Mindeleffs by recording clan migration narratives regarding ancestral Hopi ruins and gathering information on the kinds of work carried out on roof tops, the separate areas used for bartering by women and men, as well as the temporal use of plazas, kivas and other spaces for religious as well as economic activities.[668] Most importantly, they documented the social organization of architectural forms, as in Cosmos Mindeleff's "Localization of Tusayan Clans."[669]

Neither brother learned enough Hopi or Navajo to record the words for the architectural features they so skillfully represented in sketches, maps and, above all, in their models. For example, virtually all of the ethnographic material presented in Cosmos Mindeleff's "Navaho Houses" was taken, verbatim, from reports and diagrams prepared by Stephen.[670]

---

668 A. M. Stephen and Jeremiah Sullivan, [Mindeleff survey of Hopi architecture, 1887-1888], Elsie Clews Parsons Field Notebooks 32-33, Columbia University Library. Cited hereafter as ECPFN, CUL. Stephen submitted reports to the Mindeleffs based on the notebooks.

669 C. Mindeleff 1900a. While recognizing the importance of Lewis Henry Morgan's work, it can be claimed that the work of the Mindeleffs marked the beginning of the study of vernacular architecture. As a built form, vernacular architecture is viewed today as representing/embodying a plurality of symbolic orders. By symbolic order is meant those tangible/substantial means of giving expression to those ideas/values that give shape/direction to behavior/practice. For the most part these symbolic orders derive from, on the one hand, the conceptualization and practice of social relations (what is traditionally called kinship and social organization) and, on the other, from the conceptualization and practice of religion (cosmology or world view and ritual). Beyond these two, a third important area of interest concerns the house as a "mnemonic design for the remembrance of the past," that is, the importance of this kind of material culture or the use of the natural world for social memory. The literature here is extensive: e.g., Bourdieu 1972, Carsten and Hugh-Jones, eds, 1995, Fox 1993, Oliver 2007, Rapoport 1994, Waterson 1990, and Yates 1989.

670 C. Mindeleff 1898a. This report was prepared after Cosmos left the Bureau of American Ethnology in 1895. See Stephen's field notes and reports on Navajo

After submitting the completed manuscript for "A Study of Pueblo Architecture in Tusayan and Cibola" in 1890, Victor Mindeleff left the Smithsonian to pursue a career in architecture.[671] Cosmos continued to work in the modeling room and to publish reports on field research he had done in Arizona on the Hohokam great house at Casa Grande, ancestral Hopi architecture in Canyon de Chelly, as well as on a survey made in the Verde Valley. Cosmos Mindeleff's field research in the Southwest spanned fourteen years and resulted in over thirty publications in the *American Anthropologist, Journal of the American Geographical Society, Science, Scientific American* and other professional journals.[672] After his departure from the Smithsonian in 1895, Cosmos became a journalist and worked on several newspapers in New York City.

Historian Don Fowler provides this summary acknowledgement of the contributions of Victor and Cosmos Mindeleff:

> The Mindeleff brothers completed a task stemming from Lewis Henry Morgan's research agenda... thus contributing to the understanding of houses and house-life that Morgan considered so important to his scheme of social evolution. But they also contributed to the development of museology with the models of the various pueblos...[673]

Of Victor Mindeleff's "A Study of Pueblo Architecture in Tusayan and Cibola," cultural historian Peter Nabokov wrote:

> Over the years it acquired a distinguished reputation: as an unheralded classic, as a model for the study of vernacular architecture, as the principal sourcebook on traditional Western Pueblo buildings and their ancient prototypes, and as a major data base for studies of Pueblo culture change.[674]

---

architecture in Gladys Reichard Papers, MS 29-39-1, Museum of Northern Arizona.

671   Information on the careers of Victor and Cosmos Mindeleff after their departures from the Bureau of Ethnology is included below in Biographical Notes.

672   A list of Cosmos Mindeleff's anthropological publications is included in the Bibliography.

673   Fowler 2000:143.

674   Nabokov 1989:xxix-xxx.

Biographical Notes

Victor and Cosmos were sons of Dimitri Victorovitch Mindeleff (1812-1892), a chemist and inventor born in Rega, Russia, and Julia Feodorovna von Ulrich Mindeleff (1836-1918), an artist born in St. Petersberg. Their first son, Victor, was born in London on June 2, 1860, as they emigrated from Russia to the United States. The Mindeleffs sailed for the United States from Liverpool aboard the "City of Glasgow" on July 6, 1860, and settled near Washington. Their house was destroyed during the Confederate siege of Washington at the beginning of the Civil War. Cosmos was born in Washington on May 18, 1863. Another son, Charles (1867-1943), became a metallurgical and explosives chemist. By 1876 Dimitri had left his family in Washington, and moved to San Francisco where he lived until his death. He was known then as the inventor of "terrorite," an explosive said to be stronger than dynamite. Julia worked as a portrait artist and linguist, and later she was employed by the Bureau of American Ethnology.

Victor was educated in public schools and the Emerson Institute in Washington, where he received the Pickney medal for scholarship. Soon afterwards, he came in contact with William Henry Holmes who introduced Victor into the newly established Bureau of Ethnology. Like his mother, he apparently excelled in water colors and oils. Nothing is known of Cosmos before he joined his brother at the Bureau of Ethnology, except he "inherited [a] scholarly turn' from this mother."[675]

Victor, or "Vic" as he was known in the field, was employed by the Bureau from 1881 until 1890 and Cosmos, "Cos," from 1882 until 1895. Victor was placed in charge of field parties in the Southwest and often initiated research which Cosmos was subsequently assigned to complete. During most years the brothers were engaged in creating and installing models or in writing reports ("desk work"), most notably Victor's "A Study of Pueblo Architecture in Tusayan and Cibola."

Victor joined James Stevenson's Bureau of Ethnology expedition to the Southwest during the summer of 1881. Among instructions, Powell directed Stevenson to continue collecting artifacts,

make photographs and drawings for illustrative purposes

---

675   Op cit., xiv. Nabokov uses Anon. 1897 for biographical information on Cosmos and the 1929/1930 edition of *Who's Who in the Nation's Capital* for Victor. The 1880 census gives "real estate" as Cosmos's employment.

of the Indians, their houses, ground plans of the villages and scenes representative of their daily life…make investigations into their languages, customs and habits, mythology, government, architecture, etc. … To enable you to carry out these objects I have directed Mr. Victor Mindeleff to report to you for duty.[676]

A month into the field season Stevenson wrote to Powell:

Mr. Mendeleff [sic] is going to prove of great use, he will make a good man in the field & fully comprehends the work before him.[677]

Victor's "Sketch Book" of Zuni from August 1881 reveals the meticulous measurements of dimensions and angles as well as careful notation of "pot chimneys," ladders, doorways, and other features that made possible the "several thousand details" that enriched the model of the pueblo.[678] The "Governor's House," where Frank Hamilton Cushing was in residence, was the first house-block to be measured and drawn. Missing from the sketches, as well as the map and model of Zuni, were the trading post of Douglas D. Graham and the Presbyterian mission buildings at the edge of the village.[679]

On September 13, 1881, after two months at Zuni, Stevenson, Hillers, Mindeleff and Albert L. Webster, an assistant topographer with the USGS, traveled from Fort Wingate, New Mexico, to Keams Canyon and the Hopi villages where they stayed until returning to Fort Wingate a month later. Webster was assigned to "map the Moki towns." Stevenson acquired "7 wagon loads of specimens" from Thomas V. Keam who was paid $450.29. While Mindeleff helped prepare the pottery, baskets, "head-dresses" and other materials for shipment, Hillers completed a photographic survey of the Hopi villages, including "a series of fine photographic views of exteriors and interiors" at Oraibi.[680]

---

676   Powell to Stevenson, July 3, 1881, LR-BE, NAA, SI.

677   Stevenson to Powell, August 13, 1881, LR-BE, NAA, SI.

678   Victor Mindeleff, Zuni Sketchbook, 1881, MS 2138, National Anthropological Archives, Smithsonian Institution.

679   The Bureau of Ethnology was interested in the aboriginal culture of Native Americans and documentation consistently omits non-native elements in maps, photographs and narrative accounts. See Hieb 2011:160 for the development of this focus.

680   Powell 1884:xxi and Stevenson 1884. Hillers's Oraibi images have been lost.

Early in 1882 Cosmos was added to the Bureau of Ethnology payroll to assist Victor in the creation of the model of Zuni for exhibition in the U. S. National Museum. This and all subsequent models made by the Mindeleffs were in a uniform scale of 1:60 or one inch to five feet.

During the summer, Cosmos joined Victor for the field season in the Southwest.[681] During September and October, the Mindeleffs made "fully detailed architectural plans of the seven inhabited villages [and Awatobi], together with sketches and diagrams of constructive details, photographs, and, in general, such data as were necessary for the preparation of accurate large scale models of these pueblos" for use in the U. S. National Museum and at various regional and national expositions. After their survey of Awatobi and the First Mesa villages, Victor left his brother, Cosmos, in charge of the work at Oraibi and on Second Mesa, and accompanied Stevenson's expedition to Canyon de Chelly[682]

Cosmos began mapping the Hopi villages, starting at Oraibi. Jeremiah Sullivan assisted in the identification of clan ownership of house blocks at Oraibi. However, with Sullivan's arrest when they reached Second Mesa, it is likely clan ownership for the remaining six villages was not added to the drawings until the Mindeleffs returned to Second Mesa in 1885.[683] At the end of the field season the *New York Daily Tribune* reported:

> Complete surveys in minute detail were made of each village, from which models will be constructed sufficiently large to show every feature of interest. From all except one [Oraibi] large collections of household and other articles were obtained. Mr.[Victor] Mindeleff

---

The images of the Hopi villages made by Hillers were reproduced in a portfolio entitled "Photographic Illustrations of the Puebla [sic] Indian Villages in New Mexico & Arizona." See Hieb 2011a.

681   Early in 1882 Cosmos was added to the Bureau of Ethnology payroll to assist Victor in the creation of the model of Zuni for exhibition in the U. S. National Museum. When Cosmos joined the Bureau his monthly salary was $25, half that paid to a cook with a field party. James Stevenson, "executive officer," received an annual salary of $3,000; the photographer J. K. Hillers, $1,800; and Victor Mindeleff, $810. See Judd 1967:13-20.

682   See Hieb 2005 for an account of the expedition into Canyon de Chelly.

683   Tom Polacca accompanied the Mindeleffs while they were at the Second Mesa villages and he, rather than Sullivan, may have assisted in identifying the clan ownership of house units.

is the gentleman who last year [1881] made a survey of Zuni Village, from which the model now on exhibition in the National Museum was constructed.[684]

Before winter, Cosmos returned to Washington to continue work in the modeling room at the Smithsonian Institution. Victor remained with Stevenson's party. In late November, during a brief visit to the USGS camp near Holbrook, Arizona, Powell put Victor in charge of a collecting expedition to Oraibi.[685] After supervising the shipment of three wagon loads of pottery, basketry, and other materials, Victor returned to Washington in February.

Back at the Smithsonian Institution, the Mindeleff brothers began work on a series of models of the Hopi villages. Victor wrote to Holmes that he wished to "personally attend to the First Mesa model." He wanted to "make a damn big thing of it, modeling the entire mesa with the three towns on top. It would be a fine thing if executed in the same scale as the Zuni model."[686] This work was carried on until June when it was interrupted for the preparation of a series of duplicate models of "cliff ruins and pueblos" to be exhibited at the Southern Exposition in Louisville, Kentucky, in the autumn of 1883.[687]

684   Anon [J. S. Brown], The Dwellers in Cliffs, January 14, 1883, *New York Daily Tribune*; reprinted in the *Kansas City Review of Science*, March, 1883. The author clearly has congressional support for the Bureau's explorations in mind.

685   Cushing led the party to Oraibi where a conflict with the village leaders led to his "eviction." See Chapter 4 as well as Green 1990:255-260 for accounts by Cushing, Willard Metcalf, and Victor Mindeleff.

686   Quoted by Nabokov 1989:xx. Nabokov does not provide the source. Victor married Jessie Louise Randall on April 2, 1883. They had two children: Victor, Jr., born in 1885 and Natalya born in 1887.

687   Powell 1886:li.

"Victor Mindeleff, Modeler, Bureau of Ethnology," ca. 1884. Photograph by George "Ben" Wittick. Anthropology Collection, Science Museum of Minnesota. Image: Object ID A63:27:38T.

The Mindeleff party left Washington later in September and began field work at Kin-Tiel,[688] a thirteenth century ancestral puebloan "Great

688   Kin Tiel is a large masonry pueblo located about 22 miles south of present-day Ganado, half-way between Zuni and the Hopi First Mesa villages. Built ca. 1275, it has curvilinear walls, some two stories high when visited by the Mindeleffs, containing perhaps 1000 rooms. The stone work and rectangular kivas suggest

House" south of Pueblo Colorado [later renamed Ganado], Arizona, where they obtained supplies from Lorenzo Hubbell. At Kin-Tiel the party made a detailed ground plan and then explored and photographed a small ruin nearby known as Kinna-Zinde.[689] The following two months were spent exploring and mapping Canyon de Chelly and its branches; detailed ground plans "wherever possible" were made of the one hundred and thirty-four ruins they identified in the canyons. In December, the party returned to Fort Wingate, and proceeded to Acoma Pueblo where an architectural survey of the village was made:

> The ground plans were drawn to a scale of 20 feet to the inch, as had been done previously in the cases of the Zuni and the Tusayan [Hopi] villages, with the object of preparing a large model.[690]

Twelve hundred piece of pottery were obtained at Acoma. While Victor Mindeleff returned to Washington in early January, his brother remained behind until the shipment of pottery was completed later in the month.

In retrospect, the most important accomplishment of the field season was work of the Mindeleff brothers in Canyon de Chelly that laid the foundation for the eventual publication of Cosmos Mindeleff's insightful article, "The Cliff Ruins of Canyon de Chelly, Arizona."[691]

In June 1884, the brother's attention was turned to preparations for the Government exhibit at the World's Industrial and Cotton Centennial Exhibition in New Orleans to open in December.[692] In August, Victor left Washington to survey the "great house" ruins in Chaco Canyon, New Mexico.[693] His party included one "office employee," Lorenzo J.

---

it was built as the Four Corners area was being abandoned by an ancestral Pueblo people. It is ancestral Zuni according to Zuni oral traditions. See Victor Mindeleff 1891:91-94 and plate lxiii and Morgan 1994:192-193.

689   See Mindeleff 1891:91-94.

690   Powell 1883:xxv.

691   C. Mindeleff 1897b.

692   Powell, op cit., xxxvi. A much publicized exhibition, see Anon. 1884b and 1885a. Organized by the National Cotton Planters Association, the event marked what was believed to be the first export of cotton from the United States to England in 1784. It was opened by President Chester A. Arthur on December 16, 1884 and closed on June 2, 1885. The exhibition's largest building was also the largest in the country at the time.

693   The Puebloan occupation in Chaco Canyon, New Mexico, began A.D. 550 but

Hatch, and a cook, a teamster and an "Indian Guide and Herder with horse" who would be paid $1.50 per diem.[694] He was also given funds for a "photographic outfit."[695] At the end of two months in the field "five of the ruins were accurately measured and platted to scale, and a full series of sketches, plans, and photographs were secured."[696] A century later, Victor Mindeleff's drawings and photographs made in Chaco Canyon in 1884, and those made by Victor and Cosmos Mindeleff during the winter of 1887-1888, would serve as a baseline for conserving the major ruins in Chaco Canyon.[697]

During the remainder of the year Victor joined Cosmos in

---

the area is best known for the great houses known as Pueblo Bonito, Chetro Ketl, Penasco Blanco, Una Vita, Pueblo Pintado and others which were expanded or built A.D. 1040-1105. Chaco Canyon was the hub of an extensive system of roads and is thought to have been a center of trade and religious power. A series of droughts led to the abandonment of Chaco Canyon by A.D.1140. The Chacoan culture included a number of outlying communities ("outliers"), especially to the north (e.g., Salmon Ruin on the San Juan River and the Aztec Ruin complex on the Animas River in New Mexico). With the abandonment of Chaco Canyon the population center shifted to the north, and with the additional periods of drought to southwestern Colorado to communities like Sand Canyon Pueblo. Following the "Great Drought of 1276" the Four Corners area was completely abandoned and the population dispersed, probably to the area of the western Pueblos and to the Rio Grande. The literature is extensive, including significant work by Lekson (1991), and Vivian and Hilpert (2002). For an introduction, see Fagan (2005) or Frazier (1999).

694   V. Mindeleff to Powell, June 24, 1884, LR-BE, NAA, SI. The *Albuquerque Morning Journal*, August 12, 1884, lists Edwin H. Andrews and Lorenzo J. Hatch as Mindeleff's assistants.

695   V. Mindeleff to Powell, July 7, 1884, LR-BE, NAA, SI.

696   Powell 1888:xxix-xxx. For a detailed description of Victor and Cosmos Mindeleff's work in Chaco Canyon in 1887, see Mathien 2006. Shortly after Mindeleff's visit to Chaco Canyon in 1884, F. T. Bickford, a member of James Stevenson's Bureau of Ethnology expedition to the Southwest that summer, spent eight days in Chaco Canyon. See Bickford 1890. Victor returned to Washington on October 1. He then went to Cartersville, George, where Cyrus Thomas was excavating the large Etowah mound, to make a survey and scale drawing as the basis for a model. See Thomas 1894 for a summary of his Mound Builder archaeology and Fowler 2000:106. Mindeleff's visit to the Etowah mound was brief as he returned to Washington on October 1! Although Thomas was a friend of Powell, it was Spencer Baird, Secretary of the Smithsonian, who pushed for support of the Mound Builder excavations.

697   See Mathien 2006.

preparations for the New Orleans exposition.[698] Models of the seven Hopi villages were completed along with a relief map of the area. The model of Walpi included a portion of the mesa on which the village is located to illustrate the topography. Models of White House in Canyon de Chelly and the Mummy Cave ruin in Canyon del Muerto were also created. During December and January, Cosmos supervised the installation of the USGS and Bureau of Ethnology exhibits in the Government Building at the New Orleans exhibition. He returned to New Orleans in June to take charge of the packing and shipment of the exhibits for their return to Washington and for the installation of a portion of the material at the Milwaukee Industrial Exposition.[699]

In early June, Victor submitted a detailed and ambitious proposal for the 1885 field season. It included work at Walnut Canyon near Flagstaff, Arizona, the Hopi villages, additional architectural studies at Canyon de Chelly, Chaco Canyon, Jemez, Cochiti, plans and sections of 'the cave lodges excavated in the soft cliffs of the 'Rito de los Frijoles,'" visits to Laguna, Acoma and finally to Zuni, where surveys would be made of the "original cities of Cibola" and ground plans made of the Zuni farming villages at Nutria and Pescado.[700] However, once in the field Victor was forced to submit revised estimates of costs and scaled down plans of the work to be accomplished.[701]

Victor left Washington at the beginning of July and traveled via Kanab, Utah, reaching Keams Canyon on July 15. Cosmos had left Washington on June 6 and traveled via Holbrook, Arizona, to Keams Canyon, arriving a day after his brother. Cosmos brought supplies from Holbrook for a camp they established at Second Mesa near the village of Mishongnovi. Victor's monthly report indicates that during the first three weeks of August a number of ruins in the vicinity of Second and First Mesa were surveyed.[702] While Cosmos and other members of the party continued detailed studies of the architecture in "the modern villages," Victor went to Keams Canyon for three days to consult with

698   By 1885 Cosmos was placed in charge of the modeling room.

699   Powell 1888:xlvii-xlviii.

700   V. Mindeleff to Powell, June 11, 1885, LR-BE, NAA, SI.

701   V. Mindeleff to Powell, September 29, 1885, LR-BE, NAA, SI.

702   V. Mindeleff to Powell, September 29, 1885. The sites included: Pa-yup-ki, Tcu-ku-bi, Old Walpi and another mound of ruins also near First Mesa.

Navajo head men regarding their planned explorations of Canyon de Chelly. In his "Report of Field Work [for] July and August '85," Victor wrote:

> On August 17th a snake dance took place at Mashongnivi [sic]—similar in every respect to the one at Walpi, except that it was on a smaller scale. *No whites were present here except our party.* Eleven plates were exposed.
>
> The following day (Aug. 18th) the snake dance at Walpi was photographed. Seven plates were exposed, but the light was not very good. A large number of Americans were present, and 4 other cameras were at work. Owing to previous day's experience we secured the best position.[703]

As discussed in Chapter 7, Michel-Rolph Trouillot argues that "any historical narrative is a bundle of silences" and that these silences begin with the making of sources. Victor does not mention that among those attending the ceremony at Mishongovi was twenty-four year old Harriet Marion Warren, a successful musical comedy actress and wife of Walter W. Fessler, whom she had married in 1881.[704] Marion Warren,

---

703   Ibid. Emphasis added. It is clear from photographs made by Ben Wittick and [Stephen Poole?] Sanders that the afternoon was heavily overcast. The 1885 Snake Dance at Walpi is described in greater detail in Chapter Two.

704   Harriet Marion Warren (1861-1933) was the daughter of Rev. Russell Madison Warren (1833-1911), one of the founders of the Chautauqua Institution in 1873, who lived in New Castle, Pennsylvania. One of four daughters, Harriet was a gifted musician, played the organ in her father's church in Cleveland, Ohio, when she was ten, and soon aspired to become an actress. Her sister, Sarah Elizabeth Warren, became an accomplished opera singer. On August 18, 1881, Harriet married Walter W. Fessler (1854-1912), actor, playwright and sometime manager or director of plays, who was born in Sheakleyville, Pennsylvania. In 1882 Fessler's play, "The Midnight Marriage," was published by the Shenango Valley News in Greenville, the first of a number of melodramas he wrote. Henry C. Miner's *American Dramatic Directory* for 1884 lists Marion Warren and Fessler as actors with Simmonds & Brown, dramatic agents, in Greenville. According to the directory, she played a soubrette—a saucy, coquettish, intriguing maidservant in comedies; he played "leading man." Marion appeared in Gus Williams' "Captain Mishler" in 1884 and throughout 1885 and 1886 she played the role of "Peggy O'Moore" in William J. Scanlon's Irish musical comedy, "Shane-na-lane" As Peggy O'Moore the Springfield, Ohio, *Daily Republic* reported "Miss Warren is a charming little brunette, with

to use her stage name, was the guest of Cosmos and afterwards helped him writing what Cosmos claimed to be the first scientific description of that ceremony.[705] After her brief visit, Marion returned to the east where, with her husband, she was a member of the supporting cast in a comedy that opened at the Globe Theater in Boston on August 31.[706] As detailed below, Marion accompanied Cosmos on later field trips in the Southwest and eventually became his wife. In her obituary Cosmos claimed she was the first white woman to attend a Hopi Snake Dance.[707]

---

bright winsome face, exquisite form and frolicksome way about her that makes her a favorite everywhere" (November 19, 1885). Fessler was in the supporting cast and they continued to act togerther into 1888. On a trip to Arizona from December 1890 until the spring of 1891, Marion was referred to as "Mrs. Mindeleff." However, no record of their marriage has been located. In the 1900 Census Marion and Cosmos were living together in New York City. In October 1901 Fessler filed for divorce, stating that he and Marion lived together until 1889 and then she "deserted him without good cause." In 1902 Fessler, recent author of the melodrama, "The Great White Diamond," became one of the founding members of the Green Room Club, a fraternal organization in New York City for people involved in the dramatic arts. In 1905 Marion and Cosmos traveled to London and stated on their passports they would be gone 1-2 years. On July 6, 1908 "Marion Mindeleff" returned from Italy with her sister Sarah, one of several trips they made together to Europe. In the 1910 census Cosmos Mindeleff and Marion Mindeleff were living in New York City. She was listed as "wife," "married 15 years," and gave her profession as "none." They moved to Carmel, Putnam County, New York, ca. 1917. She died on April 8, 1933. Cosmos died on June 26, 1938. Bill Korstick and Carol Anderson, relatives of Marion have generously supplied the biographical information regarding Hariett Marion Warren (Fessler) Mindeleff included here.

705   Anon. 1933. Cosmos Mindeleff 1886a and 1886b. This discounts the more famous but sensationalistic account by Bourke (1884).

706   The *New Castle Weekly News* reported Marion visited her parents in western Pennsylvania from early July until the first week in August. The Snake Dance was not announced until 16 days before the public ceremony. Clearly some prior arrangement requiring an exchange of telegrams informing Marion of the date of the ceremony and Cosmos of her expected arrival date in Holbrook or Winslow had to have been made. Her return to the east would have been less complicated to arrange.

707   There were a number of women in attendance at the Snake Dance at Walpi the following day. However, I know of no other white woman attending this ceremony before then. While five photographers made images of the Walpi Snake Dance, I know of no other photographs of or photographers in attendance at any Snake Dance prior to this.

While working from the camp at Second Mesa, Cosmos is said to have "assisted in collecting...legendary information on the ruins." A narrative, recorded by Sullivan, regarding the establishment and abandonment of Payupki on Second Mesa, was clearly part of this effort.[708] Victor's report for September concludes:

> Aug 22nd [a week after the Snake Dance at Mishongnovi] the party moved into Keams canon en route for canon de Chelly. After two days spent here in overhauling outfit, shoeing horses, &c the party went north taking the trail for the mouth of canon de Chelly. ... Last two days of Aug were spent in canon del Muerte in surveys of ruins and detail diagrams.[709]

During the first three days of September, the party made a "close and accurate" survey of the "mummy cave group" in Canyon del Muerto.[710] The party then moved the camp into Canyon de Chelly where they spent four days making a detailed study of "White House group."[711]

After leaving Canyon de Chelly, the party went to Fort Defiance to gather supplies. From Navajos at the agency they learned there was no water in the Chaco region. As a result, Victor changed plans and the party proceeded to Zuni, reaching there on September 16. The following day they moved to Ojo Caliente, 15 miles south of Zuni. From there they surveyed "Ha-wi-ku"[712] and several other ruins. Ten days later, the camp

---

708   Victor Mindeleff 1891:40-41. It is ironic that although this narrative was not "up to the standard" of those used in Cosmos Mindeleff's "Traditional History of Tusayan" (Op. cit., 16-38), they were all based on narratives collected by Sullivan and copied into Stephen's notebooks.

709   V. Mindeleff to Powell, September 29, 1885, Ibid.

710   A. M. Stephen and Jeremiah Sullivan were also at Mummy Cave during the same time and probably accompanied the Mindeleff party to Canyon de Chelly. Hopi Notebooks, No. 1, Ms Coll. No. 1563, American Philosophical Society Library. Neither Stephen nor Mindeleff mention the other.

711   See Cosmos Mindeleff 1897b.

712   The ruins of the Zuni village of Hawikuh. It was here that Esteban, Fray Marco de Niza's companion, was killed in May 1539. Coronado was confronted at Hawikuh in 1540 and a Franciscan mission was established here in 1628. In 1632 the Zunis revolted, killed the priest, destroyed the church then under construction and fled to Corn Mountain where they stayed until 1635 or 1636. The church and friary were rebuilt sometime after 1642 then burned and sacked by Apaches in 1672. Apparently rebuilt, it was destroyed during the Pueblo

was moved back to Zuni and several ruins in the vicinity were surveyed. None of the reports submitted by Victor Mindeleff or published by Powell indicate when the party completed its work in the field and returned to Washington.[713] However, on October 29, Cosmos wrote to Spencer Baird, Secretary of the Smithsonian Institution, to propose the position of curator for models in the National Museum.[714]

Cosmos Mindeleff, left, and Victor Mindeleff, rear, in the Modeling Room at the U. S. National Museum, ca. 1885. Smithsonian Institution Archives. Image: #MNH-6084. At the lower left is William H. Jackson's model of Tewa (Hano). Above the Mindeleffs is W. J. Hoffman's model of Pueblo Bonito (Chaco Canyon). Models by the Mindeleffs include: on the display table, left center, is the "Puebla of Shipaulovi, Moki, Arizona" and standing on edge is a model of Shungopavi (Hopi). The Mindeleffs are working on a model of Penasco Blanco (Chaco Canyon).

Revolt of 1680. See Morgan 1994:193.

713 Powell 1891a:xxv-xxviii.

714 Cosmos Mindeleff to Spencer Baird, October 29, 1885. His proposal was rejected. Baird to Cosmos Mindeleff, November 3, 1885. RU 112, Smithsonian Institution Archives.

On his return from the Southwest, Victor resumed work on the manuscript that would become "A Study of Pueblo Architecture in Tusayan and Cibola." Cosmos, in charge of the modeling room, began construction of a series of models of the ruins in Chaco Canyon based on Victor's work there in 1884. Two new models were finished by the end of the fiscal year: Wijiji and a small ruin near Pueblo Alto. In addition, several duplicate models were made for exchange with other museums.

"Indian House at Walpi," August 18, 1885. Photograph by [Stephen Poole?] Sanders. Center for Southwest Research, University of New Mexico General Library. Image: Atlantic & Pacific Railway Collection #000-083. Visible in the photograph are some of the twenty-five Anglo visitors gathering for the Snake Dance.

In the spring of 1886, with the assistance of Marion Warren, Cosmos ("Kosmos Mendelieff") submitted an account of the 1885 Snake Dance at Mishongnovi for publication in the journal *Science*. The objectivity and empathy of this account stands in marked contrast with the descriptions of the Walpi ceremony, such as W. Cal Brown's "A Carnival of Horrors."[715]

---

715 Brown 1885; see also Burge 1885.

Work in the modeling room continued into the summer of 1886. Cosmos prepared a report on the exhibits of the Bureau of Ethnology and the USGS at the expositions in Louisville, Cincinnati (both in 1883), and New Orleans (1884-1885). This was completed in October and submitted to the Department of the Interior.[716] For the remainder of 1886/1887 fiscal year and the first two months of the following, Cosmos assisted Victor in the preparation of "a preliminary report on the architecture of Zuni and Tusayan."[717] The portion assigned to Cosmos was an introductory chapter on the "traditional history of the Tusayan," based on material "collected by Mr. A. M. Stephen, of Keam's Canyon, Arizona."[718] At the same time, Cosmos remained in charge of the modeling room where a series of duplicate models was made.

Victor, with Cosmos as his assistant, left Washington on September 1, 1887, and returned the following March. Victor hired Stephen to assist with the documentation of "details of architecture" and Stephen, in turn, hired Sullivan whose conversational knowledge of Hopi and rapport with people in all of the villages would facilitate their research.[719]

Field research began northeast of Flagstaff, where a group of "cave lodges" were explored and diagrams were made. The cliff dwellings of Walnut Canyon, southeast of Flagstaff, were also examined.[720] The Mindeleff party reached Keams Canyon near the first of October.[721] Six

---

716 I was unable to locate this report.

717 Powell 1891b:xxvii. It was termed "preliminary" as part of the year was given to preparation for a return to the Southwest in the fall of 1887.

718 As noted elsewhere Cosmos made use of the clan migration narratives collected by Sullivan and copied by Stephen into his first two field notebooks. A. M. Stephen, Notebooks 1 and 2, Elsie Clews Parsons Field Notebooks, Columbia University Library. This became Chapter I in Victor Mindeleff 1891:16-38.

719 A. M. Stephen to Washington Matthews, September 15, 1887, Frank Hamilton Cushing Manuscript Collection, MS6, Braun Research Library, Autry Museum of the American West. Stephen and Mindeleff were to meet to settle on a "plan of work."

720 Stephen reports being at "William's store," west of Flagstaff, on October 31 and Victor Mindeleff sent a telegram from Flagstaff on Novermber 17, suggesting these explorations took place after a survey of the Hopi villages moved west to Moencopi. No notes survive from Mindeleff's research in the Flagstaff area. A. M. Stephen, Field Notebook, No. 31, ECPFN, CUL. V. Mindeleff to J. W. Powell, November 17, 1887, LR-BE, NAA, SI.

721 The first entry in Stephen's Field Notebook, No. 31, is October 12, 1887.

ancestral Hopi villages located east along the northern border of the Jeditoh Valley were surveyed (designated "Ruins #1 through #6").[722] On October 20, the party camped near Oraibi and surveyed two ruins (Ruins #8 and #9) before moving on to Moencopi where the summer farming village and a number of ruins were surveyed and mapped before the end of the month (Ruins #10 through #13).[723]

During November and early December, the Mindeleff party spent six weeks at the Chaco ruins in New Mexico. Powell reported an accurate architectural survey of thirteen important ruins was made and indicated "the plans obtained will be published in articles not yet in preparation."[724] Unfortunately, the articles were never written. However, 117 photographs made during the field season at Chaco have survived, providing important base-line information regarding the state of the structures at that time. Later, the party moved east and platted the pueblo of Jemez.

After his return to Washington on February 23, 1888, Cosmos began preparations of an exhibit for the Bureau of Ethnology at the Centennial Exhibition of the Ohio Valley and Central States, Cincinnati. During the summer, Cosmos was in charge of the exhibit and later in repairing models returned after the closing of the event.

Meanwhile, in late October Victor traveled to St. John's, Arizona, where he examined the Hubbell collection of prehistoric pottery and made a series of photographs and colored drawings of the more important specimens.[725] Afterwards he revisited Zuni to obtain interior details of dwellings and other information needed for completion of his studies of the architecture of this pueblo.

Victor spent most of the 1889/1890 fiscal year preparing the report on Hopi and Zuni architecture. Near the end of November, he was asked to go to southern Arizona to view the ruins of Casa Grande and to suggest repairs necessary for its preservation.[726] A growing concern for

---

722   The designation "Ruin #7" was given to "Old Shungopavi" at Second Mesa visited by the Mindeleffs in 1885.

723   Of note here are excavations made by a trader, E. D. Stone.

724   Powell 1891b:xxx–xxxi. See Mathien 2006 on the Mindeleff's work in Chaco Canyon in 1887/1888.

725   For a biography of the trader John Lorenzo Hubblell, see Hieb 1999.

726   Casa Grande was a multi-storied "great house." It was built using calcium carbonate which accumulates in desert soils and can be dug up, mixed with water and turned into "caliche," an excellent building material. During what is

the preservation of the building had been expressed. As early as 1879, the *Weekly Arizona Miner*, a newspaper in the territorial capital of Prescott, carried a report that the people wished to have an appropriation "to improve and reserve" the Casa Grande ruins.[727] Ten years later, through the efforts of Sylvester Baxter, Mary Hemenway, Cushing and, finally, with the aid of Massachusetts Senator George F. Hoar who brought the matter to the attention of the U. S. Senate, an appropriation for repair and approval of the president to declare a reservation to protect the site from looting and vandalism.[728] On April 16, 1889 it was announced that $2,000 in repair money would be available after the beginning of the next fiscal year on July 1. The Secretary of the Interior contacted the Director of the USGS who, in turn, approached the Bureau of Ethnology and obtained the services of Victor Mindeleff.[729]

During December and early January 1890, Victor investigated the ruins at Casa Grande and other sites Cushing had examined while in charge of the Hemenway expedition.[730] He ascertained Casa Grande to be almost identical in character with the many ruins located in the valleys of the Gila and Salt Rivers.[731] Plans, diagrams, and photographs were made of the ruin. On January 8, *The Los Angeles Daily Herald*

---

called the "Classic Period" of the Hohokam which began about A.D. 1175 the population moved into larger and larger villages. These compact communities were composed of walled compounds around a central area which at Casa Grande ruins included a ball court and community plaza surrounded by four compounds. Archaeologists believe that by A.D. 1300 canal consolidation produced a centralized managerial/religious authority in a few villages where the "great houses" were constructed. See Clemensen (1992) and Houk (1996) for descriptions of the architecture of this great house and of the culture of the Hohokam.

727   Clemensen 1992, Chapter 3, p. 1.

728   The 480 acre "Casa Grande Reservation" was the first prehistoric and cultural site established by the United States Government. It is known today as Casa Grande Ruins National Monument.

729   Clemensen, op cit, Chapter 3.

730   Cushing was in charge of the Hemenway Southwestern Archaeological Expedition from 1886 to 1889. See Hinsley and Wilcox, eds. 2002.

731   Large-scale irrigation began in the Phoenix Basin in the Hohokam "Pioneer Period," A.D. 450-700, and by the Late Classic Period, A.D. 1300-1450, a number of these great houses were built along the Gila and Salt Rivers. Of these, Pueblo Grande near present-day Tempe is the best preserved (Andrews and Bostwick 1977).

reported the arrival of Victor and wife in Los Angeles,[732] suggesting Jessie had accompanied him on this field trip. Mindeleff submitted his report on July 1, 1890, the day after his employment with the Bureau of Ethnology ended.[733] He concluded that the main destruction of the ruins came from undermining of the walls but visitors had also done much damage. He advocated six measures to protect the ruins, including a fence around the ruin, providing an on-site custodian, clearing debris, and repairing and reinforcing the walls. In addition, he included a plan for a roof over the ruin.

During the summer of 1889 Cosmos assisted Victor in the final preparation of report on Hopi and Zuni architecture, his own portion of the report having been finished. In December, Cosmos began work on a series of maps showing the location of all known ruins in the "ancient Pueblo country." The maps were to be accompanied by a catalogue containing a description of each ruin and references to the literature relating to it. It was intended that the completed work would be published in the future by the Bureau of Ethnology. The work was never completed. A "Bibliographic Study" by Cosmos was submitted with Victor's completed work on February 24, 1890, but it was withheld from publication by Holmes "with the idea of extending the work to cover the literature of the whole Pueblo region and employing it in connection with the final work upon the pueblos, ancient and modern."[734]

Work in the modeling room continued throughout the year, with repairs and construction of duplicates. A large model of Penasco Blanco, one of the ruins in Chaco Canyon was completed, cut into sections for ease of shipment, and boxed. A duplicate model of Walpi was completed and deposited in the National Museum in place of the original which was destroyed.

Throughout the decade of the 1880s, Victor was the first to go to

---

732 The newspaper says "V. Mindeleff and wife, Washington, D.C." suggesting Victor, Jr. and his sister Natalya, ages 4 and 2, remained with family in Washington.

733 The precise date of the end of Victor's Bureau employment cannot be confirmed. No further reports of his work appear in the annual reports of the Bureau of Ethnology.

734 Holmes to Powell, February 24, 1890, MS.6.CM.11, Frank Hamilton Cushing Manuscript Collection, Braun Research Library, Autry Museum of the American West. Mindeleff's "Bibliographic Study" was never completed and the work referred to has been lost.

Zuni, the Hopi villages, Canyon de Chelly, Chaco Canyon and, finally, to Casa Grande. As his assistant, Cosmos always followed his brother into these areas of research the following year or years later. With the exception of his account of the Snake Dance at Mishongnovi in 1885, virtually all of his "office work" aided Victor in the completion of "A Study of Pueblo Architecture in Tusayan and Cibola." This was to change with Victor's departure from the Bureau of Ethnology in 1890.

As the next fiscal year began in July 1890, Cosmos remained in charge of the modeling room and, for the first five months, was occupied in compiling a card catalogue of ruins as a part of the project to map and document all known ancestral Puebloan structures. On November 20, Cosmos was ordered to go to Casa Grande and make as many repairs as possible within the $2000 appropriated by Congress. Before his departure, he received a detailed letter from Holmes, who had been transferred from the USGS to the Bureau of Ethnology in July 1889 and who now directed Mindeleff's work.[735] Holmes, archaeologist by title but "artist all his life," outlined the nature of the explorations to be carried out by the "ideal investigator:"

> The materials available for field study belong to a number of arts, first among which are the remains of architecture, somewhat less prominent, but hardly less important, are remains illustrating the arts of pottery, weaving and carving in bone, wood, horn, and shell, and pictography. Evidences of the horticultural arts, such as acequias and cultivated fields, deserve the closest attention. The ideal investigator covers all these branches of art with equal care and records of all visible and discoverable characters and relationships in a way to make them available to science.[736]

Only then, Holmes concluded, can we hope "to do justice to the history of our ancient peoples and to the evolution of their culture."

In the Gila Valley, Cosmos's primary responsibility was to

---

735   See Hinsley 1981:100-109 for account of Holmes' career. Holmes (1846-1933) was especially interested in pottery. In 1875, with assistance by William H. Jackson, Holmes prepared plaster and papier mache models for F. V. Hayden's exhibit at the Centennial Exhibition in Philadelphia (Hieb 2011:163) and recognized the importance of the work done by Victor and Cosmos Mindeleff.

736   Holmes to C. Mindeleff, November 28, 1890, MS 4745, NAA, SI.

"superintend the work at Casa Grande." Cosmos, with Marion Warren, arrived at Phoenix late in December 1890. The December 27, 1890 *Arizona Weekly Enterprise* reported:

After the Real Old Timers

Professor Cosmos Mindeleff of the Bureau of Ethnology, U. S. Geological Survey, who arrived last Friday with his charming wife,[737] intended to start overland to Casa Grande this morning. Some unauthorized party obtained possession of his outfit from the express office yesterday and his departure is delayed. ... An appropriation of $2,000 has been made to enclose the famous Casa Grande ruins with roof and outside wall and the Professor is in charge of this work. The loss of photographic material and personal apparel even is exceedingly embarrassing, yet Mrs. Mindeleff bore her experience cheerfully. It is her first visit to the far west.[738] After starting the work of preservation at Casa Grande, Prof. Mindeleff will follow up the Gila River and study old sites... Next spring he and his brave, bright-eyed wife expect to ask the rugged ranges of San Juan, Colorado, to give an account of themselves. –*Phoenix Herald.*

Before a bid announcement for a repair contract could be made, Cosmos made a survey of the Great House, developed plans for its stabilization, and prepared "Specifications: Preservation of the Casa Grande Ruin, Arizona, 1891."[739] Three bids were received and the contract was let on May 9, 1891, to T. L. Stouffer and C. A. Garlick of Phoenix whose low bid of $1985 was accepted.[740] The work was completed and

---

737 It was assumed Marion was Cosmos Mindeleff's wife. In fact, Marion Warren and Walter Fessler were never divorced and no record of a marriage of Marion Warren and Cosmos Mindeleff been located.

738 Marion had visited Cosmos for the Snake Dance at Mishongnovi in 1885, so this was not her "first visit to the far west." The reporter must have assumed this was the case.

739 A copy of this document wss found in Letters Received by the United States Geological Survey, 1879-1901 in the Bound Letters for 1882! See M590 (1965), Roll 13, Frame 341- with related correspondence.

740 The Specifications attached to the contract called for wire fencing and a metal

inspected before the end of November 1891. On June 22, 1892, President Benjamin Harrison proclaimed a 480 acre Casa Grande Reservation.

While waiting for the approval of the contracts for the Casa Grande work,[741] Cosmos explored the valley of the Verde River from its mouth near Fort McDowell to Camp Verde and beyond.[742] The region had never been thoroughly examined, and it was supposed that it would be rich as in archaeological remains as the area around Camp Verde. Mindeleff located a chain of ruins from Camp Verde southward nearly to Fort McDowell, but the ruins were not as numerous as in the Camp Verde area where the so-called Montezuma Castle and Clear Creek Ruin are located.[743] He recognized the significance of the Verde Valley area as being more like the ancestral Puebloan communities to the north than the remains of the Hohokam, as exemplified by the Casa Grande ruin. The culture whose distinctive cultural features Mindeleff recognized is known today as the Sinagua.[744] Although primarily interested in the

roof. Approval of the contract by the Secretary of the Interior was delayed until the end of June and these two items may have been deleted as the work was completed and inspected. As reported, "The plans provided for the excavation of the interior of the ruin and underpinning the walls with brick and cement, the use of tie-beams to hold the walls in place and render them more solid, the restoration of the lintels over door and window openings, and the filling of the cavities above the lintels with brick and cement" (Powell 1896a:xxxvii). H. C. Rizer arrived in late October to inspect and approve the work of Stouffer and Garlick. A roof was added in September 1903 and replaced in December 1932.

741   Mindeleff's field work was scheduled for completion between the 15th and 20th of March 1891 but delays in beginning work at Casa Grande extended the field season into July. See C. Mindeleff to Holmes, April 13, 1891, LR-BE, NAA, SI.

742   In his reports, Cosmos refers to the Verde River as Rio Verde and Fort Verde as Camp Verde. Fort Verde had been established in 1865 and relocated in 1871 because of a malarial outbreak. It was renamed Fort Verde in 1878. I have followed Cosmos's usage as the place is known today as Camp Verde. Camp McDowell, renamed Fort McDowell in 1867, was located about 25 miles northeast of Phoenix about 60 miles from Camp Verde.

743   Montezuma Castle, an ancestral Puebloan structure, was built by Sinagua people between A.D.1100 and A.D. 1425. Located in a rock shelter, the dwelling is five stories high and contained about 20 rooms. Clear Creek Ruin, three miles southeast of Camp Verde, is the largest of the Sinagua ruins in the Verde Valley.

744   The name, Sinagua, meaning "without water" was given to the area by Harold S. Colton in 1939, who distinguished two different culture areas, a Northern Sinagua centered in the highlands around Flagstaff and a Southern Sinagua who occupied the lower elevations across the Verde Valley in central Arizona.

masonry structures and cavate lodges (hand carved caves), Mindeleff also observed irrigation ditches, agricultural areas, and artificial depressions later identified as ball courts.[745]

At Camp Verde on March 17, Cosmos wrote a lengthy account of his explorations along with a request for additional funding to continue his research. The letter provides a glimpse of the fieldwork he was engaged in, an experience shared by Marion Warren:

> And now for the Verde work. I examined all the lower valley up to 10 miles north of McDowell, and found nothing. At that point we had to leave the river and go around some 25 miles to what they call the "upper settlements"... Nearly all of these were examined and photographed, and I secured there some photographs of one of the best ancient irrigation ditches to be found in this region. Some four miles above this place [Camp Verde], or about a mile above Limestone Creek...occurs the largest ruin on the Verde...
>
> It was while I was engaged upon the survey of this ruin—a particularly difficult survey by the way, as there was hardly a wall-line that ran continuously through the building—that the great storm came; it rained hard and without intermission for 3 days, then, after two days of fair weather, it rained again, and still harder, for 2 days more. The river rose...and near the end of February, it was easily fifteen feet deeper than when we crossed it, and in places, half a mile wide. Crossing the stream was out of the question... On the 27th I attempted to cross the river with a pack, nearly losing a couple of horses in the attempt and failing finally to get across. On the same day I met a couple of cowmen, who had been caught like us, on the east bank. It was their opinion, and they had

---

745 Cosmos Mindeleff's first account of the exploration of the Verde Valley appears in his letter to W. H. Holmes, March 17, 1891, LR-BE, NAA, SI. A brief summary appears in Powell 1894b:xxviii. Mindeleff's account, "Aboriginal Remains in Verde Valley, Arizona" (C. Mindeleff 1896a), provides the only early description of the area. Ball courts are found in Hohokam sites but not in Puebloan sites to the north.

lived in this country ten and fifteen years respectively, that the river could not be crossed for 3 days at least, and probably not for a week, and they decided not to attempt it—so I gave it up myself and packing 3 animals with instruments, beds, and provisions for a week—all they could carry—I struck out up the river for Camp Verde, some 65 miles. This was, without exception, the roughest trip I have ever made. We were confined to the east side by the high water and the whole distance was only a succession of climbing high hills and skirting deep canons for a crossing. Twice we had a pack horse fall and roll down the hill and it was only through the special providence that looks out for assistant archaeologists that we escaped without serious mishap. ... The trip occupied 8 days, though we might have made it in four, had we not stopped to survey and photograph ruins. ... The cliff ruins I have seen up to this time are rude affairs—cavate lodges always, and not to be compared to those of [Canyon] de Chelly in workmanship or finish. The "four story cliff ruin" on Beaver Creek,[746] modelled by Hoffman[747] and since described and illustrated, I have seen from a distance but have not yet examined.[748]

Cosmos concluded his letter, "Altogether I think I will have when I leave here the material for a good report on the Verde, from its mouth to this point."

The *Arizona Weekly Citizen* of April 11, 1891, reported:

Explorers Return

Al Childers and Frank Gabbert returned Saturday evening from their late government search for antique civilization under the command of Professor Mindeleff.

---

746 Montezuma Castle.
747 Walter James Hoffman (1846-1899), a physician who served with the Hayden Survey in Arizona and New Mexico in 1871, made models of Pueblo Bonito, Montezuma Well, and of Montezuma Castle entitled "Model of Cliff Fortress in Beaver Creek, Arizona."
748 C. Mindeleff to Holmes, March 17, 1891, LR-BE, NAA, SI.

A month was spent examing the ruins of Casa Grande
and arrangements were made to enclose and preserve
the wonder of a lost race. Journeying northward the
party, 35 miles beyond Ft. McDowell, was cut off from
the world by floods in the Salt and Verde rivers, at the
time Phoenix enjoyed similar misfortune. Their first
news of this deluge's doings was an item in a Prescott
paper stating that the water had risen within two feet of
the City Hall in Phoenix. Their trip beyond McDowell
was very slow and tedious, they being compelled to
travel three or four miles often, around some bluff, in
order to make a hundred yards of actual progress. They
were eight days in accomplishing fifty miles. At length
they reached Camp Verde, where the party disbanded.

Prof. Mindeleff, his wife and a Holbrook guide are
awaiting orders either to trudge on with their outfit to
San Juan, Colorado, or proceed to Flagstaff and take
the cars for Washington, D.C. Mrs. Mindeleff made a
brave record, coming as she did from the luxury of life
at the national capital. Donning a blue flannel bloomer
costume, she rode astride and bravely went up all trails
and along precipitous cliffs as fearlessly as any in the
party... She slept on the ground, with no canopy save the
starry vault of heaven, and came through the trip as fresh
and vigorous as a calla lily at the Presidio in February. –
Phoenix Herald.

On April 13, having returned to Camp Verde, Cosmos wrote
to Holmes with a revised schedule for the letting of contracts and the
completion of work at Casa Grande. In the same letter, he detailed
three "schemes" for continuing work in the field, all of which required
additional allotments of funds to cover the costs of a field party.[749] At
some point, he received approval to continue work in the field until July
15, 1891. It is not clear if Marion Warren continued to accompany him
in the field.

On his return to Washington, Cosmos spent the remainder of the

---

749   C. Mindeleff to Holmes, ibid.

1891/1892 as well as the 1892/1893 fiscal year engaged in office work[750]. During these eighteen months he completed his remarkable report, "Aboriginal Remains in Verde Valley, Arizona."[751] The study included a review of previous accounts and a physical description of the area, with detailed maps, sketches, and photographs. Although many large pueblos, such as Montezuma Castle, were not documented in his study, Clear Creek Ruin, Wingfield Mesa Pueblo, and other small sites were discussed in the report. There are separate accounts of "stone villages" (on bottom lands and on defensive sites), cavate lodges, "bowlder [sic]-marked sites," irrigation ditches and horticultural works. The largest group of cavates with ninety-eight hand carved caves is known today as the Mindeleff Cavate Lodge Group. Typical of Cosmos's approach, he compared these architectural forms with others, including the cavates in the Rio de los Frijoles.[752] Like his brother's work on the architectural forms of the Hopi and Zuni, Cosmos included detailed descriptions of structural characteristics: masonry, door and window openings, chimneys and fireplaces. Moving beyond descriptions, his interpretations of the social organization of architectural forms and land use patterns from the sites he recorded reveals a theoretical approach seventy years ahead of his time.[753]

During the summer of 1892, Cosmos completed the illustrations for the "Aboriginal Remains of Verde Valley, Arizona" and then assisted in preparing materials for the World's Fair in Chicago. At the same time, he directed the creation of four large models of Pueblo "villages and ruins" at the request of the United States Commission for exhibit at the 1892 Exposicion Historico-Americana in Madrid. He was then directed to prepare an article on "American Aboriginal Architecture"[754] as well as a report on Casa Grande that appeared in the *Fifteenth Annual Report*

---

750 See Powell 1896b:xlii where three sentences are given to reporting his work in 1892/1893. He had submitted "Work of Cosmos Mindeleff, Year Ending June 30th 1893," usually incorporated under Powell's name in the annual "Report of the Director."

751 C. Mindeleff 1896a.

752 Now in Bandelier National Monument, New Mexico

753 See Longacre 1999:365-367 for archaeological studies of the relationship between architecture and social organization initiated in the 1970s.

754 C. Mindeleff to Powell, September 13, 1893. The report was "finished and turned in" but was not published by the Bureau of [American] Ethnology. Mindeleff may have published it after he left the Bureau. See 1898f.

of the Bureau of Ethnology entitled "The Repair of Casa Grande Ruin, Arizona, in 1891."[755]

On July 14, 1893, Cosmos left Washington and returned to the Southwest for a series of explorations that lasted until the end of September 1894.[756] His work was interrupted and redirected by a number of unforeseen events: a flood on the Little Colorado River at Winslow, Arizona, a broken wagon wheel south of Flagstaff, a second flood on the Little Colorado River at Holbrook, sand storms followed by snow storms in Canyon de Chelly, and other misfortunes that followed. There is nothing to suggest if or when Marion Warren accompanied Cosmos during this extended field trip to the Southwest.

Cosmos had departed Washington with permission to spend a week at the World's Fair in Chicago. He reached Holbrook near the end of July and soon learned "an outfit was essential" for the region he proposed to explore.[757] After obtaining supplies and equipment he started for Keams Canyon "expecting there to obtain fuller information."[758]

At Keam's trading post he met J. Walter Fewkes who had worked with J. G. Owens and A. M. Stephen in 1891 to document the Snake Dance at Walpi. Fewkes planned to attend the ceremony again at Walpi on August 13.[759] Mindeleff noted two large placards Fewkes had hung over the two kivas used during the ceremony with "No Admittance" written on them.[760]

At Keams Canyon, Cosmos learned he would require additional supplies to explore the San Juan River area.[761] Because of "my limited

---

755   C. Mindeleff 1897a. This was the first of a series of articles describing the work done in 1891. See 1897g, 1897h, and 1898g.

756   There is no evidence Marion accompanied Cosmos on this extended period of field work.

757   No proposal for his field work for the 1893/1894 fiscal year has been found. Clearly he intended to return to Canyon de Chelly. However, it appears he planned to explore the San Juan River area in southern Utah first.

758   C. Mindeleff to Powell, ibid.

759   Six months later Fewkes published a detailed account (Fewkes 1894b). See Hinsley, Hieb, and Fash, n.d. for an account of his 1891 and 1893 studies of the Snake Dance.

760   The signs are not mentioned in Fewkes's or Owens's accounts of the 1891 ceremony.

761   Thomas V. Keam probably was the source of this information as he had visited

allotment" he decided to return to Camp Verde where he had stored part of his field outfit two years earlier.[762] Cosmos had hoped to cross the Little Colorado River east of Holbrook but high waters forced him to follow the north side of the river to Winslow. A mile north of Winslow he explored the location of a cluster of seven ancestral Hopi ruins called Homolovi ("place of little hills").[763] On August 28, he crossed the river east of Winslow intending to go to Camp Verde by way of Sunset and Chavez passes, Stoneman Lake, and Rattlesnake Tanks.[764]

At Camp Verde Cosmos loaded about 1200 pounds of materials on his wagon. Because of the weight and rough road, the wagon broke down 30 miles south of Flagstaff. In Flagstaff he acquired a new wheel and had another repaired. On September 15, he left Flagstaff and followed along the south bank of the Little Colorado River, but because of the rain-soaked ground he did not reach Winslow until September 20 and Holbrook four days later. At Holbrook, he laid in additional supplies but a "big storm came up and caught us here." In writing to Powell on September 30, Cosmos reported portions of the railroad were washed out east of Gallup and west of Flagstaff, telegraph lines were down, and he did not know when he would be able to cross the Little Colorado River. From information he had received at Keams Canyon, Mindeleff apparently abandoned his plans to explore the area around the San Juan River in southeastern Utah. Instead, he would begin with further explorations in Canyon de Chelly, and then proceed to the San Juan River area in northern New Mexico. However, it was not until October 4 that he began his slow trip north to investigate what was rumored to be a ruin but turned out to be a volcanic dyke. On October 12 he reached Ganado (formerly Pueblo Colorado).

Finally in Canyon de Chelly on October 18, three months after

---

southern Utah as his friend, Thomas McElmell, had a trading post at the confluence of the San Juan River and what is now known as McElmo Creek in the early 1880s.

762   It would be over one hundred and twenty miles by horse and/or wagon to travel from Keams Canyon to Camp Verde. Mindeleff must have realized it would have been impossible to carry out his explorations without the supplies and equipment stored after exploring the Verde Valley.

763   The area was occupied between A.D. 1300 and 1400—"a limited time," Mindeleff speculated.

764   C. Mindeleff to Powell, September 30, 1893, LR-BE, NAA, SI.

leaving Washington, Cosmos camped at the White House ruin and began a systematic survey of the ancestral Hopi sites.[765] From the first thirty-five ruins he examined, Cosmos soon concluded that differences in architectural features indicated "either a difference in time of occupancy or in tribal stocks."[766] A month later, after making ground plans for another thirty-three ruins, Mindeleff reported:

> I think it will be possible to classify the ruins here and to establish a chronologic sequence—a sequence commencing perhaps in pre-Columbian time, certainly in pre-Spanish time...[767]

Of particular interest to Mindeleff were four chimney structures "certainly aboriginal in execution but probably of foreign conception."[768]

Writing from Ganado on December 24, Cosmos reported having mapped Canyon de Chelly and its principle branch, Canyon del Muerto. He believed "the data thus obtained will radically change some of the accepted theories concerning the cliff ruins." The results of his research, enhanced with maps, ground plans, sections, sketches, and photographs, would be published as "The Cliff Ruins of Canyon de Chelly, Arizona."[769] In the meanwhile, he wrote:

> I am waiting information on the mountains east of here – if the reports are favorable I shall probably go up to the San Juan river, near Farmington – if unfavorable I shall probably go south toward Zuni and work around to the Rio Grande in the vicinity of Santa Clara, where the

---

765 Field parties usually included a cook and a teamster. There is no information about the make-up of Cosmos's party or when and where they were hired.

766 C. Mindeleff to Powell, October 20, 1893. LR-BE, NAA, SI. Although structural abutments and stratigraphy indicated a sequence of construction, more precise dating techniques, e.g., dendrochronology, were not developed until well into the twentieth century.

767 C. Mindeleff to Powell, Novermber 25, 1893. LR-BE, NAA, SI. With the development of dendrochronology, sites in Canyon de Chelly have been dated between AD 350 and AD 1300.

768 Ibid. The chimney structures were, in fact ventilator shafts in the kivas. They were not a part of the architecture of Zuni, the Hopi villages or other Pueblos he had examined previously. See Fewkes 1908 for the first published account of the function of this feature.

769 C. Mindeleff 1897b.

cavate lodges are very abundant.[770]

Mindeleff chose to go in the direction of the San Juan River. Powell would later report that while crossing the Tunicha Mountains in snow and wind on the way to the San Juan River in northern New Mexico,

> ...the party missed the trail and for a time were lost; among other accidents a wagon was overturned in such a manner that Mr. Mindeleff was caught beneath it and his shoulder dislocated, whereby he was disabled for some months. Fortunately the expedition was rescued by a party of ranchmen from Fort Defiance...[771]

When the party reached Olio, New Mexico, on the San Juan River a few days later, Cosmos wrote to Powell, not mentioning the accident, and to W J McGee, now his immediate supervisor, to say:

> At present I am laid up with a dislocated shoulder— wagon fell on me in crossing the mountains in the snow, but I expect to be about again in a few weeks.[772]

Cosmos moved east to the Mormon settlement of Fruitland. However, the injury was more serious than he believed. Two months later, in a letter to McGee, Cosmos wrote:

> When I found that my disabled shoulder would prevent very active work for some time—aside from dislocation (which was reduced) the muscles were crushed and they recover slowly—I reduced my outfit to practically nothing, retaining only a buckboard and team to get about with. Up to a month ago I was unable to drive myself, but I am now doing nicely and am able to feed and care for the horses myself.[773]

He hoped by the end of the fiscal year to "make a beginning on the San Juan valley." The published reports from the previous two months indicate he was confined to camp by the weather and spent his time preparing reports and maps.[774] It was not until April that a

---

770   Mindeleff to Powell, December 24, 1893, LR-BE, NAA, SI.
771   Powell 1897a:lx.
772   C. Mindeleff to Powell and C. Mindeleff to W J McGee, January 20, 1894, LR-BE, NAA, SI.
773   C. Mindeleff to W J McGee, April 5, 1894, LR-BE, NAA, SI.
774   Powell 1897:xlvii, lii, and lvi.

substantive report was submitted, as Powell summarized:

> Mr. Mindeleff finds the Pueblo country overrun by speculators in primitive pottery and other relics, which are collected and sold as products of Aztec art. The operations of these speculators are ruinous; the material is collected without adequate study of association, so that its value as a record of aboriginal conditions is largely lost; and in addition the methods employed are destructive of all material except that of portable character and commercial value. Mr. Mindeleff is making every attempt to forestall these destructive operations and to enable him to do so advantageously he is continued in field at some sacrifice in efficiency of work on reports and illustrations.[775]

In June, with time and his allotment running out, Cosmos resumed surveying the terraces along the San Juan River and made an effort to develop a sequence of occupation of the area.[776] At the beginning of September he began closing up his work, completing accounts, and making arrangements of disposing of his field outfit and equipment. Towards the end of the month he took the train from Gallup, New Mexico, and returned to Washington.[777]

After nearly a year in the field, Cosmos had little to show for his efforts, except for his work in Canyon de Chelly. The summary of this field work given by Powell in August 1894 reported:

> Mr. Mindeleff's researches have covered a large territory and will permit archeologic mapping of considerable value, even the negative results of use as indicating the territory barren of aboriginal works...[778]

---

775 Powell 1897a:lx. In his letter to McGee cited above, Mindeleff indicates most of the "Aztec pottery" was marketed in Denver.

776 C. Mindeleff to Powell, July 2, 1894, LR-BE, NAA, SI. This is the only detailed account of sites he visited on the San Juan.

777 Powell 1897b:xx, xxiii, and xxvii. Cosmos had made requests for additional allotments to continue in the field, returning to Canyon de Chelly and to Chaco Canyon. See C. Mindeleff to Powell, September 12 and September 20, 1894, LR-BE, NAA, SI.

778 Powell 1897b:xxiii.

Cosmos Mindeleff, ca. 1897. Anon., Authorities of the Southwest, *Land of Sunshine* 6: 186.

Cosmos never prepared a report on what he may have found on the terraces along the San Juan River.[779] The Salmon Ruins, occupied by several different peoples between ca. A. D. 1090 and A.D. 1280, with an elevated tower kiva and as many as 300 rooms, would have been visible to some extent. His reference to "Aztec art" indicates Cosmos knew of and probably visited the so-called Aztec Ruin, located on the

---

779 See C. Mindeleff to Powell, July 2, 1894, LR-BE, NAA, SI. In this letter Cosmos provides some detailed observations on the location of sites along the San Juan River but no detailed report was ever published.

Animas River northeast of Farmington, New Mexico.[780]

While Cosmos was in the Southwest, changes were taking place in the Bureau of Ethnology. Powell's declining health had affected his leadership and he retired from the USGS to devote full-time to the Bureau. Even so, many of Powell's duties were left to W J McGee who became "acting director." Changes were made in appropriations at the beginning of the 1894/1895 fiscal year with the consequence that many projects, including those Cosmos was working on, could no longer be extended beyond June 30, 1895.[781]

On his return to Washington, Cosmos began preparing a report on his explorations made during the period from July 1893 to September 1894. Powell's monthly reports repeat the statement, "Mr. Cosmos Mindeleff spent the month in the preparation of a report on the 'Cliff Ruins of Canyon de Chelly.'"[782] Then, abruptly, his many years of work with the Bureau of Ethnology came to an end:

> The completion of Mr. Mindeleff's report rounds out one of the lines of archaeologic research in the southwest which has been in progress for some years; and with the transmission of the report Mr. Mindeleff's connection with the Bureau terminates.[783]

On May 7, Cosmos sent a proposal to Samuel P. Langley, Secretary of the Smithsonian Institution, to continue work in Canyon de Chelly, this time to collect materials for the National Museum.[784] Nothing came of his effort, although Powell offered to continue his appointment for one month to read the proofs of his report on Canyon de Chelly.[785]

---

780 Pioneers in the area supposed the ruins were constructed by the Aztecs. The ruin is a Great House, bearing resemblances to the architecture of Chaco Canyon and may have been a Chacoan outlier. The site contained over 400 rooms and a great kiva and saw at least two periods of occupation between the 11th and 13th centuries. It was extensively "pot-hunted" as Mindeleff indicated. For information on the Aztec ruin see Morgan 1994:81-82 and 85-87 for the Salmon ruin.

781 Powell 1897b:lxi.

782 See, for example, Powell 1897b:xl.

783 Powell 1897b:lvi.

784 C. Mindeleff to S. P. Langley, May 7, 1895, RU31, Smithsonian Institution Archives.

785 C. Mindeleff to Powell, July 20, 1895, LR-BE, NAA, SI. Cosmos writes to negotiate when he will read proofs. After leaving the Bureau, Mindeleff wrote

After leaving the Bureau of American Ethnology in 1895, Cosmos turned to writing as a source of income. In July, he told Powell, "I am very much in need of money now..."[786] Soon after, he began reworking Stephen's 1888 report on Navaho architecture into "Navaho Houses," published under Cosmos's name in 1898.[787] In "Authorities on the Southwest," a series of biographical sketches in Charles Lummis's *Land of Sunshine* published in 1897, Cosmos is described as having a mass of materials on the ruins of the Southwest he was preparing for publication as well as "writing a number of essays on miscellaneous topics connected with his work in the Southwest."[788]

Late in November 1898, Cosmos wrote to W J McGee, "ethnologist in charge" but effectively "acting director," offering "for sale" an article on the "origin and development of the kiva in Pueblo architecture" for possible publication in an *Annual Report of the Bureau of American Ethnology*.[789] Apparently nothing came of the proposal. However, between 1897 and 1902, thirty publications bearing Cosmos Mindeleff's name appeared in a wide range of scientific and popular venues.[790]

Otherwise little is known of Cosmos Mindeleff's life after his Bureau of Ethnology service. In 1898 he was employed by *The Commercial Advertiser* in New York City. In the 1900 Census, Cosmos and Marion Mindeleff [sic[were living in Manhattan and Cosmos was employed as a newspaper editor. Walter Fessler filed for divorce in October 1901, claiming his wife, Marion, had "deserted him for no good reason" in 1889, the year she began to be known as "Mrs. Mindeleff." Two months later, on November 8, 1901, the *New York Times* reported "Cosmos Mindeleff, bankrupt."[791]

---

786 "Navaho Houses" (1898a) and may have received payment for this manuscript. Ibid.

787 C. Mindeleff 1898a. Cosmos apparently sold the manuscript to W J McGee for publication by the Bureau of American Ethnology. The "reports" Stephen prepared for Victor Mindeleff as well as his notes on Navaho architecture used by Cosmos have been lost. Fragments of his Navaho research are located in the Gladys Reichard Papers, MS 29-39-1, Museum of Northern Arizona.

788 Anon. 1897:187.

789 C. Mindeleff to McGee, November 23, 1898. On McGee, see Judd 1967:21-23.

790 See Bibliography.

791 *New York Times*, November 8, 1901, p. 11, and December 10, 1901, p. 11. Divorce

In 1905 Cosmos was still employed with the *The Commercial Advertiser* when he and Marion traveled to London with his mother, Julia Mindeleff.

The 1910 census reported Cosmos and Marion Mindeleff, "married 15 years," sharing a house with another family in New York City where he worked as a journalist. In about 1917 the Mindeleffs purchased "the Dr. Knudson residence" in Carmel, New York.[792] During these years the Mindeleffs resided for lengthy periods in London, Paris, and in Florence, Italy. Marion Mindeleff died on April 8, 1933. At her death it was recalled:

> When she married Mr. Mindeleff, then in the Smithsonian Institute…she accompanied him on his annual visits to the Indian country… She often lived for six months to a year on these expeditions, traveling most of the time in the saddle. She was the first white woman to see the snake dance of the Hopi Indians in Arizona and assisted her husband in writing the first scientific description and explanation of that weird ceremony ever published.[793]

When Cosmos died five years later, on June 26, 1938, *The Putnam County Courier* described him as the "well known newspaper man" who studied Indian villages and cliff ruins for the Smithsonian Institution. It noted that Cosmos commuted to New York City, a distance of 60 miles, until he retired in 1929, and that at various times he was connected with the *New York Sun, New York World,* and the *New York American,* for whom he was a foreign correspondent during World War I.

Victor Mindeleff's career, on the other hand, is well-documented. After leaving the Bureau of Ethnology in 1890 he (along with Cosmos) worked for the E. and E. Baltzley Real Estate Company, located in Montgomery County, Maryland. Victor designed several buildings for the National Chautauqua of Glen Echo, Maryland, including the Chautauqua Tower, built in 1892, as well as a number of private residences.

In 1898 Victor became architect of the United States Life-Saving

---

proceedings were not completed. Legally Marion remained Mrs. Walter Fessler until his death in 1912.

792 Her obituary indicates "she purchased" the Knudson residence (see Anon 1933).

793 Anon. 1933.

Service (USLSS) and between then and 1914 he created thirteen known designs. The Forge-River type station designed in 1914 was used on the East and West Coasts and the Great Lakes and was the dominant design used by the United States Coast Guard through the 1940s. In 1914, he entered private practice. He was noted for his domestic designs that showed house and garden as a unit. Victor was elected to membership in the Anthropological Society of Washington in 1901. In 1918 he was elected to membership in the Cosmos Club. In 1924, he was elected Member of the American Institute of Architects and became a Fellow two years later. For the 1926 Philadelphia World's Fair, the Mindeleff Studios prepared a model of Thomas Jefferson's Academical Village.[794]

Victor Mindeleff died March 26, 1948. At his death, Delos H. Smith wrote of his later years:

> ...his domestic design showed a real appreciation of house and garden as a unit, as well as the rare feeling for form and color which made his work distinctive.[795]

Acknowledgements

Through his genealogical research, Bill Korstick has provided most of what I know of the careers of Victor and Cosmos Mindeleff after they left the Bureau of [American] Ethnology in the 1890s. Without his interest in Marion Warren, I would know nothing of her role in Cosmos's documentation of the Hopi Snake Dance or of her participation in his research in the Verde Valley, Arizona. Early in my work on the Mindeleffs, Peter Nabokov generously sent me the research files he assembled in preparation for writing his insightful introductory biography to Victor Mindeleff's classic study of vernacular architecture.[796] Bill Longacre's acknowledgement of Cosmos Mindeleff's pioneering studies of the social organization of architectural form and his encouragement of my own efforts are gratefully acknowledged here.[797]

---

794   See Elizabeth Hicks, New Research on the Academical Village Model, http:// www.uvamblogs.com/jeffersons_academical_village/?p=439.
795   1948:219.
796   Nabokov 1989.
797   Longacre 1999 and 2010.

6. Accidental Anthropologist: Alexander M. Stephen and the Exploration of Tusayan, 1879-1894[798]

M. R. Trouillot reminds us "any historical narrative is a particular bundle of silences"[799] and in the histories of Southwestern anthropology none is greater than that surrounding the life of Alexander M. Stephen (1846-1894), whose legacy includes several thousand pages of manuscripts and over a dozen articles rich in descriptions of the social and ceremonial life of the Hopi and Navajo he met while living at Keams Canyon, Arizona, from 1879 to 1894. It is puzzling that none of the men who knew Stephen well—Washington Matthews, J. Walter Fewkes, and above all, Thomas V. Keam—did not write an appreciation for the life of a man who shared so much with them.

From Scotland to Keams Canyon

"Alexander Stiven"—Alexander Middleton Stephen[800]—son of James and Elizabeth Croll Stephen was born in Dundee, Forfarshire [Angus], Scotland, on October 29, 1846. In the Scottish census of 1851

---

798 In this brief chapter on A. M. Stephen I have drawn on several previous essays I have published regarding Stephen's life and work. Although known primarily for his research among the Hopi in the early 1890s, Stephen's first interest was in the Navajo (Hieb 2004a). The Keam pottery collection catalogued by Stephen was, I discovered, documented in photographs by Ben Wittick (Hieb 2009). Between 1891 and 1894 Stephen was employed by J. Walter Fewkes to record Hopi social and ceremonial life (forthcoming in Hinsley, Hieb, and Fash, eds.).

799 Trouillot 1995:27.

800 Alexander M. Stephen's middle name was "Middleton," not "MacGregor." Keam to Washington Matthews, January 27, 1897, Washington Matthews Papers, Wheelwright Museum. Cited hereafter as WMP, WM. The earliest use of "MacGregor" appears in Culin 1905:171.

his father, age 50, was said to be a joiner (a furniture maker or inside carpenter); his mother, "Betsy," was 49, and Alexander, then 5, had two older siblings, Mary, 10, and William, 14. When the Scottish census was taken in April 1861 Alexander, 15, was living with his parents in Dundee, and a millworker by profession. Like others in Scotland in the nineteenth century, Stephen received an excellent education.

Soon after the census was taken, Stephen sailed to the United States. At Hopi many years later he wrote:

> Sitting in the kiva, listening to the songs, the gale overhead whistling through the huge piles of greasewood and past the tall mast like poles of the ladder, forcibly reminded me of nights long ago when I have been down the forecastle listening to the songs of the watch below.[801]

On October 22, 1861, in Potsdam, New York, the not quite sixteen year old "Alexander Stevens" enlisted in Company A, 92nd Regiment, New York Infantry ("Second St. Lawrence Regiment"). Claiming to be eighteen, Stephen was described as being "5'4" [with] light complexion, blue eyes, light hair," born in Scotland, and a sailor by occupation. He was mustered in with the regiment on January 1, 1862, as a Private enrolled for three years.

In March 1862, the 92nd Regiment left for Washington, where it embarked with General McClellan's forces for the Virginia Peninsula. The regiment was present during the siege of Yorktown from April 17 to May 4, and the battle of Williamsburg on May 5. Between May 21 and June 1, the regiment suffered the loss of 105 killed, wounded, or missing in the battle of Fair Oaks or Seven Pines. Stephen later wrote, "I first made the acquaintance of Frank [Carter, a life-long friend] and some other rebel gentlemen in a dark-nasty-stormy-night—the night of May 31st 1862." In June the regiment shared in the Seven Days battles, and it is during this time that Stephen was first reported to be a Clerk at the regimental headquarters.

After being stationed at Camp Hamilton, Virginia, for three months, the regiment was ordered to Suffolk, and then to New Bern, North Carolina, where it participated in the Goldsboro expedition from December 11 to 20. In January 1863, still in New Bern, Stephen's name appears on the hospital muster roll as a Nurse. In April 1863 Stephen

---

801   Parsons, ed., 1936:192.

was appointed Commissary Sergeant of the regiment. For the next year the 92nd Regiment, New York Infantry performed garrison and other duties at New Bern.

On January 4, 1864, Stephen was discharged from the 92nd Regiment in order for him to re-enlist (now just 18 years old) in Company G, 96th New York Infantry Regiment ("McComb's Plattsburg Regiment") for three years as a Veteran Volunteer. He received a bounty of $160, and was appointed 1st Lieutenant and Acting Regimental Adjutant. A year later, in April 1865, he was promoted to Adjutant, and in August he was made an Acting Assistant Attorney General. While Stephen was with the 96th Regiment, it was present at various engagements in Virginia, and in May the regiment joined the Army of the Potomac at the beginning of the battle at Cold Harbor. The regiment then remained with the forces besieging Richmond until the end of the war. The 96th Regiment, including 1st Lieutenant (Adjutant) "Alexander M. Stephen," was honorably discharged and mustered out, February 6, 1866, at City Point, Virginia.[802] Stephen was 19 years old.

Stephen's whereabouts during the years following his discharge in 1866 are a mystery. Various reports suggest he came to the Southwest soon after being discharged and became a prospector in Utah, Nevada, and possibly California. He visited at Keams Canyon in April 1879, and took up permanent residence at the beginning of January 1880.[803] In

---

802   Complete Military Service Records of Private/Commissary Sergeant Alexander M. Stephen, Companies A, K, 92nd New York Regiment [and] 1st Lieutenant and Adjutant Alexander M. Stephen, Company G, 96th New York Regiment, Index to Compiled Service Records of Volunteer Union Soldiers Who Served in Organizations from the State of New York, M551 (Washington, D.C.: National Archives and Records Administration), roll 135, Steo-Stoc. Frederick Henry Dyer, *Compendium of the War of Rebellion* (Dayton, OH: Morningside, 1979), vol. 2, pp. 1441-1442. Frederick Phisterer, *New York in the War of Rebellion, 1861-1865* (Albany: Weed and Parsons, 1890), vol. 4, pp. 3094-3111. *Annual Report of the Adjutant-General of the State of New York, 1901* (New York: J. B. Lyon, 1902), p. 1034 for the Register of the Ninety-second Infantry Regiment and *Annual Report of the Adjutant-General of the State of New York, 1902* (New York: J. B. Lyon, 1903), p. 699 for the Ninety-sixth Infantry Regiment.

803   Stephen gives the dates of his visit and residence at Keam's trading post in A. M. Stephen, Deposition in Support of Thomas Keam in Response to Allegations Made by Philip Zoller, August 17, 1882, Report 257, Reports of the Field Jurisdiction of the Office of Indian Affairs, Records of the Secretary of the

the U. S. Census of 1880 Stephen declared himself an "explorer" and a "prospector."

Alexander M. Stephen at Keam's Trading Post

On January 6, 1880, an addition was made to the 1868 Navajo Treaty Reservation which included the location of Tom Keam's Fair View Trading Post. This event, combined with Billy Keam's illness and death at Fort Wingate on October 24, 1880, led Tom Keam to relocate to his Keams Canyon trading post and ranch.[804] In January 1880 Keam was joined by Stephen who would serve as clerk in charge of the trading post.

At Keam's trading post Stephen had frequent contact with Hopis and soon began compiling word and phrase lists in Hopi and Tewa. However, he was soon more interested and involved in the culture and language of the Navajos who came to trade on a daily basis.[805]

On his way to the Snake Dance at Walpi in August 1881, John G. Bourke wrote in his journal:

> At Keam's ranch we met Mr. Alexander Stevens [sic], a bright Scotchman [sic] who, during the past twelve years, has had considerable experience as a metallurgist and mining prospector in Nevada and Utah. He gave me a thrilling account of his journey westward to the country of the Cohoninos, a tribe of Indians living in the canon of Cataract Creek.[806]

The following year, Henry C. Rizer, editor of the *Eureka Herald*, wrote:

> In the absence of Mr. Keam we were welcomed by two friends and guests of his, Mr. Stephens [sic], a native of Scotland, and Mr. [Thomas] McElmell, formerly an

---

Interior, RG48, National Archives. Keam later said he had known Stephen for fifteen years, suggesting the two men had not met prior to Stephen's initial visit in 1879.

804   William Keam's death was reported in the *Santa Fe New Mexican*, October 31. The funeral took place at Fort Wingate on October 28.

805   See Hieb 2004b.

806   The Cohoninos or Coconinos, as they were often called at the time, are better known today as the Yuman-speaking Havasupai. See Schwartz 1983 for an overview of Havasupai history and culture. See Parsons, ed., 1936:1232 for Stephen's use of the name Cohonino.

officer in our navy. They are both attractive gentlemen of unusual breadth of information, intelligence and culture. They both came west quite young men upon the conclusion of the war and have followed the varied and strangely fascinating life of prospectors….in California, Nevada, Utah and this region.[807]

After many years of exploring and prospecting, Stephen would have found Keam's ranch, as it was often called, attractive as more than just a room and a source of employment. As Bourke saw in 1881, Keam's residence was furnished with the classics of English literature as well as current journals and newspapers. Keam had a garden and a cook. Stephen had his own room in the complex of buildings that comprised the trading post. Keam employed Stephen to manage the "general store." At various times, other individuals filled in for Stephen or Keam when visitors, travel, or business occupied their attention. Their arrangement was clearly one of convenience.

When taking up residence at the trading post in 1880, Stephen joined a man who had nearly fifteen years' experience working with the Navajo people as an interpreter, a trader, and an advocate. Keam boasted an excellent knowledge of Navajo language and culture, and enjoyed the trust and confidence of many important Navajo leaders. At the store, Navajos traded wool, pelts, and livestock for coffee, sugar, and other goods. Keam and Stephen carried out transactions in Navajo, with Spanish as a second language. From necessity, Stephen began learning

---

807　Bourke 1884:80, and H. C. Rizer, Editorial Correspondence, *Eureka Herald*, October 6, 1882 provide what little we know of Stephen's years as a prospector. There are few additional clues regarding Stephen's whereabouts before taking up residence at Keam's ranch. Frederick Nolan cites a single letter indicating an A. M. Stephen was appointed post trader at Fort Stanton, New Mexico, on October 14, 1870 (Frederick Nolan, *The Lincoln County War, A Documentary History*, Norman: University of Oklahoma Press, 1992, p. 42, 530, n.24). Stephen speaks of his "old chum" Walter R. "Jim" Fales (ca. 1851-?) of Wretham, Massachusetts, "a staunch man of mountain & desert," who was employed at and then took over Keam's trading post near Fort Defiance from 1883 to 1884 and worked at a trading post at Washington Pass from 1884-1885 (Stephen to J. W. Fewkes, March 18, 1892, MS 4408, National Anthropological Archives, Smithsonian Institution; cited hereafter as NAA, SI. McNitt 1962:58-59, 253). Fales visited Stephen in August 1893 and may have been a prospector with Stephen along the Colorado River in the 1870s.

the Navajo language, through which also he conducted much of his later work with the Hopi.

While Bourke was at Keam's trading post in 1881 Stephen presented him "with an almost perfect 'olla' of very old-fashioned pottery" found by a Navajo in Canyon de Chelly.[808] Through trade and excavations, the Keam brothers—first Billy, then Tom--began accumulating a large collection of ancestral Hopi pottery from sites near the trading post as well as from more distant locations, most notably Canyon de Chelly. The Keams were well aware of the commercial potential of the pottery, and soon after his arrival at Keam's trading post Stephen began numbering and classifying the ceramics.

During the Bureau of Ethnology's first expedition to the Southwest in 1879, James Stevenson and J. K. Hillers traveled from Zuni to Keams Canyon. While Hillers made stereographic photographs of Navajos and Hopis at the trading post, Stevenson purchased 323 pieces of historic pottery and Kachina dolls from "Wolpi" (Walpi, i.e., First Mesa) and twenty-one examples of prehistoric pottery from Canyon de Chelly.[809] Two years later Stevenson returned to Keams Canyon where he acquired another 1,802 pieces of pottery for $450.29. And a year later, Stevenson purchased an additional 4,643 pieces of pottery from Keam for $1,857.20.[810]

Stephen's knowledge of Navajo language and culture as well as his well-established rapport with several important Navajo "singers" is first evident in an event that took place in the fall of 1882. Stevenson used Keam's trading post as a field headquarters for an expedition he would lead into Canyon de Chelly.[811] Accompanying the party was H. C. Rizer, editor of the *Eureka* (Kansas) *Herald*. During the evening of October 20, Stephen and Rizer interviewed Guisheen Begay (*Gishi'bi'ye'*), who was an important Evilway singer (*hataali*), and other Navajo headmen "in Mr. Stephen's room at the trading post." In a letter to his newspaper, Rizer wrote:

> Being the host of the evening I placed in the circle formed

---

808   Bourke 1884:80, 92.

809   Stevenson 1881.

810   Lawson 2003:159-161.

811   See Chapter 4 for a detailed description of the 1882 Bureau of Ethnology expedition into Canyon de Chelly.

by the group a jar of tobacco and a handful of cigarette papers, to all of which they helped themselves without urgent invitation.

In the interview Rizer asked questions—the responses providing the first general account of Navajo religion, including references to one of the most complex of Navajo deities, *Begocdi'di'*—and Stephen recorded the exchange.[812]

Stephen's first journal entries and manuscripts date from the fall of 1882; they include material on a Navajo Mountainway ceremony he sent to his friend Washington Matthews.[813] Matthews was a U. S. Army surgeon stationed at Fort Wingate, New Mexico, from October 1880 until March 1884 and again from March 1890 to March 1894. While carrying out fieldwork under the auspices of the Bureau of Ethnology, Matthews occupied a position Stephen might otherwise have filled. As will become evident below, throughout the 1880s Stephen was first and foremost a student of the Navajo—an interest shared through correspondence with Matthews. Stephen's "The Navajo," published in the *American Anthropologist* is regarded as a classic of nineteenth century ethnology.[814]

It is important to remember Stephen came to Keam's Canyon as a prospector, not an ethnologist. In September 1893, while employed as an ethnologist for the Hemenway Southwestern Archaeological Expedition, Stephen reflected:

> I have not chosen this pursuit to make money in; nor scarce can I say I did choose it. Years ago it came to me almost unawares and never since will it let me be.[815]

---

812   Hieb 2005:241. The interview was published as "Indian Traditions" (Stephen 1883). The notes made by Stephen on October 20 and November 2, 1882, are now located in Alexander M. Stephen, Notes on Navajo Religion and Culture, Gladys Reichard Papers, MS 29{restricted], Museum of Northern Arizona Archives. Cited hereafter as MS 29, MNA.

813   Stephen, October 27, 1882, Notebook No. 1, Elsie Clews Parsons Field Notebooks, Columbia University Library. Cited hereafter as ECP, CUL. See Matthews 1892. The "comedy" was omitted from Matthrews 1887. The expurgation met with sharp criticism in Washington's intellectual community leading to the privately published edition of 1892. See Hieb 2004a:363 and 385-386, and Halpern and McGreevy, eds., 1997:151. For more on Matthews and his relationship with Stephen, see Chapter 4.

814   Stephen 1893b.

815   Stephen to Mary Hemenway, September 28, 1893, Hemenway Expedition

The closing of the Moqui Pueblo Indian Agency at the end of 1882 meant, among other things, that Keam had to arrange weekly mail runs; Stephen was appointed postmaster at Keams Canyon, a position he held from 1883 until 1888. More importantly, Keam learned his trading post was located on land set aside on December 16, 1882 for the Executive Order Moqui Pueblo Indian Reservation. With Stephen's architectural drawings, he approached the Secretary of the Interior with the proposal that the government purchase the buildings for an Indian Industrial School. The boarding school was opened in 1887, and Keam deeded the buildings and other "improvements" to the government in 1889 for $10,000.[816]

During the early 1880s, as Keam was selling over five thousand pieces of pottery to Stevenson for the National Museum, he reserved several hundred of the finest specimens, most of them excavated from ancestral Hopi ruins near his trading post, including Awatovi and Sikyatki. Stephen sorted the ceramics according to a typology he developed, an evolutionary framework based primarily on color, design and assumptions he made about the rise and decline of the Hopi (their "decadence and retrogression") as evidenced particularly by their pottery.[817] He began preparing a catalog of Keam's collection, and in an effort to enrich his typology with information regarding the symbolism on the pottery he sought the help of Jeremiah Sullivan.

Records, 980-2, Box 9.7, Peabody Museum Archives, Harvard University.

816   In the spring of 1884, Keam visited Washington, and met with Secretary of the Interior, Henry M. Teller. See Teller to Chairman, Committee on Appropriations, U. S. Senate, April 29, 1884, File 267, Special Files of the Office of Indian Affairs, RG 75, NA, and Graves 1998:178-186. As Graves points out, Keam also had the support of Herbert K. Welsh, of the Indian Rights Association (see also Anon. 1884). Keam's hospitality to the Stevensons also bore fruit in his efforts to sell his property. See M. C. Stevenson 1886. Plans and measurements prepared by Stephen were sent under Keam's name: Keam to John D. C. Atkins, CIA, February 10, 1886, LR-OIA, RG 75, NA.

817   Stephen was well versed in the social evolutionary thought of Lewis Henry Morgan but saw the Hopi as an instance of degeneration, both physically and culturally. See Alexander M. Stephen, Catalogue of the Keams Canyon Collection of Relics of the Ancient Builders of the Southwestern Table Lands [1891], 43-39A, Hemenway Expedition Records, Peabody Museum Archives or Edward E. Ayer, MS 839, Newberry Library, and Stephen to Keam, March 28, 1893, Ayer MS 839, Newberry Library.

Alexander M. Stephen, 1884. Photograph by George "Ben" Wittick. Museum of New Mexico, Palace of the Governors Photo Archives. Image: Neg. #149231. Stephen is surrounded by pottery from Thomas Keam's collection.

Throughout 1884 Stephen continued to work on a "Catalogue of Keam's Canon Collection Relics of the Ancient Builders of the Southwestern Table Lands," incorporating materials from Sullivan as well as a series of photographs of the pottery made in May by Ben Wittick.[818] In July Powell ordered Stevenson to the Southwest again, this time to make a collection of the arts of various tribes of Pueblo Indians

---

818   Hieb 2009.

for exhibit at the World's Industrial and Cotton Centennial Exposition which would open on December 16, 1884, in New Orleans. In November, the opportunistic Keam sent Stephen to Washington, with the catalogue, Wittick's photographs, a mummy, a large box of pottery, and a number of "sacred Moqui masks . . . obtained secretly." in anticipation the National Museum would purchase his collection for exhibit in New Orleans.[819]

Stephen returned to Keams Canyon after several months in the east. During the summer of 1885 he worked again with Guicheen Begay to record a version of the Navajo origin narrative.[820] On August 17 and 18 Stephen attended the Snake Dance at Walpi, and made the first notes on a Hopi ceremony to appear in his notebooks.[821] Publication of Bourke's *Snake Dance of the Moquis of Arizona* the previous fall created widespread interest in the ceremony and brought over two dozen spectators, including Dr. H. C. Yarrow, Assistant Surgeon, U. S. Army, on duty at the Army Medical Museum. Through the assistance of Keam and Stephen, Yarrow was able "to procure from a noted Navajo wise man [probably Guicheen Begay] an exact account of the burial customs of his people, as well as information regarding their medical practices, especially as such related to obstetrics."[822] At Yarrow's encouragement, Stephen began writing descriptions of Navajo curing ceremonies. Stephen's account of the divinations required for Hosteen Bukuki was subsequently published under Yarrow's name as "Navajo Methods of

---

819   Keam to William Henry Holmes, November 17, 1884, Folder 833, Series 17: Division of Ethnology Manuscripts and Pamphlets File, Records of the Department of Anthropology, U.S. National Museum/Museum of Natural History, NAA, SI. This is the *only* evidence of Keam acquiring an object regarded as "sacred" by the Hopi. In an article entitled "Stolen Gods," the *Albuquerque Morning Journal* reported Keam had been guided by a Hopi "priest" to a shrine and removed two "figures...rudely carved and painted sticks with feathers." The day following Keam was confronted by other religious leaders and returned the objects to them. See Keam 1883b.

820   The Navajo origin narrative, according to Guisheen Begay, was recorded by Stephen at Keams Canyon on August 5, 1885, and was later edited by Elsie Clews Parsons, with additional fragments included (Stephen 1932). See A. M. Stephen, pp. 60-87, MS 29, MNA.

821   Parsons, ed., 1936:590-593. See Chapter 5 for an account of the 1885 Snake Dance at Walpi.

822   Powell 1891a:xxix.

Curing Ague."[823] Hosteen Bukuki, a Navajo jeweler known as John the Jeweler, had an intermittent fever and Stephen provided an account of the efforts of four singers who sought to determine which ceremony was needed for a cure.

The Stevensons spent October and November in 1885 at Keam's trading post while making collections of pottery and other material culture on Second and Third Mesa. Early in their stay, "Tilly" made notes for a description of a Navajo Yeibit-cai ceremony—later published under James Stevenson's name.[824] She was assisted by Navajo John, a young interpreter from Fort Defiance, and afterwards Stephen provided the narratives appended to the account. The controversy that developed around this research and publication is explored in greater detail in Chapter 4.

Even though Stephen had income as clerk and postmaster at Keam's trading post, he was often "on the wrong side of the books" with his employer. Early in 1887 he wrote to Otis T. Mason, Curator of Ethnology and Assistant Secretary of the Smithsonian Institution, offering to assemble collections for the National Museum. Mason suggested Stephen might write "something about the shoemaking art among the Indians of the region." On February 16, Stephen responded:

> My friend Hostin N'taz (Heavy Man) happened to be in on a visit when I received your letter and I read it to him. I asked him to think over the subject & to prepare me some specimens. … On his return he unfolded the origin of the shoe. His story occupied the greater part of two nights…and I will try to give you a synopsis [from] the 50 odd pages I cull from.

Three weeks into May, G. Brown Goode, Assistant Secretary in Charge of the National Museum, responded with fifty dollars and instructions to acquire a representative collection of "tools of all kinds." In response, Stephen sent awls, needles, unfinished and finished shoes and an illustrated essay, "The Navajo Shoemaker," which described the materials, tools, and techniques employed in making various types of shoes as well as a translation of Hosteen N'tez's narrative giving the origin of shoes in Navajo culture.[825]

---

823   Stephen 1887. For another version, see Stephen 1922.
824   J. Stevenson 1891.
825   J. Brown Goode to Stephen, May 21, 1887, Outgoing Correspondence, Assistant

Stephen also approached William H. Holmes and Victor Mindeleff for possible employment with the Smithsonian Instiution. As the new fiscal year began in July 1887, Mindeleff telegraphed Stephen to make arrangements for an extended field season. Beginning on October 6, and continuing over the next six months, Mindeleff's field party completed a survey of the architecture at ancestral Hopi sites from the Jeddito Valley in the east to Moencopi in the west. Stephen paid Sullivan twenty-five dollars a month out of the salary he received to assist with Hopi research. Stephen also prepared "memoranda" on Navajo architecture. The results of their field work were two significant studies of vernacular architecture: Victor Mindeleff's "A Study of Pueblo Architecture in Tusayan and Cibola [Hopi and Zuni]" and Cosmos Mindeleff's "Navaho Houses."[826]

With Sullivan's departure during the summer of 1888, Stephen became the resident expert on the Hopi. He may not have attended the Snake Dance at Walpi in 1887, as his notebooks record only the date of the ceremony. However, at the 1889 ceremonies at Walpi, Stephen made notes and photographs with the assistance of Hernado J. Messenger, a former teacher at the Moqui Boarding School. Within weeks a full page, illustrated article on "The Snake Dance," coauthored by Stephen and Messenger, was published in sensationalized form by New York newspaper, *The World*.[17]

By 1890 a number of external agents—missionaries, government representatives, traders, ethnologists—had spent considerable time on one or more of the Hopi mesas. Hopis were increasingly conflicted as to what to take (material goods, language and education, a different religion?) and what to give (arts and craft, access to their daily life and

---

Secretary in Charge of the United States National Museum, 1879-1907, RU112, SIA. Draft of a letter from Stephen to Otis T. Mason, February 16, 1887, providing background for "The Navajo Shoemaker" (Stephen 1889) is located in MS 29, MNA.

826   V. Mindeleff 1891. Cosmos Mindeleff 1898a. V. Mindeleff to Powell, July 26, 1886, LR-BE, NAA, SI. The fieldwork is documented in A. M. Stephen and Jeremiah Sullivan, Notebooks 31 and 32, ECP, CUL. Stephen prepared "Ruins of the Southwest [1888]" (MS 1339, NAA, SI), a reworking of the "Introductory" to his "Catalogue of the Keams Canyon Collecton," for V. Mindeleff's work on Hopi architecture. Stephen also prepared several "memoranda" on Navajo architecture published, much of it verbatim, by C. Mindeleff (1898a). See, for example, Stephen to C. Mindeleff, January 6, 1889, and other materials in MS 29, MNA. For more information on the Mindeleffs' research, see Chapter 5.

ceremonies, sacred knowledge?). An uneasy, even disturbed atmosphere existed. In June, a party of Hopi leaders, including Loololma from Oraibi and Polacca from Hano, led by C. E. Vandever, the Navajo Agent, with Keam as interpreter, traveled to Washington where they met with the Commissioner of Indian Affairs and President Benjamin Harrison. The Hopis agreed to accept three things: the education program, Christian missionaries, and allotment of land as specified by the Dawes Severalty Act of 1887.[827]

Stephen's focus shifted to the Hopi in the summer of 1891, when he agreed to assist J. Walter Fewkes who had been been appointed two years before to replace Frank Hamilton Cushing as the Director of the Hemenway Southwestern Archaeological Expedition.[828] Following in Cushing's footsteps, Fewkes visited Zuni in 1890 but was frustrated in his field work. His observations were limited to public celebrations; he was denied entrance to the kivas where he believed still more important secret ceremonies were taking place simultaneously. His "ignorance of the Zuni tongue" and other circumstances led him to consider shifting is research to the neighboring Hopi villages where "possibly a more primitive representation existed."[829]

Anticipating the move to Tusayan, at the end of the 1890 field season at Zuni Fewkes made a quick exploratory trip to the Hopi villages in time to witness parts of the Flute ceremony at Walpi which Fewkes supposed to be a simpler form of the Snake Dance, "a snake dance without snakes."[830] After this brief visit to First Mesa—only the afternoon of August 20—he returned to Keams Canyon.

At the trading post he examined the ceramics, basketry, and ritual paraphernalia displayed in the "Indian Room" and learned about Keam's collection of ancestral Hopi pottery still in storage at the National Museum. In 1886 Congress failed to appropriate funds for the collection Keam had shipped to Washington two years earlier. In the interim Keam

---

827   See Whiteley 1988a:71-83 for a history of the agreement and its immediate consequences.

828   The expedition was funded by the Boston philanthropist Mary Hemenway. Cushing had been the director from 1886 to 1889. For an insightful comparison of Cushing and Fewkes, see Hinsley 1983.

829   Fewkes 1892c:1. Nineteenth century evolutionary theory included for many a search for origins, assumed to be the simplest form of an institution.

830   Fewkes 1890:107.

had sought other potential buyers, including Mary Hemenway. On a trip east in 1889 Keam wrote to Cushing about a "large and valuable" addition he would make to the collection and that Stephen would prepare a catalogue. Keam now approached Fewkes with the idea; early in 1892 the collection was purchased for $10,000 for Mrs. Hemenway's proposed Pueblo Museum in Salem, Massachusetts.[831]

On his return to Boston that summer, Fewkes quickly published two articles on the Hopi, signaling his decision to move his research to Tusayan after two seasons at Zuni, working in the shadow of Cushing's charisma, residence, and popular publications.[832] In a note accompanying his account of the "Ley-la-tuk" [Lakon, a women's society] ceremony, Fewkes noted:

> The Moquis have been studied with great profit by the Stevensons, Bourke, Stevens [i.e., Stephen], Keam and others, but much yet remains before we can get at the true significance of their religious ceremonials. There is no subject in comparative religion which will better repay investigation that that of the ceremonial life of the Moquis.[833]

The following spring, Fewkes returned to Keams Canyon accompanied (as he had been the previous summer) by a young Harvard graduate student in anthropology, J. G. Owens.[834] The two men reached Keams Canyon on May 7, with Kodak camera, a phonograph, notebooks, and other equipment. At the trading post they met Stephen, who had been in northern Mexico with Norwegian explorer and ethnographer Carl Lumholtz during their visit the previous August. Stephen gave Fewkes a copy of "The Snake Dance," the description of the 1889 ceremony he had co-authored with Messenger. In the "Indian Room," Fewkes busied himself making sketches of Kachina dolls and tiles decorated with Katsina imagery.[835] With help from "Mr. Stevens" [sic] Fewkes recorded the names of the katsinas and the elements of

831   Hieb 2004b and 2009.
832   Fewkes 1890 and 1891.
833   Fewkes 1891:107.
834   For Owens's letters describing his fieldwork and his relationship with Fewkes, see Hinsley, Hieb, and Fash, eds., forthcoming.
835   The term Kachina is used for the carved representation; Katsina, the spirit being. See Chapter 3 for a fuller discussion.

symbolism employed on ritual paraphernalia.

Keam and Stephen visited the anthropologists on several occasions, including the 4th of July when they "celebrated the 'festival' by pyrotechnic display on the top of the highest house in Walpi"[836] From Keam's trading post, Stephen wrote to Owens with information on Hopi agriculture, a subject Owens was pursuing for publication.

Fewkes had returned to Hopi in 1891 with an agenda: to document Hopi ceremonial life, "the Dances," especially the Snake Antelope ceremonies to take place at Walpi in August.

Stephen saw in Fewkes an opportunity for employment and recognition; Fewkes found in Stephen a rich and reliable source of ethnographic materials to publish. A productive scholar and a charming individual, Fewkes had no background in ethnology or archaeology. However, the two men were scientists. Much of their shared work consisted of descriptions of observations although Stephen, unlike Fewkes, enhanced his work (and Fewkes's) with an understanding of Hopi concepts of space and time, the names of ritual participants and paraphernalia, and the Hopi words for other aspects of their social and ceremonial life.

Documenting the Snake Dance was a priority for Fewkes and at the beginning of August Stephen provided Fewkes with strategies for observing the activities of the two participating men's societies— the Snakes and the Antelopes—in their separate kivas (ceremonial chambers). The celebration of the Snake Dance in 1891 lasted for nine days from August 13 until August 21. The first days were taken up with secret preparations, to which the uninitiated were not admitted, with the public ceremonies taking place on the final two days.

Matthews was among the many Anglos who attended the 1891 ceremony at Walpi and met Fewkes and Owens. In writing Cushing afterwards, Matthews remarked,

> Of course 'Steve' [Stephen] got them into the estufa [kiva] and told them all about it, and gave them the benefit of his many years of investigation but I fear he will reap scant glory and scanter money.[837]

Fewkes filled 132 pages of his notebook. He combined his

---

836   Parsons, ed., 1936:491.
837   Matthews to Cushing, April 5, 1892, WMP, WM.

notes with those of Stephen and possibly Owens's as well. These were supplemented by additional observations at the 1893 ceremonies, and then revised through an extensive correspondence between Fewkes and Stephen. The results, "The Snake Ceremonials at Walpi," comprised an entire issue of *A Journal of American Ethnology and Archaeology*.[838]

Fewkes's notes were limited to observable behavior; page after page was filled with detailed sketches of ritual paraphernalia, noting the colors and measurements of each object. Even with the addition of material supplied by Stephen and Owens, the published account remained superficial, giving little potential for grasping the meaning of the ceremony for Hopis. In his review of "The Snake Ceremonials of Walpi," Matthews wrote:

> One of the most notable deficiencies is the absence of texts and translations of the prayers and songs... Dr. Fewkes has fortunately secured many of the songs on phonographic cylinders, where they may be studied years hence, when the priests are dead and the rite forgotten. Dr. Fewkes, we believe, intends to continue the work and find out still more about the snake dance. We wish him every success; yet we fear he will be greatly hampered by the loss of his assistant, Mr. Stephens.[839]

Before leaving in September, Fewkes persuaded Stephen to continue documenting Hopi ceremonial life. Despite differences in biography, Stephen and Fewkes had much in common. Keam said Stephen lived a life "devoted to science and good works."[840] Stephen called himself a "collector" and, like Fewkes, his work with Keam's pottery was largely

---

838   The fourth volume of *A Journal of American Ethnology and Archaeology*, J. Walter Fewkes, ed., consisted of "The Snake Ceremonials at Walpi," by J. Walter Fewkes, assisted by A. M. Stephen and J. G. Owens, and was published by Houghton, Mifflin, Boston and New York, in April 1894. It was printed by The Riverside Press, Cambridge, and included a colored frontispiece by the artist Julian Scott, line drawings by Fewkes, color reproductions of the "sand mosaics," as well as photographs by Fewkes and Owens. Appendices included Stephen's text of "Legend of Ti-yo, the Snake Hero," and a bibliography. It was "gratefully dedicated to the memory of Mrs. Mary Hemenway," who had died in March 1894 as Fewkes was readying the manuscript for publication.

839   Matthews 1894.

840   The inscription on Stephen's grave marker in Keams Canyon.

descriptive and taxonomic. His accounts of Navajo and Hopi rituals were that of a detached observer. But Stephen did have something Fewkes lacked: a facility with language. Stephen's first fieldwork among the Hopi was carried out in Navajo; it was only in his third year that the attained a conversational knowledge of Hopi. Nonetheless, Stephen had an extensive vocabulary of Hopi words and he believed (like Cushing at Zuni) that a key to understanding Hopi religion lay in linguistic etymology. He gave Fewkes the names of things, enlarged a sense of their meaning and provided the former naturalist with much more in the way of detailed accounts of Hopi ritual practice and paraphernalia.

Their collaboration and co-authorship evolved quickly. Stephen soon found himself committed to research on the Hopi, a project unparalleled in nineteenth-century American ethnology. Beginning with the *Mamzrau*, a women's society ceremony, in September, Stephen began sending Fewkes accounts of ceremonies—"extracts" from his notebooks and memoranda—which Fewkes prepared for publication, giving Stephen credit but claiming first authorshiop for himself.[841] Once he had Stephen's account of a ceremony in hand, Fewkes quickly edited it, and submitted it for publication in either the *American Anthropologist* or the *Journal of American Folk-Lore*. The galley slips and page proofs sent to Fewkes for review were forwarded to Stephen who immediately sent corrections and, in his first letters to Fewkes, sought to establish an accurate orthography the two men would share in spelling Hopi words. In addition, Stephen also provided Fewkes with outlines of the Hopi calendar and ceremonial organization.

Under pressure to write up the results of his summer's research, Fewkes published "A Few Tusayan Pictographs" in the January 1892 issue of *American Anthropologist*.[842] Soon after its appearance, Matthews wrote to Cushing:

> You may expect something soon a great work on the Moquis Snake dance from the hand of a learned ethnologist [Fewkes] who has recently been there. He pumped poor Steve [Stephen] dry and promised Steve (so the later told me, poor fool!) that he would

841   See Fewkes and Stephen 1892a, 1892b, and 1893 as well as Fewkes 1894b.
842   The "pressure" appears to have been self-imposed as part of Fewkes's efforts towards professional advancement.

give him credit for all. But I see in the last number of
the Am[erican] Anthropologist an article by him on
"Tusayan Pictographs." Now this has been for years
Steve's specialty and all his information must have been
derived from Steve. Yet he mentions Steve in the most
indirect way, and in a foot note and there gives his name
incorrectly. But he will prosper! All frauds do and get
ahead of honest men.[843]

There is only one passing reference to a petroglyph in Fewkes's
notebooks from the previous summer.

On New Year's Eve 1891—at the end of a lengthy letter responding
to proofs of Fewkes' article, "A Few Summer Ceremonials…"—Stephen
asked:

> Is it possible to make any arrangement—on a salary
> basis—with your folks [i.e., Mary Hemenway]—you
> know I am always busted so it really makes no difference
> whether you can or no so don't hesitate to say No bluntly;
> our work will go on just the same.[844]

Fewkes proposed a salary of $50.00 a month. In reply, Stephen
remarked, "the sum you fixed on cannot be called extravagant…and I
am glad to note you hope of possibly being able to stretch your limit."[845]
Later in the year Stephen's salary was raised to $115 a month. In a letter
to Hemenway written in the fall of 1893, thanking her for a check for
two month's salary, Stephen gave this accounting of the costs of his field
research:

> I should tell you just how I expend the money you give
> me, and looking over my memoranda I get the following
> items on an average monthly outlay:
> $10 – Rent; $10 – Cook and Water bearers; $8 – Courier;
> $12 – Firewood. During the Summer, June to Septr.,
> additional water and the expense of visiting other
> villages about commute this item, which holds from
> Octr. to May; $35 – Food; $40 – Gifts to Kiva societies:
> to various authorities for stories and songs; for general

---

843   Matthews to Cushing, April 4, 1892, WMP, WM.
844   Stephen to Fewkes, December 30, 1891, MS 4408, NAA, SI.
845   Cushing's salary, set a decade earlier, was $100 per month.

facilities – and of course a few dollars for my own use.[846]

Between September 1891 and February 1894, Stephen filled seventeen notebooks with detailed descriptions of Hopi social and ceremonial life, recorded a number of Hopi narratives, and wrote "memoranda" which Fewkes included in his publications, often verbatim.[847] Their collaboration led to three articles for which Stephen is identified as the co-author.[848] Fewkes spent much of the summer of 1892 in Madrid, where he mounted an exhibit on the Hopi at the Historico-American Exposition.[849] Fewkes returned in time for the 1893 Snake Dance at Walpi but immediately returned to Boston to complete a monograph on that ceremony.[850] In need of more materials to publish, Fewkes asked Stephen to send the notebooks to him but Stephen was not ready to part with them:

> I would send the notebooks readily—but my boy—you must remember I have to turn to them "every hour"— but I will make excerpts *in extensor*.[851]

Stephen became ill in December 1893. In spite of his illness he continued his observations, sometimes staying throughout the night in a kiva to document ritual activities. He began his first letter of 1894 by noting:

> After several days of doubt I am now persuaded that Masauwu [a complex being in Hopi religion with power over life, death, fire, and the earth] is about to desist from tormenting me but we had a lively (deadly) row.[852]

---

846   Stephen to Mary Hemenway, September 28, 1893,

847   The contents of the seventeen notebooks were published in Parsons, ed., 1936.

848   Fewkes and Stephen 1892a, 1892b, and 1893. Fewkes had not observed any of the three ceremonies described.

849   See Fewkes 1896b.

850   Fewkes 1894b.

851   Stephen to Fewkes, March 8, 1894, MS4408, NAA, SI.

852   To Mary Hemenway, Stephen reported the death of a Tewa man, Tawi-moki, on December 4, 1893, and of his visit to his grave the following day. He wrote, "When I got home, some of the women (there eyes are everywhere) came to my quarters and asked what I had been doing at the grave, and half in jest, half-earnest, they predicted I would be haunted by Ma-sau-wu (the death God). I laughed and declared I wished to see him, that I wanted to draw his picture, and the women went away half scared." Stephen's illness continued until his death on April 17, 1894. In this letter, as well as one written to Washington Matthews,

But Masauwu did not desist, and Stephen began sending excerpts from his notebooks, including materials on the demographics of the First Mesa villages. Soon after Stephen's death, Fewkes published these under his own name.[853]

In mid-March 1894, Stephen sent Fewkes his notebook on the *Wuwutcim* (manhood initiation) ceremonies held in December at Walpi. Fewkes did not return the *Wuwutcim* notebook. He published its contents—an account of a ceremony he had never seen—as author under the title, "The Tusayan New Fire Ceremony."[854] For several years after Stephen's death, Fewkes scavenged his colleague's letters and memoranda for materials to publish—crediting Stephen in the text for collecting the information—but claiming authorship for himself.[855]

In 1893 Stephen wrote two short articles on the Hopi in response to invitations he had received. For the Congress of the International Folk-Lore Association held at the World's Columbian Exposition, Stephen sent "Pigments in Ceremonials of the Hopi" in which he described the system of correspondences—the logical structuring of categories of space, time, color and number—that informs much of Hopi ritual.[856] In another essay, "Description of the Hopi Ti-hu," Stephen provided a rich account of the significance of the small carved representations of the *Katsinas* ("Kachina dolls") given to young girls and of the role of the *katsina* in Hopi thought and ritual.[857] Shortly before his death he told Matthews, "I think with one more year up here I will have sufficient data

---

Stephen described the efforts of a Hopi Po-boc-tu to remove the illness affecting him. See Stephen to Hemenway, February 15, 1894, Hemenway Expedition Records, 980-2, Box 9.7, PMA, HU; and Stephen 1894.

853   Fewkes 1894c and 1894d. Stephen is acknowledged in the text of both articles. See Stephen to Fewkes, January 18, 1894 and March 12, 1894, MS4408, NAA, SI. In his letter of March 12, Stephen wrote "upon the ground plans [I] have marked the house groups by numbers and under these groups I have entered all the family with all the data of kinship, lineage, etc. obtainable." The ground plans and other information provided by Stephen were published in Fewkes 1906. Fewkes makes no acknowledgement of Stephen's assistance nor does he compare his findings with those of Cosmos Mindeleff (C. Mindeleff 1900).

854   Fewkes 1895a. This is the only notebook missing from the series on Hopi ceremonies.

855   See my essay in Hinsley, Hieb, and Fash, eds., forthcoming.

856   Stephen 1898.

857   Stephen 1893a; see Hieb 2015.

for a comprehensive monograph but an interruption now...would just about ruin me."[858]

On March 6, 1894, Mary Hemenway died from the diabetes that had plagued her for several years. With her death, funding for the Hemenway Southwestern Archaeological Expedition came to an abrupt end. Stephen died the following month, on April 17. During the winter Fewkes had pressed Stephen to complete revisions of the galley slips for the culminating publication of Fewkes, Owens, and Stephen's fieldwork, "The Snake Ceremonial at Walpi." Fewkes rushed it into print shortly after Hemenway's death.[859] To the end Stephen sent additions and corrections, at one point pleading, "I beseech you not to publish the account [the Legend of Tiyo] I sent you," but finally conceded "there are no vital changes necessary, but many changes in detail..."[860]

Within months after Hemenway's death, Fewkes found employment as a "special ethnologist" with the Bureau of American Ethnology, eventually becoming Chief—a position he held from 1918 to 1928.

Unlike what can be known of Cushing, Matthews, the Stevensons or Jeremiah Sullivan, the record of Stephen's fieldwork among the Hopi is extensive. In a letter to Matthews after Stephen's death, Keam wrote:

> I still have all of [Stephen's] letters and manuscripts, which Dr. Fewkes has been claiming for to complete what he calls the Hemenway papers. I have however at Steve's request before his death refus[ed] to part with them without proper compensation, part of which will be sent to his relatives in Scotland.[861]

Keam preserved Stephen's notebooks; unfortunately his correspondence—copies of letters received as well as drafts of letters he sent—was discarded along with the many "memoranda" Stephen kept on various areas of inquiry. Following the summer of 1891, Fewkes returned for a month in 1892 and again briefly, in 1893, to attend

858 Stephen 1894:214.

859 Fewkes dedicated the volume to the memory of Mary Hemenway. No mention is made of Stephen's death.

860 Stephen to Fewkes, March 29, 1894, MS4408, NAA, SI.

861 Keam to Matthews, August 8, 1896, Washington Matthews Papers, Wheelwright Museum of the American Indian.

the Snake Dance. While not together in the field, Stephen wrote to Fewkes on an almost weekly basis reporting on aspects of his work and responding to the galley slips, page proofs, and inquiries sent by Fewkes. Fewkes preserved forty-five of Stephen's letters;[862] however, we have only one side of their correspondence, so we have little knowledge of Fewkes' questions and concerns. Clearly their collaboration was one of mutual respect, although for Fewkes publication was often more important than the ethnographic and linguistic accuracy Stephen insisted on. In addition to his letters to Fewkes, Stephen also wrote letters to Mary Hemenway, providing her with a richly informative account of the research she was supporting.[863] What remained of his research was eventually published by Elsie Clews Parsons as *Hopi Journal of Alexander M. Stephen*.[864]

---

862   Stephen, Correspondence to J. Walter Fewkes, MS4408, NAA, SI.

863   Stephen, A. M., A Report of the Field Work of the Hemenway Expedition in the Autumn and Winter of 1892-1893. Hemenway Expedition Records, 980-2, Peabody Museum of Archaeology and Ethnology Archives, Harvard University. The "report" consists of a series of letters and contains accounts of barter, a wedding, and events of the Hopi year. Also included in the Hemenway Expedition Records are letters from Stephen to Mary Hemenway, September 28, 1893 – February 15, 1894. Stephen's final letter gives an account of his final sickness.

864   Parsons, ed., 1936. In ca. 1902 Keam sold Stephen's notebooks to Stewart Culin of the Brooklyn Museum. Culin, in turn, sold the manuscripts to Parsons on April 16, 1923. Parsons restructured the temporal framework of Stephen's journal, arranging his notes according to the Hopi ritual calendar.

7. Paper Trails: Rethinking History

The story of ethnological research among the Hopi had its beginnings in a collection of essays published in the *American Anthropologist* in 1922 under the title, "Contributions to Hopi History." The accounts were presented in chronological order beginning with "Oraibi in 1883" by Frank Hamilton Cushing and "Oraibi in 1890" by J. Walter Fewkes, and these were followed by "Oraibi in 1920" and "Shohmo'pavi in 1920" by the editor, Elsie Clews Parsons.

In his book, *Silencing the Past: Power and the Production of History*, historian Michel-Rolph Trouillot reminds us that "any historical narrative is a particular bundle of silences."[865] On the one hand, we are confronted with the fact that the Hopi were a people without writing and little was recorded as they voiced their responses to the interests of the ethnologists who visited them. On the other hand, there are quite literally thousands of pages of materials produced by the ethnologists (broadly defined) who visited the Hopi in the nineteenth century alone. These include the correspondence between Hopi Agents and the Commissioner of Indian Affairs and other records of the Office [Bureau] of Indian Affairs; correspondence and reports of the ethnologists sent to the Hopi under the sponsorship of the Smithsonian Institution's Bureau of [American] Ethnology; letters, diaries, and other records of Mormon and Presbyterian missionaries; letters sent by the trader Thomas V. Keam (but none of his trading post records); notebooks, reports, letters, and published articles by Alexander M. Stephen, Keam's store manager and later an ethnologist with the Hemenway Southwestern Archaeological Expedition; and dozens of published and unpublished accounts in newspapers, magazines, and books of visits by others to Keams Canyon and the Hopi villages, especially on the occasion of the

---

865   Trouillot 1995:27.

Snake-Antelope ceremonies. Rarely matter-of-fact, these documents are often self-serving, occasionally humorous, sometimes deceitful, and only occasionally sensitive to Hopi concerns.

The period under consideration here has not been ignored by historians but few have reflected on the production of history or on the tension between historical truth and narrative truth, what Trouillot describes as a distinction between history as "what happened" and history as "that which is said to have happened."[866] What interests Trouillot is the problem of how histories as stories (that which is said to have happened) are constructed from or in relation to history as sociohistorical process (what happened). Trouillot seeks to discover how power works to foreground some persons and events and to mute and silence others.

For most students of Southwestern anthropology, the key figures visiting the Hopi during the period from 1879 to 1894 are John Gregory Bourke, author of *Snake Dance of the Moquis of Arizona* (1884); Frank Hamilton Cushing, participant observer of the Zuni from 1879 to 1884; the brothers, Victor and Cosmos Mindeleff, whose "A Study of Pueblo Architecture: Tusayan and Cibiola" (1891) is a classic in the literature on vernacular architecture; and Alexander M. Stephen whose notebooks of detailed descriptions of Hopi social and ceremonial life were edited and published by Elsie Clews Parsons as *Hopi Journal of Alexander M. Stephen* (1936). There are other names that appear in many historical accounts, e.g., John Wesley Powell, James and Matilda Coxe Stevenson, Jesse Walter Fewkes, and H. R. Voth.[867] However, with one notable exception, the name of the most important ethnologist among the Hopi during the 1880s is missing, his voice silenced as well as his role in an event of lasting importance to the Hopi people.[868]

The name, of course, is that of Jeremiah Sullivan, a young doctor who lived in the First Mesa village of Sichumovi from 1881 until 1888 and who recorded Hopi songs and narratives, facilitated the research of nearly every ethnologist during that time period, and was the "immediate cause" (McCluskey) of the creation of the Executive Order Moqui Pueblo Indian Reservation on December 16, 1882.

***

---

866   Op cit, p. 2.
867   See, for example, Dockstader 1979 and Fowler 2000.
868   McCluskey 1980; see also Fewkes 1922.

On June 10, 1921, the anthropologist A. L. Kroeber sent Parsons "a notebook compiled at Hopi in [1882 and 1883] by J. Sullivan that [he] was given by a former teaching fellow, Mrs. Lucile LaPrade, in the Department of Anthropology, University of California Berkeley, who had received the notebook from her father-in-law [Fernando T. "Ferd" LaPrade], a resident of [Winslow] Arizona, who had some way got it from Sullivan." Kroeber observed the small notebook was marked "number 6." The contents include an outline of annual ceremonies, a list of katsinas, an essay on types of katsina carvings, katsina masks drawn with colored pencils by Hopi artists, vocabularies, etc. From this notebook Parsons immediately extracted and published a brief "folk-tale" and then set the notebook aside.[869] Parsons later wrote, "In 1920 I was told that 'the Doctor danced with us,'" but it is not clear what she knew of Jeremiah Sullivan at that time.[870]

At the time these events began to unfold, Parsons (1875-1941) was emerging as the preeminent student of the Pueblo Indians in New Mexico and Arizona. She had begun fieldwork at Zuni in 1915 and between 1916 and 1941 Parsons produced 95 publications concerning the Southwest, 90 of these dealing with the Puebloan peoples of New Mexico and Arizona. In the summer and fall of 1920 Parsons ventured west to the Hopi villages—especially those on First Mesa—where she was made a member of a Hopi family. This event so moved her that in *American Indian Life* she identified herself as "Elsie Clews Parsons, Member of the Hopi Tribe."[871] As the daughter of a successful banker, she had financial resources that not only permitted her to do fieldwork in the Southwest almost every year from 1915 until 1932 but to underwrite the fieldwork of others and to provide subventions for the publications of the American Anthropological Association and the American Folklore Society. In 1939 she published a work that was the summation and high point of her research, *Pueblo Indian Religion*, and the following year she became the first woman president of the American Anthropological Association. She died in 1941.

In 1922, the year following Kroeber's gift of Sullivan's notebook,

---

869   Jeremiah Sullivan 1921; Elsie Clews Parsons, Field Notebooks, vol. 31, Columbia University Library. Cited hereafter as ECP, CUL.

870   Parsons, ed., 1936:1117.

871   Parsons, ed., 1922a

Parsons edited and published the "Contributions to Hopi History" that included Fewkes' essay, "Oraibi in 1890." Fewkes, who first visited First Mesa in 1890 and began fieldwork there in 1891, wrote:

> One of the first Americans to live with the Hopi for purposes of study [sic] was Dr. Jeremiah Sullivan, or, as he was called by them, Urwica [Oyiwisha, He Who Plants Corn]. When the writer began work at Walpi, Urwica was remembered as the American who amputated the arm of the mother of Pautiwa [Pauwatiwa], the chief of the Bow priesthood [Kaletakwimkya, War society]. He slept in the pueblo, ate Hopi food, and worked on the farms with the Hopi, but he left Walpi [Sichumovi] a few years before the writer began his Hopi studies. He published a few short notes on the Hopi but no elaborate work on this interesting people.[872]

In her biography of Parsons, Desley Deacon tells us that Parsons "sounded Stewart Culin out about editing the journals [of Alexander M. Stephen] at the anthropology meetings hosted by the Brooklyn Museum in 1921, following her Hopi fieldwork in 1920 and 1921" and that on April 16, 1923 Parsons purchased Stephen's journals for $500.[873] Stephen's field notebooks and other manuscripts had been sold by Keam to Culin of the Brooklyn Museum in 1903.[874] The collection included over thirty notebooks with entries from 1882 until a few days before Stephen's death in 1894 as well as a number of loose manuscripts. While the bulk of the material concerned Hopi social and ceremonial life, and was compiled by Stephen while employed by the Hemenway Southwestern Archaeological Expedition from 1891 until 1894, the early notebooks and manuscripts also reflect Stephen's knowledge of the Navajo language and his interest in their culture. Virtually all of the manuscripts concerning the Hopi were created by Stephen in the course of his employment by Thomas V. Keam, by Victor Mindeleff (Bureau of Ethnology, 1887-1888), and by the Hemenway Southwestern Archaeological Expedition under J. Walter Fewkes (1891-1894).

Over the course of the next decade, while continuing to do field

---

872   Parsons, ed., 1922b:269.
873   Deacon, 1997:478, n.17.
874   Graves 1993:304, n.7.

research, publish, and support the development of the professions of anthropology and folklore, Parsons began preparing Stephen's notebooks for publication. In the meantime, Parsons edited *A Pueblo Indian Journal*, by Crow-Wing (the name given by Parsons to George Cochisi), the diary of a Hopi-Tewa kept during 1920-1921. In her introduction to Crow-Wing's diary Parsons noted that "about this time [ca. 1893] A. M. Stephen was living with his Navajo wife on First Mesa."[875] Immediately after publication, the artist Frederick S. Dellenbaugh, who had lived on First Mesa and then at Keam's Canyon in the fall and winter of 1884-1885, wrote to question Parsons' statement:

> In think you are in error... I knew Mr. Alexander M. Stephen very well. ... Stephen at that time was not married to a Navajo...or to any one else and had no intention of marrying. He never lived in any of the Hopi Towns [sic] and had no intention of doing so—in fact he would have spurned the idea. It is possible that he may have gone there in some of the years before his death but I never heard of it.

In fact, Stephen rented a house in Tewa for $5.00 a month while employed by the Bureau of Ethnology, from 1887 to 1888, and rented the same house for $10.00 a month in 1891-1893 while employed by the Hemenway Southwestern Archaeological Expedition. In 1893 he moved into a house in Sichumovi that had been occupied by the first Hopi Agent, Captain A. D. Palmer from 1869 to 1870. Dellenbaugh continues:

> Possibly you were thinking of "Dr." Jeremiah Sullivan who was living with the Cichumovi [Sichumovi] people—the middle town of the First Mesa—when I was there. He was the only white man in the whole region outside of Stephen, Keam and the storekeeper and a hostler then at Keam's. He was an entirely different character from Stephen. He wore his shirt outside of his trousers most of the time like the Indians and on ceremonial occasions or at the time of "dance" practicing he put a line of vermillion under each eye. During the Somaikoli ceremonial he disappeared entirely for several days. I suppose he was locked up in some initiation ceremony.

---

875   Crow-Wing 1926:6.

Sullivan provided Dr. [Daniel Garrison] Brinton with valuable notes ["Hopitu Calendar"]. He was an intelligent person but did not have the education that Stephen had. He called himself "Governor of the Mokis." He was skillful in his profession of medicine and did much good but in cases of fracture of a bone he had great difficulty in preventing the medicine men from removing the bandages. I went to Oraibi with him once and while there he went to inspect a broken arm he had set some time before our visit and found that the medicine men had again torn off the splints and bandages which he greatly deplored.

So far as I know he was not married to a Navajo or a Hopi. He lived in the house of Anawita, the "war chief" of Cichumovi...[876]

If Dellenbaugh had refreshed his memory by rereading letters he wrote from the "Ancient Province of Tusayan" he would have remembered that Sullivan was living in a house he had built for himself in 1882. In his letter to Parsons, Dellenbaugh goes on to describe Stephen and Thomas V. Keam, noting that "Stephen studied the Hopis for a long time from his home center at Tom Keam's place in Keam's Canyon. Among other results he had a large sort of blank book filled with notes." Stephen had just finished compiling the "Catalogue of Keam's Canon Collection of Relics of the Ancient Builders of the Southwestern Table Lands" which he took with him to Washington, D.C., during the time Dellenbaugh stayed at Keam's ranch.[877] Dellenbaugh finished his letter with a personal comment about Stephen:

Another note about Stephen. I have heard it said that he was a great drunkard but that is not correct. He sometimes went on a spree in one of the settlements [i.e., Holbrook or Winslow]. During the winter I was at Keam's we used often to have a nip by the fire at night with some crackers and "Finnon Haddie" of which

---

876 Frederick S. Dellenbaugh to Elsie Clews Parsons, July 31, 1926, Papers of Frederick Samuel Dellenbaugh, MS 407, Special Collections, The University of Arizona Library. Cited hereafter as MS 407, UAL.

877 See Hieb 2004, 2009.

Stephen being Scotch was extremely fond, but I never knew him to take too much of the Scotch firewater. I liked and admired Alexander M. Stephen very much. He was one of my friends which is my excuse for troubling you with this letter.[878]

Parsons replied to Dellenbaugh, "I did not confuse [Stephen] with Sullivan. ... It was [Stewart] Culin who told me he was married to a Navajo. ... I will correct this in my preface to the Stephen Journal."[879] Culin, it should be noted at the outset, was also responsible for establishing Stephen's name as "Alexander MacGregor Stephen" when it was, in fact, Alexander Middleton Stephen (Culin 1905:170, emphasis added).[880]

However, if Parsons did not "confuse" the two men, she did merge their authorship three years later when she edited and published "Hopi Tales, by Alexander M. Stephen."[881] Parsons began the process of editing the manuscripts acquired from Culin by extracting eleven Hopi narratives recorded in the two earliest notebooks, dated from 1883 to 1885.[882] To these she added seventeen narratives recorded on First Mesa in 1893 by Stephen.[883] The "earlier tales" had been copied into the notebooks and later revised by Stephen as evidenced by an undated note, probably March 1888, in which Stephen wrote, "Edit Legends – with comments of the narrators & my own exegetical notes."[884] After selecting the "Tales" she would publish and making a few additional editorial changes of her own, Parsons turned the notebooks over to her secretary. Later, in her "Preface" to "Hopi Tales, by Alexander M. Stephen," Parsons noted that the "earlier tales, although heard from some of the same informants as

---

878 Dellenbaugh, Ibid.

879 Elsie Clews Parsons to Frederick S. Dellenbaugh, August 18, 1926. MS 407, UAL.

880 Culin 1905:170, emphasis added. Thomas V. Keam to Washington Matthews, January 27, 1897, Washington Matthews Papers, Wheelwright Museum of the American Indian. Keam examined Stephen's papers after his death and informed Matthews that Stephen's middle name was "Middleton."

881 Parsons, ed., 1929.

882 Volumes 1 and 2, ECP, CUL.

883 Op. cit., volumes 23 and 24.

884 Alexander M. Stephen, Notebook I, p. 56, Ms. Coll. No. 1563, American Philosophical Society Library.

the later tales, seem in many ways different in character, almost giving the impression at times of a different culture. This is perplexing to the editor..." and Parsons then suggests the differences "may be due largely to the recorder's comparative familiarity with the Navaho..."[885] Although perplexed, Parsons apparently did not reconsider including "Sullivan's note" she had deleted at the end of one narrative nor reinstating, in light of Fewkes's and Dellenbaugh's recollections, another narrative from 1883 she had omitted. In it, Pauwatiwa speaks:

> It has been many days since this dance was observed— probably 50 years ago. It has been repeated today on the occasion of a white man becoming the first and highest ranking chief we ever had, carrying the chieftaincy into the chief gens and among the warriors, a thing that was promised to us but which we never expected to see.[886]

The "white man" was Jeremiah Sullivan who was initiated into the War Society on First Mesa within the same month Cushing was famously initiated into the Priesthood of the Bow at Zuni. Other contextual evidence regarding the authorship of the earlier tales is developed in Chapters 2 and 6 (cf. Hieb 2004). Suffice it to say here, it was Jeremiah Sullivan who recorded the "earlier" narratives that Stephen copied into Notebooks 1 and 2.

In 1932 Parsons published the manuscript of a "Navajo Origin Legend" Stephen had recorded in 1885.[887] She then gave Gladys Reichard this as well as a number of other manuscripts on Navajo religion and architecture, most of which had been published by Stephen.[888]

Parsons continued to work on Stephen's Hopi notebooks each summer from 1927 until 1934.[889] The result was *Hopi Journal of Alexander M. Stephen* published in 1936, consisting of 1417 pages in two volumes. Parsons included nearly all of the descriptions of Hopi social and ceremonial life recorded in Volumes 3-26 and 28, as they

---

885   Parsons, ed., 1929:2.
886   Alexander M. Stephen, Field Notebook, Vol. 1, p. 74, ECP, CUL; cf. Parsons, ed., 1936:1145.
887   Stephen 1932.
888   Alexander M. Stephen, [Notes on Navajo Religion and Culture], Gladys Reichard Papers, MS 29-39-1, Museum of Northern Arizona. Stephen 1883, 1887 and 1888. See also Cosmos Mindeleff 1898, 1900, 1901a, 1901b.
889   Deacon 1997:354.

are identified in the Elsie Clews Parsons Field Notebooks, Columbia University Libraries, as well as the Hopi material in five notebooks located in the American Philosophical Society Library.[890] Omitted were two volumes of notes on Hopi language (Vols. 29 and 30), and the index Stephen prepared in 1884 for the "Catalogue of the Keams Canon Collection" (Vol. 27).[891] For the most part, Parsons also omitted the notes and drawings by Stephen and Sullivan made during 1887 and 1888 while Stephen was employed by the Bureau of Ethnology (Vols. 32 and 33). Among the materials selected were narratives concerning Oraibi and Shungopavi, recorded March 28 and April 1, 1888, "probably *not* by Stephen" (Parsons's emphasis) but by Sullivan who was assisting Stephen at that time.[892] In addition, she published Sullivan's notes on Masau'wuh's house.[893]

This is now clear: with the exception of notes on Snake Dances of 1885 and 1889 and a brief note on "Tribal Boundary Marks" Stephen's Hopi ethnographic materials reflect his research undertaken after Sullivan moved to Holbrook, Arizona, in 1888.[894] The only references to Jeremiah Sullivan in the *Hopi Journal of Alexander M. Stephen* occur in three footnotes. John H. Sullivan, Jeremiah's father and Hopi Agent, 1880-1882, is mentioned in the text once and is misidentified by Parsons as Jeremiah Sullivan on one other occasion.[895]

The richness and accuracy of Stephen's accounts of Hopi ceremonial life coupled with the authoritative editorial contributions Parsons made to the two volumes, immediately and justifiably elevated Stephen to a place of prominence among early Southwestern ethnologists. In 1939 and 1940, Frederick Webb Hodge, Director of the Southwest Museum in Los Angeles, published an anonymous and untitled manuscript he found in the George Bird Grinnell Papers.[896] Hodge supplied the title, "The Hopi Indians of Arizona," attributed it to "Alexander MacGregor Stephen"

890   Alexander M. Stephen, Hopi Notebooks, 1885-1892, MS 1563 and Navaho Notebook, 1885-1891, MS 2387, American Philosophical Society Library.

891   See Hieb 2009.

892   Parsons, ed., 1936:1179-1180.

893   Op cit., 150-151.

894   Op cit., 580-589, Stephen and Messenger 1889; Stephen 1889.

895   Op cit., 196, 1402.

896   [Jeremiah Sullivan, Untitled Manuscript] George Bird Grinnell Papers, MS 5.291, Braun Research Library, Autry Museum of the American West.

and suggested it was written about 1890.[897] A note in the manuscript makes clear that it was completed soon after the Snake Dance of 1885.

A comparison of this account with those in Stephen's notebooks for 1885 and 1889 or with an article written by Stephen and Hernando J. Messenger following the 1889 Snake Dance make clear this is not Stephen's work. Stephen's manuscripts are precise in their accounts of observable behavior—of who did what and when, and exact in their descriptions of material culture—of shape, color, and use. Jeremiah Sullivan recorded the conceptual, the "inner Indian," locating practices in the context of Hopi thought. The manuscript in the Southwest Museum (now the Autry Museum of the American West) is a rich compilation of Hopi thought, songs and prayers and is clearly Sullivan's work but in 1939 it was beyond question that Alexander Middleton Stephen was the author. Proof the manuscript is Sullivan's has been located in lecture notes written by H. C. Yarrow after attending the Snake/Antelope ceremonies at Mishongnovi and Walpi in 1885. Yarrow stated, "I have here a transcript . . . in the exact words of the old man [Wiki] translated from his own language by Dr. Sullivan who resided with the Moquis."[898] The lengthy quotation is from materials included in the manuscript Hodge attributed to Stephen.

It is not known how the manuscript in the Southwest Museum came to be in the possession of George Bird Grinnell although it may have been sent in an effort to attract a patron. Attribution of authorship is muddied by the fact that the handwriting and the illustrative style are Stephen's. However, Stephen provides a clue to how this might have happened. During the summer of 1888 Jeremiah Sullivan mentioned to Cushing, "I have a vast quantity of material which is now being put in shape for publication."[899] Notations in Stephen's notebook for 1888 indicate he owed "Jere Sullivan . . . $372.20" and Stephen may have edited and made a clear copy of the "material" for Sullivan in payment. Stephen made no reference to or use of the extraordinary contents of

---

897   [Jeremiah Sullivan] 1939-1940:1.

898   Henry Crecy Yarrow, Remarks on the Hopi Snake Dance, MS 3794, National Anthropological Archives, Smithsonian Institution.

899   Jeremiah Sullivan to Frank Hamilton Cushing, July 20, 1888, Frank Hamilton Cushing Manuscript Collection, MS 6.HAE.1.52, Braun Research Library, Autry Museum of the American West.

Sullivan's manuscript in his later work.

* * *

For the first twenty-five years I worked on this project, the case for Sullivan's authorship was built primarily on circumstantial evidence and differences in voice, not on any substantial body of Sullivan's writing in his own hand. In October 2009 I noted the listing of a "book" by a Jeremiah Sullivan in WorldCat, the global on-line union catalog of books, articles, archival, and other materials located in libraries. The bibliographic citation stated simply "Hopitu Calendar" and indicated it was in the holdings of the University of Pennsylvania Library. Their catalog, in turn, showed it to be in the Daniel Garrison Brinton Collection in the Library of the University of Pennsylvania Museum of Archaeology and Anthropology (913.72 Su53). No information regarding date or pagination was given when the online record posted in 2000.

The "Hopitu Calendar" is a collection of four essays written by Jeremiah Sullivan, ca. 1884-1885, and sent to Daniel G. Brinton, Professor of Ethnology at the Academy of Natural Sciences in Philadelphia and soon (1886) to become Professor of American Linguistics and Archaeology in the University of Pennsylvania. After Brinton's death, the manuscripts, totaling 109 leaves, were bound together in one volume and located in the collections of the Library of the University of Pennyslvania Museum of Archaeology and Anthropology. A note from Sullivan dated January 11, 1886, was bound in saying, "My kind friend, Dr. Brinton, Inclosed please find Part 3, "Feast of Mu-in-wu – Hopituh" which is entitled, ""Part 3, The Pon-ya or Altar." Although in other essays special reference is made to the "Feast of Mu-in-wu" or Mamzrau, as this women's ceremony is more commonly known, it appears Parts 1 and 2 of Sullivan's account of the "Feast of Mu-in-wu" have been lost.

In 1884 Dellenbaugh knew Sullivan was sending "information" to Brinton. Sullivan's note on the final part of his account of the Mamzrau ceremony tells us nothing of the exact circumstances but it appears certain Sullivan created the accounts for Brinton—as well as for George Bird Grinnell—in an effort to get financial support for his medical practice among the Hopi. The materials sent to Brinton are important to the story told here as they confirm Sullivan's authorship through his distinctive "voice" as well as through his representation of Hopi words— e.g., Sullivan: baho, kiba; Stephen paho, kiva.

Trouillot reminds us, "Power does not enter the story once and for all, but at different times and from different angles. It precedes the narrative proper, contributes to its creation and to its interpretation."[900] The manuscripts Parsons and Hodge edited had already been shaped by various forces in the 1880s, disguising the appearance, but not completely silencing the voice, of Jeremiah Sullivan whose story is central to this book. The essays Sullivan sent to Brinton were invisible and only made partly visible by the posting of a brief record of their existence in WorldCat more than a century after they were given to the University of Pennyslvania. In a very real sense, it has been the power of the internet that has made possible this effort to restore Jeremiah Sullivan's name, his voice, and our knowledge of his contributions to and about the Hopi people.

---

900   Trouillot 1995:26-27.

Bibliography: Works Cited and Consulted

Archival Sources

American Philosophical Society Library, Philadelphia, PA.
　　　　Elsie Clews Parsons Papers. Ms Coll. No. 29.
　　　　Alexander M. Stephen. Hopi Notebooks. Ms. Coll. No. 1563.
　　　　Alexander M. Stephen. Notes and Sketches. Ms. Coll. No. 1564.
　　　　Alexander M. Stephen. Hopi Notebook. Ms. Coll. No. 2387.
Arizona Historical Society, Tucson, AZ.
　　　　Dellenbaugh Manuscript Collection. MS 0215.
Autry Museum of the American West, Braun Research Library, Los Angeles, CA.
　　　　Frank Hamilton Cushing Manuscript Collection. MS.6.
　　　　George Bird Grinnell Manuscript Collection. MS.5.
　　　　[Jeremiah Sullivan] Hopi Indians of Arizona. MS 5.291.
Church of Jesus Christ of Latter-Day Saints, Historical Department, Salt Lake City, UT.
　　　　Christian Lyngaa Christiansen Journal. Ms f170.
　　　　Heber Jeddy Grant Diary. Ms d1233.
　　　　Brigham Young, Jr. Journal. Ms f326.
Columbia University Rare Book and Manuscript Library, New York, NY.
　　　　Elsie Clews Parsons Field Notebooks [A. M. Stephen Notebooks 1-30, 32-33; Jeremiah Sullivan Notebook 31]
Harvard University. Peabody Museum of Archaeology and Ethnology Archives, Cambridge, MA.
　　　　Hemenway Expedition Records, 1886-1914.
　　　　Catalogue of Keam's Canon Collection of Relics of the Ancient Builders of the Southwestern Table Lands [A. M. Stephen].
　　　　A Report on the Field Work of the Hemenway Expedition in the Autumn and Winter of 1892-1893 [A. M. Stephen].
Huntington Free Library, New York, NY.
　　　　Papers of the Hemenway Southwestern Archaeological Expedition.
Lee County Historical Society, Keokuk, IA.
　　　　John H. Sullivan Autobiography.
Library of Congress, Washington, D.C.
　　　　P. Phillips Family Papers, MSS 36087. [W. Hallett Phillips]
Museum of New Mexico, Laboratory of Anthropology Archives, Santa Fe, NM.
　　　　James [Matilda Coxe] Stevenson Scrapbook. Archive 91 JSS 000.
Museum of Northern Arizona, Flagstaff, AZ.
　　　　Gladys Reichard Papers. Notes on Navajo Religion and Culture [A. M. Stephen]. MS 29-39-1.
　　　　Hopi Notes, A Diary Written by Miss Kate Cory, 1909-1910, at First Mesa. MS 208-2-2.

National Archives, Washington, D.C.

       Medical Histories of Posts. RG94. Vols. 820-821, Fort Wingate 1880-1884, 1890-1894 [Washington Matthews]

       Records of the Accounting Offices of the Department of the Treasury. RG 217.

       Office of the First Auditor, Settled Miscellaneous Treasury Accounts, 6 September 1790 to 29 September 1894.

       Records of the Bureau of Indian Affairs. RG 75.

       Letters Received by the Office of Indian Affairs, 1824-1881. (M234)

       Letters Received by the Office of Indian Affairs, 1882-1885.

       Letters Received by the Office of Indian Affairs, 1881-1907.

       Letters Sent by the Indian Division of the Office of the Secretary of the Interior, 1849-1903. (M606)

       Letters Sent by the Office of Indian Affairs, 1824-1881. (M21)

       Records Created by Bureau of Indian Affairs Field Agencies Having Jurisdiction Over the Pueblo Indians, 1874-1900. (M1304)

       Registers of Letters Received by the Office of Indian Affairs, 1824-1880. (M18)

       Report Books of the Office of Indian Affairs, 1838-1885. (M348)

       Reports of Inspections of the Field Jurisdiction of the Office of Indian Affairs, 1873-1900. (M1070)

       Special Case 147: Moqui [Allotment, 1890-1894]

       Special Files of the Office of Indian Affairs, 1807-1904. File 267.

       Charges Against Agent J. H. Fleming, Moqui Pueblo Agency, 1882-1883. (M574)

       Records of the Office of the Secretary of the Interior. RG 48.

       Interior Department Appointment Papers: Arizona, 1857-1907. (M576)

       Records of the U. S. Geological Survey. RG57.

       Letters Received by the United States Geological Survey, 1879-1901.

       Letters Sent by the United States Geological Survey, 1869-1895. (M152)

National Archives, Laguna Naguel, CA.

       U. S. Office of Indian Affairs. Moqui Agency Records.

       Moqui Agency Correspondence, 1875-1883. 1144.

       Moqui Agency Diary, 1880-1882. 1146.

       Moqui Agency Ledger. 1147.

       Moqui Agency Letterbook, 1882-1883. 1145.

       U. S. Office of Indian Affairs. Navajo Agency Records.

       Fort Defiance Letterbooks.

Newberry Library, Chicago, IL.

       A. M. Stephen Manuscript [Catalogue of the Keam's Canon Collection of Relics of the Ancient Builders of the Southwestern Table Lands] and Letter. Ayer MS 829.

Presbyterian Historical Society, Philadephia, PA.
> American Indian Correspondence: The Presbyterian Historical Society Collection of Missionary Letters, 1833-1893.
> The Sheldon Jackson Collection, 1835-1909.

Princeton University, Mudd Manuscript Library, Princeton, NJ.
> Alumni File and Reunion Books for 1873. (Charles A. Taylor)

Smithsonian Institution Archives, Washington, D.C.
> George Brown Goode Collection, 1798-1896. RU 7050.

Smithsonian Institution, National Anthropological Archives, Washington, D.C.
> Brown, J. Stanley, Hopi Names for Pottery and Pottery Design, November, 1882. MS 1141.
> Cushing, Frank Hamilton, Annual Reports, 1883, 1884. MS 2472.
> Cushing, Frank Hamilton, Correspondence with Spencer Baird, 1880-1883. MS 4677.
> Holmes, William Henry, Letters Received and Other Papers. MS 4745.
> Mallery, Garrick, Collection of Sign Language and Pictography. MS 2372.
> Mindeleff, Victor, Zuni Sketchbook, 1881. MS 2138.
> Mindeleff, Victor, Field Plans and Diagrams of Inhabited Pueblos and Pueblo Ruins of Arizona and New Mexico, 1881-1886. MS 2621.
> Miscellaneous Pamphlet File.
> Records of the Bureau of American Ethnology, Correspondence, Letters Received, 1879-1888.
> Records of the Department of Anthropology, U. S. National Museum/National Museum of Natural History. Series 17: Division of Ethnology, Manuscript and Pamphlet File.
> Stephen, A. M. Hopi Vocabulary. MS 791.
> Stephen, A. M. Hopi and Tewa Vocabulary. MS 793.
> Stephen, A. M. A Petition [M. C. Stevenson, collector]. MS 3967.
> Stephen, A. M. Pottery of Tusayan – Catalogue of the Keam Collection. MS 3282.
> Stephen, A. M. Ruins of the Southwest. MS 1339. [Attributed, incorrectly, to Cosmos Mindeleff]
> Stephen, A. M. Correspondence to J. W. Fewkes, 1891-1894. MS 4408.
> Stevenson, James, Catalogue of Ethnological and Archaeological Collections from Hopi Pueblos, October-November, 1885. MS 775.
> Sullivan, Jeremiah. Hopitu (Moquis Pueblo), November 1882. MS 792.
> Sullivan, Jeremiah. Snake Dance. MS 837.
> Sullivan, Jeremiah. Tewa (Moquis Pueblo), April 1883. MS 1015.
> Sullivan, Jeremiah. Genesis Myth of the Tusayan (Moki). MS 1310. [Attributed, incorrectly, to A. M. Stephen.]
> Sullivan, Jeremiah. Dances, Medicine. MS 1607.
> Sullivan, Jeremiah. Ceremony. MS 3953.
> Yarrow, H. C. Remarks on Hopi Snake Dance. MS 3794.

Thomas Gilcrease Institute of American History and Art, Tulsa, OK.
        Willard Leroy Metcalf Papers. Journal from December 2, 1882 to
        February 1, 1883.
University of Arizona Library, Special Collections, Tucson, AZ.
        Scrapbooks of Edward S. Merritt. MS. 022.
        Papers of Frederick Samuel Dellenbaugh. Ms. 407.
University of New Mexico, Center for Southwest Research, Albuquerque, NM.
        George P. Hammond Collection. MSS 55 BC. Hopi-Navajo Relations.
University of Pennsylvania Museum Library, Philadelphia, PA.
        Daniel Garrison Brinton Collection.
        Jeremiah Sullivan. Hopitu Calendar. 913.72 Su53.
Wheelwright Museum of the American Indian, Santa Fe, NM
        Washington Matthews Papers.

Published Primary Sources

Anon.

1878   The Field-Work of the United States Geological and Geographical
        Survey of the Territories, Under the Direction of Prof. F.
        V. Hayden, For the Season of 1877. *American Naturalist* 12 (2): 96-
        114.

1879   Government Surveys. *Kansas City Review of Science* 3: 5-6.

1880   The Naughty Navajos. [May] (Sheldon Jackson Correspondence 54: 58-
        59).

1881a   Mission to the Moqui Indians. *The Field is the World* (March): 186-187.

1881b   Our Friend Dr. Jere Sullivan. *Madison Daily Courier* (December 19): 3.

1882   Moquis After Medicine. *Albuquerque Morning Journal* (September 1).

1883a   Canyon de Chelly. *Albuquerque Morning Journal* (May 6).

1883b   Probably One of the Egyptian Kings. *Albuquerque Morning Journal*
        (September 11).

1883c   Relics of the Cliff Dwellers. *Albuquerque Morning Journal* (October 3).

1883d   A Visit to the Large Cave on the Mineral. *Orion Era* (November 10).

1884a   Indian Rights Association. *The Morning Journal* (Albuquerque; May
        13): 2.

1884b   Models of the Prehistoric Pueblos of New Mexico and Arizona. *Kansas
        City Review of Science* 8 (7): 374-376.

1885a   The National Exhibit at the New Orleans Exposition. *Kansas City
        Review of Science* 8 (9): 536-538.

1885b   A Cool Robbery. *Albuquerque Morning Journal* (September 3).

1886a   Cowed by a Woman [Matilda Coxe Stevenson]. *Illustrated Police News*
        (March 6).

1886b   He Rests in Peace [John H. Sullivan obituary]. *Albuquerque Morning
        Democrat* (October 17): 4.

1886c   John H. Sullivan. *Madison Daily Courier* (October 27): 3.

1888a   Holbrook Items. *St. Johns Herald* (St. Johns, Arizona; May 10): 3.

1888b   Jeremiah Sullivan, B.A., M.D. *The Apache Herald* (St. Johns, Arizona; July 11): 3.

1888c   Fire in Holbrook. The Entire Business Portion of the Town in Ashes. *The Apache Review* (June 27): 3.

1888d   Fiction in Zuni Land [Interview with Cosmos Mindeleff regarding the Hopi!]. *The Roman Citizen* [Rome, New York] (June 1, 1888).

1892   "Terrorite." Death of the Inventor of the New Explosive at San Francisco [Dimetry Mindeleff obituary]. *Democrat Chronicle* [Rochester, New York] (February 15).

1897   Authorities of the Southwest [Cosmos Mindeleff]. *Land of Sunshine* 6 (5): 186-187.

1910   Train Kills Indian Chief [Wiki]. *Winslow Mail* (April 2).

1933   Mrs. Mindeleff Dies Here on Saturday [Marion Mindeleff]. *The Putnam County Courier* [Carmel, NY] (April 14).

1938   Cosmos Mindeleff Succumbs to Shock. *The Putnam County Courier* (June 30).

Banta, A. F.

1888   Holbrook in Ruins! *St. Johns Herald* (June 28).

Barber, Edwin A.

1875   The Hayden Survey: Interesting Picture of the Moqui Towns in Arizona. *New York Herald* (October 1): 4.

Baxter, Sylvester

1881   Solved at Last: Mysteries of Ancient Aztec History Unveiled by an Explorer from the Smithsonian Institution; Wonderful Achievements of Frank H. Cushing. *Boston Herald* (June 16).

1882a   An Aboriginal Pilgrimage. *Century Illustrated Monthly Magazine* 24 (August): 526-536.

1882b   The Father of the Pueblos. *Harper's New Monthly Magazine* 65 (June): 72-91.

1882c   F. H. Cushing at Zuni. *The American Architect and Building News* 11: 56-57.

1882d   Logan's Land? [by S. B.] *Boston Herald* (December 11).

1883   Zuni Revisited. *The American Architect and Building News* 13: 124-126.

1888   The Old New World. *Boston Herald* (April 15).

Beaman, E. O.

1874   The Canon of the Colorado, and the Moquis Pueblos. *Appletons' Journal* 11 (May): 641-644.

Bickford, F. T.

1890   Prehistoric Cave-Dwellings. *The Century* 40(6): 896-911.

Bloom, Lansing B., ed.

1937   Bourke on the Southwest, IX and X. *New Mexico Historical Review* 11(1): 77-122 and 11(2): 188-207.

Bourke, John G.

1874   The Moquis of Arizona. *Alta California* (December 17); also issued as a separate.

1881a   The Snake Dance. *Military Review*, Santa Fe 1:14 (October 1); reprinted from *The Times*, Chicago (September 14).

1881b   An Indian Snake Dance. *The National Police Gazette* 39 (October 15): 6, 9.

1884   *The Snake-Dance of the Moquis of Arizona.* New York: Charles Scribner's.

1892   The Medicine-Man of the Apache. *Ninth Annual Report of the Bureau of Ethnology*, 1887-1888. Washington: Government Printing Office. Pp. 443-603.

1895   [Review of] The Snake Ceremonials at Walpi, by J. Walter Fewkes. *American Anthropologist* 8 (April): 192-196.

Bowman, John H.

1884   Reports of Agents in New Mexico: [Maquis Agency]. *Annual Report of the Commissioner of Indian Affairs...for the Year 1884.* Washington: Government Printing Office. Pp. 136-138.

1885   Report of Agents in New Mexico: [Moquis Pueblo Indians]. *Annual Report of the Commissioner of Indian Affairs...for the Year 1885.* Washington: Government Printing Office. Pp. 410-411.

Brown, W. Cal.

1885   A Carnival of Horrors. *Albuquerque Morning Journal* (August 26).

Brown, Joseph Stanley

1883   The Dwellers in Cliffs. *New York Tribune* (January 14).

Browning, D. M.

1894   Report of the Commissioner [Allotments and Patents: Moqui Reservation, Ariz.]. *Sixty-Third Annual Report of the Commissioner of Indian Affairs.* Washington: Government Printing Office. Pp. 19-20.

Burge, J. C.

1885   Dance of the Moquis. *Arizona Champion* (September 5).

Case, Theo S.

1885   The New Orleans Exposition. *Kansas City Review of Science* 8 (10): 590-595.

Colyer, Vincent

1872   The Moquis. *Report of the Commissioner of Indian Affairs...for the Year 1869.* Washington: Government Printing Office. Pp. 90-91.

Crothers, W. D.

1872a   No. 128 [Moqui Pueblo Indians]. *Report of the Commissioner of Indian Affairs...for the Year 1871.* Washington: Government Printing Office. Pp. 703-706.

1872b   No. 61 [Moqui Pueblo Indians]. *Annual Report of the Commissioner of Indian Affairs...for the Year 1872.* Washington: Government Printing Office. Pp. 324-325.

Curtis, William E.
1883a   General Logan's Ranch. *The Inter-Ocean* (May 2).
1883b   *Children of the Sun.* Chicago: Inter-Ocean.

Cushing, Frank Hamilton
1882a   The Zuni, Social, Mythic, and Religious Systems. *Popular Science Monthly* 21 (June): 186-192.
1882b   The Nation of Willows. *Atlantic Monthly* 50: 362-374, 541-559.
1882-1883   My Adventures in Zuni. *Century Illustrated Monthly Magazine* 25: 197-207, 500-511; 26: 28-47.
1883   Zuni Fetiches. *Second Annual Report of the Bureau of Ethnology, 1882-1883.* Washington: Government Printing Office. Pp. 9-45.
1884-1885   Zuni Breadstuff. *The Millstone* 9: nos. 1-12 (January-December 1884); 10: nos. 1-3 (January-March 1885); *The Millstone and the Corn Miller* 10: no. 4 (April 1885), nos. 6-8 (June-August 1885).
1886   A Study of Pueblo Pottery as Illustrative of Zuni Cultural Growth. *Fourth Annual Report of the Bureau of Ethnology, 1882-1883.* Washington: Government Printing Office. Pp. 467-521.
1888   Zuni Mysteries. *Daily Examiner,* San Francisco (July 8). [Interview with Henry B. McDowell]
1892   A Zuni Tale of the Underworld. *Journal of American Folk-Lore* 5: 49-56.
1893   Commentary of a Zuni Familiar. In *The Song of the Ancient People,* by Edna Dean Proctor. Boston: Houghton, Mifflin and Company. Pp. 25-49.
1896   Outlines of Zuni Creation Myths. *Thirteenth Annual Report of the Bureau of American Ethnology, 1891-1892.* Washington: Government Printing Office. Pp. 321-447.
1901   *Zuni Folk Tales.* Introduction by John Wesley Powell. New York: G. P. Putnam's Sons.
1920   *Zuni Breadstuff.* New York: Museum of the American Indian, Heye Foundation. [Originally published in *The Millstone,* 1884-1885]
1922   Oraibi in 1883. Contributions to Hopi History, Elsie Clews Parsons, ed. *American Anthropologist* 24 (July-September): 253-268.
1923   The Origin Myth from Oraibi, E. C. Parsons, ed. *Journal of American Folklore* 36: 163-170.
1965   *The Nation of Willows,* Robert C. Euler, ed. Flagstaff: Northland Press.

Davis, J. C., Jr.
1881a   Mr. Lo, Whose Front Name is Moquis. *Madison Evening Daily Star* (April 7).
1881b   A Corn Dance. *Madison Evening Daily Star* (June 25).
1882   Over the Rockies. *Madison Evening Daily Star* (July 6).

Defrees, W. S.

1873   No. 57 [Moqui Pueblo Indians]. *Annual Report of the Commissioner of Indian Affairs...for the Year 1873.* Washington: Government Printing Office. Pp. 285-286.

1874   Moqui Pueblo Indian Agency. *Annual Report of the Commissioner of Indian Affairs...for the Year 1874.* Washington: Government Printing Office. P. 290.

Dellenbaugh, Frederick S.

1889   An Artist's Glimpse of Northern Arizona. *St. Nicholas Magazine* 16 (11): 854-856.

1916   The Somaikoli Dance at Sichumovi [1884]. *American Museum Journal* 15 (5): 256-258.

Donaldson, Thomas

1893   *Moqui Pueblo Indians of Arizona and Pueblo Indians of New Mexico.* (Extra Census Bulletin). Washington: Government Printing Office.

Fewkes, J. Walter

1890   A Study of the Summer Ceremonials at Zuni and Moqui Pueblos. *Bulletin of the Essex Institute* 22 (7-8-9): 89-113.

1891   A Suggestion as to the Meaning of the Moki Snake Dance. *Journal of American Folk-Lore* 4 (April-June): 129-138.

1892a   A Few Tusayan Pictographs. *American Anthropologist* 5 (January): 9-26.

1892b   The Ceremonial Circuit among the Village Indians of Northeastern Arizona. *Journal of American Folk-Lore* 5 (January-March): 33-42.

1892c   A Few Summer Ceremonials at the Tusayan Pueblos. *A Journal of American Ethnology and Archaeology* 2: 1-160.

1892d   The Wa-wac-ka-tci-na, A Tusayan Foot Race. *Bulletin of the Essex Institute* 24 (7-8-9): 113-133.

1893a   A Central American Ceremony which suggests the Snake Dance of the Tusayan Villagers. *American Anthropologist* 6 (July): 285-306.

1893b   A-wa-to-bi: An Archaeological Verification of a Tusayan Legend. *American Anthropologist* 6 (October): 363-375.

1894a   On Certain Personages who appear in a Tusayan Ceremony. *American Anthropologist* 7 (January): 32-52.

1894b   The Snake Ceremonials at Walpi. Assisted by A. M. Stephen and J. G. Owens. *A Journal of American Ethnology and Archaeology* 4: 1-126.

1894c   The Kinship of a Tanoan-Speaking Community in Tusayan. *American Anthropologist* 7 (April): 162-167.

1894d   The Kinship of the Tusayan Villagers. *American Anthropologist* 7 (October): 394-417.

1894e   The Walpi Flute Observance: A Study of Primitive Dramatization. *Journal of American Folk-Lore* 7 (27): 265-288.

1894f   Dolls of the Tusayan Indians. *Internationales Archiv fur Ethnographie* 7: 45-74.

1895a   The Tusayan New Fire Ceremony. *Proceedings of the Boston Society of Natural History* 26 (January): 422-458.

1895b   Provisional List of Annual Ceremonies at Walpi. *Internationales Archiv
             für Ethnographie* 8: 215-237.
1896a   Studies of Tusayan Archaeology. *Internationales Archiv fur Ethnographie*
             9: 204-205.
1896b   Catalogue of the Hemenway Collection in the Historico-American
             Exposition of Madrid. *Report for 1892-1893 of the United States
             Commission to the Columbian Historical Exposition at Madrid.*
             Washington: Government Printing Office. Pp. 279-326.
1896c   Preliminary Account of an Expedition to the Cliff Villages of the Red
             Rock Country, and the Tusayan Ruins of Sikyatki and Awatobi,
             Arizona, in 1895. *Annual Report...of the Smithsonian
             Institution...1895.* Washington: Government Printing Office. Pp.
             557-588.
1897a   Tusayan Totemic Signatures. *American Anthropologist* 10 (January):
             1-11.
1897b   Tusayan Katcinas. *Fifteenth Annual Report of the Bureau of Ethnology,*
             1893-
1894.   Washington: Government Printing Office. Pp. 245-313.
1897c   Tusayan Snake Ceremonies. *Sixteen Annual Report of the Bureau of
             American Ethnology,* 1894-1895. Washington: Government
             Printing Office. Pp. 267-312.
1898   Archeological Expedition to Arizona in 1895. *Seventeenth Annual
             Report of the Bureau of American Ethnology,* 1895-1896.
             Washington: Government Printing Office. Pp. 519-744.
1899a   Death of a Celebrated Hopi [Kopeli]. *American Anthropologist* 1
             (January): 196-197.
1899b   Hopi Basket Dances. *Journal of American Folk-Lore* 12 (45): 81-96.
1900a   Tusayan Migration Traditions. *Nineteenth Annual Report of the Bureau
             of American Ethnology,* 1897-1898. Washington: Government
             Printing Office. Pp. 573-633.
1900b   Tusayan Flute and Snake Ceremonies. *Nineteenth Annual Report of the
             Bureau of American Ethnology,* 1897-1898. Washington:
             Government Printing Office. Pp. 957-1011.
1906a   The Sun's Influence on the Form of the Hopi Pueblos. *American
             Anthropologist* 8 (1): 88-100.
1906b   Hopi Shrines near the East Mesa, Arizona. *American Anthropologist* 8
             (2): 346-375.
1908   Ventilators in Ceremonial Rooms of Prehistoric Cliff-Dwellings.
             American Anthropologist 10 (3): 387-398.
1922   Oraibi in 1890. Contributions to Hopi History, E. C. Parsons, ed.
             American Anthropologist 24 (July-September): 268-283.
Fewkes, J. Walter, ed.
1891-1908   *A Journal of American Ethnology and Archaeology.* 5 vols. Boston:
             Houghton Mifflin.

Fewkes, J. Walter, and J. G. Owens
1892   The La-la-kon-ta: A Tusayan Dance. *American Anthropologist* 5 (April): 105-129.
Fewkes, J. Walter, and A. M. Stephen
1892a   The Mam-zrau-ti: A Tusayan Ceremony. *American Anthropologist* 5 (July): 217-245.
1892b   The Na-ac-nai-ya: A Tusayan Initiation Ceremony. *Journal of American Folk-Lore* 5 (July-September): 189-221.
1893   The Pa-lu-lu-kon-ti: A Tusayan Ceremony. *Journal of American Folk-Lore* 6 (23): 269-294.
Fleming, Jesse R.
1882a   The Moquis. *Albuquerque Morning Journal* (March 17).
1882b   Reports of Agents in Arizona: Moquis Pueblo Agency. *Annual Report of the Commissioner of Indian Affairs...for the Year 1882.* Washington: Government Printing Office. Pp. 4-6.
Green, Jesse, ed.
1979   *Zuni: Selected Writings of Frank Hamilton Cushing.* Lincoln: University of Nebraska Press.
1990   *Cushing at Zuni: The Correspondence and Journals of Frank Hamilton Cushing, 1879-1884.* Albuquerque: University of New Mexico Press.
Hough, Walter
1915   *The Hopi Indians.* Cedar Rapids: Torch Press.
Ingersoll, Ernest
1885   The Making of a Museum. *Century* 39: 354-369.
Irvine, Alex. G.
1877   Reports of Agents in New Mexico: [Moquis Pueblos]. *Annual Report of the Commissioner of Indian Affairs...for the Year 1877.* Washington: Government Printing Office. P. 160.
Kate, Herman F. C. ten
1885   *Reizen en onderzoekingen in Noord-Amerika.* Leiden: E. J. Brill.
1886   Description d'un crane d'Indien Moqui. *Archives neerdlandaises des sciences exactes et naturelles* 20: 14-19.
1900   Frank Hamilton Cushing. *American Anthropologist* 2: 768-771.
2004   *Travels and Researches in Native North America, 1882-1883,* Pieter Hovens, William Orr, and Louis A. Hieb, eds. Albuquerque: University of New Mexico Press.
Keam, Thomas V.
1883a   An Indian Snake Dance. *Chambers's Journal* (January 6).
1883b   Stolen Gods! An Enthusiastic Antiquarian Carries Off a Couple of Indian Gods—Great Consternation Among the Tribe is a Consequence Thereof. *Albuquerque Morning Journal* (October 31).
1884   The Cliff-Houses of Canon de Chelly. *Chambers's Journal* (January 19).

King, Henry
1883   Reality vs. Romance. *Topeka Daily Capital* (January 18).

Lange, Charles H., and Carroll L. Riley, eds.
1966   *The Southwestern Journals of Adolph F. Bandelier, 1880-1882.*
            Albuquerque: University of New Mexico Press.

Lange, Charles H., Carroll L. Riley, and Elizabeth M. Lange, eds.
1970   *The Southwestern Journals of Adolph F. Bandelier, 1883-1884.*
            Albuquerque: University of New Mexico Press.

Loew, Oscar
1874a   The Moquis Indians of Arizona. *Popular Science Monthly* 5 (3): 351-
            369.
1874b   Lieutenant Wheeler's Expedition nach Neu-Mexiko und Arizona.
            Petermann's Geographische Mittheilungen 20: 401-416 and 453-461.

Lumholtz, Carl
1891   Explorations in the Sierra Nevada. *Scribner's Magazine* 10 (November):
            531-548.

Lummis, Charles F.
1892   Some Strange Corners of Our Country, III: The Snake-Dance of the
            Moquis [1891]. *St. Nicholas* 19 (April): 421-428.

Mateer, William R.
1878   Reports of Agents in Arizona: Moquis Pueblo Indian Agency. *Annual
            Report of the Commissioner of Indian Affairs...for the Year 1878.*
            Washington: Government Printing Office. Pp. 8-10.
1879a   The Snake Dance [1879]. *Long-Islander* (October 10).
1879b   An Uncanny Crew. *The National Police Gazette* (October 11).

Matthews, Washington
1883a   The Zuni Dispute. *Topeka Capital* (February 14).
1883b   Navajo Silversmiths. *Second Annual Report of the Bureau of Ethnology,*
            1881-1882. Washington: Government Printing Office. Pp. 167-178.
1884a   Navajo Weavers. *Third Annual Report of the Bureau of Ethnology,* 1882-
            1883. Washington: Government Printing Office. Pp. 371-391.
1884b   A Night with the Navajos, by Zay Elini [pseud.]. *Field and Stream* 6
            (November): 282-283.
1885   Mythic Dry-Paintings of the Navajos. *American Naturalist* 19
            (October): 931-939.
1887   The Mountain Chant: A Navajo Ceremony. *Fifth Annual Report of the
            Bureau of Ethnology,* 1883-1884. Washington: Government
            Printing Office. Pp. 379-467.
1892   *The Suppressed Part of "The Mountain Chant: A Navajo Ceremony."* Fort
            Wingate: [The Author].
1894   [Review of] The Snake Ceremonials at Walpi, by J. Walter Fewkes.
            American Anthropologist 7 (October): 420-422.
1897   *Navajo Legends.* Memoirs of the American Folk-Lore Society, 5. New
            York: Houghton, Mifflin and Company.

1902   *The Night Chant: A Navaho Ceremony*. Memoirs of the American
            Museum of Natural History, Anthropology, vol. 6. New York:
            American Museum of Natural History.

Mindeleff, Cosmos

1886a   An Indian Snake-Dance [1885], by Kosmos Mindelieff. *Science* 7 (June
            4): 507-514.

1886b   An Indian Snake-Dance [1885]. *Science* 8 (July 2): 12-13.

1888   Fiction in Zuni Land [Interview with Cosmos Mindeleff]. *The Roman
            Citizen* (Rome, New York; June 1).

1889   Topographic Models. *National Geographic* 1 (July): 12-13.

1891   The Traditional History of Tusayan. *In* A Study of Pueblo Architecture
            in Tusayan and Cibola, by Victor Mindeleff. *Eighth Annual Report
            of the Bureau of Ethnology*, 1886-1887. Washington: Government
            Printing Office. Pp. 16-41.

1895   The Cliff Ruins of Canyon de Chelly, Arizona. *American Anthropologist*
            8 (April): 153-174.

1896a   Aboriginal Remains in Verde Valley, Arizona. *Thirteenth Annual Report
            of the Bureau of Ethnology*, 1891-1892. Washington: Government
            Printing Office. Pp. 179-261.

1896b   Casa Grande Ruin. *Thirteenth Annual Report of the Bureau of Ethnology*,
            1891-1892. Washington: Government Printing Office. Pp. 289-319.

1897a   The Repair of Casa Grande Ruin, Arizona, in 1891. *Fifteenth
            Annual Report of the Bureau of Ethnology*, 1893-1894. Washington:
            Government Printing Office. Pp. 315-349.

1897b   The Cliff Ruins of Canyon de Chelly, Arizona. *Sixteenth Annual
            Report of the Bureau of American Ethnology*, 1894-1895.
            Washington: Government Printing Office. Pp. 73-198.

1897c   The Influence of the Geographic Environment. *Journal of the
            Geographical Society of New York* 29 (1): 1-12.

1897d   Recent Irrigation Work on the Navaho Reservation. *Scientific American*
            76 (January 23): 52-54.

1897e   Models of the United States. *Scientific American* Supplement 42 (March
            20): 17698-17699.

1897f   Pueblo Architecture. *American Architect and Building News* 56 (April
            17): 19-21; (May 22): 59-61; 57 (July 24): 31-33; (September 11):
            87-88; "to be continued" but no additional installments appeared.

1897g   The Casa Grande Ruin, Southern Arizona. *Scientific American
            Supplement* No. 1118 (June 5): 17877-17878.

1897h   The Casa Grande of Arizona. *New England Magazine* 16 (July): 570-
            582.

1897i   House Building by Ritual. *Scientific American* 77 (September 4): 153-
            154.

1898a   Navaho Houses. *Seventeenth Annual Report of the Bureau of American Ethnology*, 1895-1896. Washington: Government Printing Office. Pp. 469-517.

1898b   Pueblo Arts and Industries. *Scientific American* 78 (January 5): 42-43; 78 (April 16): 249-250; 79 (July 30): 75.

1898c   Origin of the Cliff Dwellings. *Journal of the American Geographical Society of New York* 30: 111-123.

1898d   Ghost Dance. *Scientific American* Supplement 46 (October 22): 19071-19074; (October 29): 19088-19089.

1898e   Native Architecture in Africa and New Mexico. *Scientific American* 79 (November 12): 313-314.

1898f   Aboriginal Architecture in the United States. *Journal of the American Geographical Society of New York* 30: 414-427.

1898g   Repair of the Casa Grande Ruin, Arizona. *American Architect and Building News* 40 (April 23): 28-29.

1899a   Superstitions of the Navajo Indians. *Current Literature* 26 (September): 250. Reprinted from the *Denver Republican*.

1899b   Navajo Sweat Baths. *The Phoenix Republican* (Commercial Advertiser).

1899c   Navaho Indian Gamblers. *Scientific American* 81 (July 8): 27.

1900a   Localization of Tusayan Clans. *Nineteenth Annual Report of the Bureau of American Ethnology*, 1897-1898. Washington: Government Printing Office. Pp. 635-653.

1900b   Houses and House Dedication of the Navahos. *Scientific American* 82 (April 14): 233-234.

1900c   White Indians of New Mexico. *Scientific American* 83 (August 18): 107.

1900d   Geographical Relief Maps: Their Use and Manufacture. *Journal of the American Geographical Society of New York* 32 (4): 367-380.

1901a   A Cliff-Dwelling Park in Colorado. *Scientific American* 84 (May 11): 297-298.

1901b   The Navaho Reservation: Sweat Houses. *The Indian Advocate* (Sacred Heart, OK) 13 (1): 319-324. [Note: "continued from the October Number," i.e., 1900]

1901c   The Navaho Reservation. *The Indian Advocate* 13 (8): 225-231.

1901d   The Navaho Reservation: Habits of the People. *The Indian Advocate* 13 (9): 255-264.

1901e   The Navaho Reservation: Legendary and Actual Winter Hogans. *The Indian Advocate* 13 (10): 287-293. [Note: "To be Continued"]

1902   Rites of the Navaho. *New York Times* (August 16): 18.

1909   The Right Line of Approach [for life underwriters]. *Life Association News* 4 (4): 1-3.

Mindeleff, Victor

1887   Origin of Pueblo Architecture. *Science* 9 (June 17): 593-595.

1891   A Study of Pueblo Architecture: Tusayan and Cibola. *Eighth Annual Report of the Bureau of Ethnology,* 1886-1887. Washington: Government Printing Office. Pp. 3-228.

Moffet, Charles R.

1889a   A Day in Cherelon Canyon. *Overland Monthly* 13 (February): 145-152.

1889b   In the Moqui Country. *Overland Monthly* 14 (September): 243-256.

Mooney, James

1893   Recent Archaeological Find in Arizona. *American Anthropologist* 6 (July): 283-284.

1896   The Ghost-Dance Religion and the Sioux Outbreak of 1890. *Fourteenth Annual Report of the Bureau of Ethnology,* 1892-1893. Washington: Government Printing Office. Pp. 641-1110.

Morgan, Lewis Henry

1869   'The Seven Cities of Cibola.' *North American Review* 108: 457-498.

1877   *Ancient Society, or Researches in the Lines of Human Progress from Savagery through Barbarism to Civilization.* New York: Henry Holt.

1880   A Study of the Houses of the American Aborigines with a Scheme of Exploration of the Ruins in New Mexico and Elsewhere. *First Annual Report of the Executive Committee, with Accompanying Papers, Archaeological Society of America, 1879-1880.* Cambridge: Archaeological Institute of America. Pp. 29-80.

1881   *Houses and House-Life of the American Aborigines.* Contributions to North American Ethnology, Vol. 4. Washington: Government Printing Office.

Ober, Fred A.

1882   How a White Man Became the War Chief of the Zunis. *Wide Awake* (June): 382-388.

Owens, J. G.

1892   Natal Ceremonies of the Hopi Indians. *A Journal of American Ethnology and Archaeology* 2: 161-176.

Palmer, A. D.

1870   No. 38 [Moquis Indians]. *Annual Report of the Commissioner of Indian Affairs...for the Year 1870.* Washington: Government Printing Office. Pp. 132-136.

Parsons, Elsie Clews, ed.

1922   Contributions to Hopi History. *American Anthropologist* 24 (3): 253-298.

1929   Hopi Tales, by A. M. Stephen. *Journal of American Folk-Lore* 42: 3-72. [Narratives recorded by A. M. Stephen: 3-35, 50-57, and 60-66; all others were recorded by Jeremiah Sullivan.]

1936   *Hopi Journal of Alexander M. Stephen.* Columbia University Contributions to Anthropology, vol. 23). New York: Columbia University Press.

Patterson, S. S.
1886   Reports of Agents in New Mexico: [Moquis Indians]. *Annual Report of the Commissioner of Indian Affairs...for the Year 1886.* Washington: Government Printing Office. P. 205.

1887   Reports of Agents in New Mexico: [Moquis Pueblo Indians]. *Annual Report of the Commissioner of Indian Affairs...for the Year 1887.* Washington: Government Printing Office. Pp. 177-178.

1888   Reports of Agents in New Mexico: [Moquis Pueblo Indians]. *Annual Report of the Commissioner of Indian Affairs...for the Year 1888.* Washington: Government Printing Office. Pp. 196-197.

Pilling, James Constantine
1885   *Proof-Sheets for a Bibliography of the Languages of North American Indians.* Washington: Government Printing Office.

Plummer, E. H.
1897   The Moqui Indian Snake Dance in Arizona [1893]. *Frank Leslie's Popular Monthly* 44 (November): 500-505.

Poston, Charles D.
1864   Arizona Superintendency: The Moquins. *Report of the Commissioner of Indian Affairs for the Year 1863.* Washington: Government Printing Office. P. 388.

1865   Arizona Superintendency: Moquis. *Report of the Commissioner of Indian Affairs for the Year 1864.* Washington: Government Printing Office. Pp. 150-151.

Powell, John Wesley
1875   The Ancient Province of Tusayan. *Scribner's Monthly* 11:2 (December): 193-213.

1880   *Introduction to the Study of Indian Languages; With Words, Phrases and Sentences to be Collected.* 2d ed. Washington: Government Printing Office.

1881   Report of the Director. *First Annual Report of the Bureau of Ethnology, 1879-1880.* Washington: Government Print Office. Pp. xi-xxxiii.

1883   Report of the Director. *Second Annual Report...1880-1881.* Pp. xv-xxxvii.

1884   Report of the Director. *Third Annual Report...1881-1882.* Pp. xii-lxxiv.

1886   Report of the Director. *Fourth Annual Report...1882-1883.* Pp. xxvii-lxiii.

1887   Report of the Director. *Fifth Annual Report...1883-1884.* Pp. xvii-liii.

1888   Report of the Director. *Sixth Annual Report...1884-1885.* Pp. xxiii-lviii.

1891a   Report of the Director. *Seventh Annual Report...1885-1886.* Pp. xv-xli.

1891b   Report of the Director. *Eighth Annual Report...1886-1887.* Pp. xiii-xxxvi.

1892   Report of the Director. *Ninth Annual Report...1887-1888.* Pp. xix-xlvi.

1893   Report of the Director. *Tenth Annual Report...1888-1889.* Pp. iii-xxx.

1894a   Report of the Director. *Eleventh Annual Report...1889-1890.* Pp. xxi-xlvii.

1894b   Report of the Director. *Twelfth Annual Report...1890-1891.* Pp. xix-xlviii.

1896a   Report of the Director. *Thirteenth Annual Report...1891-1892.* Pp. xix-lix.

1896b   Report of the Director. *Fourteenth Annual Report...1892-1893.* Pp. xxv-lxi.

1897a   Report of the Director. *Fifteenth Annual Report...1893-1894.* Pp. xv-cxxi.

1897b   Report of the Director. *Sixteenth Annual Report of the Bureau of American Ethnology,* 1894-1895. Compiled by F. W. Hodge. Washington: Government Printing Office. Pp. xiii-cxix.

Riordan, M. J.
1890   The Navajo Indians. *Overland Monthly* 16 (October): 373-380.

Rizer, Henry Clay
1882a   Recent Rambles: Natives. *Eureka Herald* (December 21): 1.
1882b   The Home of the Zunis. *New York Tribune* (October 21).
1883a   Hosh-Kon: Description of a Great Navajo Festival. *Topeka Daily Capital* (January 14):3; reprinted in the *Eureka Herald* (January 25): 1.
1883b   Ga-Bi-Tcai: A Graphic Description of a Dance by that Name among the Navajoe [sic] Indians in New Mexico [i.e., Arizona]. *Eureka Herald* (November 29): 1.

Robinson, Charles M., III, ed.
2013   *The Diaries of John Gregory Bourke,* Vol. 5, May 23, 1881-August 26, 1881. Denton: University of North Texas Press.

Roberts, Edwards
1886   A Moqui Indian Fete. *Overland Monthly* 8 (September): 261-266.

Shipley, David L.
1891   Reports of Agents in New Mexico: Report of Moqui Sub-Agency. *Annual Report of the Commissioner of Indian Affairs - 1891.* Washington: Government Printing Office. Pp. 310-311.
1892   Reports of Agents in Arizona: Report of the Moqui Subagency. *Annual Report of the Commissioner of Indian Affairs - 1892.* Washington: Government Printing Office. Pp. 211-212.

Shufeldt, Robert W.
1891   Snake Dance of the Moquis [1889]. *Great Divide* 6 (October): 24.

Steck, M.
1865   New Mexico Superintendency: No. 41 [Moqui Indians]. *Report of the Commissioner of Indian Affairs for the Year 1865.* Washington: Government Printing Office. Pp. 170-171.

Stephen, Alexander M.
1883   Indian Traditions [Navajo]. *Eureka Herald* (March 29).

1887   Navajo Methods of Curing Ague, H. C. Yarrow, ed. *Forest and Stream*
           28 (March 3): 104-105.
1888   Legend of the Snake Order of the Moquis, as Told by Outsiders. *Journal*
           of American Folklore 1: 109-114. [Recorded by Jeremiah Sullivan.
           Attributed to Stephen by Washington Matthews.]
1889a   The Navajo Shoemaker. *Proceedings of the United States Museum.*
           Washington: Government Printing Office. Pp. 131-136.
1889b   Tribal Boundary Marks [Hopi]. *American Anthropologist* 2 (July): 214.
1890a   Marriage among the Navajoes. *Our Forest Children* 4: 222.
1890b   Navajo Dress. *Our Forest Children* 4: 222-223.
1890c   Navajo Dwellings. *Our Forest Children* 4: 223.
1890d   Notes about the Navajoes. *The Canadian Indian* 1 (October): 15-16.
1893a   Description of a Hopi Ti-hu. *The Folk-Lorist; Journal of the Chicago*
           Folk-Lore Society 1 (July): 83-88.
1893b   The Navajo. *American Anthropologist* 6 (October): 345-362.
1894a   The Legend of Tiyo, The Snake Hero. *A Journal of American Ethnology*
           and Archaeology 4: 106-119.
1894b   The Po-boc-tu among the Hopi. *The American Antiquarian and*
           Oriental Journal 16 (4): 212-214.
1898   Pigments in Ceremonials of the Hopi. (Archives of the International
           Folk-Lore Association, vol. 1) *International Folk-Lore Congress of*
           the World's Columbian Exposition 1: 260-265.
1922   When John the Jeweler was Sick. *American Indian Life*, Elsie Clews
           Parsons, ed. New York: B. W. Huebsch. Pp. 153-156.
1932   Navajo Origin Legend. *Journal of American Folk-Lore* 43: 88-104.
Stephen, Alexander M., and H. J. Messenger
1889   The Snake Dance. *The World* [New York] (September 8): 9.
Stevenson, James
1881   Illustrated Catalogue of the Collections Obtained from the Indians of
           New Mexico and Arizona in 1879. *Second Annual Report of the*
           Bureau of Ethnology, 1880-1881. Washington: Government
           Printing Office. Pp. 307-422.
1884   Illustrated Catalogue of the Collections Obtained from the Pueblos of
           Zuni, New Mexico, and Wolpi, Arizona, in 1881. *Third*
           Annual Report of the Bureau of Ethnology, 1881-1882. Washington:
           Government Printing Office. Pp 511-594.
1886   Ancient Habitations of the Southwest [1882]. *Journal of the American*
           Geographical Society of New York 18: 329-342.
1891   Ceremonial of Hasjelti Dailjis and Mythical Sand Painting of the Navajo
           Indian. *Eighth Annual Report of the Bureau of Ethnology,*1886-1887.
           Washington: Government Printing Office. Pp. 229-285. [Written
           by Matilda Coxe Stevenson]
Stevenson, Matilda Coxe
1886   An Arizona School Site. *Lend a Hand* 1 (February) 121.

1904   The Zuni Indians: Their Mythology, Esoteric Fraternities, and Ceremonies. *Twenty-third Annual Report of the Bureau of American Ethnology*, 1902-1903. Washington: Government Printing Office. Pp. 1-608.

Sullivan, Jeremiah

1881a The Madisonians in the Far West. *Madison Evening Courier* (January 21).

1881b Interesting Legends of the Moquis Indians. *Madison Daily Evening Star* (May 16).

1882   Letters from the People. Jerry Sullivan in a New Role. *Madison Evening Courier* (December 6).

1886   The Cliff Dwellers. *Madison Courier* (August 27).

1887   Moqui Snake Dance. *Apache County Critic* (August 27).

1888   The Moquis. *Apache Review* (July 4); reprinted from the San Fernando, California *Sun*.

1891a Supplementary Legend. *In* A Study of Pueblo Architecture: Tusayan and Cibola, by Victor Mindeleff. *Eighth Annual Report of the Bureau of Ethnology*, 1886-1887. Washington: Government Printing Office. Pp. 40-41.

1891b The Snake Dance. *San Francisco Chronicle* and *The Times*, Los Angeles (August 6).

1891c Moquis Celebrate the Great Snake Dance. *The Times*, Los Angeles (August 26)

1921   Spanish Folk-Tale Recorded on First Mesa in 1885, E. C. Parsons, ed. *Journal of American Folk-Lore* 34: 221.

1929   Hopi Tales, by A. M. Stephen, E. C. Parsons, ed. *Journal of American Folk-Lore* 42: 35-50, 57-60, and 67-72. [Attributed, incorrectly, to A. M. Stephen.]

1940   *Hopi Indians of Arizona*. Southwest Museum Leaflets, No. 14. Los Angeles: Southwest Museum. First published in *The Masterkey*, 1939-1940. [Attributed, incorrectly, to A. M. Stephen by F. W. Hodge.]

Sullivan, John H.

1880a The Indian Question. *Indianapolis Daily Sentinel* (January 14).

1880b The Far West. *Madison Evening Courier* (November 5).

1880c Trip to the Indian Agency. *Madison Evening Courier* (November 10).

1881a A Peculiar People. *Madison Evening Courier* (March 7).

1881b The Moquis Indians. *Madison Evening Courier* (June 23).

1881c Reports of Agents in Arizona: Moquis Pueblo Indian Agency. *Annual Report of the Commissioner of Indian Affairs...for the Year 1881*. Washington: Government Printing Office. Pp. 3-5.

1883a Albuquerque. *Albuquerque* Morning *Journal* (February 1).

1883b New Mexico Mining. *Madison Evening Courier* (May 12).

1884   The Moquis Indians. *American Antiquarian and Oriental Journal* 6: 101-103.

Taylor, Charles A.
1880   The Moqui Indians. *Rocky Mountain Presbyterian* 9 (December): 189-
            190.
1881a   Our Journey to Moqui. *Presbyterian Home Missions* 10 (April): 269-
            270.
1881b   The Great Snake Dance of the Moquis. *Rocky Mountain Presbyterian* 10
            (April): 176.
1881c   Moqui Mission, Arizona. *Presbyterian Home Missions* 10 (November):
            359.
1882   New Mexico. [Clipping in Sheldon Jackson Correspondence 58: 124;
            dated January 2]

Taylor, Mrs. Charles A.
1881   A Seven Weeks Journey. *Women's Executive Committee Home Missions*
            10: 202.

Thomas, Cyrus
1894   Report on the Mound Explorations of the Bureau of Ethnology. *Twelfth
            Annual Report of the Bureau of Ethnology*, 1890-1891. Washington:
            Government Printing Office. Pp. 3-730.

Truax, W. B.
1875   Reports of Agents in Arizona: Moquis Pueblo Indian Agency. *Annual
            Report of the Commissioner of Indian Affairs...for the Year 1875*.
            Washington: Government Printing Office. Pp. 211-212.
1876   Reports of Agents in Arizona: Moquis Pueblo Indian Agency. *Annual
            Report of the Commissioner of Indian Affairs...for the Year 1876*.
            Washington: Government Printing Office. Pp. 5-6.

Tylor, Edward B.
1871   *Primitive Culture: Researches into the Development of Mythology,
            Philosophy, Religion, Language, Art and Custom*. London: J.
            Murray.
1889   *Primitive Culture: Researches into the Development of Mythology,
            Philosophy, Religion, Language, Art and Custom*. New York: H.
            Holt.

Vandever, C. E.
1889   Reports of Agents in New Mexico: Report of Agent for Moqui
            Pueblos. *Annual Report of the Commissioner of Indian Affairs -
            1889*. Washington: Government Printing Office. Pp. 261-262.
1890   Reports of Agents in New Mexico: Report of Moqui Pueblo Indians.
            Annual Report of the Commissioner of Indian Affairs – 1890.
            Washington: Government Printing Office. Pp. 167-172.

Voth, H. R.
1901   *The Oraibi Powamu Ceremony*. Field Columbian Museum Publication
            No. 61; Anthropological Series No. 3(2). Chicago: Field Columbian
            Museum.

1905   *The Traditions of the Hopi.* Field Columbian Museum Publication No. 96; Anthropological Series No. 8. Chicago: Field Columbian Museum.

1912   *The Oraibi Marau Ceremony.* Field Museum of Natural History Publication No. 156; Anthropological Series No. 9(1). Chicago: Field Museum of Natural History.

Ward, John

1865   New Mexico Superintendency. *Report of the Commission of Indian Affairs, 1864.* Washington: Government Printing Office. Pp. 187-195.

Welsh, Herbert

1885   *Report on a Visit to the Navajo, Pueblo, and Hualapais Indians of New Mexico and Arizona.* Philadelphia: Indian Rights Association.

Wheeler, Olin D.

1906   In the Land of the Moki [1876]. *Talisman* (October). Reprinted in *New Mexico Historical Review* 86 (2): 176-184.

Whipple, Amiel W.

1854-1855   Itinerary, Explorations, and Surveys for a Railroad Route from the Mississippi to the Pacific Ocean War Route Near the Thirty-fifth Parallel... in 1853 and 1854. Pacific Survey Reports, Vol. 3. *33d Cong., 2d sess. Exec. Doc. No. 78 (Serial No. 760).* Washington: Beverley Tucker.

Winship, George Parker

1896   *The Coronado Expedition, 1540-1542.* Nineteenth Annual Report of the Bureau of Ethnology, 1892-1893. Washington: Government Printing Office. pp.329-613.

Yarrow, H. C.

1885   [Anon.] A Moqui Snake Dance [Interview with H. C. Yarrow]. *The Evening Star* [Washington, DC] (October 17): 2.

1887   re Matthews/Stevenson collaboration...p. see D. Miller

1888   Snake Bite and Its Antidote. *Forest & Stream* 30 (May 17): 327-328.

Secondary Literature

Adams, E. Charles

1991   *Origin and Development of the Pueblo Katsina Cult.* Tucson: University of Arizona Press.

Adams, E. Charles, and M. Nieves Zedeno

1999   BAE Scholars as Documenters of Diversity and Change at Hopi, 1870-1895. *Journal of the Southwest* 41 (3): 311-334.

Banker, Mark T.

1982   Presbyterians and Pueblos: A Protestant Response to the Indian Question, 1872-1892. *Journal of Presbyterian History* 60 (Spring): 23-41.

1993   *Presbyterian Missions and Cultural Interaction in the Far Southwest, 1850-1950.* Urbana: University of Illinois Press.

Bartlett, Richard A.

1997   Scientific Exploration of the American West, 1865-1900. *North American Exploration*, vol. 3, *A Continent Comprehended*, John Logan Allen, ed. Lincoln: University of Nebraska Press. Pp. 461-520.

Batkin, Jonathan

1998   Some Early Curio Dealers of New Mexico. *American Indian Art Magazine* 23 (2): 68-81.

1999   Tourism is Overrated: Pueblo Pottery and the Early Curio Trade, 1880-1910. *Unpacking Culture: Art and Commodity in Colonial and Postcolonial Worlds*, Ruth B. Phillips and C. B. Steiner, eds. Berkeley: University of California Press. Pp. 282-297.

Beesley, Kenneth R., and Dirk Elzinga

2015   *An 1860 English-Hopi Vocabulary Written in the Deseret Alphabet.* Salt Lake City: University of Utah Press.

Bender, Norman J.

1984   *Missionaries, Outlaws, and Indians: Taylor F. Ealy at Lincoln and Zuni, 1878-1881.* Albuquerque: University of New Mexico Press.

1996   *Winning the West for Christ: Sheldon Jackson and Presbyterianism on the Rocky Mountain Frontier, 1869-1880.* Albuquerque: University of New Mexico Press.

Black, Mary E.

1984   Maidens and Mothers: An Analysis of Hopi Corn Metaphors. *Ethnology* 23 (4): 279-288.

Blair, Mary Ellen, and Laurence Blair

1999   *The Legacy of a Master Potter: Nampeyo and Her Descendents.* Tucson: Treasure Chest.

Bloch, Maurice

1998   *How We Think They Think: Anthropological Studies in Cognition, Memory and Literacy.* Boulder: Westview.

Bourdieu, Pierre

1972   The Berber House or the World Reversed. *Social Sciences Information* 9 (2): 151-170.

1977   *Outline of a Theory of Practice.* Cambridge: Cambridge University Press.

Bradfield, Richard Maitland

1995   *An Interpretation of Hopi Culture.* Duffield, England: The Author.

Brandes, Raymond S.

1965   Frank Hamilton Cushing: Pioneer Anthropologist. Unpublished PhD dissertation, University of Arizona, Tucson.

Brown, Arthur Judson

1936   *One Hundred Years: A History of the Foreign Missionary Work of the Presbyterian Church in the U. S. A.* New York: Fleming H. Revell.

Brunet, Francois
2007   "With the Compliments of F. V. Hayden, Geologist of the United States."
            In *Images of the West: Survey Photography in French Collections,
            1860-1880*, Francois Brunet and Bronwyn Griffith, eds. Giverny:
            Musee d'art Americain. Pp. 11-29.
Carsten, Janet, and Stephen Hugh-Jones, eds.
1995   *About the House: Levi-Strauss and Beyond.* Cambridge: Cambridge
            University Press.
Clemenson, A. Berle
2002   *Casa Grande Ruin National Monument, Arizona: A Centennial History
            of the First Prehistoric Reserve, 1892-1992.* Washington: National
            Park Service, Department of the Interior. Online version accessed
            July 8, 2016. https:www.nps.gov/parkhistory/online_books/cagr/
            adi0b.htm [citations omitted]
Connelly, John C.
1979   Hopi Social Organization. *Handbook of North American Indians,* vol. 9,
            Southwest, Alfonso Ortiz, ed. Washington: Smithsonian Institution.
            Pp. 539-553.
Connerton, Paul
1989   *How Societies Remember.* New York: Cambridge University Press.
Crow-Wing
1925   *A Pueblo Indian Journal, 1920-1921.* Elsie Clews Parsons, ed. Memoir
            of the American Anthropological Association, no. 32. Menaha:
            American Anthropological Association.
Culin, Stewart
1905   Thomas Varker Keam. *American Anthropologist* 7 (1): 171-172.
Darnell, Regna
1988.   *Daniel Garrison Brinton: The "Fearless Critic" of Philadelphia.*
            Philadelphia: Department of Anthropology, University of
            Pennsylvania.
Deiss, William A.
1980   Spencer Baird and His Collectors. *Journal of the Society for the
            Bibliography of Natural History* 9: 635-645.
Dilworth, Leah
1996   *Imagining Indians in the Southwest: Persistent Visions of a Primitive Past.*
            Washington: Smithsonian Institution Press.
Dozier, Edward P.
1954   *The Hopi-Tewa of Arizona.* University of California Publications
            in American Archaeology and Ethnology, vol. 44, no. 3. Berkeley:
            University of California Press.
1966   *Hano: A Tewa Indian Community in Arizona.* New York: Holt, Rinehart
            and Winston.

Eggan, Fred
1950   *The Social Organization of the Western Pueblos*. Chicago: University of
            Chicago Press.
1983   Comparative Social Organization. *Handbook of North American
            Indians*, vol. 10, *Southwest*, Alfornso Ortiz, ed. Washington:
            Smithsonian Institution. Pp. 723-742.
Ellis, Bruce T.
1958   Santa Fe's Tertio Millennial, 1883. *El Palacio* 65:121-135.
Evans, Brad
1997   Cushing's Zuni Sketchbooks: Literature, Anthropology, and American
            Notions of Culture. *American Quarterly* 49 (4): 717-745.
Fagan, Brian
2005   *Chaco Canyon: Archaeologists Explore the Lives of an Ancient Society*.
            New York: Oxford University Press.
Faris, James C.
1990   *The Nightway: A History and a History of Documentation of a Navajo
            Ceremonial*. Albuquerque: University of New Mexico Press.
Farr, F. C., ed.
1918   *The History of Imperial County, California*. Berkeley: Elms and Franks.
            [Biography of H. J. Messenger]
Ferguson, Thomas J., and E. R. Hart
1985   *A Zuni Atlas*. Norman: University of Oklahoma Press.
Fernlund, Kevin J.
2000   *William Henry Holmes and the Rediscovery of the American West*.
            Albuquerque: University of New Mexico Press.
Foster, Don
2000   *Author Unknown: On the Trail of Anonymous*. New York: Henry Holt.
Fowler, Don D.
2000   *A Laboratory for Anthropology: Science and Romanticism in the
            American Southwest, 1846-1930*. Albuquerque: University of New
            Mexico Press.
Fox, James J.
1993   Comparative Perspectives on Austronesian Houses. *Inside Austronesian
            Houses: Perspectives on Domestic Designs for Living*, James J. Fox,
            ed. Canberra: Department of Anthropology, Research School of
            Pacific Studies. Pp. 1-28.
Frazier, Kendrick
1999   *The People of Chaco: A Canyon and Its Culture*. Rev. ed. New York: W.
            W. Norton.
Frigout, Arlette
1979   Hopi Ceremonial Organization. *Handbook of North American Indians*,
            vol. 9, *Southwest*, Alfonso Ortiz, ed. Washington: Smithsonian
            Institution. Pp. 564-576.

Frisbee, Charlotte J.
1997   Washington Matthews' Contributions to the Study of Navajo
            Ceremonialism and Mythology. *Washington Matthews: Studies
            of Navajo Culture, 1880-1894*, Katherine Spencer Halpern and
            Susan Brown McGreevy, eds. Albuquerque: University of New
            Mexico Press. Pp. 28-41.

Fritz, Henry E.
1963   *The Movement for Indian Assimilation, 1860-1890*. Philadelphia:
            University of Pennsylvania Press.

Geraets, Gertrude
1980   *E. L. Conklin, MD, Pioneer Woman Doctor of Madison, Indiana.*
            [Madison: The Author]

Glowacka, Maria D.
1998   Ritual Knowledge in *Hopi* Tradition. *American Indian Quarterly* 22 (3):
            386-392.
1999   The Concept of *Hikwsi* in Traditional Hopi Philosophy. *American
            Indian Culture and Research Journal* 23 (2): 137-143.

Glowacka, Maria, and Emory Sekaquaptewa
2009   The Metaphorical Dimensions of Hopi Ethics. *Journal of the Southwest*
            51 (2): 165-186.

Glowacka, Maria, Dorothy Washburn, and Justin Richland
2009   *Nuvatukyaʹovi*, San Francisco Peaks. *Current Anthropology* 50 (4): 547-
            561

Goody, Jack
2000   *The Power of the Written Tradition*. Washington: Smithsonian
            Institution Press.

Graves, Laura
1998   *Thomas Varker Keam, Indian Trader*. Norman: University of Oklahoma
            Press.

Green, Jesse D., ed.
1979   *Zuni: Selected Writings of Frank Hamilton Cushing*. Lincoln: University
            of Nebraska Press.
1990   *Cushing at Zuni: The Correspondence and Journals of Frank Hamilton
            Cushing, 1879-1884*. Albuquerque: University of New Mexico
            Press.

Hafner, A. W., F. W. Hunter, and F. M. Tarpay
1993   *Directory of Deceased American Physicians, 1804-1929*. Chicago:
            American Library Association.

Haile, Berard
1917   The Meaning of "Tusayan." *American Anthropologist* 19 (1): 151.

Halbwacks, Maurice
1992   *On Collective Memory*, Lewis A. Coser, ed. Chicago: University of
            Chicago Press.

Halpern, Katherine Spencer
1997   Washington Matthews: Army Surgeon and Field Anthropologist in
            the American West, 1843-1905. In *Washington Matthews: Studies
            of Navajo Culture, 1880-1894*, K. S. Halpern and S. B. McGreevy,
            eds. Albuquerque: University of New Mexico Press. Pp. 3-15.

Halpern Katherine Spencer, and S. B. McGreevy, eds.
1997   *Washington Matthews: Studies of Navajo Culture, 1880-1894.*
            Albuquerque: University of New Mexico Press.

Hart, E. Richard
2003   *Pedro Pino, Governor of Zuni Pueblo, 1830-1878.* Logan: Utah State
            University Press.

Hieb, Louis A.
1994a   The Meaning of Katsina: Towards a Cultural Definition of a 'Person'
            in Hopi Religion. *Kachinas in the Pueblo World*, Polly Schaafsma,
            ed. Albuquerque: University of New Mexico Press. Pp. 23-33.

1994b   Hopi Thought and Archaeological Theory: The Sipapu Reconsidered.
            American Indian Religions: An Interdisciplinary Journal 1 (1): 17-
            36.

1999a   John Lorenzo Hubbell. *American National Biography*. New York:
            Oxford University Press. Vol. 11, pp. 391-393.

1999b   Ma'sau's World: Katsinas in the Pueblo World, 1275-1325. Unpublished
            paper presented to the Archaeological Society of New Mexico,
            Albuquerque.

2004a   A. M. Stephen and the Navajos. *New Mexico Historical Review* 79 (3):
            353-395.

2004b   A Question of Authorship: A. M. Stephen's Catalogue of the Keam
            Collection [1884]. *Kiva: The Journal of Southwestern Anthropology
            and History* 69 (4): 399-421.

2005   'The Flavor of Adventure Now Rare': H. C. Rizer's Account of James
            Stevenson's 1882 Bureau of Ethnology Expedition to Canyon de
            Chelly. *The Journal of Arizona History* 46 (3): 205-248.

2008   The Hopi Clown Ceremony (*tsukulalwa*). *American Indian Culture and
            Resarch Journal* 32 (4): 107-124.

2009   Ben Wittick and the Keam Pottery Collection. *American Indian Art
            Magazine* 34 (3): 38-49.

2010   *The Indians of Arizona and New Mexico; Nineteenth Century
            Ethnographic Notes of Archbishop John Baptist Salpointe*, Patricia
            Fogelman Lange, Louis A. Hieb, and Thomas J. Steele, eds. Los
            Ranchos: Rio Grande Books.

2011a   Expeditionary Photography and the Hopi, 1872-1881: E. O. Beaman, J.
            K. Hillers, and W. H. Jackson. *Essays in Honor of David Kirkpatrick
            and Meli Duran*, Carol Condie, ed. Albuquerque: Archaeological
            Society of New Mexico. Pp. 131-144.

2011b   Collecting for the Centennial Indian Exhibition: The J. K. Hillers – Olin
             D. Wheeler Expedition to the Hopi in 1876. *New Mexico Historical
             Review* 86 (2): 157-195.

Hinsley, Curtis M.

1981   *Savages and Scientists: The Smithsonian Institution and the Development
             of American Anthropology 1846-1920.* Washington: Smithsonian
             Institution Press.

1983   Ethnographic Charisma and Scientific Routine: Cushing and Fewkes
             in the American Southwest, 1879-1893. *Observers Observed: Essays
             on Ethnographic Fieldwork*, George Stocking, ed. Madison:
             University of Wisconsin Press. Pp. 53-69.

1989   Zunis and Brahmins: Cultural Ambivalence in the Guilded Age.
             Romantic Motives: Essays on Anthropological Sensibility, George W.
             Stocking, Jr., ed. Madison: University of Wisconsin Press. Pp. 169-
             207.

1992   Collecting Cultures and the Cultures of Collecting: The Lure of the
             Southwest, 1880-1915. *Museum Anthropology* 16 (1): 12-20.

1996   Boston Meets the Southwest: The World of Frank Hamilton Cushing
             and Sylvester Baxter. *The Southwest in the American Imagination:
             The Writings of Sylvester Baxter, 1881-1889*, Curtis M. Hinsley and
             David R. Wilcox, eds. Tucson: University of Arizona Press. Pp.
             3-33.

1999a   Life on the Margins: The Ethnographic Poetics of Frank Hamilton
             Cushing. *Journal of the Southwest* 41 (Autumn): 371-382.

1999b   Hopi Snakes, Zuni Corn: Early Ethnography in the American
             Southwest. *Colonial Subjects: Essays on the Practical History
             of Anthropology*, Peter Pels and Oscar Salemink, eds. Ann Arbor:
             University of Michigan Press. Pp. 180-195.

Hinsley, Curtis M., Louis A. Hieb and Barbara Fash, eds.

n.d.   *Zuni, Hopi, Copan: John G. Owens's Letters from the Field, 1890-1893.*
             Cambridge: Peabody Museum Press. Forthcoming.

Hinsley, Curtis M., and David R. Wilcox, eds.

1996   *The Southwest in the American Imagination: The Writings of Sylvester
             Baxter, 1881-1889.* Tucson: The University of Arizona Press.

2002   *The Lost Itinerary of Frank Hamilton Cushing.* Tucson: The University of
             Arizona Press.

Hopi Dictionary Project

1998   *Hopi Dictionary/Hopiikwa Lavaytutuven: A Hopi-English Dictionary of
             the Third Mesa Dialect.* Tucson: University of Arizona Press.

Houk, Rose

1996   *Casa Grande Ruins National Monument.* 2nd ed. Tucson: Southwest
             Parks and Monuments Association.

Hovens, Pieter
1988   The Anthropologist as Enigma: Frank Hamilton Cushing. *European Journal of Native American Studies* 1 (1): 1-5.

Jenkins, Leigh, T. J. Fergusson, and Kurt Dongoske
1994   A Reexamination of the Concept of *Hopitutsqwa*. Unpublished paper presented at the Annual Meeting of the American Society for Ethnohistory, Tempe, Arizona.

Judd, Neil M.
1967   *The Bureau of American Ethnology: A Partial History.* Norman: University of Oklahoma Press.

Kaemlein, Wilma R.
1967   *An Inventory of Southwestern American Indian Specimens in European Museums.* Tucson: Arizona State Museum, The University of Arizona.

Kramer, Barbara
1996   *Nampeyo and Her Pottery.* Albuquerque: University of New Mexico Press.

Ladd, Edmund J.
1994   Cushing among the Zuni: A Zuni Perspective. *Gilcrease Journal* 2 (2): 20-35.

Laird, W. David
1977   *Hopi Bibliography: Comprehensive and Annotated.* Tucson: University of Arizona Press.

Lawson, Michael J.
2003   Baskets, Pots, and Prayer Plumes: The Southwest Ethnographic Collections of the Smithsonian Institution. Unpublished PhD dissertation, Arizona State University, Tempe.

Lee, Ronald E.
1970   *The Antiquities Act of 1906. Washington: National Park Service, U. S. Department of the Interior.*

Lekson, Stephen H.
1991   Settlement Patterns and the Chaco Region. *Chaco and Hohokam: Prehistoric Regional Systems in the American Southwest,* Patricia L. Crown and W. James Judge, eds. Santa Fe: School of American Research Press. Pp. 31-55.

Loftin, John D.
1991   *Religion and Hopi Life in the Twentieth Century.* Bloomington: Indiana University Press.

Longacre, William A.
1999   Why did the BAE Hire an Architect? *Journal of the Southwest* 41 (3): 358-369.
2010   Archaeology as Anthropology Revisited. *Journal of Archaeological Method and Theory* 17 (2): 81-100.

Mardock, Robert Winston
1971   *The Reformers and the American Indian.* Columbia: University of
            Missouri Press.
Mark, Joan
1980   *4 Anthropologists: An American Science in its Early Years.* New York:
            Science History Publications.
Mathien, Frances Joan
2006   Archaeological Studies of Victor and Cosmos Mindeleff in Chaco
            Canyon, New Mexico. *Southwestern Interludes: Papers in Honor of
            Charlotte J. and Theodore R. Frisbee,* R. N. Wiseman, T. C.
            O'Laughlin, C. T. Snow, and D. M. Brugge, eds. Albuquerque:
            Archaeological Society of New Mexico. Pp. 103-114.
McCluskey, Stephen C.
1977   The Astronomy of the Hopi Indians. *Journal of the History of Astronomy*
            8:174-195.
1980   Evangelists, Educators, Ethnographers, and the Establishment of the
            Hopi Reservation. *Journal of Arizona History* 21 (4): 363-390.
1981   Transformations of the Hopi Calendar. *Archaeoastronomy in the
            Americas,* Ray A. Williamson, ed. Los Altos: Ballena Press. Pp. 173-
            182.
1982   Historical Archaeoastronomy: The Hopi Example. *Archaeoastronomy
            in the New World,* A. F. Aveni, ed. Cambridge: Cambridge
            University Press. Pp. 31-57.
McGee, W J, William H. Holmes, J. W. Powell, Alice C. Fletcher, Washington
            Matthews, Stewart Culin, and Joseph D. McGuire
1900   In Memoriam: Frank Hamilton Cushing. *American Anthropologist* 2
            (2): 354-380.
McIntire, Elliot G.
1971   Changing Patterns of Hopi Indian Settlement. *Annals of the Association
            of American Geographers* 61: 510-521.
1982   First Mesa in 1900. *Journal of Cultural Geography* 2 (2): 58-71.
McIntire, Elliot G., and Sandra R. Gordon
1968   Ten Kate's Account of the Walpi Snake Dance: 1883. *Plateau* 41: 27-33.
McNitt, Frank
1962   *The Indian Traders.* Norman: University of Oklahoma Press.
Merrill, William L., and Richard E. Ahlborn
1997   Zuni Archangels and Ahayu:da; A Sculpted Chronicle of Power
            and Identity. *Exhibiting Dilemmas: Issues of Representation at
            the Smithsonian,* Amy Henderson and Adrienne L. Kaeppler, eds.
            Washington: Smithsonian Institution Press. Pp. 176-205.
Miller, Darlis A.
2007   *Matilda Coxe Stevenson: Pioneering Anthropologist.* Norman: University
            of Oklahoma Press.

Montgomery, Ross Gordon, Watson Smith, and John Otis Brew
1949   *Franciscan Awatovi: The Excavation and Conjectural Reconstruction of a 17th Century Spanish Mission Established at the Hopi Indian Town in Northeastern Arizona.* Papers of the Peabody Museum, 36. Cambridge: The Museum.

Morgan, William N.
1994   *Ancient Architecture of the Southwest.* Austin: University of Texas Press.

Morris, Earl H.
1938   Mummy Cave. *Natural History* 42 (September): 127-138.
1941   Prayer Sticks in Walls of Mummy Cave Tower, Canyon del Muerto. *American Antiquity* 6 (3): 227-230.

Murry, David
1987   "They Love Me and I Learn": Frank Hamilton Cushing and Ethnographic Method. *European Review of Native American Studies* 1 (2): 3-8.

Nabokov, Peter
1989   Introduction. *A Study of Pueblo Architecture in Tusayan and Cibola*, by Victor Mindeleff. Washington: Smithsonian Institution Press. Pp. ix-xli.

Nandy, Ashis
1995   History's Forgotten Doubles. *History and Theory* 34 (2): 44-66.

Oliver, Paul
2007   *Dwellings: The Vernacular House Worldwide.* London: Phaidon.

Pandy, Triloki Nath
1972   Anthropologists at Zuni. *Proceedings of the American Philosophical Society* 116 (4): 321-337.

Parezo, Nancy J.
1985   Cushing as Part of the Team: the Collecting Activities of the Smithsonian Institution. *American Ethnologist* 12 (4): 763-774.
1987   The Formation of Ethnographic Collections: The Smithsonian Institution in the American Southwest. *Advances in Archaeological Method and Theory* 10:1-46.
1997   Washington Matthews and the Discovery of Navajo Drypaintings. *Washington Matthews: Studies in Navajo Culture, 1880-1894*, Katherine Spencer Halpern and Susan Brown McGreevy, eds. Albuquerque: University of New Mexico Press. Pp. 53-73.

Parsons, Elsie Clews, ed.
1922a   *American Indian Life.* New York: B. W. Huebsch.
1922b   Contributions to Hopi History. *American Anthropologist* 24 (3): 253-298.

Peterson, Charles S.
1971   The Hopis and the Mormons: 1858-1873. *Utah Historical Quarterly* 39 (2): 179-194.

1973 *Take Up Your Mission: Mormon Colonizing Along the Little Colorado River 1870-1900.* Tucson: University of Arizona Press.

Porter, Joseph C.
1986 *Paper Medicine Man: John Gregory Bourke and His American West.* Norman: University of Oklahoma Press.

Quebbeman, Frances E.
1966 *Medicine in Territorial Arizona.* Phoenix: Arizona Historical Foundation.

Rabbitt, Mary C.
1979-1980 *Minerals, Lands, and Geology for the Common Defence and General Welfare: United States Geological Survey.* 2vols. Washington: United States Government Printing Office.

Rapoport, Amos
1994 Spatial Organization and the Built Environment. *Comparative Encyclopedia of Anthropology,* Tim Ingold, ed. London: Routledge. Pp. 460-502.

Rebord, Bernice Ann
1947 A Social History of Albuquerque, 1880-1885. Unpublished MA thesis, University of New Mexico, Albuquerque.

Rockland Centennial Book Committee
1980 *Rockland Valley, 1879-1979.* Rockland, ID: The Committee.

Schroeder, Albert H., and Ives Goddard
1979 [Hopi] Synonymy. *Handbook of North American Indians,* vol. 9, *Southwest,* Alfonso Ortiz, ed. Washington: Smithsonian Institution. P. 551.

Schauinger, Joseph H.
1941 Jeremiah C. Sullivan, Hoosier Jurist. *Indiana Magazine of History* 37 (3): 217-236.

Schwartz, Douglas W.
1983 Havasupai. *Handbook of North American Indians,* vol. 10, *Southwest,* Alfonso Ortiz, ed. Washington: Smithsonian Institution. Pp. 13-24.

Secrest, William B.
1975 The Saga of John Moss. *True West* 22 (6): 8-12, 53-54.

Sekaquaptewa, Emory
1972 Preserving the Good Things of Hopi Life. *Plural Society in the Southwest,* Edward H. Spicer and Raymond H. Thompson, eds. New York: Interbook. Pp. 239-260.

Sekaquaptewa, Emory, and Dorothy Washburn
2004 *They Go Along Singing*: Reconstructing the Hopi Past from Ritual Metaphors in Song and Image. *American Antiquity* 69 (3): 457-486.

2009 As a Matter of Practice … Hopi Cosmology in Hopi Life: Some Considerations for Theory and Method in Southwestern Archaeology. *Time and Mind: The Journal of Archaeology, Consciousness and Culture* 2 (2): 195-214.

Sekaquaptewa, Emory, Kenneth C. Hill, and Dorothy Washburn
2015   Hopi Katsina Songs. Lincoln: University of Nebraska Press.
Smith, Delos H.
1948   Victor Mindeleff, 1861-1848 [obituary]. Journal of The American
            Institute of Architects 9 (5): 219-220.
Snead, James
2001   Rivals and Ruins: The Making of Southwestern Archaeology. Tucson:
            University of Arizona Press.
Stanislawski, Michael B.
1979   Hopi-Tewa. Handbook of North American Indians, vol. 9, Southwest,
            Alfonso Ortiz, ed. Washington: Smithsonian Institution.
            Pp. 587-602.
Stephens, Lester D., and Dale R. Calder
2010   The Zoological Career of Jesse Walter Fewkes (1850-1930). Archives of
            Natural History 37: 255-273.
Sykes, Godfrey
1944   A Westerly Trend. Tucson: Arizona Pioneers Historical Society.
Taylor, Bruce Lee
1990   Presbyterians and "the People": A History of Presbyterian Missions
            and Ministries to the Navajos. Unpublished Ph.D. dissertation,
            Union Theological Seminary of Virginia, Richmond.
Titiev, Mischa
1944   Old Oraibi: A Study of the Hopi Indians of Third Mesa. Peabody
            Museum of American Archaeology and Ethnology, Papers, 22(1).
            Cambridge: The Museum.
Titterton, Robert J.
1997   Julian Scott: Artist of the Civil War and Native America. Jefferson, NC:
            McFarland.
Trouillot, Michel-Rolph
1995   Silencing the Past: Power and the Production of History. Boston: Beacon
            Press.
Vivian, Gwinn, and Bruce Hilpert
2002   The Chaco Handbook: An Encyclopedic Guide. Salt Lake City: University
            of Utah Press.
Wade, Edwin L., and Lea S. McChesney
1980   America's Great Lost Expedition: The Thomas Keam Collection of Hopi
            Pottery from the Second Hemenway Expedition, 1890-1894.
            Phoenix: Heard Museum.
1981   Historic Hopi Ceramics: The Thomas V. Keam Collection of the Peabody
            Museum of Archaeology and Ethnology, Harvard University.
            Cambridge: Peabody Museum Press.
Waterson, Roxana
1990   The Living House: An Anthropology of Architecture in South-East Asia.
            Oxford: Oxford University Press.

Wayte, Harold C.
1962   A History of Holbrook and the Little Colorado Country, 1540-1962.
            Unpublished MA thesis, University of Arizona, Tucson.
Whiteley, Peter
1988a   *Deliberate Acts: Changing Hopi Culture through the Oraibi Split.* Tucson:
            University of Arizona Press.
1988b   *Bacavi: Journey to Reed Springs.* Flagstaff: Northland Press.
1998   *Rethinking Hopi Ethnography.* Washington: Smithsonian Institution
            Press.
2001   Hopi Histories. *Katsina: Commodified and Appropriated Images of*
            Hopi Supernaturals, Zena Pearlstone, ed. Los Angeles: UCLA
            Fowler Museum of Cultural History. Pp. 22-33.
2002   Re-imagining Awat'ovi. *Archaeologies of the Pueblo Revolt: Identity,*
            Meaning, and Renewal in the Pueblo World, Robert W. Preucel, ed.
            Albuquerque: University of New Mexico Press. Pp. 147-166.
2008   "The Orayvi Split: A Hopi Transformation." 2 vols. *American Museum*
            of Natural History Anthropological Papers, No. 87. New York:
            American Museum of Natural History.
2012   Crow-Omaha Kinship in North America: A Puebloan Perspective.
            Crow-Omaha: New Light on a Classic Problem in Kinship Analysis,
            Thomas R. Trautmann and Peter M. Whiteley, eds. Tucson:
            University of Arizona Press. Pp. 83-108.
Wilcox, David R.
2003   Restoring Authenticity: Judging Frank Hamilton Cushing's Veracity.
            Philadelphia and the Development of Americanist Archaeology, Don
            D. Fowler and David R. Wilcox, eds. Tuscaloosa: University of
            Alabama Press. Pp. 88-112.
Woolf, Charles M., and Frank C. Dukepoo
1969   Hopi Indians, Inbreeding, and Albinism: The High Frequency of
            Albinism among the Hopi is an Intriguing Problem in Population
            Genetics. *Science* 164 (3875; April 4): 30-37.
Worster, Donald
2001   *A River Running West: The Life of John Wesley Powell.* New York: Oxford
            University Press.
Wyman, Leland C.
1983   Navajo Curing System. *Handbook of North American Indians,* vol. 10,
            Southwest, Alfonso Ortiz, ed. Washington: Smithsonian Institution.
            Pp. 536-557.
Yates, Timothy
1989   Habitus and Social Space: Some Suggestions about Meaning in the
            Saami [Yapp] Tent. *The Meaning of Things: Material Culture and*
            Symbolic Expression, Ian Hodder, ed. London: Unwin Hyman. Pp.
            249-262.

Index

CPSIA information can be obtained
at www.ICGtesting.com
Printed in the USA
FSHW011832140419
57182FS